ANALYSIS AND
SYNTHESIS OF
COMPUTER SYSTEMS

2ND EDITION

Advances in Computer Science and Engineering: Texts

Editor-in-Chief: Erol Gelenbe *(Imperial College)*
Advisory Editors: Manfred Broy *(Technische Universitaet Muenchen)*
Gérard Huet *(INRIA)*

Published

Vol. 1 Computer System Performance Modeling in Perspective:
A Tribute to the Work of Professor Kenneth C. Sevcik
edited by E. Gelenbe (Imperial College London, UK)

Vol. 2 Residue Number Systems: Theory and Implementation
by A. Omondi (Yonsei University, South Korea) and
B. Premkumar (Nanyang Technological University, Singapore)

Vol. 3: Fundamental Concepts in Computer Science
edited by E. Gelenbe (Imperial College Londo, UK) and
J.-P. Kahane (Université de Paris Sud - Orsay, France)

Vol. 4: Analysis and Synthesis of Computer Systems (2nd Edition)
by Erol Gelenbe (Imperial College, UK) and
Isi Mitrani (University of Newcastle upon Tyne, UK)

Advances in Computer Science and Engineering: Texts   Vol. 4

ANALYSIS AND SYNTHESIS OF COMPUTER SYSTEMS

2ND EDITION

Erol Gelenbe

Imperial College, UK

Isi Mitrani

University of Newcastle upon Tyne, UK

Imperial College Press

ICP

Published by

Imperial College Press
57 Shelton Street
Covent Garden
London WC2H 9HE

Distributed by

World Scientific Publishing Co. Pte. Ltd.
5 Toh Tuck Link, Singapore 596224
USA office: 27 Warren Street, Suite 401-402, Hackensack, NJ 07601
UK office: 57 Shelton Street, Covent Garden, London WC2H 9HE

British Library Cataloguing-in-Publication Data
A catalogue record for this book is available from the British Library.

ANALYSIS AND SYNTHESIS OF COMPUTER SYSTEMS (2nd Edition)
Advances in Computer Science and Engineering: Texts — Vol. 4

Desk Editor: Tjan Kwang Wei

ISBN-13 978-1-84816-395-9

Typeset by Stallion Press
Email: enquiries@stallionpress.com

Printed in Singapore.

Preface to the Second Edition

The book has been revised and extended, in order to reflect important developments in the field of probabilistic modelling and performance evaluation since the first edition. Notable among these is the introduction of queueing network models with positive and negative customers. A large class of such models, together with their solutions and applications, is described in Chapter 4. Another recent development concerns the solution of models where the evolution of a queue is controlled by a Markovian environment. These Markov-modulated queues occur in many different contexts; their exact and approximate solution is the subject of Chapter 5. Finally, the queue with a server of walking type described in Chapter 2 is given a more general treatment in Chapter 10.

Erol Gelenbe
Isi Mitrani
February 2010

Contents

Chapter 1

Basic Tools of Probabilistic Modelling

1.1. General background

On a certain level of abstraction, computer systems belong to the same family as, for example, job-shops, supermarkets, hairdressing salons and airport terminals; all these are sometimes described as "mass service systems" and more often as "queueing systems". Customers (or tasks, or jobs, or machine parts) arrive according to some random pattern; they require a variety of services (execution of arithmetic and logical operations, transfer of information, seat reservations) of random durations. Services are provided by one or more servers, perhaps at different speeds. The order of service is determined by a set of rules which constitutes the "scheduling strategy", or "service discipline".

The mathematical analysis of such systems is the subject of queueing theory. Since A. K. Erlang's studies of telephone switching systems, in 1917–1918, that theory has progressed considerably; today it boasts an impressive collection of results, methods and techniques. Interest in queueing theory has always been stimulated by problems with practical applications. In particular, most of the theoretical advances of the last decade are directly attributable to developments in the area of computer systems performance evaluation.

Because customer interarrival times and the demands placed on the various servers are random, the state $S(t)$ of a queueing system at time t of its operation is a random variable. The set of these random variables $\{S(t), t \geq 0\}$ is a stochastic process. A particular realisation of the random variables — that is, a particular realisation of all arrival events, service demands, etc. — is a "sample path" of the stochastic process. For example, in a single-server queueing system where all customers are of the same type, one might be interested in the stochastic process $\{N(t), t \geq 0\}$, where $N(t)$ is the number of customers waiting and/or being served at time t. A portion

1

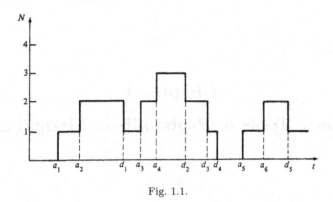

Fig. 1.1.

of a possible sample path for this process is shown in Fig. 1.1: customers arrive at moments a_1, a_2, ... and depart at moments d_1, d_2, ...

An examination of the sample paths of a queueing process can disclose some general relations between different quantities associated with a given path. For instance, in the single-server system, if $N(t_1) = N(t_2)$ for some $t_1 < t_2$, and there are k arrivals in the interval (t_1, t_2), then there are k departures in that interval. Since a sample path represents a system in operation, relations of the above type are sometimes called "operational laws" or "operational identities" (Buzen [1]). We shall derive some operational identities in section 1.7. Because they apply to individual sample paths, these identities are independent of any probabilistic assumptions governing the underlying stochastic process. Thus, the operational approach to performance evaluation is free from the necessity to make such assumptions. It is, however, tied to specific sample paths and hence to specific runs of an existing system where measurements can be taken.

The probabilistic approach involves studying the stochastic process which represents the system. The results of such a study necessarily depend on the probabilistic assumptions governing the process. These results are themselves probabilistic in nature and concern the population of all possible sample paths. They are not associated with a particular run of an existing system, or with any existing system at all. It is often desirable to evaluate not only the expected performance of a system, but also the likely deviations from that expected performance. Dealing with probability distributions makes this possible, at least in principle.

We shall be concerned mainly with steady-state system behaviour — that is, with the characteristics of a process which has been running for a long time and has settled down into a "statistical equilibrium regime". Long-run performance measures are important because they are stable;

being independent of the early history of the process, and independent of time, they are also much easier to deal with. We shall, of course, be interested in the conditions which ensure the existence of steady-state.

This chapter introduces the reader to the rudiments of stochastic processes and queueing theory. Results used later in the book will be derived here, with the emphasis on explaining important methods and ideas rather than on rigorous proofs. In discussing queueing systems, we shall use the classic descriptive notation devised by D. G. Kendall:

$$\cdot / \cdot / \cdot$$

(arrival pattern)   (service pattern)   (number of servers)

e.g. $D/M/2$ describes a queueing system with Deterministic (constant) interarrival times, Markov (exponential) service times and 2 servers.

1.2. Markov processes. The exponential distribution

Let $S(t)$ be a random variable depending on a continuous parameter t $(t \geq 0)$ and taking values in the set of non-negative integers $\{0, 1, 2, \ldots\}$. We think of t as time and of $S(t)$ as the system state at time t. The requirement that the states should be represented as positive integers is not important; it is essential that they should be denumerable. Later, we shall have occasions to use vectors of integers as state descriptors.

The collection of random variables $\{S(t), t \geq 0\}$ is a stochastic process. That collection is said to be a "Markov process" if the probability distribution of the state at time $t + y$ depends only on the state at time t and not on the process history prior to t:

$$P(S(t + y) = j | S(u); u \leq t)$$
$$= P(S(t + y) = j | S(t)), \quad t, y \geq 0, \ j = 0, 1, \ldots. \quad (1.1)$$

The right-hand side of (1.1) may depend on t, y, j and the value of $S(t)$. If, in addition, it is independent of t, i.e. if

$$P(S(t + y) = j | S(t) = i) = p_{i,j}(y) \quad \text{for all } t, \quad (1.2)$$

then the Markov process is said to be "time-homogeneous" (for an excellent treatment of stochastic processes see Cinlar [3]). From now on, whenever we talk of a Markov process, we shall assume that it is time-homogeneous.

Thus, for a Markov process, the probability $p_{i,j}(y)$ of moving from state i to state j in time y is independent of the time at which the process was in state i and of anything that happened before that time. This very important property will be referred to as the "memoryless property".

The probability $p_{i,j}(y)$, regarded as a function of y, is called the "transition probability function". The memoryless property immediately implies the following set of functional equations:

$$p_{i,j}(x + y) = \sum_{k=0}^{\infty} p_{i,j}(x)p_{k,j}(y), \quad x, y \geq 0, \quad i, j = 0, 1, \dots. \qquad (1.3)$$

These equations express simply the fact that, in order to move from state i to state j in time $x + y$, the process has to be in some state k after time x and then move to state j in time y (and the second transition does not depend on i and x). They are the Chapman–Kolmogorov equations of the Markov process. Introducing the infinite matrix $\mathbf{P}(y)$ of transition functions $p_{i,j}(y)$, we can rewrite (1.3) as

$$\mathbf{P}(x + y) = \mathbf{P}(x)\mathbf{P}(y), \quad x, y \geq 0. \qquad (1.4)$$

We shall assume that the functions $p_{i,j}(y)$ are continuous at $y = 0$:

$$\lim_{y \to 0} p_{i,j}(y) = \begin{cases} 1 & \text{if } i = j \\ 0 & \text{otherwise.} \end{cases} \qquad (1.5)$$

That assumption, together with (1.3), ensures that $p_{i,j}(y)$ is continuous, and has a continuous derivative, for all $y \geq 0$; $i, j = 0, 1, \dots$ (we state this without proof).

A special role is played by the derivatives $a_{i,j}$ of the transition functions at $t = 0$. By definition,

$$a_{i,i} = \lim_{y \to 0} \frac{p_{i,i}(y) - 1}{y}, \quad i = 0, 1, \dots$$

$$a_{i,j} = \lim_{y \to 0} \frac{p_{i,j}(y)}{y}, \quad i \neq j = 0, 1, \dots. \qquad (1.6)$$

Hence, if h is small,

$$p_{i,j}(h) = a_{i,j}h + o(h), \quad i \neq j = 0, 1, \dots, \qquad (1.7)$$

where $o(x)$ is a function such that $\lim_{x \to 0}[o(x)/x] = 0$.

In other words, if the Markov process is in state i at some moment t, then the probability that at time $t + h$ it is in state j is nearly proportional to h, with coefficient of proportionality $a_{i,j}$. That is why $a_{i,j}$ is called the "instantaneous transition rate from state i to state j", $i \neq j$. The probability that the process leaves state i by $t + h$ is approximately equal to

$$1 - p_{i,i}(h) = -a_{i,i}h + o(h), \quad i = 0, 1, \ldots, \quad (1.8)$$

so $-a_{i,i}$ is the instantaneous rate of transition out of state i. Of course, we must have

$$-a_{i,i} = \sum_{\substack{j=0 \\ j \neq i}}^{\infty} a_{i,j}. \quad (1.9)$$

In fact, since $\mathbf{P}(y)$ is a stochastic matrix (its rows sum up to 1), the rows of $\mathbf{P}'(y)$ must sum up to 0 for all $y \geq 0$.

Let $\mathbf{A} = [a_{i,j}]$, $i, j = 0, 1, \ldots$ be the matrix of instantaneous transition rates. Differentiating (1.4) with respect to x and then letting $x \to 0$ yields a system of equations known as the Chapman–Kolmogorov backward differential equations:

$$\mathbf{P}'(y) = \mathbf{A}\mathbf{P}(y). \quad (1.10)$$

Similarly, differentiating (1.4) with respect to y and letting $y \to 0$ yields the Chapman–Kolmogorov forward differential equations

$$\mathbf{P}'(x) = \mathbf{P}(x)\mathbf{A}. \quad (1.11)$$

Either (1.10) or (1.11) can be solved for the transition probability functions, subject to the initial conditions $\mathbf{P}(0) = \mathbf{I}$ (the identity matrix) and $\mathbf{P}'(0) = \mathbf{A}$. In a purely formal way, treating $\mathbf{P}(y)$ as a numerically valued function and $\mathbf{A}$ as a constant, (1.10) and (1.11) are satisfied by

$$\mathbf{P}(y) = e^{\mathbf{A}y}. \quad (1.12)$$

This turns out, indeed, to be the solution, provided that (1.12) is interpreted as

$$\mathbf{P}(y) = \sum_{n=0}^{\infty} \frac{y^n}{n!}\mathbf{A}^n, \quad y \geq 0. \quad (1.13)$$

Thus, the transition probability functions are completely determined by their derivatives at $y = 0$. It should be clear, however, that to find them in practice is by no means a trivial operation. The matrix $\mathbf{P}(y)$, for finite values of y, is referred to as the "transient solution" of the Markov process. As far as closed-form expressions are concerned, transient solutions are unobtainable for all but a few very simple Markov processes.

Let $\{S(t), t \geq 0\}$ be a Markov process with instantaneous transition rate matrix $\mathbf{A}$. Suppose that at time t the process is in state i. What is the distribution of the interval η_i until the first exit from state i (that interval is called the "holding time")? And what is the probability $q_{i,j}$ that the next state to be entered will be state j? According to the memoryless property, the answers to both these questions are independent of t and of the process history prior to t. In particular, they are independent of how long the process has already spent in state i. Consider first the holding time; denote by $\hat{H}_i(x)$ the complementary distribution function of η_i : $\hat{H}_i(x) = P(\eta_i > x)$. From the memoryless property, if the process stays in state i for time x, the probability that it will remain there for at least another interval y is independent of x. Therefore,

$$\hat{H}_i(x + y) = \hat{H}_i(x)\hat{H}_i(y), \quad x, y \geq 0. \tag{1.14}$$

Any distribution function which satisfies (1.14) must fall into one of the following three categories:

(i) $\hat{H}_i(x) = 1$ for all $x \geq 0$. If this is the case, once the process enters state i it remains there forever (properly speaking, the holding time does not have a distribution function then). States of this type are called "absorbing".

(ii) $\hat{H}_i(x) = 0$ for all $x \geq 0$. In this case the process bounces out of state i as soon as it enters it. Such states are called "instantaneous".

(iii) $\hat{H}_i(x)$ is monotone decreasing from 1 to 0 on the interval $[0, \infty)$ and is differentiable. States in this category are called "stable".

From now on, we shall assume that all states are stable. Differentiating Eq. (1.4) with respect to y and letting $y \to 0$ we obtain $\hat{H}_i'(x) = -\lambda_i \hat{H}_i(x)$, where $\lambda_i = -\hat{H}_i'(0)$. Hence

$$\hat{H}_i(x) = \mathrm{e}^{-\lambda_i x}, \quad x \geq 0,$$

and the distribution function $H_i(x) = P(\eta_i \leq x)$ is given by

$$H_i(x) = 1 - \mathrm{e}^{-\lambda_i x}, \quad x \geq 0. \tag{1.15}$$

To determine the parameter λ_i in terms of the matrix $\mathbf{A}$, note that according to (1.15) the probability of leaving state i in a small interval h is equal to $H_i(h) = \lambda_i h + o(h)$. Comparing this with (1.8) shows that λ_i is exactly the instantaneous transition rate out of state i:

$$\lambda_i = -a_{i,i}, \quad i = 0, 1, \ldots. \tag{1.16}$$

From (1.15), (1.7) and the memoryless property it follows that the probability that the process remains in state i for time x and then moves to state j in the infinitesimal interval $(x, x + dx)$ is equal to

$$\mathrm{e}^{-\lambda_i x} a_{i,j} \mathrm{d}x, \quad x \geq 0, \quad j \neq i.$$

Integrating this expression over all $x \geq 0$ gives us the probability that the next state to be entered will be state j:

$$q_{i,j} = \int_0^\infty \mathrm{e}^{-\lambda_i x} a_{i,j} \mathrm{d}x = \frac{a_{i,j}}{\lambda_i} = -\frac{a_{i,j}}{a_{i,i}}, \quad i \neq j = 0, 1, \dots. \tag{1.17}$$

We derived (1.15) and (1.17) under the assumption that the Markov process was observed at some arbitrary, but fixed, moment t. These results continue to hold if, for example, the process is observed just after it enters state i. Moreover, a stronger assertion can be made (we state it without proof): given that the process has just entered state i, the time it spends there and the state it enters next are mutually independent.

The behaviour of a Markov process can thus be described as follows: at time $t = 0$ the process starts in some state, say i; it remains there for an interval of time distributed exponentially with parameter λ_i (average length $1/\lambda_i$); the process then enters state j with probability $q_{i,j}$, remains there for an exponentially distributed interval with mean $1/\lambda_j$, enters state k with probability $q_{j,k}$, etc. The successive states visited by the process form a "Markov chain" — that is, the next state depends on the one immediately before it, but not on all the previous ones and not on the number of moves made so far. This Markov chain is said to be "embedded" in the Markov process.

We shall conclude this section by examining a little more closely the exponential distribution defined in (1.15). That distribution plays a central role in most probabilistic models that are analytically tractable. It owes its preeminent position to the memoryless property. If the duration η of a certain activity is distributed exponentially with parameter λ, and if that activity is observed at time x after its beginning, then the remaining duration of the activity is independent of x and is also distributed exponentially with parameter λ:

$$P(\eta > x + y \mid \eta > x) = \frac{P(\eta > x + y)}{P(\eta > x)} = \frac{\mathrm{e}^{-\lambda(x+y)}}{\mathrm{e}^{-\lambda x}} = \mathrm{e}^{-\lambda y} = P(\eta > y).$$

$$\tag{1.18}$$

On the other hand, we have seen in the derivation of (1.15) that (excluding the degenerate cases) the memoryless property implies the exponential distribution. There are, therefore, no other distributions with that property.

Let η_1 and η_2 be two independent random variables with distribution functions

$$F_1(x) = 1 - e^{-\lambda_1 x}; \quad F_2(x) = 1 - e^{-\lambda_2 x},$$

and density functions

$$f_1(x) = \lambda_1 e^{-\lambda_1 x}; \quad f_2(x) = \lambda_2 e^{-\lambda_2 x},$$

respectively. Think of η_1 and η_2 as the durations of two activities which are in progress simultaneously. The two activities are observed at a given moment; neither of them has completed. It is then of interest to know the distribution of the interval, η, until the first completion of an activity and the probability, q_i, that the i-th activity will complete first $(i = 1, 2)$. Denote the distribution function and the density function of η by $F(x)$ and $f(x)$, respectively. Using the conventional notation $P(\eta = x)/dx$ in place of $\lim_{\Delta x \to 0} [P(x \leq \eta < x + \Delta x)/\Delta x]$, and the memoryless property, we can write

$$\begin{aligned}
f(x)dx &= P(\eta = x) = P(\min(\eta_1, \eta_2) = x) \\
&= P(\eta_1 = x)P(\eta_2 \geq x) + P(\eta_1 \geq x)P(\eta_2 = x) \\
&= f_1(x)dx[1 - F_2(x)] + f_2(x)dx[1 - F_1(x)] \\
&= \lambda_1 e^{-\lambda_1 x} e^{-\lambda_2 x} dx + \lambda_2 e^{-\lambda_2 x} e^{-\lambda_1 x} dx \\
&= (\lambda_1 + \lambda_2) e^{-(\lambda_1 + \lambda_2)x} dx.
\end{aligned} \tag{1.19}$$

The time until the first completion is thus distributed exponentially with parameter $(\lambda_1 + \lambda_2)$. The probability that activity 1 will complete first is given by

$$q_1 = P(\eta_1 < \eta_2) = \int_0^\infty f_1(x)[1 - F_2(x)]dx = \lambda_1/(\lambda_1 + \lambda_2). \tag{1.20}$$

Similarly, $q_2 = P(\eta_2 > \eta_1) = \lambda_2/(\lambda_1 + \lambda_2)$. Moreover, it is easily seen that the time until the nearest completion does not depend on which activity completes first. For instance,

$$P(\eta = x \mid \eta_1 < \eta_2) = (\lambda_1 + \lambda_2) e^{-(\lambda_1 + \lambda_2)x} dx = P(\eta = x). \tag{1.21}$$

These results, which can be generalised in an obvious way to any (even infinite) number of activities, give an intuitive meaning to expressions (1.15) and (1.17) concerning the holding times and transition probabilities of a Markov process.

When the process enters state i, we can imagine exponentially distributed activities, representing the transitions from state i to state j ($j = 0, 1, \ldots$), being started all at once. The parameter of the j-th distribution is $a_{i,j}$. The holding time in state i is then the time until the first completion of an activity; the next state entered is the index of that first activity.

1.3. Poisson arrival streams. Important properties

The telephone calls received at a switchboard, the impacts by molecules to which a small particle immersed in liquid is subjected, the breakdown of machines in a large factory — all these, and many other physical phenomena, give rise to Poisson processes. In general, a Poisson process is used to model a sequence of events — we shall refer to them as "arrivals" — whose moments of occurrence satisfy certain probabilistic conditions. In textbooks on stochastic processes, the definition and treatment of the Poisson process usually precede those of general Markov processes. Here, however, we wish to be as economical as possible; having developed some Markov process theory, we shall apply it to this very special case.

The Poisson process, $\{N(t), t \geq 0\}$, is a Markov process which satisfies the following restrictions:

(i) $N(0) = 0$ with probability 1,
(ii) from state i ($i = 0, 1, \ldots$) the process moves to state $i + 1$ with probability 1; the instantaneous transition rate $a_{i,i+1}$ does not depend on i ($a_{i,i+1} = \lambda, i = 0, 1, \ldots$).

We have thus defined a counting process: the value of $N(t)$ is equal to the number of moves, or the number of arrivals, in the interval $(0, t]$. The distribution of that number, $p_k(t) = P(N(t) = k \mid N(0) = 0)$, $k = 0, 1, \ldots$, constitutes the first row of the transition probability matrix $\mathbf{P}(t)$ defined in the last section. We are now in the happy position of being able to use the general result (1.12) to find the desired distribution; the Poisson process is just simple enough to permit such an approach.

Restriction (ii), together with (1.9) and (1.17), imply that the instantaneous transition matrix of the Poisson process has the form

$$\mathbf{A} = \begin{bmatrix} -\lambda & \lambda & 0 & 0 & \cdots \\ 0 & -\lambda & \lambda & 0 & \cdots \\ 0 & 0 & -\lambda & \lambda & \cdots \\ & & \cdots\cdots\cdots & & \end{bmatrix} = \lambda(-\mathbf{I} + \mathbf{U}). \tag{1.22}$$

Here, $\mathbf{I}$ is the (infinite) identity matrix and $\mathbf{U}$ is the matrix which has ones on the first upper diagonal and zeros everywhere else:

$$\mathbf{U} = \begin{bmatrix} 0 & 1 & 0 & 0 & \cdots \\ 0 & 0 & 1 & 0 & \cdots \\ 0 & 0 & 0 & 1 & \cdots \\ & & \cdots\cdots\cdots & & \end{bmatrix}.$$

Substituting (1.22) into (1.12) yields

$$\mathbf{P}(t) = e^{\lambda(\mathbf{U}-\mathbf{I})t} = e^{-\lambda t} e^{\lambda \mathbf{U} t} = e^{-\lambda t} \sum_{n=0}^{\infty} \frac{(\lambda t)^n}{n!} \mathbf{U}^n. \tag{1.23}$$

Now, the matrix $\mathbf{U}^n$ has ones on the n-th upper diagonal and zeros everywhere else. Therefore, the first row of the matrix defined by the series on the right-hand side of (1.23) is $(1, \lambda t, (\lambda t)^2/2!, \ldots)$. The probability of k arrivals in the interval $(0, t]$ is equal to

$$p_k(t) = \frac{e^{-\lambda t}(\lambda t)^k}{k!}, \quad k = 0, 1, \ldots. \tag{1.24}$$

Because of the memoryless property, the probability of k arrivals in any interval of length t is also given by (1.24). In a small interval of length h, there is one arrival with probability $p_1(h) = \lambda h + o(h)$. The probability that there are two or more arrivals in an interval of length h is $P_{>1}(h) = o(h)$. These last properties (plus the memoryless one) are sometimes given as defining axioms for the Poisson process.

Since the Poisson process is a Markov process, the holding times, i.e. the intervals between consecutive arrivals, are independent and distributed exponentially with parameter λ. This property too, can be taken as a definition of the Poisson process; it implies the Markov property and everything else. The expected length of the interarrival intervals is $1/\lambda$. Therefore, the average number of arrivals per unit time is λ. For that reason, the parameter λ is called the "rate" of the Poisson process. The average number of arrivals in an interval of length t is

$$E[N(t)] = \lambda t, \tag{1.25}$$

as can also be seen directly from (1.24).

Often in practice, arrival streams from two or more different sources merge before reaching a single destination. We shall see this happening, for example, in queueing networks (Chapter 3). Now, if the component processes are Poisson, then the result of this merging, or superposition operation is also Poisson. Indeed, let $\{N_1(t), t \geq 0\}$ and $\{N_2(t), t \geq 0\}$ be two independent Poisson processes with rates λ_1 and λ_2, respectively, and let $\{N(t) = N_1(t) + N_2(t), t \geq 0\}$ be their superposition. Consider the interval η between an arbitrary moment t_0 and the next arrival instant of $\{N(t)\}$. Clearly, $\eta = \min(\eta_1, \eta_2)$, where η_i is the interval between t_0 and the next arrival instant of $\{N_i(t)\}, i = 1, 2$. Since the component processes are Poisson, η_1 and η_2 are exponentially distributed with parameters λ_1 and λ_2, respectively; also they are mutually independent. By (1.19), η is exponentially distributed with parameter $\lambda = \lambda_1 + \lambda_2$. This, in turn, implies that $\{N(t), t \geq 0\}$ is Poisson with rate λ.

The above argument generalises easily. The superposition of an arbitrary number of independent Poisson processes is Poisson, with rate equal to the sum of the component rates. Moreover, the superposition is approximately Poisson even if the individual components are not, as long as they are independent and there is a large number of them. This explains why Poisson arrival processes are frequently observed in practice. For example, if each user of a computing facility submits jobs independently of the others, and there are many users, the total stream of jobs will be approximately Poisson.

Consider now the splitting, or "decomposition", of a Poisson process $\{N(t), t \geq 0\}$ into two components $\{N_1(t), t \geq 0\}$ and $\{N_2(t), t \geq 0\}$. The decomposition is performed by a sequence of independent Bernoulli trials: every arrival of the process $\{N\}$ is assigned to the process $\{N_i\}$ with probability α_i $(i = 1, 2; \alpha_1 + \alpha_2 = 1)$. The joint distribution of $N_1(t)$ and $N_2(t)$ can be obtained as follows:

$$
\begin{aligned}
P(N_1(t) = n_1, N_2(t) = n_2) &= P(N_1(t) = n_1, N_2(t) \\
&= n_2 \mid N(t) = n_1 + n_2)P(N(t) = n_1 + n_2) \\
&= \frac{(n_1 + n_2)!}{n_1! n_2!} \alpha_1^{n_1} \alpha_2^{n_2} \frac{\mathrm{e}^{-\lambda t}(\lambda t)^{n_1 + n_2}}{(n_1 + n_2)!} \\
&= \frac{\mathrm{e}^{-\alpha_1 \lambda t}(\alpha_1 \lambda t)^{n_1}}{n_1!} \frac{\mathrm{e}^{-\alpha_2 \lambda t}(\alpha_2 \lambda t)^{n_2}}{n_2!}, \tag{1.26}
\end{aligned}
$$

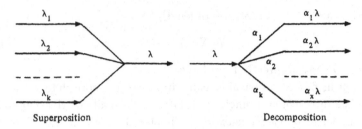

Fig. 1.2.

where we have used (1.24). We see that the processes resulting from the decomposition are both Poisson (with rates $\alpha_1\lambda$ and $\alpha_2\lambda$, respectively). Not only that, these processes are independent of each other. This result, too, generalises to arbitrary number of components.

The superposition and decomposition of Poisson processes are illustrated in Fig. 1.2.

In analysing system performance, we frequently employ the technique of "tagging" an incoming customer and following his progress through the system. It is therefore important to know something about the system state distribution that customers see when they arrive. In this respect, Poisson arrivals have a very useful, and apparently unique property: they behave like random observers. More precisely, let $\{S(t), t \geq 0\}$ be a stochastic process representing the state of a queueing system. That system is fed with customers by one or more arrival streams. Consider an arbitrary moment t_0; let $S(t_0^-)$ be the system state just prior to t_0. Then, if the arrival streams are Poisson, the random variable $S(t_0^-)$ is independent of whether there is an arrival at t_0 or not (Strauch [8]). This is because $S(t_0^-)$ is influenced only by the past history of the arrival processes, and that is independent of whether there is an arrival at t_0 (looking backwards in time, the interarrival intervals are still exponentially distributed and hence memoryless).

Thus, an arrival from a Poisson stream sees the same system state distribution as someone who just happens to look at the system, having otherwise nothing to do with it (a random observer).

To appreciate this remarkable property better, let us take a contrasting example where the arrival stream is decidedly not Poisson. Imagine a conveyor belt bringing machine parts to an operator at intervals ranging between 20 and 30 minutes; the operation performed on each part lasts between 10 and 18 minutes. Two hours after starting the belt, a random observer (the shop floor supervisor?) may well see the operator diligently at work. But if a machine part arrives at that time, it is guaranteed to find him idle!

Before leaving the topic of Poisson processes, let us derive the distribution of the time T_n until the n-th arrival instant. That random variable — the sum of n independent exponentially distributed intervals with the same mean — plays an important role in modelling. Denote its distribution function by $G_n(x)$. From the definition of T_n, and from (1.24), we have

$$G_n(x) = P(T_n \leq x) = P(N(x) \geq n) = \sum_{k=n}^{\infty} e^{-\lambda x} (\lambda x)^k / k!$$

$$= 1 - \sum_{k=0}^{n-1} e^{-\lambda x} (\lambda x)^k / k!.$$

That function is called "the n-stage Erlang distribution function". Its derivative

$$g_n(x) = G_n'(x) = \lambda e^{-\lambda x} (\lambda x)^{n-1} / (n-1)!,$$

is "the n-stage Erlang density function". The mean and variance of T_n are, respectively, n/λ and n/λ^2.

1.4. Steady-state. Balance diagrams. The "Birth and Death" process

So far, we have been concerned with time-dependent properties of stochastic processes. The chief objects of interest in a Markov process were the transition probability functions $p_{i,j}(y)$ relating the state of the process at a given moment to its state at time y later. Now, although the process state at time t depends on the initial state (at time 0), we feel intuitively that in a "well-behaved" system that dependence should weaken as t increases. In the long run, the probability of finding the process in a given state should be independent of where the process started and should cease to vary with time.

Let us give these intuitive ideas a more precise meaning. Consider a Markov process $\{S(t), t \geq 0\}$ with state space $\{0, 1, \ldots\}$ and instantaneous transition rate matrix $\mathbf{A} = [a_{i,j}]$, $i, j = 0, 1, \ldots$. The time-dependent behaviour of the process is described by the matrix of transition probability functions $\mathbf{P}(t) = [p_{i,j}(t)], i, j = 0, 1, \ldots$. We say that steady-state (or equilibrium, or long-run) regime exists for that process if (i), the limits

$$\pi_j = \lim_{t\to\infty} p_{i,j}(t) = \lim_{t\to\infty} P(S(t) = j \mid S(0) = i), \quad j = 0, 1, \ldots, \quad (1.27)$$

exist and are independent of the initial state, and (ii), these limits constitute a probability distribution:

$$\sum_{j=0}^{\infty} \pi_j = 1. \tag{1.28}$$

To justify the term "steady-state", suppose that the distribution $\pi = (\pi_0, \pi_1, \ldots)$ exists and let $x \to \infty$ in the Chapman–Kolmogorov equations (1.4). Since every row of $\mathbf{P}(x)$ tends to π, and every row of $\mathbf{P}(x+y)$ tends to π, this yields

$$\pi \mathbf{P}(y) = \pi, \quad y \geq 0. \tag{1.29}$$

In other words, if at any moment the process state has the steady-state distribution, then it has the steady-state distribution at time y later, no matter how large or small y is. The state distribution becomes invariant with respect to time.

There are two important questions which arise in this connection. First, under what conditions does a steady-state regime exist for a Markov process? Second, how does one determine the steady-state distribution of the process? We shall leave the question of existence until the end of this section and concentrate now on the determination of the vector π, assuming that it exists.

Differentiating (1.29) at $y = 0$, and remembering that $\mathbf{P}'(0) = \mathbf{A}$, we obtain a system of linear equations for π:

$$\pi \mathbf{A} = \mathbf{0}. \tag{1.30}$$

This is known as the system of "balance equations", for reasons which will become apparent shortly. Being homogeneous, that system determines the vector π up to a multiplicative constant; the normalising equation (1.28) then completes the determination.

The balance equations have a strong intuitive appeal. To see this, let us write the i-th equation in the form

$$-a_{i,i}\pi_i = \sum_{\substack{j=0 \\ j\neq i}}^{\infty} a_{j,i}\pi_j. \tag{1.31}$$

Now, we can think of π_j as the proportion of time (in the steady-state) that the process spends in state j. While the process is in state j, it moves to state i at rate $a_{j,i}$ (since $a_{j,i}$ is the instantaneous transition rate from state j to state i; see (1.7)). Therefore, the product $\pi_j a_{j,i}$ is equal to the average number of transitions from state j to state i per unit time. The right-hand side of (1.31) thus represents the average number of times that the process enters state i per unit time. Similarly, the left-hand side of (1.31) represents the average number of times that the process leaves state i per unit time (since $-a_{i,i}$ is the instantaneous transition rate out of state i; see (1.8)). If the process is in equilibrium, these two averages must be equal. More generally, if $I = (i_1, i_2, \ldots)$ is any group of states, finite or infinite, then the average number of times that the process enters group I per unit time is equal, in the steady-state, to the average number of times that the process leaves group I per unit time. The balance equations obtained by considering groups of states are not, of course, independent of the system (1.30); however, they are sometimes simpler and easier to deal with.

It is very convenient to describe a Markov process in equilibrium by means of a marked directed graph. This representation, called a "balance diagram", makes it easier to visualise the process structure and often helps to select the set of balance equations best suited for determining the steady-state distribution. The nodes of the balance diagram correspond to the process states. With node i is associated the steady-state probability π_i ($i = 0, 1, \ldots$). There is an arc from node i to node j ($i \neq j$) if the instantaneous transition rate $a_{i,i}$ is non-zero; that arc is labelled $a_{i,j}$. To obtain a balance equation from the diagram, cut off a group of nodes from the rest of the diagram by an imaginary closed curve. If an arc from node i to node j crosses the curve we say that there is a flow $\pi_i a_{i,j}$ across the cut. The total flow out of the cut (from nodes inside to nodes outside) is then equal to the total flow into the cut (from nodes outside to nodes inside). For instance, making a cut around node i alone, we obtain the balance equation (1.31). Note that the term "flow" used here is simply an abbreviation for "average number of transitions per unit time".

Consider, as an example, the celebrated "Birth and Death" Markov process. As well as illustrating the methods of analysis, this example is of interest in its own right since a number of queueing system models turn out to be special cases of it. We think of the Birth and Death process $\{N(t), t \geq 0\}$ as representing the size of a certain population at time t. The only possible transitions out of state i are to states $i + 1$ and $i - 1$, with instantaneous transition rates λ_i, and μ_i, respectively (these are the

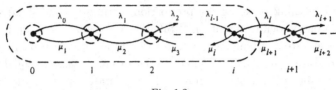

Fig. 1.3.

rates of "Birth" and "Death" when the population size is i), $i = 1, 2, \ldots$.
From state 0 the process moves to state 1, with instantaneous rate λ_0. The
balance diagram for the Birth and Death process is shown in Fig. 1.3.

Making a cut around each node in succession we obtain the system of
balance equations (1.30);

$$\lambda_0 \pi_0 = \mu_1 \pi_1$$
$$(\lambda_1 + \mu_1)\pi_1 = \lambda_0 \pi_0 + \mu_2 \pi_2$$
$$\ldots\ldots\ldots\ldots \tag{1.32}$$
$$(\lambda_i + \mu_i)\pi_i = \lambda_{i-1}\pi_{i-1} + \mu_{i+1}\pi_{i+1}$$
$$\ldots\ldots\ldots\ldots$$

(there are two arcs going out and two arcs coming into each cut, except
for node 0). Alternatively, cutting off the group of states $(0, 1, \ldots, i)$, for
$i = 0, 1, \ldots$, we obtain an equivalent system of balance equations:

$$\lambda_0 \pi_0 = \mu_1 \pi_1$$
$$\lambda_1 \pi_1 = \mu_2 \pi_2$$
$$\ldots\ldots\ldots\ldots \tag{1.33}$$
$$\lambda_i \pi_i = \mu_{i+1}\pi_{i+1}$$
$$\ldots\ldots\ldots\ldots$$

(one arc going out and one arc coming into each cut). The general solution
of (1.33) is easily obtained by successive elimination:

$$\pi_i = \frac{\lambda_0 \lambda_1 \ldots \lambda_{i-1}}{\mu_1 \mu_2 \ldots \mu_i}\pi_0, \quad i = 1, 2, \ldots. \tag{1.34}$$

This leaves one unknown constant, π_0, which is determined from the
normalising condition (1.28):

$$\pi_0 = \left(1 + \frac{\lambda_0}{\mu_1} + \frac{\lambda_0 \lambda_1}{\mu_1 \mu_2} + \cdots\right)^{-1}. \tag{1.35}$$

Note that we have here a necessary condition for equilibrium of the Birth and Death process in order for the solution given by (1.34) and (1.35) to be a probability distribution, the infinite series on the right-hand side of (1.35) must converge. We shall see that the inverse implication also holds: if the series converges, the Birth and Death process has a steady-state. However, in order to state the general result, some preliminaries are needed.

The state j of a Markov process is said to be "reachable" from state i if there is a non-zero probability of finding the process in state j at time t, given that it started in state i : $p_{i,j}(t) > 0$ for all $t > 0$. Since transition probability functions are zero either everywhere or nowhere on the open half-line, the state j is not reachable from i if $p_{i,j}(t) = 0$ for all $t > 0$. A subset σ of process states is said to be "closed" if no state outside σ is reachable from a state in σ. Thus, if the process once enters a closed subset of states, it remains in that subset for ever afterwards. A set of states is said to be "irreducible" if no proper and non-empty subset of it is closed. As far as the long-run behaviour of the process is concerned, an irreducible set of states can be treated in isolation, so we can assume that the set of all states, i.e. the Markov process, is irreducible.

Every state of an irreducible Markov process is reachable from every other state. Indeed, suppose that this is not so, and let i and j be two states such that j is not reachable from i. Consider the set σ of all states reachable from i. That set is closed, since any state k reachable from a state in σ is also reachable from i (this follows from (1.3)) and hence $k \in \sigma$. But σ does not contain j, which contradicts the irreducibility of the process.

The states of a Markov process $\{S(t), t \geq 0\}$ can be classified according to the time the process spends in them. Let $R_{i,j}(t)$ be the average amount of time spent in state j during the interval $[0, t)$, given that $S(0) = i$. Introducing the indicator function of a Boolean B

$$I_B = \begin{cases} 1 & \text{if } B \text{ is true} \\ 0 & \text{if } B \text{ is false} \end{cases}$$

we can write

$$R_{i,j}(t) = E\left[\int_0^t I_{(S(u)=j)}\mathrm{d}u \mid S(0) = i\right]$$

$$= \int_0^t E[I_{(S(u)=j)} \mid S(0) = i]\mathrm{d}u$$

$$= \int_0^t P(S(u) = j \mid S(0) = i)\mathrm{d}u = \int_0^t p_{i,j}(u)\mathrm{d}u. \qquad (1.36)$$

Further, let $R_{i,j}$ be the total average amount of time spent in state j, given that $S(0) = i$:

$$R_{i,j} = \lim_{t \to \infty} R_{i,j}(t) = \int_0^\infty p_{i,j}(u)\mathrm{d}u. \qquad (1.37)$$

A state j is said to be "transient" if $R_{i,j}$ is finite; otherwise j is "recurrent". Since the average time the process remains in state j on every visit is finite (it is equal to $-1/a_{j,j}$), the average number of visits to state j is finite if j is transient and it is infinite if j is recurrent. Denote by $f_{i,j}$ the probability that, starting in state i, the process will ever be in state j. From the remarks above it follows that if state j is recurrent, then $f_{j,j} = 1$ and if state j is transient, then $f_{j,j} < 1$. The inverse implications also hold.

If the Markov process is irreducible, and if $R_{i,j} = \infty$ for some pair of states i and j, then $R_{r,k} = \infty$ for any pair of states r, k. Indeed, taking two arbitrary positive constants v and w, we can write

$$R_{r,k} = \int_0^\infty p_{r,k}(u)\mathrm{d}u \geq \int_0^\infty p_{r,k}(v + u + w)\mathrm{d}u$$

$$\geq \int_0^\infty p_{r,i}(v)p_{i,j}(u)p_{j,k}(w)\mathrm{d}u = p_{r,i}(v)p_{j,k}(w)R_{i,j} = \infty.$$

(The first inequality is obvious; the second follows from the Chapman–Kolmogorov equations (1.3); the irreducibility of the process ensures that $p_{r,i}(v) > 0$ and $p_{j,k}(w) > 0$.) Hence, either all states are transient, or all states are recurrent.

The case of all transient states can be disposed of quickly: if $R_{i,j}$ is finite for all i, j then, according to (1.37),

$$\lim_{t \to \infty} p_{i,j}(t) = 0, \quad i, j = 0, 1, \ldots.$$

In that case, steady-state does not exist.

Suppose now that the Markov process is recurrent, as well as irreducible. Every state is guaranteed to be visited, no matter what the initial state is (if the probability of eventually moving from state i to state j were not 1, there would be a non-zero probability of moving from j to i and not returning to j; state j would not be recurrent). Having once visited a state, the process keeps returning to it *ad infinitum*. Let m_j be the average length of the intervals between consecutive returns to state j, $j = 0, 1, \ldots$. That average length may be finite, in which case state j is said to be "recurrent non-null", or it may be infinite, and then j is "recurrent null".

The moments $t_1, t_2, \ldots$ of successive visits to state j are "regeneration points" for the Markov process: the process behaviour in the interval $[t_n, t_{n+1})$ is a probabilistic replica of that in the interval $[t_{n-1}, t_n)$. The average time spent in state j during each of these intervals is $-1/a_{j,j}$. Therefore, in the long run, the fraction of time that the process spends in state j is independent of the initial state and is given by

$$\lim_{t \to \infty} \frac{R_{i,j}(t)}{t} = \frac{-(1/a_{j,j})}{m_j}, \quad i, j = 0, 1, \ldots. \tag{1.38}$$

On the other hand, that fraction of time is equal to the long-run probability of finding the process in state j:

$$\lim_{t \to \infty} p_{i,j}(t) = \frac{-(1/a_{j,j})}{m_j}, \quad i, j = 0, 1, \ldots. \tag{1.39}$$

Equations (1.38) and (1.39) seem intuitively clear, yet to prove them rigorously is not easy. Some fundamental results from renewal theory are involved (see, for example, Cinlar [3]).

It follows from (1.39) that the limiting probability of state j is zero if $m_j = \infty$, i.e. if j is recurrent null, and vice versa. Moreover, if one state, j, is recurrent null, then all other states are also recurrent null. Choose an arbitrary state k ($k \neq j$) and two positive constants v and w. The following inequality follows from the Chapman–Kolmogorov equations (1.3):

$$p_{j,j}(v + t + w) \geq p_{j,k}(v) p_{k,k}(t) p_{k,j}(w).$$

Since $p_{j,j}(t)$ tends to 0 as $t \to \infty$, so must $p_{k,k}(t)$; hence, state k is recurrent null.

Let us recapitulate the results obtained so far. In an irreducible Markov process, either all states are transient, or all states are recurrent null, or all states are recurrent non-null. In the first two cases, all limiting probabilities are equal to 0; steady-state does not exist. In the last case, all limiting probabilities are non-zero; steady-state exists.

We have seen already that if a steady-state distribution vector $\boldsymbol{\pi}$ exists, it satisfies the system of balance equations (1.30) and the normalising equation (1.28). Now we shall demonstrate that if equations (1.30) and (1.28) have a solution, $\boldsymbol{\pi}$, then steady-state exists.

First, taking the known expression (1.13) for the transition probability matrix

$$\mathbf{P}(t) = \sum_{n=0}^{\infty} \mathbf{A}^n t^n / n!$$

and multiplying both sides by π on the left, we see that if $\pi\mathbf{A} = \mathbf{0}$, then

$$\pi\mathbf{P}(t) = \pi \quad \text{for all} \quad t \geq 0. \tag{1.40}$$

Let $t \to \infty$ in this section. If the Markov process were transient or recurrent null, then every column of $\mathbf{P}(t)$ would tend to $\mathbf{0}$ and we would have $\pi = \mathbf{0}$. That, however, is impossible since π satisfies (1.28). Therefore, the process must be recurrent non-null and hence steady-state exists. In the latter case, all elements of the j-th column of $\mathbf{P}(t)$ tend to the same constant, γ_j (given by (1.39)). The j-th equation in (1.40) becomes, in the limit,

$$\pi_j = \sum_{i=0}^{\infty} \pi_i \gamma_j = \gamma_j, \quad j = 0, 1, \ldots.$$

In other words, if a solution of (1.30) and (1.28) exists, then it is unique and is precisely the steady-state distribution of the process.

So, an irreducible Markov process $\{S(t), t \geq 0\}$ has a steady-state regime if, and only if, the balance equations (1.30) have a solution $\pi = (\pi_0, \pi_1, \ldots)$ whose elements sum up to 1; that solution is then unique and represents the steady-state distribution of the process:

$$\pi_j = \lim_{t \to \infty} P(S(t) = j), \quad j = 0, 1, \ldots.$$

This important result is the point of departure for most analytic and numerical studies of systems modelled by Markov processes.

Returning to the Birth and Death process considered earlier, we can assert now that the necessary and sufficient condition for existence of steady-state is the convergence of the series appearing on the right-hand side of (1.35); when it exists, the steady-state distribution is given by (1.34) and (1.35). That assertion follows from the result above and from the fact that the Birth and Death process is irreducible; the probability $p_{i,j}(t)$ of moving from state i to state j in time t is obviously non-zero, for all i, j and all $t > 0$.

1.5. The $M/M/1$, $M/M/c$ and related queueing systems

We shall examine here several models which fit easily into the framework of the theory developed in the last section. Although these models are rather simple, they manage to capture and display some essential features of mass-service systems. In particular, they illustrate very clearly the way in which

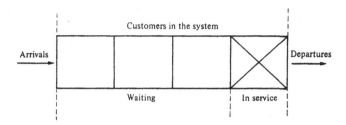

Fig. 1.4.

system performance is influenced by the level of user demand and by the capacity and availability of servers.

Consider a single-server queueing system where all customers are of the same type and are served in order of arrival (that service discipline is usually referred to as FIFO, first-in-first-out, or FCFS first-come-first-served). There is no restriction on the size of the queue that may develop and no customer leaves the queue before completing service (Fig. 1.4). Such a system can be used to model a counter at a bank, a car-washing station, a uniprogrammed computer, etc. Under a suitable set of assumptions the model becomes a Markov process which lends itself to analysis. The simplest way to ensure that the memoryless property holds is to assume that consecutive interarrival times are independent and distributed exponentially with mean $1/\lambda$ (i.e. the arrival stream is Poisson with rate λ), and consecutive service times are independent and distributed exponentially with mean $1/\mu$; also, the arrival and service processes are mutually independent. We thus obtain the $M/M/1$ queueing model. Let $N(t)$ be the number of customers in the system (waiting and in service) at time t. From the memoryless property of the exponential distribution it follows that

$$P(N(t+y) = j \mid N(t) = i) = P_{i,j}(y), \quad i,j = 0,1,\ldots$$

independently of t and of the past history $\{N(u), u < t\}$. Therefore, $\{N(t), t \geq 0\}$ is a Markov process. The only possible transitions out of state i $(i = 1,2,\ldots)$ are to states $i+1$ (if an arrival occurs before a service completion) and $i-1$ (if a service completion occurs before an arrival). The instantaneous transition rates are $a_{i,i+1} = \lambda$ and $a_{i,i-1} = \mu$. From state 0 the process always moves to state 1, with instantaneous rate $a_{0,1} = \lambda$.

We recognise here a special case of the Birth and Death process introduced in the last section, with $\lambda_i = \lambda$ $(i = 0,1,\ldots)$ and $\mu_i = \mu$ $(i = 1,2,\ldots)$.

Denoting $(\lambda/\mu) = \rho$, the general solution (1.34) of the balance equations becomes

$$\pi_i = \rho^i \pi_0, \quad i = 0, 1, \dots. \tag{1.41}$$

The necessary and sufficient condition for the existence of a solution whose elements sum up to 1, and hence for the existence of steady-state, is $\rho < 1$. When the system is in equilibrium, the number of customers in it is distributed geometrically:

$$P(N = i) = \pi_i = \rho^i (1 - \rho), \quad i = 0, 1, \dots. \tag{1.42}$$

The expectation, $E[N]$, and the variance, $\text{Var}[N]$, of that number are given by

$$E[N] = \sum_{i=1}^{\infty} i\pi_i = \rho/(1 - \rho), \tag{1.43}$$

and

$$\text{Var}[N] = E[N^2] - E^2[N] = \sum_{i=1}^{\infty} i^2 \pi_i - E^2[N] = \rho/(1 - \rho)^2. \tag{1.44}$$

In order to give physical meaning to these results, it is helpful to distinguish the amount of service required by a customer, or the "job length", from the speed of the server. Job lengths are measured in "units of work" (in computer systems the unit of work is usually a machine instruction), while the speed of the server is measured in "units of work per unit time". The time unit can always be chosen so that the server speed is 1; then the service time of a customer is simply the amount of work that he requires.

The average number of customers arriving into the system per unit time is λ. The average amount of work required by a customer is $1/\mu$. Hence, the quantity ρ represents the average amount of work brought into the system per unit time; for that reason, it is referred to as "traffic intensity". The condition for existence of steady-state now reads: the average amount of work brought into the system per unit time must be less than the speed of the server (the amount of work that it can do per unit time). This is a very natural requirement; we shall come across it many times, under much more general assumptions.

When the traffic intensity is less than 1, the process $\{N(t), t \geq 0\}$ is recurrent non-null. Every state, and in particular the state $N = 0$, occurs infinitely many times, at intervals whose expectations are finite. The system goes through alternating "busy" and "idle" periods. We shall see at the end of this section that the steady-state distribution can, in fact, be determined directly from these regeneration cycles.

As $\rho \to 1$, the steady-state average number of customers in the system tends to infinity. The state $N = 0$ occurs less and less often. The variance of N also tends to infinity, which means that a randomly observed queue size is likely to be very far from the expected one.

When $\rho = 1$, the process is recurrent null (we state this without proof). Every state is still visited infinitely many times but the intervals between visits are infinitely long on the average. The long-run mean and variance of N are infinite, and the probability of observing any given N is zero.

When $\rho > 1$, the process is transient (again we give no proof). The number of jobs in the system grows eventually above any finite number, never to drop below it again. Not only is the fraction of time that the system spends in any given state zero in the long run, but the total time it spends in any state is finite.

We shall sometimes use the terms "non-saturated system" and "saturated system" to describe the cases $\rho < 1$ and $\rho \geq 1$, respectively.

A random variable of central importance in a queueing system is the steady-state response time, w (the time a customer spends in the system). The average response time is often taken as a measure of system performance.

We now proceed to find the probability density function $f_w(x)$ of the response time in an $M/M/1$ system in equilibrium. First, from the random observer property of the Poisson stream (see section 1.3), it follows that an arriving customer sees the steady-state distribution (1.42) of the number of customers in the system. Next, from the memoryless property of the exponential distribution, if the new arrival finds a customer in service, the remaining service time of that customer is distributed exponentially with mean $1/\mu$. The response time of a customer who finds n customers in the system is therefore the sum of $n + 1$ independent exponentially distributed random variables. Such a sum has the $n + 1$ stage Erlang density function $g_{n+1}(x)$ defined in section 1.3:

$$g_{n+1}(x) = \mu(\mu x)^n e^{-\mu x}/n!. \tag{1.45}$$

Combining (1.42) and (1.45), and remembering that $\rho = \lambda/\mu$, we obtain

$$f_w(x) = \sum_{n=0}^{\infty} \pi_n g_{n+1}(x) = (1 - \rho)\mu e^{-\mu x} \sum_{n=0}^{\infty} (\rho\mu x)^n/n! = (\mu - \lambda)e^{-(\mu-\lambda)x}. \tag{1.46}$$

The response time is thus distributed exponentially. No matter how long a customer has already spent in the system, his remaining time there still has the same distribution. The average response time $W = E[w]$ is equal to

$$W = \frac{1}{\mu - \lambda} = \frac{1}{\mu(1 - \rho)}. \tag{1.47}$$

Note that this performance measure differs from those in (1.43) and (1.44) in that it depends on λ and μ not just through their ratio ρ. It is possible for a system to be nearly saturated, with large queue sizes, and yet to have a very short expected response time.

Let us now generalise the model by allowing c parallel servers (each of unit speed), keeping the other assumptions as before. This is the $M/M/c$ queueing system. If at a given moment there are i customers in the system, the number of customers in service is $\min(i, c)$. Since each service time is distributed exponentially with parameter μ, the interval until the nearest service completion is distributed exponentially with parameter $\mu \min(i, c)$. The process representing the number of customers in the system, $\{N(t), t \geq 0\}$, is therefore a Birth and Death process with constant birth rate, $\lambda_i = \lambda$ $(i = 0, 1, \ldots)$, and state-dependent death rate, $\mu_i = \mu \min(i, c)$. The general solution (1.34) of the balance equations is

$$\pi_i = \begin{cases} (\rho^i/i!)\pi_0, & i = 0, 1, \ldots, c \\ [\rho^i/(c!c^{i-c})]\pi_0 = (\rho/c)^{i-c}\pi_c, & i > c. \end{cases} \tag{1.48}$$

Steady-state exists if, and only if, $\rho < c$. As before, this is a requirement that the average amount of work brought into the system per unit time should be less than the amount of work that can be done per unit time. When $\rho \geq c$ the system is saturated (recurrent null if $\rho = c$ and transient if $\rho > c$).

To determine the steady-state distribution we need the probability of the idle state:

$$\pi_0 = \left[\sum_{i=0}^{c-1} (\rho^i/i!) + (\rho^c/c!)c/(c - \rho) \right]^{-1}. \tag{1.49}$$

Various performance measures can now be obtained, although the expressions tend to be complicated. In general, an $M/M/c$ system is less efficient than an $M/M/1$ system with an equivalent service capacity. Let us carry out the comparison between an $M/M/2$ system with parameters λ and μ, and $M/M/1$ system with parameters λ and 2μ. The non-saturation condition is, in both cases, $\lambda < 2\mu$. We shall use the expected number of customers in the system, $E[N]$, as a measure of performance. In the $M/M/1$ system we have, from (1.43),

$$E[N]_{M/M/1} = \frac{\lambda}{2\mu - \lambda}.$$

For the $M/M/2$ system, we find first

$$\pi_0 = [1 + \rho + \rho^2/(2 - \rho)]^{-1} = (2 - \rho)/(2 + \rho).$$

The expression for $E[N]$ now becomes

$$E[N]_{M/M/2} = \sum_{i=1}^{\infty} i\pi_i = \frac{4\lambda\mu}{(2\mu - \lambda)(2\mu + \lambda)}.$$

The non-saturation condition implies that

$$\frac{4\mu}{2\mu + \lambda} > 1.$$

Therefore

$$E[N]_{M/M/2} > E[N]_{M/M/1}.$$

A similar inequality holds for any number of servers. The reason for the worse performance of the $M/M/c$ system is that its full service capacity is not always utilised: when there are less than c customers in the system, some servers are idle. The $M/M/c$ system is, in its turn, more efficient than c independent servers with separate queues (i.e. c $M/M/1$ systems), where each new arrival joins any of the queues with equal probability. We leave that comparison as an exercise to the reader. The lesson that emerges from all this is that, other things being equal, a pooling of resources leads to improved performance.

A limiting case of the $M/M/c$ system is the system with infinitely many servers, $M/M/\infty$. Clearly, there can be no queue of waiting customers here. The solution of the balance equations is as in (1.48), top case, for all i:

$$\pi_i = (\rho^i/i!)\pi_0, \quad i = 0, 1, \dots. \tag{1.50}$$

That solution can always be normalised:

$$\pi_0 = \left[\sum_{i=0}^{\infty} (\rho^i/i!) \right]^{-1} = e^{-\rho}.$$

Hence, steady-state always exists. This, of course, is hardly surprising since the service capacity is infinite. The expected number of customers in the system is $E[N] = \rho$.

Other members of the Birth and Death family are models with limited waiting room: there is a maximum number K of customers that can be allowed into the system at any one time. All new arrivals who find K customers in the system are turned away and are lost. Steady-state always exists in these systems because the number of states is finite. When a limit on the waiting room is imposed, it is included in the Kendall notation as another descriptor after the number of servers, e.g. $M/G/1/K$. We shall mention here two systems of this type. The first is the $M/M/1/K$ system, where there can be one customer in service and at most $K - 1$ waiting.

For us the interest of this model lies in the fact that it is equivalent to the following closed cyclic system: K customers circulate endlessly between two servers, 1 and 2, whose service times are distributed exponentially with means $1/\mu$ and $1/\lambda$, respectively. The order of service is FIFO at both servers (Fig. 1.5). The cyclic model can be applied, for example, to a computer system consisting of one CPU and one Input/Output device, with K jobs sharing the main memory.

To see the equivalence between the $M/M/1/K$ and the cyclic system note that as long as the number of customers at server 1 is less than K, customers arrive there at intervals distributed exponentially with mean $1/\lambda$; when all K customers are at server 1, the arrivals stop. This is the same as having a Poisson arrival stream which is turned off in state K.

The steady-state distribution of the $M/M/1/K$ system state is given by

$$\pi_i = \rho^i \pi_0, \quad i = 0, 1, \ldots, K, \tag{1.51}$$

where $\rho = \lambda/\mu$ and $\pi_0 = (1 - \rho)/(1 - \rho^{K+1})$; when $\rho = 1$, $\pi_i = 1/(K + 1)$, $i = 0, 1, \ldots, K$.

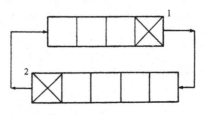

Fig. 1.5.

Our other example is the $M/M/c/c$ system, where only customers who find idle servers are admitted. The classic application for such a model is a telephone exchange with c lines. The steady-state distribution of the number of busy servers is

$$\pi_i = (\rho^i/i!)\pi_0, \quad i = 0, 1, \ldots, c, \tag{1.52}$$

where

$$\pi_0 = \sum_{i=0}^{c} (\rho^i/i!)^{-1}.$$

A measure of performance for this system is the fraction of customers that is lost. Since Poisson arrivals behave like random observers, that fraction is equal to

$$\pi_c = (\rho^c/c!) \left/ \left[\sum_{i=0}^{c} (\rho/i!) \right] \right. . \tag{1.53}$$

Expression (1.53) is known as "Erlang's loss formula".

Let us now return to the $M/M/1$ queueing system and analyse it in the steady-state by applying a renewal theory argument. We have mentioned that when $\rho < 1$, every state is entered infinitely many times at intervals whose expectation is finite. Let $t_1, t_2, \ldots$ be the consecutive moments when the queueing process $\{N(t), t \geq 0\}$ enters state 0. These moments are regeneration points for the process: the behaviour of $N(t)$ on the interval $[t_j, t_{j+1})$ is an independent probabilistic replica of its behaviour on the interval $[t_{j-1}, t_j), j = 2, 3, \ldots$. In particular, the interval lengths $(t_{j+1} - t_j), j = 1, 2, \ldots$, are independent and identically distributed. Denote their expectation by T:

$$T = E[t_{j+1} - t_j].$$

Let T_i be the total expected amount of time that the process spends in state i during a regeneration period $(i = 0, 1, \ldots)$. By the same argument that led to equations (1.38) and (1.39) it can be shown that the long-run fraction of time that the process spends in state i, and hence the steady-state probability of state i, is given by

$$\pi_i = T_i/T, \quad i = 0, 1, \ldots . \tag{1.54}$$

Now we proceed to find the expectations T_i. Denote by M_i the average number of visits to state i during a regeneration period. Then, since the average time the process remains in state 0 on each visit is $1/\lambda$, and the average time it remains in state i ($i > 0$) on each visit is $1/(\lambda+\mu)$, we have

$$
\begin{aligned}
T_0 &= M_0/\lambda \\
T_i &= M_i/(\lambda+\mu), \quad i = 1, 2, \ldots
\end{aligned}
\tag{1.55}
$$

But a visit to state i is either a result of a transition from state $i-1$, with probability $\lambda/(\lambda+\mu)$, or a result of a transition from state $i+1$, with probability $\mu/(\mu+\lambda)$, $i = 1, 2, \ldots$. State 0 can be entered only from state 1, with probability $\mu/(\mu+\lambda)$ (for the transition probabilities, see (1.17)). Hence,

$$
\begin{aligned}
M_0 &= \frac{\mu}{\lambda+\mu} M_1 \\
M_i &= \frac{\lambda}{\lambda+\mu} M_{i-1} + \frac{\mu}{\lambda+\mu} M_{i+1}, \quad i = 1, 2, \ldots
\end{aligned}
\tag{1.56}
$$

Substituting (1.55) into (1.56) we obtain

$$
\begin{aligned}
\lambda T_0 &= \mu T_1 \\
(\lambda+\mu) T_i &= \lambda T_{i-1} + \mu T_{i+1}, \quad i = 1, 2, \ldots
\end{aligned}
\tag{1.57}
$$

These last equations, together with $T_0 = 1/\lambda$ (there is only one visit to state 0 during a regeneration interval) can be solved by successive elimination:

$$
T_i = \rho^i/\lambda, \quad i = 0, 1, \ldots
\tag{1.58}
$$

The average length of a regeneration interval is, of course, equal to

$$
T = \sum_{i=0}^{\infty} T_i = 1/[\lambda(1-\rho)].
\tag{1.59}
$$

Substituting (1.58) and (1.59) into (1.54) we finally obtain the desired distribution

$$
\pi_i = \rho^i(1-\rho), \quad i = 0, 1, \ldots
$$

Note that the above approach can be applied to the general Birth and Death process as well, with obvious minor modifications.

1.6. Little's result. Applications. The $M/G/1$ system

We shall derive here a simple relation between the average response time and the average number of customers in a queueing system in equilibrium.

The first rigorous proof of that relation was given by Little [6]; hence, it is known as "Little's result", or "Little's theorem". However, the validity of the result had been realised earlier and there were also proofs for some special cases.

Consider an arbitrary queueing system in equilibrium, and let N, W and λ be the average number of customers in the system, the average time customers spend in the system and the average number of arrivals per unit time, respectively. Little's theorem states that

$$N = \lambda W, \tag{1.60}$$

regardless of the interarrival and service time distributions, the service discipline and any dependencies within the system. Note that we have not even specified what constitutes "the system", nor what customers do there. It is just a place where customers arrive, remain for some time and then depart. The only requirement is that the processes involved should be stationary (independent of time).

Let us first give an intuitive justification for (1.60). Suppose that the system receives a reward (or penalty) of 1 for every unit of time that a customer spends in it. Then the total expected reward per unit time is equal to the average number of customers in the system, N. On the other hand, the average number of customers coming into the system per unit time is λ; the expected reward contributed by each customer is equal to his average residence time, W. Since it does not matter whether the reward is collected on arrival or continuously, we must have $N = \lambda W$. (This, and the following argument and proof, are due to Foster [5].)

A different interpretation of relation (1.60) is obtained by rewriting it in the form $\lambda = (N/W)$. Since a customer in the system remains there for an average time of W, his average rate of departure is $1/W$. The total average departure rate is, therefore, N/W. Thus, the relation holds if the average arrival rate is equal to the average departure rate. But the latter is clearly the case since the system is in equilibrium.

The above arguments should suffice to convince us that Little's result holds in its full generality. To prove it formally (admittedly in a slightly less general case: arrivals in batches will be excluded), denote by $F_w(x)$ the probability distribution function of the response time. The average response time is given by

$$W = \int_0^\infty (1 - F_w(x)) \mathrm{d}x.$$

Fix an arbitrary moment t in the steady-state. The customers who are in the system at that moment are those who arrived before t and will depart after t. Since the arrival process is stationary with rate λ and customers arrive one at a time, the probability that there was an arrival at time $t - u$ is $\lambda\,\mathrm{d}u$. Such an arrival is still in the system at time t with probability $1 - F_w(u)$. Therefore, point $t - u$ contributes an average of $\lambda(1 - F_w(u))\mathrm{d}u$ customers to the ones present at time t. Integrating over all values of u yields

$$N = \int_0^\infty \lambda(1 - F_w(u))\mathrm{d}u = \lambda W,$$

thus establishing the result.

Little's original proof of the relation contained another, more basic assertion: if the space averages N, λ and W are replaced by time averages — that is, averages over an individual realisation of the queueing process — then in every such realisation (1.60) holds with probability 1. This is an instance of an operational identity.

Let us now turn to some applications. Consider first a queueing system where customers are served by a number (finite or infinite) of identical servers of unit speed. Denote, as before, the arrival rate by λ and the average service time by $1/\mu$. The relevant distributions can be general, as can be the scheduling discipline. Assume further that customers do not leave before receiving service. Define the set of servers, σ, as "the system", for the purpose of Little's theorem. Since every incoming customer enters a server eventually, the rate of arrivals into σ is also λ. The average time a customer spends in σ is equal to $1/\mu$. According to the theorem, the average number of customers in σ is λ/μ.

Thus, in any $G/G/c$ or $G/G/\infty$ system in equilibrium, the average number of busy servers is equal to the traffic intensity, ρ. One consequence of this is that the condition $\rho < c$ is necessary for the existence of equilibrium in the general case (we have already seen that it is necessary and sufficient in the case $M/M/c$). When $c = 1$, the average number of busy servers is equal to the probability that the server is busy. Therefore, in any single-server system in the steady-state we have

$$P \text{ (there are customers in the system)} = \rho,$$

$$P \text{ (idle system)} = 1 - \rho.$$

(1.61)

Suppose that the customer population is split into classes, numbered $1, 2, \ldots$, with different characteristics. Let the arrival rate and the average service time of class i customers be λ_i and $1/\mu_i$, respectively $(i = 1, 2, \ldots)$. Then, applying Little's theorem to the class i customers only, we find (in exactly the same way as above) that the average number of class i customers in service is $\rho_i = (\lambda_i/\mu_i)$, and it is necessary that $\sum_i \rho_i < c$.

In single-server systems we have

$$P \text{ (a customer of class } i \text{ is in service)} = \rho_i,$$

$$P \text{ (idle system)} = 1 - \sum_i \rho_i.$$

(1.62)

As our next example, we shall find the steady-state average number of customers, N, and the average response time, W, in a single-server system with Poisson arrivals and generally distributed service times $(M/G/1)$. The scheduling discipline is FIFO; interarrival and service times are assumed to be mutually independent; there is a single-customer class. The techniques of the previous sections cannot be applied to this system (at least not directly), because the process $\{N(t), t \geq 0\}$ representing the number of customers in the system is not Markov in general. When the distribution of service times is not exponential, the process behaviour after a given moment depends on its history prior to that moment. However, here we are only interested in the averages N and W, which can be obtained by a rather simple argument. A more detailed study of the $M/G/1$ system will be presented in Chapter 2.

By the random observer property of the Poisson stream, a new arrival into the system finds an average of N customers there. Of these, we saw that an average of ρ are being served and $N - \rho$ are waiting in the queue. Each of the waiting customers will take an average of $1/\mu$ to serve, as will the new arrival himself. Denote by W_0 the expected remaining service time of a customer found in service by a random observer. We can then write, for the expected residence time of the new arrival,

$$W = \rho W_0 + (N - \rho)(1/\mu) + (1/\mu).$$

Substituting Little's result, $W = N/\lambda$, in this equation, and solving for N, we obtain

$$N = \rho + \lambda W_0 \frac{\rho}{1 - \rho}. \qquad (1.63)$$

It remains to determine the quantity W_0. To do this, imagine the consecutive service intervals laid end-to-end on the time axis, thus eliminating any idle periods. The resulting sequence of independent and identically

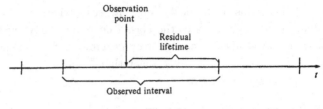

Fig. 1.6.

distributed intervals forms a "renewal process". The end-points of the renewal intervals are called "renewal epochs". We are interested in the random variable representing the time between a random observation point and the next renewal epoch (Fig. 1.6); this is the "residual lifetime" of the renewal interval (also sometimes called "random modification" or "forward recurrence time").

Let $f(x)$, m and M_2 be the probability density function, the mean and the second moment of the renewal interval, respectively (in our case, $m = 1/\mu$). Consider the renewal process over a very long period of time, T. Since, on average, there are T/m renewal intervals during T, and since a renewal interval is of length x with probability $f(x)\mathrm{d}x$, the average number of renewal intervals of length x during the period T is equal to $[Tf(x)\mathrm{d}x]/m$. Hence, the average portion of T covered by renewal intervals of length x is equal to $[Txf(x)\mathrm{d}x]/m$. The random observation point is, by definition, equally likely to fall anywhere in T; therefore, the probability $\tilde{f}(x)\mathrm{d}x$ that the observed renewal interval is of length x is given by

$$\tilde{f}(x)\mathrm{d}x = (xf(x)\mathrm{d}x)/m. \tag{1.64}$$

From (1.64) we obtain the average length, $\tilde{m}$, of the observed renewal interval:

$$\tilde{m} = \int_0^\infty x\tilde{f}(x)\mathrm{d}x = M_2/m. \tag{1.65}$$

Note that $\tilde{m}$ is always greater.than or equal to m, with equality only when $M_2 = m^2$, i.e. when the variance of the renewal interval is zero. This is because a renewal interval which receives the observation point is more likely to be long than one which does not. Since the observation point is equally likely to fall anywhere in the observed interval, the expected residual lifetime is equal to

$$W_0 = \tilde{m}/2 = M_2/(2m). \tag{1.66}$$

It is interesting that, in some cases, the expected residual lifetime can be greater than the expected lifetime!

We can now substitute (1.66) with $m = 1/\mu$, into (1.63). This yields

$$N = \rho + \frac{\lambda^2 M_2}{2(1 - \rho)}. \tag{1.67}$$

The above expression is known as Pollaczek-Khintchine's formula. It is usually written in the form

$$N = \rho + \frac{\rho^2(1 + C^2)}{2(1 - \rho)}. \tag{1.68}$$

where $C^2 = \mathrm{Var}[s]/(E[s])^2 = (\mu^2 M_2) - 1$ is the squared coefficient of variation of the service time s. Here, as in the $M/M/1$ system, we note the appearance of $(1 - \rho)$ in the denominator; the expected number of customers in the system approaches infinity as $\rho \to 1$. For fixed λ and μ, the value of N is determined by the coefficient of variation of the service times. When $C^2 > 1$, the $M/G/1$ system performance is worse than that of the $M/M/1$ system ($C^2 = 1$ for the exponential distribution); when $C^2 < 1$ it is better. The average response time W in the $M/G/1$ system can, of course, be determined easily from Little's theorem: $W = N/\lambda$.

For the last example we return to a topic covered twice already: the steady-state distribution $\{\pi_0, \pi_1, \ldots\}$ of the number of customers in the $M/M/1$ system. An ingenious derivation, using Little's theorem, was, proposed by Foster [5]. Its interest lies in the conjuring trick whereby a distribution is pulled out of a hat containing only averages.

Identify individual queue positions by numbering them $1, 2, \ldots$: 1 is the service position, 2 is the first waiting position, etc. The steady-state probability q_j that the j-th position is occupied is equal to the probability that there are j or more customers in the system:

$$q_j = \pi_j + \pi_{j+1} + \ldots; \quad j = 1, 2, \ldots.$$

This is also the average number of customers in the j-th position.

After a service completion, every customer in the system moves by one queue position to the next lower index. Every customer who finds, on arrival, $j - 1$ or more customers in the system, passes eventually through position j. Therefore, the rate of arrivals into position j is λq_{j-1} ($j = 1, 2, \ldots$; $q_0 = 1$ by definition). The average time that customers remain in position j is equal to $1/\mu$, regardless of whether they arrive there directly or from position $j + 1$ (this is because of the memoryless property of the exponential distribution). Applying Little's theorem to the "system" consisting of the j-th queue position gives

$$q_j = \lambda q_{j-1}/\mu = \rho q_{j-1}; \quad j = 1, 2, \ldots .$$

This, together with $q_0 = 1$, yields

$$q_j = \rho^j \; j = 1, 2, \ldots, \quad \text{or} \quad \pi_j = q_j - q_{j+1} = \rho^j(1 - \rho), \quad j = 0, 1, \ldots ;$$

the same expression as (1.42).

1.7. Operational identities

It will be instructive, at this point, to examine more closely the sample path behaviour of a general queueing process, $\{N(t), t \geq 0\}$, representing the number of customers in a system. Any such sample path is a step function of the type illustrated in Fig. 1.1: the function jumps up by one at arrival instants and it jumps down by one at service completion instants (bulk arrivals and departures are excluded). In this section only, $N(t)$ will denote a sample path function; it should be remembered that this is not now a random variable, but an ordinary function of t describing a particular realisation of the queueing process.

Consider a sample path $N(t)$ over a time interval $[a, b]$ such that $N(a) = N(b)$ (Buzen [2]). Let m and M be, respectively, the minimum and the maximum values reached by $N(t)$ on $[a, b]$. Since all jumps are of unit magnitude, every value n in the range $m \leq n \leq M$ is attained at least once during that interval. For each such n, denote:

$T(n)$, the total amount of time the sample path remains at level n during $[a, b]$;

$A(n)$, the number of jumps from n to $n + 1$ during $[a, b]$ (i.e. the number of arrivals who find n customers in the system);

$D(n)$, the number of jumps from n to $n - 1$ during $[a, b]$ (i.e. the number of departures who leave $n - 1$ customers behind). Clearly, $A(n) > 0$ for $n = m, m + 1, \ldots, M - 1$ and $D(n) > 0$ for $n = m + 1, m + 2, \ldots M$.

From the "operational equilibrium" condition $N(a) = N(b)$ it follows that

$$A(n) = D(n + 1), \quad n = m, m + 1, \ldots, M - 1. \tag{1.69}$$

This equation yields, in a straightforward manner,

$$\frac{A(n)}{T(n)}\frac{T(n)}{T} = \frac{D(n+1)}{T(n+1)}\frac{T(n+1)}{T}, \quad n = m, m+1, \ldots, M-1, \quad (1.70)$$

where $T = b - a$ is the length of the observation interval. Now, $A(n)/T(n)$ is the observed average number of arrivals per unit time in state n; denote it by $\lambda(n)$. Similarly, $\mu(n) = D(n)/T(n)$ is the observed average number of service completions per unit time in state n. The ratio $T(n)/T$, which we shall denote by $p(n)$, represents the observed proportion of time that the system remains in state n. In this notation, (1.70) becomes

$$\lambda(n)p(n) = \mu(n+1)p(n+1), \quad n = m, m+1, \ldots, M-1. \quad (1.71)$$

Note the similarity of form between (1.71) and the balance equations (1.33) of the Birth and Death process. It should be realised, however, that the content is very different. The relations (1.33) were between the parameters λ_i, μ_i of a certain stochastic process, and the probabilities π_i, taken over the set of all sample paths of that process. Those relations could be used to determine the probabilities. Here, on the other hand, we have identities valid for any sample path of any queueing process. The equations (1.71) can also be solved for $p(n)$:

$$p(n) = p(m) \prod_{k=m}^{n-1} \frac{\lambda(k)}{\mu(k+1)}, \quad n = m+1, \ldots, M, \quad (1.72)$$

where $p(m)$ is obtained from the normalising equation

$$\sum_{n=m}^{M} p(n) = 1.$$

The fractions $p(n)$ can thus be determined in terms of the fractions $\lambda(n)$ and $\mu(n)$. The latter are not, however, parameters of the process; they are characteristics of the same sample path for which the former are sought. Knowing the values of $\lambda(n)$ and $\mu(n)$ for one sample path does not help to find the values of $p(n)$ for another sample path.

Suppose now that the sample path $N(t)$ is observed over longer and longer periods of time, and that during those periods it attains wider and wider ranges of values. In other words, let $T \to \infty$, $m \to 0$, $M \to \infty$. Suppose further, that the limits

$$\lambda_n = \lim_{T \to \infty} \frac{A(n)}{T(n)}; \quad \mu_n = \lim_{T \to \infty} \frac{D(n)}{T(n)}; \quad p_n = \lim_{T \to \infty} \frac{T(n)}{T} \qquad (1.73)$$

exist and are non-zero for all $n = 0, 1, \ldots$ (except for μ_0). Continuing the analogy with the Birth and Death process, one would naturally expect the fractions p_n to be the unique solution of the infinite system of equations

$$\sum_{n=0}^{\infty} p_n = 1 \qquad (1.74)$$
$$\lambda_n p_n = \mu_{n+1} p_{n+1}, \quad n = 0, 1, \ldots.$$

This is not necessarily the case, as can be seen from the following example.

Consider the sample path illustrated in Fig. 1.7. $N(t)$ goes through alternating busy and idle periods of unit length. During the i-th busy period $(i = 2, 3, \ldots)$, it spends time $\varepsilon/2^{n-1}$ at level n, $n = 1, 2, \ldots, i-1$, and the rest of the time at level i $(0 < \varepsilon < \frac{1}{2})$. It is easily seen that the limits (1.73) for this sample path are

$$\lambda_0 = 1, \quad \lambda_n = \mu_n = 2^{n-1}/\varepsilon, \quad n = 1, 2, \ldots$$
$$p_0 = 1/2, \quad p_n = \varepsilon/2^n, \quad n = 1, 2, \ldots.$$

Equations (1.74), on the other hand, yield

$$p_n = (\varepsilon/2^{n-1})p_0, \quad p_0 = 1/(1 + 2\varepsilon).$$

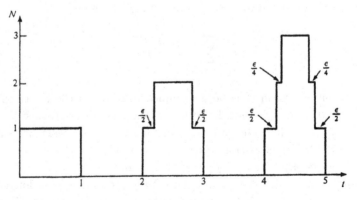

Fig. 1.7.

If we were dealing with a Birth and Death process with the above parameters, then a sample path should spend, in the long run, a fraction $1/(1 + 2\varepsilon)$ of its time in state 0, with probability 1. A pathological sample path like the one in Fig. 1.7 may occur, but the probability of such an event is zero.

1.8. Priority queueing

Let us now move away from the First-In-First-Out scheduling discipline and study some queueing models where the order of service is determined by externally assigned priorities. The customer population is split into a set R of distinct classes, numbered $1, 2, \ldots$ That set may be finite or infinite. The class indices are used as priority levels: customers of class i have priority over those of class j if $i < j$.

The models that we shall consider have several common features. In all cases, customers of different classes are assumed to arrive into the system according to independent Poisson streams, with rate λ_i for class i $(i = 1, 2, \ldots)$. Service is given by a single server of unit speed and within each class customers are served in FIFO order. The server cannot be idle when there are customers in the system. If customers of different classes are waiting for service, the ones with higher priority (lower class index) will be served first.

There are several possibilities concerning the action to be taken when a higher-priority customer arrives to find a lower-priority one in service. In our first model, the new arrival waits until the current service is completed before beginning his own. This is the "non-pre-emptive" or "head-of-the-line" priority discipline (Cobham [4]): after each service completion, the customer with the highest priority among those waiting is selected and served to completion. The service times for class i customers may be generally distributed, with mean $1/\mu_i$ and second moment M_{2i} $(i = 1, 2, \ldots)$. We shall denote, as usual, the traffic intensity for class i by $\rho_i = \lambda_i/\mu_i$; this is the expected amount of work of class i brought into the system per unit time.

The condition for non-saturation is that the server should be able to cope with the work brought in:

$$\sum_{i \in R} \rho_i < 1.$$

Under that condition, we shall be interested in the steady-state average number of class i customers in the system, N_i, and the average response time for class i, W_i.

It was shown in section 1.6 that the expected number of class i customers in service is ρ_i (this is also the probability that a new arrival finds a class i customer being served). If a class i customer is found in service, his expected remaining service time W_{0i} is given by equation (1.66):

$$W_{0i} = \frac{1}{2}\mu_i M_{2i}; \quad i \in R.$$

Therefore, the overall expected delay W_0 caused by any customer that might be found in service is equal to

$$W_0 = \sum_{i \in R} \frac{1}{2}(\rho_i \mu_i M_{2i}) = \frac{1}{2} \sum_{i \in R} \lambda_i M_{2i}. \qquad (1.75)$$

Consider the expected total delay, W_1, to which a top-priority customer is subjected. Apart from W_0, that delay comprises the service times of all class 1 customers that our customer finds in the queue (their average number is $N_1 - \rho_1$), plus his own service time. Hence,

$$W_1 = W_0 + (N_1 - \rho_1)/\mu_1 + 1/\mu_1.$$

Substituting, from Little's theorem, $N_1 = \lambda_1 W_1$, and solving for W_1, we obtain

$$W_1 = 1/\mu_1 + W_0/(1 - \rho_1). \qquad (1.76)$$

Let us examine now the total average delay, W_2, suffered by a class 2 customer. First we make the following remark: suppose that a class 2 customer has to wait for time T (no matter for what reason). All class 1 customers who arrive during T will be served before him. Since class 1 work is brought into the system at rate ρ_1 per unit time, this causes an additional delay of $\rho_1 T$. But all class 1 customers who arrive during that additional delay will be served before our customer, causing a further delay $\rho_1^2 T$, etc. Thus any delay T inflicted on a class 2 customer is stretched to

$$T(1 + \rho_1 + \rho_1^2 + \cdots) = T/(1 - \rho_1)$$

due to the continuing arrival of class 1 customers.

On arrival, a class 2 customer is subjected to delays by the customer in service (average of W_0), the class 1 customers in the queue (average of $(N_1 - \rho_1)/\mu_1$) and the class 2 customers in the queue (average of $(N_2 - \rho_2)/\mu_2$). Each of these delays is stretched by a factor of $1/(1 - \rho_1)$ because of subsequent class 1 arrivals. On top of all that, there is the customer's own service time. The expression for W_2 takes the form

$$W_2 = [W_0 + (N_1 - \rho_1)/\mu_1 + (N_2 - \rho_2)/\mu_2]/(1 - \rho_1) + 1/\mu_2.$$

Substituting $N_1 = \lambda_1 W_1$ (where W_1 is given by (1.76)) and $N_2 = \lambda_2 W_2$, and solving for W_2 yields

$$W_2 = \frac{1}{\mu_2} + \frac{W_0}{(1 - \rho_1)(1 - \rho_1 - \rho_2)}. \tag{1.77}$$

We can now write a similar formula for an arbitrary customer class, j. Note that if customer classes $1, 2, \ldots, j - 1$ are lumped together into a single class, H, and are served in FIFO order, this will not affect in any way the customers of class j. Class H would then be the top-priority class and class j the second-priority class. The value of W_0 will remain the same. The traffic intensity for class H, ρ_H is equal to

$$\rho_H = \rho_1 + \rho_2 + \cdots + \rho_{j-1}.$$

Applying formula (1.77) to class j gives

$$\begin{aligned} W_j &= \frac{1}{\mu_j} + \frac{W_0}{(1 - \rho_H)(1 - \rho_H - \rho_j)} \\ &= \frac{1}{\mu_j} + \left[\sum_{i \in R} \lambda_i M_{i2}\right] \bigg/ \left[2\left(1 - \sum_{i=1}^{j-1} \rho_i\right)\left(1 - \sum_{i=1}^{j} \rho_i\right)\right], \end{aligned} \tag{1.78}$$

where we have used (1.75). The average number of class j customers in the system is obtained, of course, from Little's theorem: $N_j = \lambda_j W_j$.

It is intuitively clear that, with priority scheduling, higher-priority customers receive better treatment at the expense of lower-priority ones. The above expressions make that intuition quantitative. They also allow one to address various optimisation problems. For instance, given the arrival and service characteristics, and a cost function of the form

$$C = \sum_{i \in R} c_i W_i,$$

how should one assign priorities to classes in order to minimise C? We shall solve this problem in Chapter 6.

As an application of formulae (1.78), consider the $M/G/1$ system under the Shortest-Processing-Time-first (SPT) scheduling discipline. Service times are assumed to be known in advance and, after each service completion, the customer with the shortest service time of those waiting is selected and served to completion. Customers arrive in a Poisson stream with rate λ; the probability distribution function of their service times is $F(x)$.

This model can be reduced to the one with head-of-the-line priorities by introducing an infinity of "artificial" customer classes, using the service time x as a class index (for a rigorous derivation, service times should be first assumed discrete and then a limit taken). Customers of class x arrive at rate $\lambda_x = \lambda \mathrm{d}F(x)$; the first and second moments of their service times are, of course, x and x^2, respectively. The traffic intensity for class x is $\rho_x = \lambda x \mathrm{d}F(x)$. Substituting these parameters into (1.78) and replacing the sums by integrals we obtain the conditional expected response time W_x of a customer whose service time is x (Phipps [7]):

$$W_x = x$$

$$+ \left[\int_0^\infty \lambda u^2 \mathrm{d}F(u) \right] \Big/ \left[2 \left(1 - \int_0^{x^-} \lambda u \mathrm{d}F(u) \right) \left(1 - \int_0^{x^+} \lambda u \mathrm{d}F(u) \right) \right]$$

$$= x + (\lambda M_2/2) \Big/ \left[\left(1 - \int_0^{x^-} \lambda u \mathrm{d}F(u) \right) \left(1 - \int_0^{x^+} \lambda u \mathrm{d}F(u) \right) \right],$$

$$(1.79)$$

where M_2 is the second moment of $F(x)$ and x^- and x^+ denote limits from the left and from the right (if $F(u)$ is continuous at point x, the two are identical). The unconditional expected response time W is given by

$$W = \int_0^\infty W_x \mathrm{d}F(x). \qquad (1.80)$$

We shall see in Chapter 6 that, of all non-pre-emptive scheduling disciplines, SPT yields the least average response time W.

Let us now return to the priority model with classes $1, 2, \ldots$. Suppose that when a higher-priority customer finds a lower-priority one in service, he interrupts the service in progress and starts his own immediately. This is a pre-emptive priority discipline: customers of class j are served only when there are no customers of classes $1, 2, \ldots, j - 1$ in the system. To define the discipline completely, one should specify what happens to a pre-empted customer. Does he later continue his service from the point of interruption (pre-emptive-resume discipline), or does he restart the same service from the beginning (pre-emptive-repeat without resampling), or does he request a new independent service (pre-emptive-repeat with resampling)? To avoid these complications, and to make the analysis easier, we shall assume that class i service times are distributed exponentially with mean $1/\mu_i$ $(i = 1, 2, \ldots)$. Now, it does not matter which of the above policies is chosen, because of the memoryless property.

Again, we are interested in the expected response time W_j for customers of class j $(j = 1, 2, \ldots)$. Because priorities are pre-emptive, class j customers are not affected in any way by the existence of classes $j + 1, j + 2, \ldots$. In particular, class 1 customers behave as they would in a single-class $M/M/1$ system with parameters λ_1 and μ_1. Their expected response time is given by expression (1.47):

$$W_1 = \frac{1}{\mu_1(1 - \rho_1)}.$$

Following a similar argument as before, we note that every delay to which a class 2 customer is subjected is stretched by a factor of $1/(1 - \rho_1)$ because of subsequent class 1 arrivals. The delays that should be included in this calculation are due to the class 1 customers he finds in the system (average number N_1 each taking an average of $1/\mu_1$ to serve), the class 2 customers he finds in the system (average N_2/μ_2) and his own service time (average $1/\mu_2$). Hence,

$$W_2 = \frac{(N_1/\mu_1) + (N_2/\mu_2) + (1/\mu_2)}{(1 - \rho_1)}.$$

Substituting $N_1 = \lambda_1 W_1$, $N_2 = \lambda_2 W_2$, using the known expression for W_1 and then solving for W_2 yields

$$W_2 = \frac{1}{\mu_2(1 - \rho_1)} + \frac{(\rho_1/\mu_1) + (\rho_2/\mu_2)}{(1 - \rho_1)(1 - \rho_1 - \rho_2)}.$$

This expression generalises easily to an arbitrary class j:

$$W_j = 1 \left/ \left[\mu_j \left(1 - \sum_{i=1}^{j-1} \rho_i \right) \right] \right.$$

$$+ \left[\sum_{i=1}^{j} (\rho_i/\mu_i) \right] \left/ \left[\left(1 - \sum_{i=1}^{j-1} \rho_i \right) \left(1 - \sum_{i=1}^{j} \rho_i \right) \right] \right. . \quad (1.81)$$

Note the similarity between (1.81) and (1.78). The numerator in the second term of (1.81) also represents expected residual service, this time averaged over classes $1, 2, \ldots, j$ only.

References

1. Buzen, J. P. (1976). Fundamental operational laws of computer system performance. *Acta Informatica*, **7**, 167–182.
2. Buzen, J. P. (1977). "Operational Analysis: An Alternative to Stochastic Modelling." Research Report, Harvard University.
3. Cinlar, E. (1954). "Introduction to Stochastic Processes." Prentice-Hall, Englewood Cliffs, New Jersey.
4. Cobham, A. (1954). Priority assignment in waiting-line problems. *Operations Research*, **9**, 383–387.
5. Foster, F. G. (1972). "Stochastic Processes" Proc. IFORS Conference, Dublin.
6. Little, J. D. C. (1961). A proof for the queueing formula $L = \lambda W$. *Operations Research*, **9**, 383–387.
7. Phipps, T. E. (1961). Machine repair as a priority waiting-line problem. *Operations Research*, **9**, 732–742.
8. Strauch, R. E. (1970). When a queue looks the same to an arriving customer as to an observer. *Man. Sci.*, **17**, 140–141.

Chapter 2

The Queue with Server of Walking Type
and Its Applications to Computer System
Modelling

2.1. Introduction

Several important classes of computer subsystems can be modelled in
a unified manner using a single server queue, whose service becomes
unavailable in a manner which depends on the queue length after each
service epoch. Such models are particularly useful in the study of the
performance of certain secondary memory devices (paging disks or drums,
for instance) and in evaluating the behaviour of multiplexed data communication channels.

In this chapter we shall first examine the properties of the basic
theoretical model, and then develop various applications. This will provide
us with a more economical presentation of the results. The performance
measures of each application will thus be obtained as special instances of
the more general results which will be derived first.

Section 2.2 will be devoted to the presentation and analysis of the
queue with server of walking type which serves as the metamodel for
the computer system models. We first derive the stationary queue length
distribution related to a special Markov chain embedded in the general
queue length process. Then, using general results from Markov renewal
theory, we obtain the stationary probability distribution for the model at
arbitrary instants. We prove that the latter is identical to the stationary
distribution at instants of departure (and hence at the instants of arrival of
customers); this generalises a similar result (due to Khintchine) which has
been proved for the $M/G/1$ queue. We also show in this section how the
$M/G/1$ queue's analysis can be immediately obtained from the preceding

results. The basic theorem we derive concerning the stationary queue length distribution of the queue with server of walking type also reveals an interesting interpretation of the relationship between the stationary waiting time of a customer in this system and the corresponding quantity for the ordinary $M/G/1$ queue: these two quantities differ only (in probability distribution) by a term which has the form of a "forward recurrence time" which can be easily computed. This general relationship holds, in fact, even when arrivals are not Poisson (see Gelenbe and Iasnogorodski [11]).

In section 2.3 we develop, in detail, the application of these results to the paging drum (or fixed-head disk) which was first analysed by Coffman [6]. However, the work done in section 2.2 eliminates the need for a separate analysis. The results obtained allow us to compare numerically the performance of a sectored paging drum with that of a first-come-first-served drum. The performance measures considered are the average queue length at each sector and the average response time. The same approach is then developed in order to evaluate a charge-coupled device memory and a bubble memory system. Some attention is paid to the problem of optimising the angular velocity as a function of queue length for a charge-coupled device, this problem being of importance in view of the introduction of such devices as circulating shift registers or as replacements for paging drums. Some new results related to this question are presented at the end of section 2.3.2.

Section 2.4 contains an application of the queue with server of walking type to the analysis of a multiplexed computer communication channel used for transmitting packets from several sources to one receiver. This type of behaviour is typical of certain computer systems in which several terminals send data to a central computer via a single channel.

2.2. The queue with server of walking type with Poisson arrivals, and the $M/G/1$ queue

Consider the service algorithm shown in Fig. 2.1. Each time the queue is non-empty $(Q > 0)$, the server serves one customer for a service time s, then takes a rest period T after which it returns to examine the queue again. If it discovers that the queue is empty $(Q = 0)$ it takes off for an absence period $\bar{S}$, after which it will return once again to examine the queue. This model has numerous applications to computer systems, some of which will be examined in this chapter. It was introduced in this form by Skinner [15], although it had been examined earlier (Miller [14]). Application of this model to computer systems can be found in [6, 9, 12].

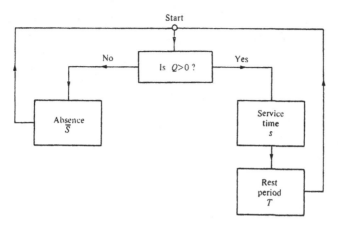

Fig. 2.1. Service algorithm of walking type server.

We shall assume that the queue is served in first-in-first-out order and in this section we suppose that arrivals to the queue occur in a Poisson stream of rate λ. Other assumptions are that $\bar{S}$ the absence period, s the service time and T the rest period are positive and finite (with probability one) random variables whose distribution functions will be noted $\bar{S}(x)$, $s(x)$ and $T(x)$, respectively: $\bar{S}(0) = s(0) = T(0) = 0$. Furthermore, we suppose that $\bar{S}$ is independent of $s + T$, and write $S = s + T$.

2.2.1. *The embedded Markov chain*

Consider the queue length process $\{Q_t\}_{t \geq 0}$, at instants $t = t_0, t_1, \ldots$ when the server arrives at the "Start" position in Fig. 2.1, i.e. *just before* testing whether $Q > 0$. Let $Q_0, Q_1, \ldots$ denote the values taken by queue length at those instants.

Denote by p_k the stationary probability

$$p_k = \lim_{n \to \infty} P[Q_n = k], \quad k = 0, 1, 2, \ldots$$

associated with the queue length at those instants. Under the present assumptions it is easy to see that $\{Q_n\}_{n \geq 0}$ is a Markov chain. Therefore the p_k, if they exist, must satisfy

$$p_0 = p_0 \bar{\pi}_0 + p_1 \pi_0$$

$$p_k = p_0 \bar{\pi}_k + \sum_{j=0}^{k} p_{k-j+1} \pi_j, \quad k \geq 1 \tag{2.1}$$

where $\bar{\pi}_k$ is the probability of k external arrivals in time $\bar{S}$, and π_k is the probability of k external arrivals in time S. Let $G(x)$ be the generating function

$$G(x) = \sum_{k=0}^{\infty} p_k x^k, \quad |x| \leq 1$$

and define for $|x| \leq 1$:

$$U(x) = \sum_{k=0}^{\infty} \bar{\pi}_k x^k$$

$$V(x) = \sum_{k=0}^{\infty} \pi_k x^k.$$

Then from (2.1)

$$G(x) = p_0 U(x) + \frac{1}{x} \sum_{i=0}^{\infty} \pi_i x^i \sum_{j=1}^{\infty} p_j x^j = p_0 U(x) + \frac{1}{x} V(x)[G(x) - p_0]$$

or

$$G(x)[x - V(x)] = p_0[x U(x) - V(x)]. \tag{2.2}$$

The quantities $U(x)$, $V(x)$ are readily obtained. Notice that due to the Poisson arrivals of rate λ we have

$$\bar{\pi}_k = \int_0^{\infty} \frac{(\lambda y)^k}{k!} e^{-\lambda y} d\bar{S}(y)$$

so that

$$U(x) = E\left[e^{\lambda(x-1)\bar{S}}\right] \tag{2.3}$$

where E denotes the expectation. Similarly, for $S = s + T$, we have

$$V(x) = E\left[e^{\lambda(x-1)S}\right]. \tag{2.4}$$

Since p_0 in (2.2) is as yet unknown we take $x \to 1$ in (2.2) and use l'Hôpital's rule since $G(1) = U(1) = V(1) = 1$:

$$\lim_{x \to 1} G(x) = 1 = \lim_{x \to 1} \left[\frac{x U'(x) + U(x) - V'(x)}{1 - V'(x)}\right] p_0.$$

But

$$\lim_{x \to 1} U'(x) = \lambda E[\bar{S}], \quad \lim_{x \to 1} V'(x) = \lambda E[S]$$

so that

$$\lim_{x \to 1} G(x) = p_0 \frac{1 + \lambda(E[\bar{S}] - E[S])}{1 - \lambda E[S]}.$$

Therefore

$$p_0 = \frac{(1 - \lambda E[S])}{1 + \lambda(E[\bar{S}] - E[S])}$$

yielding

$$G(x) = \frac{1 - \lambda E[S]}{1 + \lambda(E[\bar{S}] - E[S])} \cdot \left[\frac{x E[e^{\lambda(x-1)\bar{S}}] - E[e^{\lambda(x-1)S}]}{x - E[e^{\lambda(x-1)S}]} \right].$$

Notice that $p_0 > 0$ implies $\lambda E[S] < 1$; this is the stability condition for a queue with server of walking type.

Consider the stationary queue length distribution g_k, $k = 0, 1, \ldots$, measured at instants just *after* a departure occurs, i.e. when the server has just left the service time block of Fig. 2.1. The following relation is obtained because a departure takes place given that $Q > 0$ in Fig. 2.1:

$$g_k = \sum_{j=0}^{k} p_{k-j+1} \pi'_j / (1 - p_0), \quad k = 0, 1, \ldots$$

where π'_j is the probability of j arrivals to the queue during the service time s. Let $H(x)$ denote the generating function, for $|x| \le 1$,

$$H(x) = \sum_{k=0}^{\infty} g_k x^k.$$

We will then have

$$H(x) = (1/x)[G(x) - p_0] W(x)/(1 - p_0) \tag{2.6}$$

where

$$W(x) = \sum_{k=0}^{\infty} \pi'_k x^k = E[e^{\lambda(x-1)s}].$$

Let us now consider the single-server queue with Poisson arrivals of rate λ, and independent service times S of probability distribution function $S(x)$.

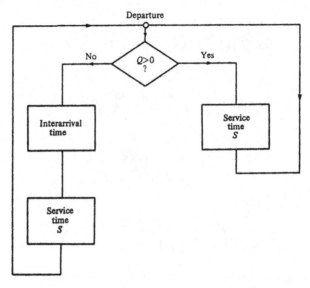

Fig. 2.2.   Service mechanism for $M/G/1$ queue.

Consider the queue length process at instants $\tau_0, \tau_1, \ldots$ just *after* a departure from the queue. The behaviour of the server may be represented as in Fig. 2.2. We see that after a departure, if the queue is empty, the server will enter an enforced idle period which corresponds to an interarrival time; this will then be followed by a service time before the server enters the cycle once again.

Let p'_k, $k = 0, 1, 2, \ldots$ denote the stationary probability that the queue length is k in the stationary state just after a departure. If π_j, $j = 0, 1, 2, \ldots$ denotes again the probability of j arrivals in time S, then

$$p'_0 = p'_0 \pi_0 + p'_1 \pi_0$$

$$p'_k = p'_0 \pi_k + \sum_{j=0}^{k} p'_{k-j+1} \pi_j, \quad k \geq 1. \tag{2.7}$$

Notice that if the queue length is zero after a departure, the following departure will correspond to the first customer which will arrive. Let $F(x)$ be the generating function, for $|x| \leq 1$,

$$F(x) = \sum_{k=0}^{\infty} p'_k x^k.$$

We then obtain after some algebra ($V(x)$ being given by (2.4))

$$F(x) = \frac{(1 - \lambda E[S])E[e^{\lambda(x-1)S}](x-1)}{x - E[e^{\lambda(x-1)S}]} = p_0' \frac{V(x)(x-1)}{x - V(x)}. \qquad (2.8)$$

Notice that $G(x)$ of (2.5) is identical to $F(x)$ when $S = \bar{S}$.

The expressions (2.5) and (2.8) give the generating functions for the stationary queue length probability distribution at instants of time embedded in the queue length process for the queue with server of walking type, and for the $M/G/1$ queue, respectively. What we really would like to have for both systems is the stationary distribution defined as

$$\lim_{t \to \infty} P(Q_t = k) \qquad (2.9)$$

which we shall derive using some general results from Markov renewal theory.

2.2.2. *The stationary queue length process*

Consider first the notion of a *Markov renewal process*. It is defined as a sequence of pairs of random variables $\{Q_n, T_n\}_{n \geq 1}$ satisfying the relationship

$$P[Q_{n+1} = j, T_{n+1} \leq t \mid Q_0 = i_0, Q_1 = i_1, \ldots, Q_n = i_n]$$
$$= P[Q_{n+1} = j, T_{n+1} \leq t \mid Q_n = i_n].$$

For our purposes the Q_n will take integer values and the T_n will be real-valued; furthermore, both will be non-negative and Q_0 corresponds to the initial state at time zero. In our queueing models Q_n will be the queue length at the instant $\sum_1^n T_i$. Notice that

$$\lim_{t \to \infty} P[Q_{n+1} = j, T_{n+1} \leq t \mid Q_n = i]$$

is simply the transition probability from state i to j of the Markov chain $\{Q_n\}_{n \geq 1}$; call it $p(i, j)$. Further, $P[Q_{n+1} = j, T_n \leq t \mid Q_n = i]$ is merely the probability that the time between the n-th and $(n+1)$-th instant of the Markov renewal process is less than or equal to t, and that the state it will enter into at the end of this interval is j, given that at the beginning of the interval the state is i. That probability is assumed to be independent of n.

A more useful quantity in this context is

$$A(i,j,t) = P[Q_t = j, T_1 > t \mid Q_0 = i] \tag{2.10}$$

which is the probability that at some instant t between two instants of the Markov renewal process the state is j, given that it was i just after the most recent instant. By the term *instant* we refer to a time $\sum_1^n T_i$, $n \geq 1$.

The result we seek will be obtained by applying the *key renewal theorem* [5]. It states that

$$\lim_{t \to \infty} P[Q_t = k] = \sum_j \frac{v(j)}{m} \int_0^\infty A(j,k,t)\mathrm{d}t \tag{2.11}$$

where $v(j)$ is the stationary probability of state j associated with the Markov chain $\{Q_n\}_{n \geq 1}$:

$$v(j) = \sum_i v(i)p(i,j), \quad \text{for all } j$$

$$\sum_j v(j) = 1.$$

Further, m is the average time between instants $\sum_1^n T_i$ and $\sum_1^{n+1} T_i$ of the Markov renewal process in stationary state:

$$m = \sum_j v(j)E[T_{n+1} \mid Q_n = j]. \tag{2.12}$$

Of course, (2.11) has a meaning only when the various quantities of which it is composed exist. In fact it has a very intuitive form since

$$\int_0^\infty A(j,k,t)\mathrm{d}t$$

is the average time the process spends in state k between two successive instants, given that it was in state j at the most recent instant. Also, m is the average time between instants. Thus the right-hand side of (2.11) is merely the average time spent in state k between each successive pair of instants, divided by m.

Let us now apply this result to the two queueing systems which we are examining here.

Stationary queue length process for the M/G/1 system: For this system, we see that the queue length process just after each departure (see Fig. 2.2) is Markov renewal. This is because the time between two successive departures is totally determined by the state just after a departure, as is the queue length just after the following departure. The stationary probability $v(j)$ in (2.11) is therefore replaced by p'_j of (2.7). Also we see from Fig. 2.2 that m of (2.12) is given by

$$m = p'_0(1/\lambda + E[S]) + (1 - p'_0)E[S] = 1/\lambda. \qquad (2.13)$$

We can obtain the $A(j, k, t)$ as follows

$$A(j,k,t) = \begin{cases} e^{-\lambda t}, & \text{if } j = k = 0 \\[2mm] \dfrac{(1 - S(t))e^{-\lambda t}(\lambda t)^{k-i}}{(k-j)!}, & \text{if } k \geq j > 0 \\[3mm] \displaystyle\int_0^t (1 - S(y))\lambda e^{-\lambda(t-y)} \frac{(\lambda y)^{k-1}}{(k-1)!} e^{-\lambda y} \mathrm{d}y, & \text{if } k > j = 0 \\[3mm] 0, & \text{if } k < j. \end{cases}$$

$$(2.14)$$

The case $j = k = 0$ is simply when no arrivals have occurred up to time t. If $k \geq j > 0$, then at time t the service is not yet ended with probability $(1 - S(t))$, and $(k - j)$ arrivals have occurred in this time. Finally, if $j = 0$ and $k > 0$, then there is an initial interval of length $(t - y)$, which is exponentially distributed, when no arrivals occur; the first arrival occurs at $(t - y)$ and the $(k - 1)$ following arrivals take place during the remaining interval of length y during which the service of the first customer to arrive does not finish with probability $(1 - S(y))$; y varies, of course, between 0 and t.

For the $M/G/1$ queue call f_k the left-hand side of (2.11), which is the stationary probability we are seeking and let

$$L(x) = \sum_{k=0}^{\infty} f_k x^k, \quad |x| \leq 1$$

be the corresponding generating function. From (2.11) and our definition of $F(x)$ (see (2.8)), we obtain

$$L(x) = \frac{1}{m} \sum_{k=0}^{\infty} \sum_{j=0}^{\infty} x^k \int_0^{\infty} A(j,k,t) p'_j \mathrm{d}t. \qquad (2.15)$$

We will now show that $L(x) = F(x)$; i.e. *the stationary queue length distribution* (2.11) *is identical to the stationary distribution just after departure instants*, for the $M/G/1$ queue.

Using (2.14) in (2.15) we have

$$L(x) = p_0' \left[1 + \int_0^\infty dt \sum_{k=0}^\infty x^k \int_0^t (1 - S(y)) \lambda^2 e^{-\lambda t} \frac{(\lambda y)^{k-1}}{(k-1)!} dy \right]$$

$$+ \int_0^\infty \sum_{k=1}^\infty \sum_{j=1}^\infty \lambda p_j' x^k (1 - S(t)) \frac{(\lambda t)^{k-j}}{(k-j)!} e^{-\lambda t} dt$$

$$= p_0' \left[1 + \int_0^\infty \lambda e^{-\lambda t} dt \int_0^t (1 - S(y)) e^{\lambda xy} \lambda x \, dy \right]$$

$$+ \lambda (F(x) - p_0') \int_0^\infty e^{\lambda t(x-1)} (1 - S(t)) dt. \qquad (2.16)$$

Notice that

$$\int_0^\infty \lambda e^{-\lambda t} dt \int_0^t (1 - S(y)) e^{\lambda xy} \lambda x \, dy = \int_0^\infty \lambda x e^{\lambda t(x-1)} (1 - S(t)) dt.$$

Therefore

$$L(x) = p_0' \left[1 + \lambda(x-1) \int_0^\infty e^{\lambda t(x-1)} (1 - S(t)) dt \right]$$

$$+ \lambda F(x) \int_0^\infty e^{\lambda t(x-1)} (1 - S(t)) dt.$$

But

$$\int_0^\infty e^{\lambda t(x-1)} (1 - S(t)) dt = \frac{-1}{\lambda(x-1)} + \frac{1}{\lambda(x-1)} E[e^{\lambda(x-1)S}]$$

$$= \frac{1}{\lambda(x-1)} [V(x) - 1].$$

Hence

$$L(x) = p_0' V(x) + \frac{F(x)}{(x-1)} [V(x) - 1] \qquad (2.17)$$

and substituting (2.8) we obtain

$$L(x) = p_0' \left[V(x) + \frac{V(x)(V(x) - 1)}{x - V(x)} \right] = p_0' V(x) \left[\frac{x-1}{x - V(x)} \right] \qquad (2.18)$$

which is identical to $F(x)$. Thus, since the equality of the generating functions implies that the corresponding probability distribution functions are identical we have proved the result:

$$\lim_{t \to \infty} P[Q_t = k] = p'_k \quad \text{for all } k \geq 0. \tag{2.19}$$

This is usually known as Khintchine's theorem [13].[†]

A useful quantity to have in many situations is the *average queue length* in stationary state for the $M/G/1$ queue. It can be obtained directly from (2.18) and (2.19) using the simple property of generating functions:

$$\lim_{x \to 1} \frac{\mathrm{d}}{\mathrm{d}x} L(x) = \sum_{k=0}^{\infty} k p'_k.$$

After some algebra we obtain

$$\lim_{t \to \infty} E[Q_t] = \sum_{k=0}^{\infty} k p'_k = \lambda E[S] \left[1 + \frac{\lambda E[S](1 + C_S^2)}{2(1 - \lambda E[S])} \right] \tag{2.20}$$

where C_S^2 is the squared coefficient of variation of S:

$$C_S^2 = [E[S^2] - (E[S])^2]/(E[S])^2.$$

Expression (2.20) is the Pollaczek–Khintchine formula derived by a different method in Chapter 1, section 1.6.

Stationary queue length process for the queue with Poisson arrivals and server of walking type: The queue length process just before the server tests whether the queue is non-empty (see Fig. 2.1) is Markov renewal for the system with Poisson arrivals and server of walking type. Notice that the queue length at these instants determines the distribution of the time until the next such instant, and therefore also the queue length.

The quantity m, or average time between two such instants, is

$$m = p_0 E[\bar{S}] + (1 - p_0)(E[s] + E[T]) = p_0 E[\bar{S}] + (1 - p_0)E[S]$$

[†]In fact, Khintchine's result is that the stationary queue length distribution and the stationary distribution at instants of arrival are identical; but the latter is identical to the stationary queue length distribution at departure instants.

where p_0 is given by (2.5). Therefore

$$m = \frac{E[\bar{S}]}{1 + \lambda(E[\bar{S}] - E[S])}. \tag{2.21}$$

The quantities $A(j,k,t)$ for this system are obtained as follows:

$$A(j,k,t) = \begin{cases} (1 - \bar{S}(t))e^{-\lambda t}\dfrac{(\lambda t)^k}{k!}, & k \geq j = 0 \\[2ex] \dfrac{(1 - s(t))e^{-\lambda t}(\lambda t)^{k-j}}{(k-j)!} & \\[2ex] + [(1 - S(t)) - (1 - s(t))]e^{-\lambda t}\dfrac{(\lambda t)^{k-j+1}}{(k-j+1)!}, & \text{if } k \geq j > 0 \\[2ex] [(1 - S(t)) - (1 - s(t))]e^{-\lambda t}, & k = j - 1 \text{ and } j > 0. \end{cases} \tag{2.22}$$

The case $k \geq j = 0$ in (2.22) corresponds to an instance of the server entering an idle period after finding the queue empty; therefore some time $t < \bar{S}$ later, before it tests once again whether the queue is empty, there will be k customers in queue only if all of them have arrived in that time. The case $k \geq j > 0$ contains two terms, where the first corresponds to an interval of length t shorter than a service period s (with probability $(1 - s(t))$), and the second corresponds to an interval of length t so that $s \leq t < s + T$ (with probability $[(1 - S(t)) - (1 - s(t))]$). In the former term we have the probability of $(k - j)$ arrivals, while in the latter there is an additional arrival to compensate for the departure at the end of the service period. Finally, the case $k = j - 1$ and $j > 0$ corresponds to an instant after the service period has ended with no arrivals in the interval.

Denoting Q_t the queue length at time t for this system, we apply (2.11) to obtain

$$\lim_{t \to \infty} P[Q_t = k] = \sum_{j=0}^{\infty} \frac{p_j}{m} \int_0^{\infty} A(j,k,t)\mathrm{d}t. \tag{2.23}$$

Call q_k the left-hand side of this expression and define the generating function

$$M(x) = \sum_{k=0}^{\infty} q_k x^k, \quad |x| \leq 1. \tag{2.24}$$

Therefore $M(x)$ can be obtained from (2.22) and (2.23) as follows:

$$M(x) = \sum_{k=0}^{\infty} \sum_{j=0}^{\infty} \frac{x^j p_j}{m} \int_0^{\infty} A(j,k,t)x^{k-j}\,\mathrm{d}t.$$

Consider this expression separately for each case of (2.22). Take first $k \geq j = 0$; this contributes the following term to $M(x)$:

$$\sum_{k=0}^{\infty} \frac{p_0}{m} \int_0^{\infty} (1 - \bar{S}(t)) e^{-\lambda t} \frac{(\lambda t x)^k}{k!} \, dt = \frac{p_0}{m} \int_0^{\infty} (1 - \bar{S}(t)) e^{\lambda t(x-1)} \, dt$$

$$= \frac{p_0}{\lambda m(x-1)} (U(x) - 1).$$

The two cases of (2.22) covered by $k \geq j-1, j > 0$, contribute the expression

$$\frac{1}{m} \sum_{j=1}^{\infty} p_j x^j \int_0^{\infty} e^{-\lambda t} (1 - s(t)) \sum_{k=j}^{\infty} \frac{(\lambda t x)^{k-j}}{(k-j)!} \, dt$$

$$+ \frac{1}{mx} \sum_{j=1}^{\infty} p_j x^j \int_0^{\infty} e^{-\lambda t} [(1 - S(t)) - (1 - s(t))] \sum_{k=j-1}^{\infty} \frac{(\lambda t x)^{k-j+1}}{(k-j+1)!} \, dt$$

$$= \left(\frac{G(x) - p_0}{\lambda m(x-1)} \right) \left[W(x) - 1 + \frac{V(x) - W(x)}{x} \right].$$

Therefore

$$M(x) = \frac{p_0}{\lambda m(x-1)} \left[U(x) - 1 + \left(\frac{G(x)}{p_0} - 1 \right) \left(W(x) - 1 + \frac{V(x) - W(x)}{x} \right) \right].$$

We can now use (2.2) to write

$$\frac{G(x)}{p_0} - 1 = \frac{x U(x) - V(x)}{x - V(x)} - 1 = \frac{x(U(x) - 1)}{x - V(x)}$$

so that, using $p_0/\lambda m = (1 - \lambda E[S])/\lambda E[\bar{S}]$,

$$M(x) = \frac{1 - \lambda E[S]}{\lambda E[\bar{S}]} \left(\frac{U(x) - 1}{x - 1} \right) \left(\frac{x - 1}{x - V(x)} \right) W(x) \qquad (2.25)$$

which is identical everywhere, except perhaps at $x = 1$, to (see (2.6) and notice that $p_0/(1 - p_0) = p_0/\lambda m$):

$$H(x) = \frac{1 - \lambda E[S]}{\lambda E[\bar{S}]} \left(\frac{U(x) - 1}{x - V(x)} \right) W(x). \qquad (2.26)$$

To verify that (2.25) and (2.26) are identical at $x = 1$ it suffices to take limits and to compare the expressions obtained. Therefore we have, once again,

$$M(x) = H(x) \qquad (2.27)$$

or *the stationary queue length distribution is identical to the stationary queue length distribution at instants of departure* for the queue with server of walking type and Poisson arrivals. This is similar to the result obtained for the $M/G/1$ queue.

In fact, $H(x)$ given in (2.26) has a very intuitive interpretation which is worth examining. First recall that for two discrete random variables A and B which are independent, the probability generating function $G(x)$ of their sum $A + B$ is the product of the generating functions $G_A(x)$, $G_B(x)$ of A and B, respectively. That is:

$$G(x) = G_A(x)G_B(x).$$

Therefore the quotient of two generating functions corresponds to the subtraction of independent random variables. Now consider the stationary queue length probability generating function $L(x)$ of the $M/G/1$ queue given by (2.18); the service time S of the $M/G/1$ queue is taken to be identical to the quantity $S = s + T$ of the queue with server of walking type. $H(x)$ can then be rewritten as

$$H(x) = \frac{L(x)}{V(x)} \left[\frac{U(x) - 1}{\lambda(x - 1)E[\bar{S}]} \right] W(x) \tag{2.28}$$

and is the product of three probability generating functions $W(x)$, $[(U(x)-1)/\lambda(x-1)E[\bar{S}]]$, and $L(x)/V(x)$. Each of these terms has a special significance. $W(x)$ is obviously the probability generating function for the number of arrivals to the queue during a service time s (see (2.6)). The second term is the generating function of the number of arrivals in an interval which is distributed as the forward recurrence time $\bar{S}^*$ related to $\bar{S}$, as we shall see presently. The forward recurrence time is defined as follows. Consider the sequence of instants $0, \bar{S}_1, \bar{S}_1 + \bar{S}_2, \bar{S}_1 + \bar{S}_2 + \bar{S}_3, \ldots$ where the $\bar{S}_i, i \geq 1$, are independent and distributed identically to $\bar{S}$. Consider an instant of time τ and define

$$P[\bar{S}^* < t] = \lim_{\tau \to \infty} \sum_{k=1}^{\infty} P\left[\sum_{1}^{k} \bar{S}_i - \tau < t \text{ and } \sum_{1}^{k-1} \bar{S}_i \leq \tau < \sum_{1}^{k} \bar{S}_i \right].$$

It is well known that the density function of $\bar{S}^*$ is given by

$$\frac{\mathrm{d}P[\bar{S}^* < t]}{\mathrm{d}t} = P[\bar{S} \geq t]/E[\bar{S}] = [1 - \bar{S}(t)]/E[\bar{S}].$$

For a proof the reader may see Cox [7]. Intuitively, $\bar{S}^*$ is the amount of time that a person arriving at a bus-stop will have to wait if buses pass by at epochs $0, S_1, S_1 + S_2, \ldots$ and all the S_i are independent and identically distributed with common probability distribution function $\bar{S}(t)$. This is also the residual lifetime of Chapter 1, section 1.6.

Now notice that

$$\sum_{k=0}^{\infty} x^k \int_0^{\infty} e^{-\lambda t} \frac{(\lambda t)^k}{k!} [1 - \bar{S}(t)]/E[\bar{S}] = \frac{E[e^{\lambda(x-1)\bar{S}}] - 1}{\lambda(x-1)E[\bar{S}]} = \frac{U(x) - 1}{\lambda(x-1)E[\bar{S}]}.$$

Therefore let Q' denote the number in queue in stationary state for the queue with server of walking type and let Q be the corresponding quantity for the $M/G/1$ queue (2.28) leads immediately to the following important identity:

$$Q' = Q + a(\bar{S}^*) + a(s) - a(S) \tag{2.29}$$

where $a(z)$ is the random variable representing the number of arrivals (from the Poisson arrival stream of rate λ) during an interval distributed as the random variable z. Since (2.28) is a relationship between probability distributions, (2.29) is an identity in the sense of the probability distributions. We can now compute directly $E[Q']$ using the Pollaczek–Khintchine formula (2.20) for $E[Q]$:

$$E[Q'] = \frac{(\lambda E[S])^2(1 + K_S^2)}{2(1 - \lambda E[S])} + \lambda E[s] + \frac{\lambda}{E[\bar{S}]} \int_0^{\infty} t(1 - \bar{S}(t))\mathrm{d}t. \tag{2.30}$$

Another deeper and more general result is concealed in (2.29). We shall state this fact without proof; the result is due to Gelenbe–Iasnogorodski [11]. Let W' be the limit as $n \to \infty$ of the waiting time W_n' of the n-th customer arriving at a queue with server of walking type and with *general* independent interarrival times, and let W be the limit as $n \to \infty$ of W_n the waiting time of the n-th customer arriving at the corresponding $GI/G/1$ queue. The service time of this $GI/G/1$ queue is $S = s + T$ (as in the case of the $M/G/1$ queue corresponding to the queue with Poisson arrivals and server of walking type). The result obtained in [11] is that

$$W' = W + \bar{S}^* \tag{2.31}$$

and that W and $\bar{S}^*$ are independent, the equality being in the sense of the probability distributions of the random variables on the left- and right-hand sides of (2.31).

Let us see how (2.31) implies the result given in (2.29) when arrivals are Poisson. In this case, the number of arrivals to the system during disjoint intervals of time are independent. As in (2.29), let $a(z)$ denote the number of arrivals in time z for the Poisson arrival process. Then (2.31) implies that

$$a(W') = a(W) + a(\bar{S}^*)$$

and we can also write

$$a(W') + a(s) = a(W) + a(\bar{S}^*) + a(s).$$

But $a(W') + a(s)$ and $a(W) + a(S)$ are the numbers of customers remaining in queue just after the departure of a customer in stationary state for the queue with server of walking type and for the $M/G/1$ queue, respectively.

We have shown that, for both systems, the stationary queue length distribution is identical to the stationary queue length distribution just after departure instants; therefore

$$Q' = a(W') + a(s)$$
$$Q = a(W) + a(S),$$

and

$$Q' = Q - a(S) + a(\bar{S}^*) + a(s)$$

follows, which is (2.29).

These theoretical results will be very useful in the system models which will be examined in the following sections.

2.3. Evaluation of secondary memory device performance

The results derived in the previous sections can be directly applied to the performance evaluation of secondary memory devices such as the paging drum or bubble memory systems. A considerable amount of work has been done in this area, and we shall show how the analysis of the queue with server of walking type and of the $M/G/1$ system can be used directly in this context.

2.3.1. *Application to a paging drum model*

The paging drum (PD) is a secondary memory device which is used to store information in blocks of fixed size called pages. This device plays an important role in paged virtual memory computer systems since it is used to store those portions of active programs for which space is unavailable in central memory. Measurements taken directly on existing systems show that the saturation of the PD is often the cause or indication of poor system performance. This is why there has been much interest in analysing its behaviour.

Coffman [6] has given a mathematical model of the PD, assuming that requests for transfer follow a Poisson process. With the same hypothesis, Gelenbe, Lenfant and Potier [12] studied the case in which transfers are sets of grouped and contiguous pages of the PD. A complete performance study of this device may be found in [9].

The PD is a fixed-head disk composed of concentric tracks which are divided into N equal-sized sectors, each able to contain a page of the main memory as shown on Fig. 2.3. The switching of reading to writing can be done in the interval between the passage of the end of a sector and the passage of the beginning of the next sector, while the PD rotates at a constant velocity.

In order to increase the PD's throughput, a queue is associated to each sector, rather than a single queue for the whole PD. An equivalent representation is obtained by assuming that the PD is fixed and that the read/write heads turn around at constant speed (see Fig. 2.3): when each read/write head comes in front of a sector whose queue is not empty, the corresponding transfer request is initiated and the transfer is completed when the head reaches the end of the sector.

Consider the instants just *before* the read/write head passes in front of the beginning of the k-th sector of the drum, where k is some sector we have fixed arbitrarily. If the k-th sector queue is non-empty, then a page will be transferred while the read/write heads scan the sector. After this, no more transfers will occur from or to this sector until the heads visit it once again.

If the time for one complete PD rotation is Y, and if there are N sectors, the service viewed from the k-th sector appears as a service time Y/N, followed by an idle period whose duration is $Y(N-1)/N$. On the other hand, if the k-th sector queue is empty when the read/write head reaches the beginning of the sector no transfer can occur until a time Y has elapsed (one full PD rotation) when the sector is once again visited, even if arrivals occur in the interval. Notice that we do not make a distinction between page reads or writes since both are equivalent from the point of view of the sector queues, and with respect to the utilisation of the PD.

The following relationship exists between the service mechanism for the k-th sector queue being examined, and the queue with server of walking

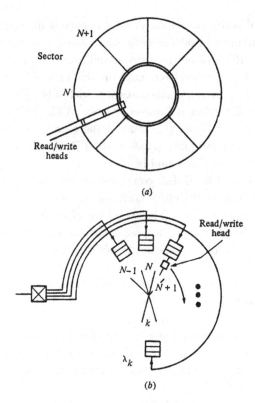

Fig. 2.3. (a) The physical model. (b) The mathematical model.

type of Fig. 2.1. The instant at which the test "is $Q > 0$?" is performed corresponds to the time when the beginning of the k-th sector passes under the read/write heads. The service time s is Y/N, the time necessary for transferring a page. The rest period T after a service is $Y(N-1)/N$, the time necessary for the beginning of the k-th sector to return under the read/write heads. Finally, the idle period $\bar{S}$ if the queue is empty after the rest in Fig. 2.1 is simply the time Y for one complete rotation of the PD. Therefore, the model of a PD sector queue will be a special case of the queue with server of walking type with

$$s = Y/N, \quad T = Y(N-1)/N, \quad S = \bar{S} = Y \qquad (2.32)$$

all of which are deterministic quantities in this system.

Now let the global arrival process of transfer requests to the PD be Poisson of parameter λ, and suppose that it is composed of N independent

Poisson streams of rates $\lambda_1, \ldots, \lambda_N$ corresponding to arrivals to the N sector queues so that

$$\lambda = \sum_{k=1}^{N} \lambda_k.$$

We may now immediately apply (2.26) and (2.27) to the analysis of the k-th sector queue. Let $M_k(x)$ denote the generating function for its stationary queue length probability distribution. Then, using (2.32), we have

$$M_k(x) = \left(\frac{1 - \lambda_k Y}{\lambda_k Y}\right) \left(\frac{e^{\lambda_k Y(x-1)} - 1}{x - e^{\lambda_k Y(x-1)}}\right) e^{\lambda_k Y(x-1)/N} \qquad (2.33)$$

so that the average queue length n_k in stationary state is obtained as

$$n_k = \lim_{x \to 1} \frac{\mathrm{d}}{\mathrm{d}x} M_k(x) = \rho_k \left(\frac{N+2}{2N}\right) + \frac{\rho_k^2}{2(1 - \rho_k)} \qquad (2.34)$$

where $\rho_k = \lambda_k Y$. The stationary probability that the k-th sector queue is empty is given by

$$M_k(0) = \left(\frac{1 - \rho_k}{\rho_k}\right) (e^{\rho_k} - 1)e^{-\rho_k/N}. \qquad (2.35)$$

The stationary average queue length for transfer requests arriving at the PD will be

$$n = \sum_{k=1}^{N} n_k \frac{\lambda_k}{\lambda}.$$

When transfer requests are uniformly distributed over the N sectors we have $\lambda_k = \lambda/N$, so that n in this case becomes

$$n = \frac{\lambda Y}{N} \left(\frac{N+2}{2N}\right) + \frac{\lambda^2 Y^2/N^2}{2(1 - \lambda Y/N)}. \qquad (2.36)$$

The average response time R in stationary state can now be obtained using Little's formula as

$$R = \frac{n}{\lambda} = \frac{Y}{N} \left(\frac{N+2}{2N}\right) + \frac{\lambda Y^2/N^2}{2(1 - \lambda Y/N)}.$$

Suppose now that instead of organising the PD so that page transfers are queued separately for each sector, we constitute a single queue for all the transfers and serve them in their order of arrival (FIFO order).

Assuming, again, that the requests have a uniform probability, $1/N$, to refer to any one of the sectors and that the sector addresses of successive transfers are independent of each other, we can model the PD as an $M/G/1$ queue if transfer requests arrive in a Poisson stream. The service time of the queue will consist of the time necessary for the read/write heads to reach the beginning of the sector concerned by the page transfer, followed by the time necessary to transfer the page. This is in fact only an approximation since the service time would be slightly different for a page transfer arriving at an empty queue. Using the Pollaczek–Khintchine formula (2.20) to evaluate the average queue length n' in this case, we obtain

$$n' = \rho' \left[1 + \frac{\rho'(1 + C^2)}{2(1 - \rho')} \right] \qquad (2.37)$$

where $\rho' = \lambda Y(N+1)/2N$, since the total time for serving a page transfer will be uniformly distributed over the set of values $Yk/N, k = 1, 2, \ldots, N$; C^2 is the squared coefficient of variation of this service time, so that

$$\left[\frac{Y(N+1)}{2N} \right]^2 (1 + C^2) = \sum_{k=1}^{N} \left(\frac{Yk}{N} \right)^2 \frac{1}{N} = \frac{2}{3}(N+1)(2N+1) \left(\frac{Y}{2N} \right)^2$$

and

$$1 + C^2 = \frac{2}{3} \left(\frac{2N+1}{N+1} \right).$$

Clearly, if no sector queueing is used the PD will saturate if $\rho' = 1$, while the saturation point will be obtained with sector queueing when $\lambda Y/N = 1$. In the former case this gives $\lambda' = 2N/Y(N+1)$ while, in the latter case, we have $\lambda = N/Y$. It is interesting to compare λ' and λ:

$$\lambda/\lambda' = (N+1)/2$$

so that the PD with sector queueing can support $(N+1)/2$ times as much page traffic as the PD without sector queueing, provided the page traffic is uniformly distributed among all of the sectors.

These results are illustrated on Fig. 2.4, where we show the average queue lengths n' and n for a PD with eight sectors.

In fact, the sector queueing policy may be viewed as a "shortest access (or service) time first" scheduling policy; such policies tend to optimise the performance of service systems, as we shall see in Chapter 6.

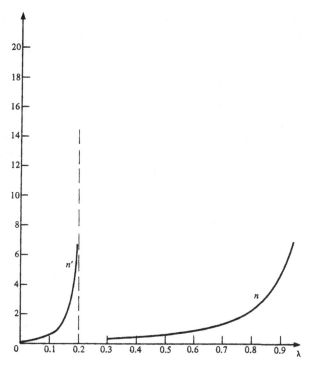

Fig. 2.4.   Average queue length for paging drum with and without sector queueing ($N = 8$).

Further discussion of the PD system can be found in Chapter 4 where diffusion approximations are used to predict queue lengths when arrival streams are no longer Poisson.

2.3.2. *Solid-state secondary memory devices*

Solid-state secondary devices with characteristics resembling those of paging drums or disks have emerged [3, 8] recently as means of supplementing or even replacing rotating secondary memory devices. These solid-state devices are an order of magnitude faster than paging disks [3] and have the additional advantage of having no mechanical parts. Their analogy to paging disks comes from the fact that, from a logical point of view, they behave as circulating shift registers. This means that the information has to pass in front of a read/write area in order to be accessed. Two types of technology have been used for these devices: magnetic bubble memory technology and charge-coupled semiconductor device technology.

In the case of a magnetic bubble memory, the information circulates inside the device under the effect of a magnetic field; it is possible to stop this magnetic field so that the corresponding server, representing the transfer of information, can be "stopped" on a page (or sector) boundary when the sector queues are empty, if the device is organised in page sectors. For charge-coupled semiconductor devices the information content must be periodically refreshed. That is, a minimum clock rate is imposed so that every bit of the stored data can be refreshed before it is lost, by making it circulate under the read/write area. Thus the device behaves as a circulating shift register loop. It also has a maximum clock rate determined by the speed of the semiconductor device. Let r_m and r_M, be the minimum and maximum clock times, respectively. Therefore, if the charge-coupled device has L bits stored on its circumference, a complete rotation time for the information will lie between $r_m L$ and $r_M L$ seconds.

The lack of mechanical inertia in these devices makes it possible to vary the clocking time between the two limits r_m and r_M for the charge-coupled device and to stop or start the rotation of the magnetic bubbles at will in the case of the magnetic bubble memory.

In this section we shall analyse the behaviour of the queue of transfer requests at a charge-coupled device secondary memory. Again, we shall assume that the device is organised in N sectors just as a paging disk. We shall examine the queue of transfer requests at the k-th sector. The unit of data being transferred will be relatively small compared to the page which is transferred at a paging drum or disk; it will be a block of L/N bits, where L is usually less than 1024 bits in present-day devices [3, 8].

We shall assume that $r(\theta)$, the clock time of the charge-coupled device, can be a function of the angular position θ of the circulating shift register, where

$$1 \le \theta \le L, \quad r_m \le r(\theta) \le r_M.$$

The clock time, or time necessary for moving one bit in the shift register, may be varied at will by appropriate electronic circuitry between the two limits, as indicated earlier. Therefore, if the need arises, a variable clock rate can be implemented in this system.

To simplify the discussion, and with no loss of generality, we shall assume that the k-th sector which we are examining begins at $\theta_1 = 1$ and ends at $\theta_2 = L/N$. Notice that these are cell positions (each cell containing one bit) rather than units of rotation time as was the case with the paging drum. If we use the queue with server of walking type to model the k-th queue we must take

$$s = \int_1^{L/N} r(\theta)\mathrm{d}\theta, \quad T = \int_{(L/N)+1}^L r(\theta)\mathrm{d}\theta, \quad \bar{S} = \int_1^L r(\theta)\mathrm{d}\theta$$

for the corresponding service time and idle times. The integrals in the above expressions should be, in the strict sense, summations. The loss in accuracy in treating θ as a continuous random variable will be insignificant, however, since L/N can be expected to be of the order of magnitude of 100 bits.

In view of (2.31), and the corresponding results (2.29) and (2.30) in the case of Poisson arrivals of transfer requests to each sector, we see that system performance will be optimised by setting $r(\theta)$ to its minimum value r_m leading to a minimisation of queue length and transfer times. If the arrivals of transfer requests to the k-th sector form a Poisson stream of rate λ_k, we can use (2.30) to obtain its average queue length n_k:

$$n_k = \frac{(\lambda_k r_m L)}{2(1 - \lambda_k r_m L)} + \lambda_k r_m L/N + \lambda_k r_m L/2.$$

In the previous analysis we assumed that the charge-coupled device speed could be varied only as a function of angular position but not of queue length. The obvious conclusion was that its rotation speed should be maintained at its highest possible level at all times. The performance of this device can be improved, however, if its speed can be varied as a function of angular position, and *also* of queue length. This possibility has been analysed in [8].

Let us assume for the time being that transfers to and from the device occur in blocks of L bits so that there is only one queue of transfer requests ($N = 1$). Consider now an idle period for the device, that is one in which the queue is empty. It is clear that during such periods the initial address $\theta = 1$ should dwell as long as possible in the vicinity of the read/write head so that as soon as a transfer request occurs it may advance at maximum speed to the head in order to minimise the latency delay preceding the beginning of the transfer. Furthermore, as soon as the initial address passes under the read/write head, the information cells of the device should be moved as quickly as possible to the vicinity of the read/write head once again if no arrivals have occurred.

In order to examine this behaviour more closely, assume that an idle period begins at an instant which we arbitrarily fix at $t = 0$ just after the cell $\theta = 1$ passes under the read/write head. Let $D(t)$ be the number of cells separating the address at time t from the initial address, this number being counted in the direction of the motion of the cells. Thus $D(0^+) = L$. We shall assume that, as long as there are no transfer requests, the address $\theta = 1$ visits the read/write head every T seconds (T being fixed).

Suppose that $f(t)\mathrm{d}t$ is the probability that an arrival occurs, ending the idle period, in the interval $(t, t + \mathrm{d}t)$ for some $t \geq 0$. Then the average distance, in number of cells to be traversed, to the starting address for the arriving transfer request is

$$\bar{D} = \int_0^\infty D(t)f(t)\mathrm{d}t.$$

Our problem is to choose the function $D(t)$ which will minimise $\bar{D}$, since as soon as an arrival occurs the optimum strategy will be to rotate the charge-coupled device using the minimum clock time r_m. The average latency, or delay before the arriving request can begin its transfer, is then $r_m\bar{D}$.

Since both $f(t)$ and $D(t)$ are non-negative quantities, $\bar{D}$ is minimised simply by letting $D(t)$ be as small as possible for each value of t. We know that $D(kT^-) = 0$, and $D(kT^+) = L$ for $k = 0, 1, \ldots$; furthermore, $D(t)$ is a decreasing function for every other value of t. It cannot decrease any faster than $1/r_m$ because of the limitation on rotation speed, and any slower than $1/r_M$ because of the need to refresh the contents of each cell at least each r_M time units. This leads immediately of the optimum form for $D(t)$ shown in Fig. 2.5. This form guarantees that $D(t)$ is as small as possible within the given constraints so that $\bar{D}$ is minimised.

The time τ at which the speed of rotation must be changed during each rotation is easily obtained from

$$(T - \tau)/r_M = L - \tau/r_m$$

yielding

$$\tau = r_m(T - Lr_M)/(r_m - r_M)$$

which corresponds to the cell number, or angular position

$$\theta(\tau) = (T - Lr_M)/(r_m - r_M).$$

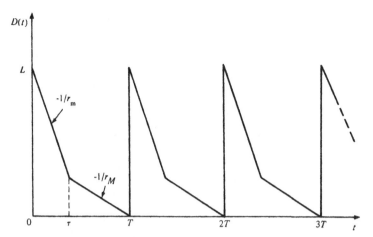

Fig. 2.5. Optimum form for $D(t)$, the number of cells separating the initial address from the read/write heads during an idle period of the charge-coupled device memory.

The preceding analysis concerns the optimum choice of $D(t)$ once T is fixed. We still have to provide guidelines for choosing T. Since $D(t)$ is periodic, we may write

$$\bar{D} = \sum_{k=0}^{\infty} \int_{kT}^{(k+1)T} D(x) f(kT + x) \mathrm{d}x.$$

Therefore the value of T which will minimise the average distance $\bar{D}$ to the starting address will depend on $f(t)$. Since $f(t)$ is the density of the instant of the first arrival after the queue of transfer requests is empty, it will depend on the arrival process and will in general be difficult to compute. If the arrival process of transfer requests is Poisson, however, $f(t)$ is the same as the interarrival time density. Let us examine the optimum choice of T for this case. We then have

$$f(t) = \lambda \mathrm{e}^{-\lambda t}$$

when there are λ arrivals per second to the system. This yields

$$\bar{D} = \sum_{k=0}^{\infty} \lambda \mathrm{e}^{-\lambda kT} \left(\int_0^T D(x) \mathrm{e}^{-\lambda x} \mathrm{d}x \right).$$

Therefore

$$\bar{D} = \frac{(L+1)}{(1 - \mathrm{e}^{-\lambda T})} \left(\frac{\mathrm{e}^{-\lambda \tau} - 1}{\lambda r_m} + \frac{\mathrm{e}^{-\lambda T} - \mathrm{e}^{-\lambda \tau}}{\lambda r_M} \right)$$

which may be written as

$$\bar{D} = \frac{L}{1 - e^{-\lambda T}} - \frac{1}{\lambda r_M}\left(1 - \left(\frac{r_m - r_M}{r_m}\right)\left(\frac{1 - e^{-\lambda \tau}}{1 - e^{-\lambda \tau}}\right)\right).$$

The first term in this expression is minimised by taking T as large as possible, which is obtained when $\tau = 0$. On the other hand, $\tau = 0$ will also make the second term (which is negative) as small as possible. Thus $\bar{D}$ is obviously minimised when $\tau = 0$ or for T equal to

$$T^* = L r_M$$

which yields

$$\bar{D}^* = L/(1 - e^{-\lambda L r_M}) - 1/\lambda r_M.$$

This result is counterintuitive, since it states that in order to minimise the latency the CCD memory must be rotated *as slowly as possible* during idle periods until an arrival occurs. After an arrival occurs it will be rotated at maximum speed to the initial address. This conclusion is dependent, of course, on the Poisson assumption concerning the arrival process and will not be valid in general. It is interesting to notice here that T^* does not depend on λ, the arrival rate of transfer requests.

The analysis so far has assumed that $N = 1$, i.e. that there is only one "sector" queue at the CCD device. In the case of multiple sectors, matters become more complicated but the same general principles can be applied to the analysis of the optimisation problem.

2.4. Analysis of multiplexed data communication systems

Many data communication systems multiplex a simple communication channel among a set of transmitting or receiving stations. Consider, for instance, the system shown in Fig. 2.6. N transmitting stations are connected to a receiver via a simple channel. The channel is multiplexed among the N stations in the following manner. A station, say the first, is polled at some instant; if it has data to transmit, it is allowed to send a packet of fixed length Y along the channel. Otherwise the second station is polled, and so on, until the N-th station is examined. The whole process starts once again with the first station after the N-th has been treated.

The situation we have just described is quite common in data communication systems, although it is not the most general scheme one may imagine. In particular, it is often the case that messages being transmitted are not

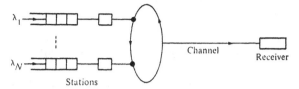

Fig. 2.6. A multiplied data communication channel with polling time y and fixed message (packet) transmission time Y.

of fixed length. For several papers on multiplexed data communication schemes the reader is referred to [4].

We shall assume that there is a fixed polling time y for each station which is independent of the fact that it may or may not have data to transmit; during that time the channel is allocated to the station being polled. We shall let Y also be the (fixed) time it takes to transmit a packet; if the station has no data to transmit the channel will be switched over immediately to the next station for polling. Each station has a buffer of packets waiting to be transmitted; their arrival to the k-th station will be modelled by a Poisson stream of rate λ_k.

The queue with server of walking type can be used to model the k-th station queue. However, the idle times $\bar{S}$ and T of Fig. 2.1 for the service at any one station depend in fact on whether the other station queues are empty or not. For instance, if they are all empty then $T = (N-1)y$ while if they are full we obtain $T = (N-1)(y+Y)$. The analysis which we shall carry out here will assume that the k-th queue has no influence on all the other queues. This is merely an approximation which simplifies the analysis since the remark concerning the values T may take show clearly that the service mechanisms at each station depend on what is happening at the remaining stations.

Let us assume initially that the probabilities $r_j, 1 \le j \le N-1$, that j stations are busy besides the k-th station being analysed are known and given. The idle times $\bar{S}$ and T for the model of the k-th buffer queue will be chosen as follows:

$$
\begin{aligned}
T &= (N-1)y + jY & \text{with probability } r_j, \\
S &= Ny + (j+1)Y & \text{with probability } r_j, \\
\bar{S} &= Ny + jY & \text{with probability } r_j, \quad 1 \le j \le N-1.
\end{aligned}
$$

The service time of Fig. 2.1 will take the value Y. As far as the k-th buffer queue is concerned, we can also identify two cases which yield the best and worst case performance:

(i) best case: $T = (N-1)y$, $\bar{S} = Ny$,
(ii) worst case: $T = (N-1)(y+Y)$, $\bar{S} = Ny + (N-1)Y$.

These two limiting cases can be analysed exactly and will provide performance bounds for the k-th buffer queue.

2.4.1. *Best and worst case analysis for the buffer queues*

Let us first consider the best case analysis for the k-th buffer queue. Here we will have $s = Y + y$, $T = (N-1)y$ and $\bar{S} = Ny$ for the queue with server of walking type model of the buffer service mechanism. The average queue length will be the measure of performance which we will examine; let b_k be this quantity for the best case. Using (2.30) we can write

$$b_k = \frac{[\lambda_k(Y + Ny)]^2}{2(1 - \lambda_k(Y + Ny))} + \lambda_k(Y + y) + \lambda_k Ny/2$$

where λ_k is the rate of arrival of packets to the k-th buffer.

For the worst case we have again $s = Y + y$, while $T = (N-1)(y+Y)$ and $\bar{S} = Ny + (N-1)Y$. If we denote by B_k the worst case average queue length we have, again using (2.30),

$$B_k = \frac{[\lambda_k N(y+Y)]^2}{2(1 - \lambda_k N(y+Y))} + \lambda_k(Y + y) + \lambda_k[Ny + (N-1)Y]/2.$$

We see that the difference between the best and worst cases is due both to the values of the arrival rate of packets which will saturate the system, which are $[Y + Ny]^{-1}$ and $[N(y+Y)]^{-1}$, respectively, and to the additional terms which appear in the formulae. On Fig. 2.7 we show the form of these results.

2.4.2. *Approximate analysis of buffer queue length*

In this section we are concerned with the behaviour of the k-th buffer queue in the presence of interference from activity at other buffers. We shall assume that j of the $N-1$ "other" buffers are non-empty, so that the time during which the channel is transferring data for the other stations is influenced by this quantity. It will be assumed that the k-th buffer queue does not influence the value j. This is, of course, inexact since when the k-th buffer queue is empty the remaining buffers receive better service and

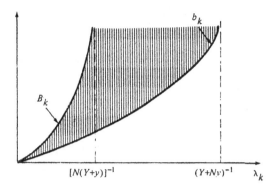

Fig. 2.7. Range of values taken by the average queue length of the k-th buffer.

therefore have a greater tendency to be idle themselves. It is a reasonable approximation, however, if N is relatively large and when the traffic arriving at the k-th station is not much larger than that which arrives at the remaining stations.

Thus, in addition to the quantities we have already computed for the k-th buffer queue which are

$$E[S] = Ny + (j + 1)Y$$
$$E[\bar{S}] = Ny + jY$$
$$s = y + Y$$

we shall also need

$$E[\bar{S}^*] = \frac{1}{2}[Ny + jY].$$

We may now use (2.30) to determine the average queue length of the k-th buffer $b_k(j)$ when there are j non-empty buffers:

$$b_k(j) = \frac{\lambda_k^2[Ny + (j + 1)Y]^2}{2(1 - \lambda_k[Ny + (j + 1)Y])} + \frac{1}{2}\lambda_k[(N + 2)y + (j + 2)Y].$$

References

1. Adams, C., Gelenbe, D. and Vicard, J. (1977). "An Experimentally Validated Model of the Paging Drum." IRIA Research Report, No. 229.
2. Borovkov, A. A. (1976). "Stochastic Processes in Queueing Theory." Springer, New York.

3. Chang, H. (1976). "Magnetic Bubble Technology — Present and Future." Symposium on Advanced Memory Concepts, Stanford Institute, Menlo Park, California, v–496, v–517.

4. Chu, W. W. (ed.) (1974). "Advances in Computer Communications." Arted House, Dedham, Massachusetts.

5. Cinlar, E. (1975). "Introduction to Stochastic Processes." Prentice-Hall, Englewood Cliffs, New Jersey.

6. Coffman, E. G. (1969). Analysis of a drum input-output queue under scheduled operation. *J.A.C.M.*, **16**(1), 73–90.

7. Cox, D. R. (1962). "Renewal Theory." Methuen, London.

8. Fuller, S. H. (1977). "Direct Access Device Modelling." Performance Modelling and Prediction, State-of-the-Art Conference, Infotech, London.

9. Fuller, S. H. and Baskett, F. (1972). "An analysis of Drum-storage Units." Technical Report, No. 29, Digital Syst. Lab., Stanford University, California.

10. Gelenbe, E. (1979). On the optimum checkpoint interval. *J.A.C.M.*, **26**(2), 259–270.

11. Gelenbe, E. and Iasnogorodski, R. (2009) A queue with server of walking type. *Annales de l'Institut Henri Poincaré*, Probabilités et Statistiques.

12. Gelenbe, E., Lenfant, J. and Potier, D. (1975). Response time of a fixed-head disk to transfers of variable length. *SIAM J. on Computing*, **4**(4), 461–473.

13. Khintchine, A. Y. (1960). "Mathematical Methods in the Theory of Queueing." Griffin, London.

14. Miller, L. W. (1964). "Alternating Priorities in Multiclass Queues." Ph.D. Thesis, Cornell University, Ithaca, New York.

15. Skinner, C. E. (1967). A priority queueing model with server of walking type. *Operations Research*, **15**, 278–285.

Chapter 3

Queueing Network Models

3.1. General remarks

The queueing models that we have examined so far — single-server models, or many servers with a common queue — have all had a common feature: every customer demands one service and leaves the system after obtaining it. Often, however, in complex systems like airport terminals, job-shops and large computers, a customer may need several different services provided by different servers, and he may have to wait in several different queues before leaving the system. A computing job, for example, may consist of some arithmetic operations (a CPU service), followed by reading of records from a disk file (disk I/O service), followed by more arithmetic operations (a second CPU service), followed by a fetch of a new virtual memory page (a drum I/O service), etc. Moreover, if the computing system is multiprogrammed, then at each of the servers it requires the job may be delayed by other jobs waiting and/or being served.

To model systems of the above type one is naturally led to define a network of service stations with a separate queue at each node. Customers (or jobs) move from node to node in the network, waiting and receiving service; they may or may not eventually leave the system. These "queueing networks" were first introduced and studied by J. R. Jackson and R. R. P. Jackson [12, 13, 14] in connection with job-shop type systems. The advent of multiprogrammed computers sparked off new interest in them, with the result that studies of queueing network models have multiplied in recent years. In this chapter, we shall concentrate on closed-form analytical solutions. When the model is too complicated and/or general to allow exact analysis, one has to apply approximate methods, some of which will be presented in Chapters 4 and 5.

The simplest way to describe a queueing network (QN) is by means of a directed graph. The nodes (all except one) of the graph represent service stations and the arcs indicate possible paths which jobs may take when moving around the network. There is one special node — node 0 — which represents the "outside world". An arc from node 0 to node i indicates that jobs arrive into node i from the outside world; an arc from node i to node 0 indicates that jobs may depart from node i, never to be seen again. If there are no arcs coming into or going out of node 0, the network is called "closed". Otherwise it is "open".

The graph defines the QN topology. In order to describe the behaviour of the system in time, one needs to specify the following:

(i) the nature of each node: how many servers there are, how fast they are, what scheduling strategy is employed there;

(ii) the nature of the jobs: their arrival patterns, their routing patterns, the amounts of service they demand from nodes on their route. Typically, there will be different classes of jobs in the system, with different characteristics.

The specifications in group (i) are deterministic in character, while those in group (ii) involve (in the type of models that concern us) probabilistic assumptions. Note that we make a distinction here between the speed of a server (say C instructions per unit time) and the service required from that server (say x instructions), rather than talking directly about service times. This distinction will be useful in defining certain scheduling strategies.

It should be obvious from this general formulation that queueing networks are very well suited to the modelling of multiprogrammed computer systems. Let us take as a simple, yet non-trivial, example a time-sharing system with M terminals, a CPU, a paging drum and a filing disk. Suppose that we are interested in the system behaviour under heavy load, i.e. when all the terminals are occupied all the time. We can then use the QN shown in Fig. 3.1 as a model.

Since none of the nodes communicates with the outside world, this is a closed network: there are always exactly M jobs circulating inside. Node 1 contains M servers representing the terminals. Each of the jobs in the network is associated with one of these servers and goes to it whenever it visits node 1 (i.e. there can be no queueing there). The "service" rendered

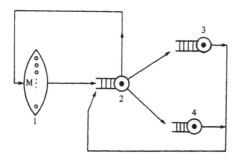

Fig. 3.1.

at this node represents the time users spend thinking between receiving a response to one job and submitting the next.

Node 2 contains a single server representing the CPU. A queue may form here and, this being a time-sharing system, let us say that the scheduling discipline is processor-sharing (we shall discuss processor-sharing strategies in detail later). Nodes 3 and 4 are also single-server nodes, representing the drum and the disk, respectively. The scheduling strategy at both nodes is FIFO (first-in-first-out).

To model the fact that job execution consists of alternating CPU and Input/Output intervals (the latter correspond to either page or file record transfers) we impose the following routing rules: after leaving nodes 1, 3 or 4 jobs always go to node 2; after leaving node 2 they may go to nodes 1, 3 or 4 with certain probabilities. These probabilities will be assumed fixed normally but may, in some applications, be allowed to depend on past job history. Think times, CPU times and I/O intervals are also governed by probabilistic assumptions.

There may be jobs of different types in the system. For example, k of the M terminals may be reserved for users with short, I/O-bound jobs while the others are occupied by users with long, CPU-bound jobs. This can be modelled by introducing two jobs classes with different routing probabilities, think and service time distributions.

What do we expect to learn from the model? Some system performance measures one may be interested in are: the average response time (the time between leaving node 1 and returning to it) for jobs of class i; the proportions of time that the CPU, the drum and the disk spend servicing jobs of class i, the marginal and joint distributions of queue sizes at the various nodes, etc.

We shall return to this model at the end of the chapter, after the tools of analysis have been developed. We shall then be able to write down expressions for these performance measures in terms of the system parameters.

3.2. Feedforward networks and product-form solution

If the removal of node 0 from the graph of a queueing network leaves an acyclic graph, the network is called "feedforward". Stated in terms of job routing, this definition means that between their arrival from the outside and their departure to the outside, jobs never visit any node twice. An example of a feedforward QN (with node 0 removed) is shown in Fig. 3.2.

From now on, whenever we talk about a feedforward QN we shall assume that its nodes $1, 2, \ldots, N$ are numbered in such a way that if there is a path *from* node i *to* node j then $i < j : i, j = 1, 2, \ldots, N$ (this is always possible with acyclic graphs). Thus, only jobs from outside arrive into node 1; only jobs from outside and/or node 1 arrive into node 2; etc. Consider now a feedforward QN with the following specifications.

Case 1. There is a single job class. Jobs arrive into node i from outside in a homogeneous Poisson stream with rate λ_{0i}; $i = 1, 2, \ldots, N$. The amount of service they require at node i is distributed exponentially with mean $1/\mu_i$. After service at node i ($i = 1, 2, \ldots, N$) jobs take an exit arc to node j ($j = 0$ or $j > i$) with fixed probability p_{ij} ($p_{ij} \geq 0, \sum_j p_{ij} = 1$). Node i contains c_i identical servers of unit speed (the last is not an important restriction, it is made only to avoid extra notation), with a common queue served in FIFO order. All external arrival and service processes are independent.

The state of the QN at any given time is defined as the integer vector

$$\mathbf{n} = (n_1, n_2, \ldots, n_N), \quad n_i \geq 0, \ i = 1, 2, \ldots, N$$

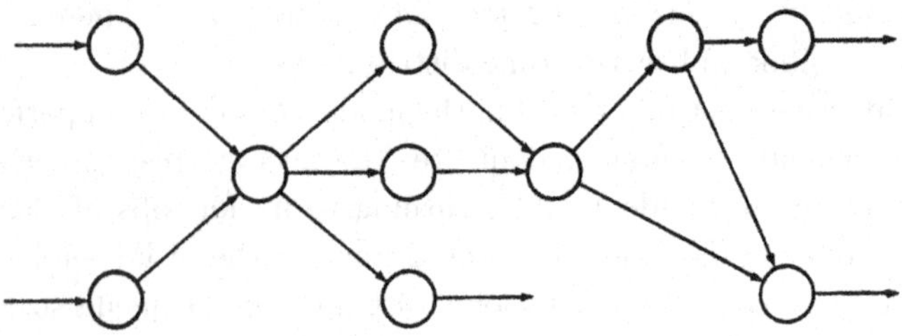

Fig. 3.2.

where n_i is the number of jobs waiting and/or being served at node i, $i = 1, 2, \ldots, N$. Denote

$$p(\mathbf{n}, t) = P[\text{the QN is in state } \mathbf{n} \text{ at time } t].$$

We are interested in the stationary distribution of the QN state, i.e. in the limit

$$p(\mathbf{n}) = \lim_{t \to \infty} p(\mathbf{n}, t)$$

when it exists.

We begin by observing that node 1 is entirely unaffected by nodes $2, 3, \ldots, N$. It behaves like the classic $M/M/c$ queue with parameters $\lambda = \lambda_{01}$, $\mu = \mu_1$ and $c = c_1$; the stationary distribution of the latter exists when $\lambda < c\mu$ and is given by (see Chapter 1)

$$p(n) = \alpha(n) \Big/ \sum_{k=0}^{\infty} \alpha(k); \quad n = 0, 1, \ldots \tag{3.1}$$

where

$$\alpha(0) = 1, \quad \alpha(k) = \lambda^k \Big/ \prod_{j=1}^{k} \mu(j), \quad \mu(j) = \mu \min(j, c), \quad j, k = 1, 2, \ldots.$$

Thus (3.1) can be used to obtain the marginal stationary distribution $p_1(n_1)$ of the number of jobs at node 1.

If the stream of arrivals into node 2 is also Poisson, say with total rate λ_2, then node 2 would also behave like an $M/M/c$ queue with parameters λ_2, μ_2 and c_2; the stationary distribution of the number of jobs at node 2, $p_2(n_2)$, would exist if $\lambda_2 < c_2\mu_2$ and we could again use (3.1) to write an expression for it. Furthermore, if n_1 and n_2 were mutually independent in the steady-state, we could obtain their joint distribution by multiplying $p_1(n_1)$ and $p_2(n_2)$.

What constitutes the input into node 2? It is formed in general by splitting off part of the output from node 1 (a fraction p_{12}) and merging it with the external arrivals into node 2. Since Poisson streams remain Poisson after splitting and merging (if the streams are independent), it will be sufficient, and necessary, to show that the total departure stream from node 1 must be Poisson in order for the total arrival stream into node 2 to be Poisson.

Perhaps the best way to approach this problem is via the notion of reversibility, introduced by Reich [20]. He observed that, in equilibrium, the state process of the $M/M/c$ queue with time reversed is indistinguishable from the original state process, i.e. that transitions from one state to another in reverse time occur with the same rates as the same transitions in forward time. This fact will be referred to as the *reversibility theorem*. Before we prove this, let us see what conclusions can be drawn from it.

A departure, or a "step down" transition, in the original state process, corresponds to a "step up" transition, or an arrival, in the reverse time process. Thus, the original departure stream is equivalent in all respects to the arrival stream in reverse time. But the latter is, according to the reversibility theorem, equivalent to the arrival stream in forward time, which is Poisson with parameter λ. Hence the original departure stream is Poisson with parameter λ.

Further, the state of the $M/M/c$ queue at time t is obviously independent of the arrival stream after t (although it depends on the arrivals before t). By the above duality, the state of the queue at time t is independent of the departure stream before t (although it depends on the departures after t). This independence, together with the Poisson character of the departure process, is referred to as the *output theorem* which was first proved (through a different argument) by Burke [4].

To prove the reversibility theorem we have to show that, for the $M/M/c$ queue with arrival and service parameters λ and μ, in equilibrium, the transition rates in reverse time from state n to state $n + 1$ $(n = 0, 1, \ldots)$ and from state n to state $n - 1$ $(n = 1, 2, \ldots)$ are λ and $\mu(n)$, respectively, where $\mu(n) = \mu \min(c, n)$. These are the only non-zero transition rates in forward time. The transition rate in reverse time from n to $n+1$ is defined as

$$\lim_{\Delta t \to 0} \frac{P(\text{state at } t - \Delta t \text{ is } n + 1 \mid \text{state at } t \text{ is } n)}{\Delta t}$$

which is equal to

$$\lim_{\Delta t \to 0} \frac{P(\text{state at } t \text{ is } n \mid \text{state at } t - \Delta t \text{ is } n + 1) \cdot p(n + 1)}{\Delta t p(n)}$$

$$= \frac{\mu(n + 1)p(n + 1)}{p(n)} = \lambda$$

after substitution of (3.1). Similarly, the transition rate in reverse time from state n to state $n - 1$ is equal to

$$\frac{\lambda p(n - 1)}{p(n)} = \mu(n),$$

completing the proof.

Going back to our feedforward network, the output theorem shows that the total arrival stream into node 2 is Poisson with rate $\lambda_2 = \lambda_{02} + p_{12}\lambda_{01}$. Thus the marginal stationary distribution of the number of jobs at node 2, $p_2(n_2)$ is given by (3.1) with $\lambda = \lambda_2$, $\mu = \mu_2$ and $c = c_2$. The theorem also shows that, at any time t in the steady-state, the number of jobs at node 2 is independent of the number of jobs at node 1. This is because only departures from node 1 prior to t influence the state of node 2 at t and those departures are independent of the state of node 1 at t.

These arguments carry through to all other nodes in the network. The total arrival stream into node j is Poisson with rate

$$\lambda_j = \lambda_{0j} + \sum_{i=1}^{j-1} \lambda_i p_{ij}, \quad j = 2, 3, \ldots, N \tag{3.2}$$

where λ_i is the total arrival (and hence departure) rate for node $i, i = 1, 2, \ldots, j - 1$. The derivation of (3.2) is obvious; it takes into account the external arrivals into node j and those parts of the departure streams from other nodes which are directed to node j. Furthermore, at any moment in the steady-state, the states of the various nodes are independent of each other because we have shown that the past departure stream is independent of the present state at a node. Therefore, the stationary distribution of the network state is equal to

$$p(\mathbf{n}) = p_1(n_1)p_2(n_2)\ldots p_N(n_N) \tag{3.3}$$

where $p_i(n_i)$ is given by (3.1) with $\lambda = \lambda_i$, $\mu = \mu_i$ and $c = c_i$, provided that $\lambda_i < c_i\mu_i$, $i = 1, 2, \ldots, N$.

Thus, under the feedforward topology and the assumptions of case 1 the QN has the so-called "product form" solution: the distribution of the network state decomposes completely into a product of individual node distributions. We shall see in later sections that both the topology and the other assumptions can be generalised considerably without losing that form of the solution. One should be careful, however, in interpreting the meaning of the product form. In particular, the fact that the node states are independent does not imply that the times a job spends at various nodes (the sojourn times) are also independent. Consider, for example, the feedforward QN in Fig. 3.3. Suppose that node 3 is much faster than node 2 ($\mu_3 \gg \mu_2$). Let J be a job with a long sojourn time at node 1; it is quite likely that when J leaves node 1 there will be a queue behind; with a finite probability J will go to node 4 via node 2, while some jobs from the

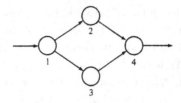

Fig. 3.3.

queue behind it will go to node 4 via node 3, in which case they will arrive there before J and cause it to wait longer. Thus the conditional probability of a long sojourn time at node 4 given a long sojourn time at node 1 is higher than the corresponding unconditional probability, i.e. the two are not independent.

There is only one known case of a QN where the sojourn times of a given job at different nodes are all independent: N nodes strictly in tandem; all except the first and the last contain a single exponential server; the first node is an $M/M/c$ queue and the last can be an $M/G/c$ queue (Burke [5]; Reich [20]). Another curious aspect of this problem is that if waiting times are defined to exclude service times, then even in the above case the waiting times at different nodes are not independent (Burke [5]).

3.3. Jackson networks

Of the restrictions imposed on the networks of the last section, the most unpalatable was clearly the one forbidding jobs to visit the same node twice. We shall remove that restriction now, and study the following model.

Case 2. The topology of the network can be represented by an arbitrary graph. All other assumptions are as in case 1, except that on leaving node i ($i = 1, 2, \ldots, N$) a job may go to any node j ($j = 0, 1, \ldots, N$) with probability

$$p_{ij} \left(p_{ij} \geq 0, \sum_{j=0}^{N} p_{ij} = 1 \right).$$

Queueing networks of the type covered by case 2 are known as "Jackson networks". The main results concerning them were obtained by J. R. Jackson in two pioneering papers [12,13]. Queues strictly in tandem had previously been studied by R. R. P. Jackson [14].

Again, the state of the QN at a given moment in time is defined by the vector $\mathbf{n} = (n_1, n_2, \ldots, n_N)$ where n_i is the number of jobs (waiting and being served) at node i $(i = 1, 2, \ldots, N)$. We are interested in the steady-state distribution of $\mathbf{n}$. The existence and uniqueness of that distribution are determined completely by the following system of linear equations, known as "traffic equations" or "flow balance equations":

$$\lambda_j = \lambda_{0j} + \sum_{i=1}^{N} \lambda_i p_{ij}, \quad j = 1, 2, \ldots, N. \tag{3.4}$$

We saw a special case of the traffic equations in (3.2); there, the associated matrix was triangular and the equations always had a unique solution; the steady-state distribution existed if, and only if, that solution satisfied $\lambda_i > c_i \mu_i$ $(i = 1, 2, \ldots, N)$.

It is readily seen that if a general Jackson QN has a steady-state regime then the corresponding traffic equations have a solution. Indeed, they are satisfied by the total rates of input (number of arrivals per unit time), $\lambda_1, \lambda_2, \ldots, \lambda_N$ into nodes $1, 2, \ldots, N$. To justify that statement it is enough to observe that, in the steady-state, λ_i is also the total rate of output from node i $(i = 1, 2, \ldots, N)$. The right-hand side of (3.4) then contains the rate of external input into node j (λ_{0j}), plus all the output rate fractions which are directed to node j $(\lambda_i p_{ij}, i = 1, 2, \ldots, N)$ i.e. the total rate of input into node j. Thus the existence of a solution to (3.4) is a necessary condition for the existence of a steady-state distribution of the Jackson QN. A rigorous proof of this can be found in [12].

Before examining the sufficiency of that condition we shall introduce a classification of the individual nodes of the network. This follows loosely the one adopted by Melamed [18]. A node is called "open" if any job which visits it is certain (will do so with probability 1) to leave the network eventually. A node is called "closed" if any job which visits it is certain to remain in the network forever. A node is called "recurrent" if any job which visits it is certain to return to it eventually (clearly all recurrent nodes are closed but not vice versa). For example, in the network of Fig. 3.4, nodes 5 and 6 are open, nodes 3 and 4 are closed and recurrent, node 2 is closed and non-recurrent (transient), and node 1 is neither open nor closed.

Let A be the set of open nodes in the network, B be the set of the non-open nodes and R be the set of the recurrent nodes. It can be demonstrated that the traffic equations (3.4) have a solution if, and only if, $\lambda_{0j} = 0$ for all $j \in B$ [18].

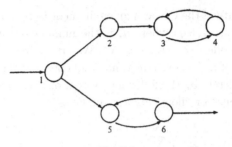

Fig. 3.4.

We shall give an outline of the proof. Suppose that $\lambda_{0j} > 0$ for some $j \in B$ and that j is either recurrent or has a path leading from it to some node $r \in R$ (otherwise j would be open). In either case, a fraction (perhaps all) of the external arrivals into j find their way to some recurrent node r and hence keep on visiting it *ad infinitum*. Therefore r saturates in the long run; the traffic through it does not balance and (3.4) does not have a solution. If, on the other hand, $\lambda_{0j} = 0$ for all $j \in B$, one solution of (3.4) can be obtained by setting $\lambda_j = 0$ for all $j \in B$ and solving only those equations in (3.4) corresponding to $j \in A$. That will be possible because all nodes $j \in A$ are transient (in Markov chain terminology) and therefore the submatrix of (3.4) associated with them has an inverse.

If the traffic equations (3.4) have a solution, $\lambda_1, \lambda_2, \ldots, \lambda_N$, then, necessarily $\lambda_j = 0$ for all $j \in B - R$ [18]. This can be explained intuitively by remarking that jobs may leave the set of nodes $B - R$ but never arrive into it (from the definitions of A and R and from the fact that $\lambda_{0j} = 0$, $j \in B$). Hence that set of nodes eventually drains of jobs completely and the traffic through it, when balanced, is zero.

Bearing in mind that $p_{ij} = p_{ji} = 0$ for all $i \in A$ and $j \in R$, we can summarise the above results in the following manner.

Theorem 3.1. The traffic equations (3.4) have a solution if, and only if, they are equivalent to the three independent sets of equations

$$\lambda_j = \lambda_{0j} + \sum_{i \in A} \lambda_i p_{ij}, \quad j \in A, \tag{3.5}$$

$$\lambda_j = 0, \qquad\qquad j \in B - R \tag{3.6}$$

$$\lambda_j = \sum_{i \in R} \lambda_i p_{ij}, \qquad j \in R. \tag{3.7}$$

Note that (3.5) always has a unique solution because its matrix has an inverse (due to $\sum_{j \in A} p_{ij} < 1$ for all $i \in A$). (3.7), if present, has infinitely many solutions because it is homogeneous and its matrix is singular $(\sum_{j \in R} p_{ij} = 1, i \in R)$. Therefore, if we want the traffic equations to have a unique solution, R must be the empty set. Since $R = \emptyset$ iff $B = \emptyset$, we have:

Corollary 3.1. The traffic equations have a unique solution if, and only if, all nodes of the network are open.

If the set R of the recurrent nodes is not empty, there is (after all the jobs have drained from the nodes in $B - R$) a constant number of jobs circulating in it. Furthermore, R is split into non-intersecting equivalence classes by the relation "communicate" (nodes i and j communicate if there is a path from i to j and a path from j to i). There is a constant number of jobs circulating in each of these communicating classes and the system of equations (3.7) splits into independent subsystems, one for each communicating class.

Thus, in order to understand the steady-state behaviour of general Jackson networks it is important to study two special cases:

(i) open networks all of whose nodes are open (we shall call these networks "completely open");

(ii) closed networks consisting of a single communicating class, with a fixed number of jobs circulating inside (we shall call such networks "completely closed").

Let us write the balance equations for the equilibrium probability distribution of the general Jackson network state:

$$p(n_1, n_2, \ldots, n_N) \left[\sum_{j=1}^{N} \lambda_{0j} + \sum_{j=1}^{N} \mu_j(n_j) I_{(n_j > 0)} (1 - p_{jj}) \right]$$

$$= \sum_{j=1}^{N} p(n_1, \ldots, n_j - 1, \ldots, n_N) I_{(n_j > 0)} \lambda_{0j}$$

$$+ \sum_{j=1}^{N} p(n_1, \ldots, n_{j+1}, \ldots, n_N) \mu_j(n_j + 1) p_{j0}$$

$$+ \sum_{j=1}^{N} \sum_{\substack{i=1 \\ i \neq j}}^{N} p(n_1, \ldots, n_i + 1, \ldots, n_j - 1, \ldots, n_N) \mu_i(n_i + 1)$$

$$\times I_{(n_j > 0)} p_{ij} \quad \text{for all } (n_1, n_2, \ldots, n_N) \geq 0. \tag{3.8}$$

where $\mu_j(n) = \mu_j \min(n, c_j)$ and I_B is the indicator function of the Boolean B:

$$I_B = \begin{cases} 1 & \text{if } B \text{ is true} \\ 0 & \text{if } B \text{ is false.} \end{cases}$$

In the left-hand side of (3.8) is the instantaneous transition rate out of state $\mathbf{n} = (n_1, n_2, \ldots, n_N)$; the right-hand side contains the transition rates into state $\mathbf{n}$ due to: external arrivals (first line), departures to the outside (second line) and transfers from one node to another (third line).

Suppose that the network is completely open. Jackson's classic result can be stated as follows:

Theorem 3.2. (Jackson) If the unique solution to (3.5) satisfies the inequalities

$$\lambda_j < c_j \mu_j, \quad j = 1, 2, \ldots, N \tag{3.9}$$

then the steady-state distribution of the network state exists and has the form

$$p(n_1, n_2, \ldots, n_N) = p_1(n_1) p_2(n_2) \ldots p_N(n_N), \quad n_j \geq 0, \ j = 1, 2, \ldots, N \tag{3.10}$$

where $p_j(n_j)$ is the steady-state probability of having n_j customers in an $M/M/c$ queueing system with parameters $\lambda = \lambda_j, \mu = \mu_j, c = c_j$ ($j = 1, 2, \ldots, N$); it is given by (3.1).

Proof. First we verify that (3.10) satisfies the balance equations (3.8). We substitute (3.10) into (3.8) and use the identities (see (3.1)):

$$\alpha_j(n_j - 1) = \frac{\mu_j(n_j)}{\lambda_j} \alpha_j(n_j), \quad n_j > 0;$$

$$\alpha_j(n_j + 1) = \frac{\lambda_j}{\mu_j(n_j + 1)} \alpha_j(n_j), \quad n_j \geq 0.$$

The factors $\alpha_j(n_j) / \sum_{k=0}^{\infty} \alpha_j(k)$, $j = 1, 2, \ldots, N$, cancel out and (3.8) is reduced to

$$\sum_{j=1}^{N} \lambda_{0j} + \sum_{j=1}^{N} \mu_j(n_j) I_{(n_j > 0)} (1 - p_{jj})$$

$$= \sum_{j=1}^{N} \lambda_{0j} I_{(n_j > 0)} \frac{\mu_j(n_j)}{\lambda_j} + \sum_{j=1}^{N} \lambda_j p_{j0} + \sum_{j=1}^{N} \frac{\mu_j(n_j)}{\lambda_j} I_{(n_j > 0)} \sum_{\substack{i=1 \\ i \neq j}}^{N} \lambda_i p_{ij}.$$

This last equation always holds. Indeed, individual terms on the left- and right-hand sides can be equated: from (3.4) we have

$$1 - p_{jj} = \frac{1}{\lambda_j} \left[\lambda_{0j} + \sum_{\substack{i=1 \\ i \neq j}}^{N} \lambda_i p_{ij} \right], \quad j = 1, 2, \ldots, N,$$

and hence, for $j = 1, 2, \ldots, N$,

$$\mu_j(n_j) I_{(n_j>0)}(1 - p_{jj}) = \lambda_{0j} I_{(n_j>0)} \frac{\mu_j(n_j)}{\lambda_j} + \frac{\mu_j(n_j)}{\lambda_j} I_{(n_j>0)} \sum_{\substack{i=1 \\ i \neq j}}^{N} \lambda_i p_{ij}.$$

Also from (3.4), by summing all equations, we obtain

$$\sum_{j=1}^{N} \lambda_{0j} = \sum_{j=1}^{N} \lambda_j p_{j0}$$

thus completing the verification. □

As an important aside, we should point out that the last two identities mean, in effect, that

(i) the rate of transition out of state **n**, due to a job leaving node j, is equal to the rate of transition into state **n**, due to a job arriving into node j; and

(ii) the total rate of arrivals into the network is equal to the total rate of departures from the network.

Property (i) is usually called "local balance" (to distinguish it from the "global balance" equations (3.8)) and it appears to be intimately connected with the existence of product-form solutions.

Having established that (3.10) satisfies (3.8), we next verify, by direct summation, that it also satisfies the normalising equation

$$\sum_{\mathbf{n} \geq 0} p(\mathbf{n}) = 1$$

when (3.9) holds. Jackson's theorem now follows from the theorem in section 1.4 which states that if the balance equations of an irreducible Markov process have a positive solution which satisfies the normalising equation then the steady-state distribution of the Markov process exists and is given by that solution. The state process of a completely open Jackson

QN is, indeed, irreducible; this follows from the fact that the state $\mathbf{n} = 0$ is accessible from every state [18].

Jackson's theorem implies that the states n_j of individual nodes $(j = 1, 2, \ldots, N)$ at a given moment in the steady-state are independent random variables. This is an even more remarkable result than in the case of feedforward networks because, *a priori*, it would seem that the nodes of a general Jackson network have more opportunities to influence each other. Furthermore, as we shall see at the end of this section, the total input process into a given node is no longer Poisson, in general. Yet the node behaves as if it were!

Remark: The theorem states that conditions (3.9) are sufficient for the existence of a steady-state distribution. Clearly, they are also necessary because if steady-state exists the total rate of output from node j is λ_j ($j = 1, 2, \ldots, N$) and, since the servers there are occasionally idle, the rate of output is less than $c_j \mu_j$ (which is what it would be if all the servers were busy all the time).

Suppose now that we are dealing with a completely closed network with K jobs circulating inside. The state process of the network is a finite Markov chain, it is irreducible (since all nodes communicate) and therefore always has a steady-state distribution. The form of that distribution was discovered by Gordon and Newell [11] (although it can be derived as a special case from one of Jackson's theorems).

Theorem 3.3 (Gordon–Newell). Let λ_j^*, $j = 1, 2, \ldots, N$, be any non-zero solution of the traffic equations (3.7). The steady-state distribution of the network state is given by

$$p(n_1, n_2, \ldots, n_N) = \frac{1}{G(K)} \alpha_1(n_1) \alpha_2(n_2) \cdots \alpha_N(n_N),$$

$$n_j \geq 0, \quad n_1 + \cdots + n_N = K \qquad (3.11)$$

where $\alpha_j(n_j)$ are obtained as in (3.1) with $\lambda = \lambda_j^*$, $\mu = \mu_j$, $c = c_j$ ($j = 1, 2, \ldots, N$) and the normalising factor $[G(K)]^{-1}$ is chosen so that all probabilities sum up to one:

$$G(K) = \sum_{n_1 + \cdots + n_N = K} \alpha_1(n_1) \alpha_2(n_2) \cdots \alpha_N(n_N). \qquad (3.12)$$

The proof of this theorem is also by direct substitution of (3.11) into (3.8) and verifying that the latter are satisfied.

We encounter again a product-form distribution. This time, however, it is not a product of individual node distributions and we cannot conclude that the node states are independent of each other. In fact, they are obviously not independent since the total number of jobs in the network is fixed.

What can we say about the steady-state distribution of general (not completely open and not completely closed) Jackson networks? The state process of such a network is not necessarily an irreducible Markov chain. Even if the balance equations have a solution summing up to 1, steady-state distribution may not exist because the long-run behaviour of the network will depend, in general, on the initial conditions. For example, different initial assignments of jobs to the nodes in the set $B - R$ will lead to different numbers of jobs draining into the communicating classes of recurrent nodes and hence different long-run distributions.

Many measures of network performance can be derived directly from the steady-state distributions (3.10) and (3.11). Let us obtain some for completely open networks; closed networks present special computational problems which will be tackled in a separate section.

The total throughput of the network is, of course,

$$\lambda = \sum_{j=1}^{N} \lambda_{0j}.$$

Since jobs are being served at node j for an average of $1/\mu_j$ and they arrive there at rate λ_j, the average number of jobs being served at node j is, according to Little's theorem, $\rho_j = \lambda_j/\mu_j$ ($j = 1, 2, \ldots, N$). If there is only one server at node j then ρ_j is its utilisation factor (the fraction of time the server is busy). The total average number of jobs being served (not waiting in queues) in the network is $\rho_1 + \rho_2 + \cdots + \rho_N$ and hence, again according to Little's theorem, the total average amount of service a job obtains during its residence in the network is

$$E[S] = \left[\sum_{j=1}^{N} \rho_j \right] \Big/ \lambda.$$

If e_j is the average number of visits a job makes to node j ($j = 1, 2, \ldots, N$) then, since an average of λ jobs arrive into the network from outside per unit time and each of them visits node $j e_j$ times on the average, the rate of input into node j should be λe_j. Thus we have

$$e_j = \lambda_j/\lambda.$$

So far we have not used the distribution of the network state; the same arguments would apply, for example, if interarrival and service times had general distributions. One needs the state distribution if one is interested in the numbers of jobs at various nodes or the time jobs spend there. In particular, the average number of jobs at node j is equal to

$$E[n_j] = \sum_{k=1}^{\infty} k p_j(k).$$

The total average number of jobs in the network is

$$E[n] = \sum_{j=1}^{N} E[n_j]$$

which gives, once more according to Little's theorem, the average response time W (the time between the arrival of a job into, and its departure from the network):

$$W = E[n]/\lambda.$$

Let us now look at some traffic processes of jobs between nodes. Very little is known about these and the results that are available are mostly of a negative nature. For example, the total input process into a node is not, in general, Poisson. To demonstrate this, consider the single-node network of Fig. 3.5 (Burke [6]). There is a single server at node 1; upon completion of service a job leaves with probability p_{10} and is fed back with probability $p_{11} = 1 - p_{10}$. The traffic equation is $\lambda_1 = \lambda_{01} + p_{11}\lambda_1$, yielding $\lambda_1 = \lambda_{01}/p_{10}$. Steady-state exists when $\lambda_1 < \mu_1$ and the system, as far as the queue size distribution is concerned, is equivalent to an $M/M/1$ queue with traffic intensity $\rho = \lambda_1/\mu_1$:

$$p(n) = \rho^n(1 - \rho), \quad n = 0, 1, \ldots.$$

Now, the queue size distribution left behind by departing (not fed-back) jobs is the same as that seen by jobs arriving from the outside; the latter

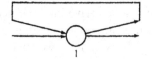

Fig. 3.5.

is the same as the steady-state distribution because the exogenous arrivals form a Poisson stream. On the other hand, fed-back jobs see the same queue size distribution (conventionally, the queue seen by a fed-back job does not include the job itself) as departing jobs, since the feedback decision is made independently of the system state. Hence, the state distribution at input instants (exogenous or feedback) is also given by $p(n)$.

Let $F(x)$ be the distribution function of the interval T between consecutive input instants: $1 - F(x)$ is the probability that $T > x$. Let $1 - G(x)$ be the probability that the time until the first feedback following an input instant is greater than x. Denote by $f(x)$ and $g(x)$ the density functions associated with $F(x)$ and $G(x)$, respectively, and let $g_n(x)$ be the latter density conditioned upon the number n of jobs in the system just before an input instant. We have

$$g_n(x) = \sum_{j=1}^{n+1} p_{10}^{j-1} p_{11} \mu_1 e^{-\mu_1 x} (\mu_1 x)^{j-1} / (j-1)!.$$

The j-th term in the sum is equal to the probability that the j-th customer in the queue will be the first to be fed back, multiplied by the density function of j service times (Erlang with parameters j, μ_1). Next,

$$g(x) = \sum_{n=0}^{\infty} p(n) g_n(x) = p_{11} \mu_1 e^{-(\mu_1 - \lambda_{01})x}$$

after substitution of $p(n)$ and $g_n(x)$ and inverting the order of summation. This gives

$$G(x) = \int_0^x g(t)\mathrm{d}t = \frac{p_{11}\mu_1}{\mu_1 - \lambda_{01}}[1 - e^{-(\mu_1 - \lambda_{01})x}].$$

The distribution function $F(x)$ is determined by observing that, for the interval between inputs to be greater than x, there must be no exogenous arrivals and no feedbacks before x:

$$1 - F(x) = e^{-\lambda_{01}x}[1 - G(x)]$$
$$= [(p_{10}\mu_1 - \lambda_{01})e^{-\lambda_{01}x} + p_{11}\mu_1 e^{-\mu_1 x}]/(\mu_1 - \lambda_{01}).$$

We see that the mean of $F(x)$ is $1/\lambda_1$ (as expected), but $F(x)$ is not exponential and hence the input stream is not Poisson.

This situation raises the question of what is the network state distribution at the moments when jobs move from one node to another (or arrive from the outside). If the total input into a node is Poisson, and independent of the network state, then the network state distribution at input instants is the same as the steady-state distribution. We saw in an example that the input process is not necessarily Poisson but we also saw that input jobs may still see the steady-state distribution. This is, in fact, the case for any completely open Jackson network: jobs arriving into a node (externally or internally) do not, in general, form a Poisson process but they see the steady-state distribution of the network state (Sevcik and Mitrani [23]). In a closed network with K jobs circulating in it, a job coming into a node sees the steady-state distribution of a network with $K-1$ jobs. These results are generalised in [23] to a large class of networks with many job classes; the networks may be open with respect to some job classes and closed with respect to others.

A generalisation of the output theorem holds for the processes of departure from Jackson networks in equilibrium: the stream of jobs leaving the network from node j is Poisson with rate $\lambda_j p_{j0}$ and its past is independent of the network state. Moreover, these streams are mutually independent [18].

3.4. Other scheduling strategies and service time distributions

Executing jobs in order of arrival has the obvious advantages of fairness, simplicity and ease of implementation. It is also efficient in the sense of yielding small average queue sizes and waiting times, when the variation in the required service times is small. However, the FIFO scheduling strategy has disadvantages, too. Its performance is far from optimal when the variation in the required service times is large (we shall return to these questions in the chapters on design). It is inherently unsuitable for certain applications, like time-sharing (where jobs are served in parallel) or stack processing (where the last arrival is served first). It cannot be used in situations where it is desirable to give some jobs priority over others.

Clearly, the utility of queueing network models would be enhanced significantly if different scheduling disciplines were allowed at different nodes. The enhancement would be even greater if one could drop the rather restrictive assumption that all service times are distributed exponentially. There are certain jobs scheduling strategies and a certain type of probability distribution which make such generalisations possible.

3.4.1. *The egalitarian processor-sharing strategy*

This servicing discipline was introduced [16] in connection with computer time-sharing models. It was formulated originally as a limiting case of the Round-Robin discipline which allocates service in quanta of fixed size Q; if a job does not complete within a quantum, it returns to the end of the queue and waits until its turn comes again. The smaller the quantum size, the faster the jobs circulate and, in the limit $Q \to 0$, one obtains a mode of operation without queueing where all jobs requiring service are being served in parallel at a rate inversely proportional to their number. This is the classic processor-sharing strategy. It is usually defined directly by saying that if the capacity (or speed) of the processor is C instructions per unit time and if at time t there are n jobs requiring service, then in a small interval $(t, t + \Delta t)$ (during which nobody arrives or leaves) each of the n jobs increases its attained service by $(C/n)\Delta t$ instructions. We call this processor-sharing strategy "egalitarian" because it divides the processing capacity equally among the jobs present, without regard to class or other distinctions.

Consider an $M/M/1$ processor-sharing system with R job classes and unit processor speed $(C = 1)$. Jobs of class r arrive in a Poisson stream at rate λ_r and have required service times distributed exponentially with mean $1/\mu_r$ $(r = 1, 2, \ldots, R)$. The system state is defined by the vector $(k_1, k_2, \ldots, k_R)$ where k_r is the number of class r jobs requiring service. The steady-state distribution of $(k_1, k_2, \ldots, k_R)$ is determined from the balance equations

$$p(k_1, k_2, \ldots, k_R) \left[\sum_{r=1}^{R} \lambda_r + \sum_{r=1}^{R} (k_r/k)\mu_r \right]$$

$$= \sum_{r=1}^{R} p(k_1, \ldots, k_r - 1, \ldots, k_R) I_{(k_r > 0)} \lambda_r$$

$$+ \sum_{r=1}^{R} p(k_1, \ldots, k_r + 1, \ldots, k_R) \mu_r (k_r + 1)/(k + 1),$$

$$(k_1, k_2, \ldots, k_R) \geq 0, \qquad (3.13)$$

where $k = k_1 + k_2 + \cdots + k_R$.

It is not difficult to verify, by direct substitution, that the solution of (3.13) which satisfies the normalising equation

$$\sum_{\mathbf{k} \geq 0} p(\mathbf{k}) = 1$$

is given by

$$p(k_1, k_2, \ldots, k_R) = (1 - \rho)k! \prod_{r=1}^{R} (\rho_r^{k_r}/k_r!), \quad (k_1, k_2, \ldots, k_R) \geq 0 \quad (3.14)$$

where $\rho_r = \lambda_r/\mu_r$ and $\rho = \rho_1 + \rho_2 + \cdots + \rho_R$ (steady-state exists when $\rho < 1$). The easiest way of performing the verification is by showing that (3.14) satisfies the local balance equations: each term in the first sum on the left-hand side of (3.13) is equal to the corresponding term in the second sum on the right-hand side and vice versa.

Note that, as far as the total number (k) of jobs is concerned, the processor-sharing queue is equivalent to a FIFO queue with traffic intensity ρ: by summing (3.14) over all $(k_1, k_2, \ldots, k_R)$ such that $k_1 + k_2 + \cdots + k_R = k$, we obtain $p(k) = (1 - \rho)\rho^k, k = 0, 1, \ldots$.

3.4.2. The pre-emptive-resume LCFS strategy

If the resource being modelled is (or behaves like) a stack, a scheduling discipline under which the last arrival is served first is appropriate. In many cases this would involve pre-emptions, i.e. if a job is in service when a new job arrives, the service is interrupted until the new job departs (which, in turn, may be interrupted) and then resumed from the point of interruption. We use the name "pre-emptive resume LCFS" (last-come-first-served) when referring to this scheduling strategy.

Let us take again an $M/M/1$ system with R job classes (same assumptions and notations as before) and study it under the pre-emptive-resume LCFS scheduling strategy. The system state is defined by the variable-length vector $(r_1, r_2, \ldots, r_k)$, where the number of elements is equal to the total number of jobs requiring service and the i-th element is the class index of the i-th job in the LCFS order: the first of these jobs is being served and all others are waiting (having been interrupted). We use the notation (0) for the empty state.

The steady-state balance equations are

$$p(r_1, r_2, \ldots, r_k) \left[\sum_{j=1}^{R} \lambda_j + \mu_{r_1} I_{(r_1 > 0)} \right]$$

$$= p(r_2, \ldots, r_k)\lambda_{r_1} I_{(r_1 > 0)} + \sum_{j=1}^{R} p(r_j, r_1, \ldots, r_k)\mu_{r_j} \quad (3.15)$$

and their solution, subject to the normalising equation, is

$$p(r_1, r_2, \ldots, r_k) = (1 - \rho) \prod_{i=1}^{k} \rho_{r_i} \qquad (3.16)$$

provided that $\rho < 1$, where the product is defined as 1 if the vector $(r_1, \ldots, r_k)$ consists of the single element 0 (i.e. represents the empty state). Again (3.16) satisfies the local balance subequations of (3.15).

If we wish to find the steady-state distribution of the aggregate system state $(k_1, k_2, \ldots, k_R)$, where k_r is the number of class r jobs in the system $(k_r \geq 0, r = 1, 2, \ldots, R)$, we have to sum (3.16) over all vectors $(r_1, r_2, \ldots, r_k)$ which have k_1 elements equal to 1, k_2 elements equal to 2, \ldots k_R elements equal to R. This gives

$$p(k_1, k_2, \ldots, k_R) = (1 - \rho)k! \prod_{r=1}^{R} (\rho_r^{k_r} / k_r!) \qquad (3.17)$$

where $k = k_1 + k_2 + \cdots + k_R$. We observe that the pre-emptive-resume LCFS discipline and the egalitarian processor-sharing discipline yield identical steady-state distributions of the numbers of jobs of various classes in the system.

3.4.3. *The server-per-job strategy*

In order to operate this scheduling strategy one needs as many servers as there may be jobs requiring service. As soon as a job arrives, a separate server is assigned to it for the duration of the service. All servers are assumed identical and of unit speed. For example, the collection of user terminals in a computer system can be modelled by a node with the server-per-job scheduling discipline.

In the case which we have been considering (R jobs classes arriving in Poisson streams and with exponentially distributed service requirements), the server-per-job scheduling strategy would involve infinitely many servers (since there is no bound to the number of jobs in the system). The system state is defined by the vector $(k_1, k_2, \ldots, k_R)$, k_r being the number of jobs of class r in the system $(k_r \geq 0, r = 1, 2, \ldots, R)$. The steady-state balance equations take account of the fact that the departure rate for class r is proportional to the number of class r jobs present:

$$p(k_1, k_2, \ldots, k_R) \left[\sum_{r=1}^{R} \lambda_r + \sum_{r=1}^{R} k_r \mu_r \right]$$

$$= \sum_{r=1}^{R} p(k_1, \ldots, k_r - 1, \ldots, k_R) \lambda_r I_{(k_r > 0)}$$

$$+ \sum_{r=1}^{R} p(k_1, \ldots, k_r + 1, \ldots, k_R)(k_r + 1)\mu_r. \qquad (3.18)$$

Their solution, subject to the normalising equation, is given by

$$p(k_1, k_2, \ldots, k_R) = \prod_{r=1}^{R} [(\rho^{k_r}/k_r!)e^{-\rho_r}]. \qquad (3.19)$$

Steady-state exists for all values of the parameters.

Note that although (3.14), (3.17) and (3.19) are all product-form solutions, only the last one factorises completely into a product of distributions for the individual job classes (the right-hand side of (3.19) is the product of R single class $M/M/\infty$ distributions). The random variables $k_1, k_2, \ldots, k_R$ are mutually independent in a server-per-job system (that is intuitively obvious, too) but they are not independent in a single-server processor-sharing or pre-emptive-resume LCFS system.

We shall define now a family of probability distributions which are, to all intents and purposes, general and which will allow us to relax the assumption that required service times are distributed exponentially. The idea, due initially to Erlang and generalised later by Cox [10], is to use the response time of a simple exponential network to represent the service time required from a single server.

Consider the network with L nodes in Fig. 3.6. There can never be more than one job in the network. Jobs enter via node 1. After receiving service from node l (distributed exponentially with mean $1/\mu_l$) a job leaves

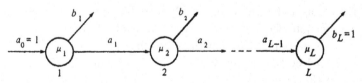

Fig. 3.6.

the network with probability b_l, or proceeds to node $l+1$ with probability a_l $(a_l + b_l = 1, l = 1, 2, \ldots, L-1)$. After node L jobs leave the network. The probability that a job reaches node l is $A_l = a_0 a_1 \cdots a_{l-1}$ ($l = 1, 2, \ldots, L; a_0 = 1$) and the probability that a job visits nodes $1, 2, \ldots, l$ and leaves the network is equal to $A_l b_l$. Hence, the time τ a job spends in the network is, with probability $A_l b_l$, the sum of l independent, exponentially distributed random variables. The expected value of τ is equal to

$$E[\tau] = \sum_{l=1}^{L} A_l b_l \sum_{i=1}^{l} (1/\mu_i) = \sum_{i=1}^{L} (A_i/\mu_i). \tag{3.20}$$

Let $f(x)$ be the probability density function of τ and let $f^*(s)$ be its Laplace transform. Since the Laplace transform of the node l service time is $\mu_l/(\mu_l + s)$, we can write

$$f^*(s) = \sum_{l=1}^{L} A_l b_l \prod_{i=1}^{l} [\mu_i/(\mu_i + s)]. \tag{3.21}$$

The right-hand side of (3.21) is a rational function of s: it can be rewritten as $P(s)/Q(s)$, where $P(s)$ and $Q(s)$ are polynomials. Furthermore, all roots of $Q(s)$ are real, the degree of $Q(s)$ is higher than the degree of $P(s)$ and $P(0)/Q(0) = f^*(0) = 1$. Conversely, any rational function of s which satisfies the above conditions can be expressed in the form (3.21) and, therefore, any distribution whose Laplace transform is such a rational function can be represented by a network of exponential stages as in Fig. 3.6. Distributions which are representable in this way are called *Coxian distributions*.

The exponential, hyperexponential and Erlang distributions are Coxian, and any distribution function which is a linear combination of Coxian distributions is also Coxian. Moreover, any probability distribution function $F(x)$ can be approximated arbitrarily closely by Coxian distribution functions. This can be done, for example, by first constructing a staircase approximation to $F(x)$ of the form

$$\tilde{F}(x) = \sum_{i=1}^{m} d_i I_{(x \geq ih)}$$

where the increment h, the staircase steps d_i and their number m are chosen so that $\tilde{F}(x)$ approximates $F(x)$ with the desired accuracy. Each of the unit step functions $I_{(t \geq ih)}$ is the distribution function of a constant (ih)

and can, therefore, be approximated by an Erlang distribution arbitrarily closely (if we take an Erlang distribution with parameters n, μ and let $n \to \infty$, $\mu \to \infty$ so that $n/\mu \to$ const. $= k$, the Erlang distribution function approaches $I_{(x \geq k)}$). Thus $F(x)$ is approximated by a linear combination of Erlang distributions, which is the Coxian.

Let us now revisit the three models considered in this section and assume, in each case, that the required service time for class r jobs $(r = 1, 2, \ldots, R)$ has a Coxian distribution with parameters L_r (number of stages), $1/\mu_{rl}$ (mean of l-th stage, $l = 1, 2, \ldots, L_r$), a_{rl} (probability of proceeding to the $j + 1$ stage, $l = 0, 1, \ldots, L_r - 1, a_{r0} = 1$) and b_{rl} (probability of exiting after the j-th stage, $l = 1, 2, \ldots, L_r, b_{rL_r} = 1$). The average required service time for class r jobs is, according to (3.20),

$$1/\mu_r = \sum_{l=1}^{L_r} (A_{rl}/\mu_{rl}), \quad r = 1, 2, \ldots, R$$

where $A_{rl} = a_{r0} a_{r1} \cdots a_{rl-1}$ is the probability that a class r job reaches the l-th stage of its service.

When the required service times are not distributed exponentially, the stochastic process defined by the number (or vector of numbers) of jobs in the system is not Markov and one cannot find its steady-state distribution by means of balance equations. However, if those distributions are Coxian, the Markov property can be reinstated by a suitable redefinition of the system state. The new process can then be studied in the usual way.

In the case of the processor-shared server, define the system state as a vector of vectors $(\mathbf{v}_1, \mathbf{v}_2, \ldots, \mathbf{v}_R)$, where $\mathbf{v}_r = (k_{r1}, k_{r2}, \ldots, k_{rL_r})$ is a vector whose l-th element is the number of class r jobs which are in the l-th stage of their service. As defined, the system state forms a Markov process because all stages are distributed exponentially. We can therefore write a set of balance equations for the steady-state distribution of $(\mathbf{v}_1, \mathbf{v}_2, \ldots, \mathbf{v}_R)$. These equations take into account transitions out of and into a state due to arrivals of class r jobs and due to completions of stage l of a class r service $(r = 1, 2, \ldots, R; l = 1, 2, \ldots, L_r)$. The solution of the balance equations, subject to the normalising equation, is given by

$$p(\mathbf{v}_1, \mathbf{v}_2, \ldots, \mathbf{v}_R) = (1 - \rho) k! \prod_{r=1}^{R} \left\{ \lambda_r^{k_r} \prod_{l=1}^{L_r} [(A_{rl}/\mu_{rl})^{k_{rl}}/k_{rl}!] \right\} \qquad (3.22)$$

where $k_r = k_1 + \cdots + k_{rL_r}$ is the number of class r jobs, $k = k_1 + \cdots + k_R$ is the total number of jobs in the system and

$$\rho = \sum_{r=1}^{R} (\lambda_r/\mu_r) = \sum_{r=1}^{R} \left[\lambda_r \sum_{l=1}^{L_r} (A_{rl}/\mu_{rl}) \right].$$

Steady-state exists when $\rho < 1$.

The verification that the balance equations are satisfied is carried out by showing that (3.22) satisfies the following set of local balance equations: the rate of flow out of state $(\mathbf{v}_1, \ldots, \mathbf{v}_R)$ due to a class r job completing stage l of its service is equal to the rate of flow into that state due to a class r job entering stage l of its service ($r = 1, 2, \ldots, R$; $l = 1, 2, \ldots, L_r$); and vice versa. This allows individual terms to be cancelled out on both sides of the balance equations.

If we sum (3.22) over all states $(\mathbf{v}_1, \ldots, \mathbf{v}_R)$ such that $k_{r1} + \cdots + k_{rL_r} = k_r$ ($r = 1, 2, \ldots, R$) we obtain the distribution of the aggregate system state $(k_1, k_2, \ldots, k_R)$, where only the numbers of jobs of various classes are considered and not the stages of service. This yields

$$p(k_1, k_2, \ldots, k_R) = (1-\rho)k! \prod_{r=1}^{R} \left\{ (\lambda_r^{k_r}/k_r!) \left[\sum_{l=1}^{L_r} (A_{rl}/\mu_{rl}) \right]^{k_r} \right\}$$

$$= (1-\rho)k! \prod_{r=1}^{R} [(\lambda_r/\mu_r)^{k_r}/k_r!] = (1-\rho)k! \prod_{r=1}^{R} (\rho_r^{k_r}/k_r!).$$

We have obtained the same expression as (3.14)! In other words, the distribution of the vector $(k_1, k_2, \ldots, k_R)$ depends only on the average required service times, not on the shape of the required service time distributions.

When the scheduling strategy is pre-emptive-resume LCFS, we define the system state as the vector of pairs $((r_1, l_1), (r_2, l_2), \ldots, (r_k, l_k))$, where k is the number of jobs present and (r_j, l_j) describes the j-th job in the LCFS order: r_j is the class and l_j the service stage of that job ($r_j \in \{1, 2, \ldots, R\}, l_j \in \{1, 2, \ldots, L_{r_j}\}, j = 1, 2, \ldots, k$). The empty state is conventionally denoted $((0,0))$.

Thus defined, the state forms a Markov process. Following a path which is becoming familiar, we find that its steady-state distribution is given by

$$p((r_1, l_1), (r_2, l_2), \ldots, (r_k, l_k)) = (1-\rho) \prod_{j=1}^{k} (\lambda_{r_j} A_{r_j l_j}/\mu_{r_j l_j}), \qquad (3.23)$$

using the same notation as in the previous case (and assuming that $\rho < 1$). The product on the right-hand side is defined as 1 if $(r_1, l_1) = (0, 0)$. Aggregating over all states such that the class index of the first job in the LCFS order is r_1, that of the second job is r_2, etc., gives

$$p(r_1, r_2, \ldots, r_k) = (1 - \rho) \prod_{j=1}^{k} (\lambda_{r_j} / \mu_{r_j}) = (1 - \rho) \prod_{j=1}^{k} \rho_{r_j}$$

which is the same expression as (3.16). A further aggregation would yield (3.17). Again, the distribution of $(k_1, k_2, \ldots, k_R)$ turns out to be insensitive to the shape of the required service time distributions and to depend only on their means.

We have a similar result for the server-per-job discipline. Defining the system state by a vector of vectors $(\mathbf{v}_1, \mathbf{v}_2, \ldots, \mathbf{v}_R)$, exactly as in the processor-sharing case, we obtain

$$p(\mathbf{v}_1, \mathbf{v}_2, \ldots, \mathbf{v}_R) = \mathrm{e}^{-\rho} \prod_{r=1}^{R} \prod_{l=1}^{L_r} [(\lambda_r A_{rl} / \mu_{rl})^{k_{rl}} (1/k_{rl}!)]. \qquad (3.24)$$

Steady-state exists for all values of the parameters. In this case, since $\exp(-\rho)$ factorises into a product of $\exp(-(\lambda_r A_{rl} / \mu_{rl}))$ over all r and l, the random variables k_{rl} (the number of class r jobs in the l-th stage of their service) are mutually independent. Aggregation of (3.24) yields (3.19).

3.5. The BCMP theorem

We are now ready to formulate one of the most general queueing network models which have been analysed to date. The development and analysis of the model was due to the combined effort, over several years, of Baskett, Chandy, Muntz and Palacios [2, 3, 8]; the result bears their initials.

Case 3 (BCMP). The network topology is represented by an arbitrary graph with N nodes (excluding the "outside world" node). There are R job classes and jobs may change class as they move from one node to another. More precisely, a job of class r, when completing service at node i, goes to node j as a job of class s with probability $p_{ir,js}$; that job leaves the network with probability

$$p_{ir,0} = 1 - \sum_{j,s} p_{ir,js} \quad (i,j = 1,2,\ldots,N;\ r,s = 1,2,\ldots,R).$$

The pair (i,r) associated with a job at a node is called "job state". The set of job states is split into one or more non-intersecting subsets (or "subchains") in the following way: two job states belong to the same subchain if there is a non-zero probability that a job will be in both job states during its life in the network. Denote these subchains by $E_1, E_2, \ldots, E_m (m \geq 1)$. (For example, if jobs never change class when they go from node to node, there will be at least R subchains.)

It may be that some subchains are closed, having a constant number of jobs in them at all times, while others are open with external arrivals and departures. Moreover, the external arrival processes may be state-dependent in a restricted way. Let $\mathbf{S}$ be the state of the network (to be defined later), let $M(\mathbf{S})$ be the total number of jobs in the network in state $\mathbf{S}$ and let $M(\mathbf{S}, E_k)$ be the number of jobs in subchain E_k when the network is in state $\mathbf{S}$. The external arrivals may be generated in either, but not both, of the following two ways:

(i) by a single non-homogeneous Poisson process whose instantaneous rate, $\lambda(M(\mathbf{S}))$, depends on the system state via the total number of jobs in the network. A new arrival joins node i as a class r job with probability $p_{0,ir} (\sum_{i,r} p_{0,ir} = 1)$;

(ii) by m independent non-homogeneous Poisson processes, one for each subchain. The instantaneous rate of the k-th process, $\lambda_k(M(\mathbf{S}, E_k))$, depends on the system state via the number of jobs in the subchain E_k. A new arrival in the k-th stream joins node i as a class r job with probability $p_{0,ir} (\sum_{(i,r) \in E_k} p_{0,ir} = 1)$.

It remains to describe node i of the queueing network and to define its state, $\mathbf{S}_i (i = 1,2,\ldots,N)$. There are four possibilities, as will now be described.

Type 1 *node*: The service requirements for all job classes are distributed exponentially with mean $1/\mu_i$. Jobs are served in order of arrival. The state $\mathbf{S}_i$ of the node is defined as the vector $(r_1, r_2, \ldots, r_{n_i})$, where n_i is the number of jobs present and r_j is the class index of the j-th job in the FCFS order. There is a single server whose speed $C_i(n_i)$ depends on the number of jobs and satisfies $C_i(1) = 1$ (multiple servers can be modelled by setting

$C_i(n_i) = \min(n_i, c_i))$. Thus the instantaneous completion rate at node i in state $\mathbf{S}_i$ is $\mu_i C_i(n_i)$.

Type 2 node: This consists of a single processor-shared server as described in the last section. The required service times for class r jobs ($r = 1, 2, \ldots, R$) have Coxian distribution with parameters $a_{irl}, b_{irl}, \mu_{irl}, L_{ir}$ ($l = 1, 2, \ldots, L_{ir}$) and mean $\sum_{l=1}^{L_{ir}} (A_{irl}/\mu_{irl})$, where A_{irl} is the probability that a class r job at node i will reach stage l of its service. The node state $\mathbf{S}_i$ is defined as the vector $(\mathbf{v}_1, \mathbf{v}_2, \ldots, \mathbf{v}_R)$ where $\mathbf{v}_r = (n_{ir1}, n_{ir2}, \ldots, n_{irL_{ir}})$ is a vector whose l-th element n_{irl} denotes the number of class r jobs at node i which are in the l-th stage of their service ($l = 1, 2, \ldots, L_{ir}$). The numbers of class r jobs at node i is $n_{ir} = n_{ir1} + \cdots + n_{irL_{ir}}$ and the total number of jobs is $n_i = n_{i1} + \cdots + n_{iR}$. The speed of the server may depend on n_i as for type 1 nodes. Thus the rate of completion for class r jobs in stage l of their service, when the node is in state $\mathbf{S}_i$, is $(n_{irl}/n_i)\mu_{irl}C_i(n_i)$; after such completion, the job leaves node i with probability b_{irl} and proceeds to the next stage with probability a_{irl}.

Type 3 node: The scheduling strategy is server-per-job (it was defined and analysed in the last section). The assumptions regarding the required service time distributions, and the definition of the node state $\mathbf{S}_i$ are the same as for type 2 nodes. Since in the server-per-job discipline the speed of service already depends on the numbers n_{irl} (the completion rate for class r jobs in stage l is $n_{irl}\mu_{irl}$; $r = 1, 2, \ldots, R$; $l = 1, 2, \ldots, L_{ir}$) there seems little point in introducing further dependencies, although it is possible.

Type 4 node: A single server is scheduled according to the preemptive-resume LCFS discipline (see last section). The required service times have Coxian distributions, as for type 2 and 3 nodes. The state of the node, $\mathbf{S}_i$, is defined as the vector of pairs $((r_1, l_1), (r_2, l_2), \ldots, (r_{n_i}, l_{n_i}))$ whose j-th element describes the j-th job in the LCFS order ($j = 1, 2, \ldots, n_i$): r_j is its class index and l_j is its service stage. The speed of the server may depend on n_i as for type 1 nodes. The stage completion rate in state $\mathbf{S}_i$, is $\mu_{ir_1 l_1}C_i(n_i)$.

The total network state $\mathbf{S}$ is defined as the vector $(\mathbf{S}_1, \mathbf{S}_2, \ldots, \mathbf{S}_N)$. The above definitions and assumptions ensure that $\mathbf{S}$ (regarded as a function of time) is a Markov process. We are interested in the steady-state distribution $p(\mathbf{S})$ of that Markov process. To find it, it suffices (since the process is irreducible) to find a solution to the balance equations:

$$p(\mathbf{S})[\text{instantaneous transition rate out of } \mathbf{S}]$$

$$= \sum_{\mathbf{S}'} p(\mathbf{S}') [\text{instantaneous transition rate from } \mathbf{S}' \text{ to } \mathbf{S}] \qquad (3.25)$$

which satisfies the normalising equation

$$\sum_{\mathbf{S}} p(\mathbf{S}) = 1. \tag{3.26}$$

The existence of the steady-state distribution depends on the solution of the following set of equations:

$$e_{js} = p_{0,js} + \sum_{i,r} e_{ir} p_{ir,js}; \quad i,j = 1, 2, \ldots, N; \ r, s = 1, 2, \ldots, R.$$

In this model, the equations play the role which the traffic equations played in Jackson networks. The quantity e_{ir} is proportional to the total arrival rate of class r jobs into node i ($i = 1, 2, \ldots, N; r = 1, 2, \ldots, R$). Since $p_{ir,js} = 0$ when the job states (i, r) and (j, s) belong to different subchains, there are in fact m independent subsystems.

$$e_{js} = p_{0,js} + \sum_{(i,r) \in E_k} e_{ir} p_{ir,js}; \quad (j, s) \in E_k, \ k = 1, 2, \ldots, m. \tag{3.27}$$

If $p_{0,js} = 0$ and $p_{js,0} = 0$ for all $(j, s) \in E_k$ then the subchain E_k is closed and there is, at all times, a fixed number of jobs in it. If $p_{0,js} > 0$ for some $(j, s) \in E_k$ and $p_{ir,0} > 0$ for some $(i, r) \in E_k$ then E_k is open. The corresponding subsystem in (3.27) has a unique solution if all nodes in E_k are open (see section 3.3), i.e. if E_k is completely open. We shall assume that all subchains are either completely open or completely closed.

The following result is known as the BCMP theorem.

Theorem 3.4 (BCMP). Let $e_{ir}(i = 1, 2, \ldots, N; r = 1, 2, \ldots, R)$ be any solution of (3.27). The general solution of the balance equations (3.25) has the form

$$p(\mathbf{S}) = (1/G)d(\mathbf{S})f_1(\mathbf{S}_1)f_2(\mathbf{S}_2) \cdots f_N(\mathbf{S}_N) \tag{3.28}$$

where:

(a) G is an arbitrary constant;
(b) if there are external arrivals and they are of type (i) (see the model specification), then

$$d(\mathbf{S}) = \prod_{n=0}^{M(\mathbf{S})-1} \lambda(n),$$

otherwise, if there are external arrivals and they are of type (ii) then

$$d(\mathbf{S}) = \prod_{k=1}^{m} \left[\prod_{n=0}^{M(\mathbf{S},E_k)-1} \lambda_k(n) \right],$$

and, if there are no external arrivals, $d(\mathbf{S}) = 1$;

(c) the factor $f_i(\mathbf{S}_i)$ depends on the type of node i ($i = 1, 2, \ldots, N$): if node i is of type 1 then

$$f_i(\mathbf{S}_i) = \prod_{j=1}^{n_j} [e_{ir_j}/(\mu_i C_i(j))],$$

if node i is of type 2 then

$$f_i(\mathbf{S}_i) = n_i! \left\{ \prod_{r=1}^{R} \prod_{l=1}^{L_{ir}} [(e_{ir}A_{irl}/\mu_{irl})^{n_{irl}}/n_{irl}!] \right\} \Big/ \prod_{j=1}^{n_j} C_i(j),$$

if node i is of type 3 then

$$f_i(\mathbf{S}_i) = \prod_{r=1}^{R} \prod_{l=1}^{L_{ir}} [(e_{ir}A_{irl}/\mu_{irl})^{n_{irl}}/n_{irl}!],$$

if node i is of type 4 then

$$f_i(\mathbf{S}_i) = \prod_{j=1}^{n_i} [e_{ir_j}A_{ir_j l_j}/(\mu_{ir_j l_j} C_i(j))].$$

Moreover, if the constant G can be chosen so that the normalising equation (3.26) is satisfied, i.e. if the sum $\sum_{\mathbf{S}} [d(\mathbf{S})f_1(\mathbf{S}_1)f_2(\mathbf{S}_2)\cdots f_N(\mathbf{S}_N)]$ converges, then the steady-state distribution exists and is given by (3.28) with what choice of G.

The proof of the theorem is by substituting (3.28) into (3.25) and verifying that the latter are satisfied. The verification is performed by showing that (3.28) satisfies a rather detailed set of local balance equations: the rate of transition out of state $\mathbf{S}$ due to a class r job completing stage l of its service at node i is equal to the rate of transition into state $\mathbf{S}$ due to a class r job entering stage l of its service at node i; also, the rate of transition out of $\mathbf{S}$ due to a class r job coming into node i is equal to the rate of transition into $\mathbf{S}$ due to a class r job leaving node i. These local balance equations (which, in turn, are established with the aid of (3.27) in a similar way as we demonstrated in the case of Jackson networks) allow individual terms to be cancelled out on both sides of the global balance equations.

In practical applications one is usually interested not so much in the node states $\mathbf{S}_i$ as we have defined them, but rather in the aggregate node states $\mathbf{n}_i = (n_{i1}, n_{i2}, \ldots, n_{iR})$ specifying the number of class r jobs at node i ($i = 1, 2, \ldots, N; r = 1, 2, \ldots, R$). Let $\mathbf{n} = (\mathbf{n}_1, \mathbf{n}_2, \ldots, \mathbf{n}_N)$ be the aggregate network state. Its steady-state distribution can be obtained (assuming that the steady-state distribution of $\mathbf{S}$ exists) by summing $p(\mathbf{S})$ over all states $\mathbf{S}$ which yield $\mathbf{n}$. Because of the product-form of $p(\mathbf{S})$, this is equivalent to summing the factors $f_i(\mathbf{S}_i)$ over all node states $\mathbf{S}_i$ which yield $\mathbf{n}_i$, and then multiplying the resulting factors together (note that $d(\mathbf{S})$, in (3.28), depends only on the total number of jobs in the network, or in the subchains, and hence is the same for all $\mathbf{S}$ which yield $\mathbf{n}$; we can denote it $d(\mathbf{n})$). Performing these calculations we obtain

$$p(\mathbf{n}) = (1/G)d(\mathbf{n})g_1(\mathbf{n}_1)g_2(\mathbf{n}_2)\cdots g_N(\mathbf{n}_N), \qquad (3.29)$$

where G is the same constant as in (3.28); $d(\mathbf{n})$ is defined in the same way as $d(\mathbf{S})$ in (3.28); the factor $g_i(\mathbf{n}_i)$ depends on the type of node i ($i = 1, 2, \ldots, N$):

if node i is of type 1 then

$$g_i(\mathbf{n}_i) = \left[n_i! \prod_{r=1}^{R} (e_{ir}^{n_{ir}}/n_{ir}!) \right] \bigg/ \prod_{j=1}^{n_i} [\mu_i C_i(j)],$$

if node i is of type 2 or 4 then

$$g_i(\mathbf{n}_i) = n_i! \left\{ \prod_{r=1}^{R} [(e_{ir}/\mu_{ir})^{n_{ir}}/n_{ir}!] \right\} \bigg/ \prod_{j=1}^{n_i} C_i(j),$$

if node i is of type 3 then

$$g_i(\mathbf{n}_i) = \prod_{r=1}^{R} [(e_{ir}/\mu_{ir})^{n_{ir}}/n_{ir}!];$$

$1/\mu_{ir}$ is the average required service time for class r jobs at node i (node types 2, 3 and 4):

$$1/\mu_{ir} = \sum_{l=1}^{L_{it}} (A_{irl}/\mu_{irl}).$$

Once again we observe (see previous section) that the distribution of the aggregate system state does not depend on the shape of the required service time distributions (for node types 2, 3 and 4), only on their means. Only the latter need to be estimated, therefore, when applying the model in practice.

An even higher level of aggregation would involve defining the network state simply as the vector $(n_1, n_2, \ldots, n_N)$, where n_i is the total number of jobs (of all classes) at node i $(i = 1, 2, \ldots, N)$. Rather simpler expressions can be obtained for the distribution of this aggregate state in the case when the network does not contain any closed subchains, the speed of the servers is independent of the node states, and the external arrival rate λ is independent of the network state. Then equations (3.27) have a unique solution e_{ir} $(i = 1, 2, \ldots, N; r = 1, 2, \ldots, R)$ which can be interpreted as the average number of times a job visits node i with a class index r, during its life in the network. The total average number of class r jobs coming into node i per unit time is $\lambda_{ir} = \lambda e_{ir}$ and the overall traffic intensity for node i is

$$
\rho_i =
\begin{cases}
\displaystyle\sum_{r=1}^{R} (\lambda_{ir}/\mu_i) & \text{if node } i \text{ is of type 1} \\[2mm]
\displaystyle\sum_{r=1}^{R} (\lambda_{ir}/\mu_{ir}) & \text{if node } i \text{ is of type 2, 3 or 4.}
\end{cases}
$$

The steady-state distribution of $(n_1, n_2, \ldots, n_N)$ now factorises completely into a product of individual node distributions:

$$
p(n_1, n_2, \ldots, n_N) = p_1(n_1) p_2(n_2) \ldots p_N(n_N), \tag{3.30}
$$

where

$$
p_i(n_i) =
\begin{cases}
(1 - \rho_i)\rho_i^{n_i} & \text{if node } i \text{ is of type 1, 2 or 4} \\[2mm]
e^{-\rho_i} \rho_i^{n_i}/n_i! & \text{if node } i \text{ is of type 3,}
\end{cases}
$$

provided that $\rho_i < 1$ for nodes of type 1, 2 or 4. We see that in this case the nodes behave like N independent $M/M/1$ (for types 1, 2 and 4) or $M/M/\infty$ (for type 3) queues.

Some remarks are in order concerning the assumptions, generality and usefulness of the BCMP model. Clearly, the introduction of different job classes and node types widens considerably the field of application of the model. We shall give two examples of systems which can be modelled as BCMP but not as Jackson networks.

Consider a Jackson network where a job transition from node i to node j is not instantaneous but takes a random time with Coxian distribution (in computer systems transitions are rarely instantaneous, due to supervisor overheads). This model can be included in the BCMP framework by adding N^2 "artificial" nodes (i,j) of type 3 whose service times will represent the transit times between nodes in the original network. The new routing probabilities should be defined in terms of the old as $\tilde{p}_{i,(i,j)} = p_{ij}$, $\tilde{p}_{(i,j),j} = 1$, $\tilde{p}_{0i} = p_{0i}$, $\tilde{p}_{i0} = p_{i0}$ and zero otherwise. The state description of the new network includes jobs at the (i,j) nodes (i.e. in transit), as well as jobs at the original nodes.

Our second example is of a network where the destination of a job after leaving a node depends not only on the node just left but also on nodes visited previously (i.e. the job states represent a higher-order rather than a first-order Markov chain). This generalisation can be reduced to a standard BCMP model by introducing new job classes, where the class index would include the nodes previously visited. Thus, the higher-order transition probabilities with the old job classes, $p_{i_1 i_2 \ldots i_h r, js}$, become first-order transition probabilities with the new job classes, $\tilde{p}_{i_h \tilde{r}, j\tilde{s}}$, where $\tilde{r} = (i_1 i_2 \ldots i_{h-1} r)$ and $\tilde{s} = (i_2 i_3 \ldots i_h s)$.

Regarding the assumptions of the BCMP model, one can legitimately ask the questions "Why these particular four node types?", "What is so special about the processor-sharing, the server-per-job and the preemptive-resume LCFS disciplines?", "Is there no hope of generalising the model even further by allowing, for instance, nodes with priority disciplines or FIFO nodes with different required service time distributions for the different job classes?". Some answers to these questions are gradually emerging. Muntz [19] has shown that the four node types in the BCMP model all have a certain property which ensures that when they are taken in isolation, with Poisson inputs for each class, the departure process for each class is also Poisson. He calls this the M$\Rightarrow$M property (Markov implies Markov). The M$\Rightarrow$M property (which, briefly, states that the class r arrival process in reverse time is equivalent to the class r arrival process in forward time and hence is Poisson) is sufficient for the existence of a product-form solution and these four node types are, at present, the only ones known to possess it.

We have already seen that local balance is closely connected with product form. A recent work (Chandy *et al.*, [9]) defines a property called "station balance" which equates transition rates in and out of a particular position in a queue, rather than in and out of the whole queue. It turns out that station balance is necessary, as well as sufficient, for the existence of a product-form solution. Many interesting scheduling disciplines (e.g. priority ones) do not satisfy station balance; it seems, therefore, that the chances of generalising the BCMP model with respect to the scheduling strategies allowed at each node are very slim.

Other generalisations exist, however. Kelly [15] allowed jobs to take arbitrary paths through the network (rather than paths governed by the transfer probabilities $p_{ir,js}$). He also conjectured that, where Coxian distributions are admitted, one can allow arbitrary distributions — which has been proved to be true by Barbour [1]. Lam [17] considered a model where arrivals to the network can be lost and departures from the network can trigger an arrival.

3.6. The computation of performance measures

If the solution for the stationary distribution of a queueing network state is to be of any practical use, one should be able to extract from it numerical values for specific measures of system performance like node utilisations, throughputs, average response times, etc. Furthermore, one should be able to do this at a computational cost which compares favourably with that of a simulation.

The easiest cases to deal with are those of completely open Jackson networks or BCMP networks all of whose subchains are open with state-independent arrival rates. In those cases each node can be considered as a separate, independent $M/M/1$ or $M/M/\infty$ queue, perhaps with different job classes and server speed depending on the number of jobs requiring service. The relevant quantities of interest can be obtained either explicitly (see sections 3.3 and 3.4) or with a minimum of computational effort.

Consider now a closed network with a single job class, a single (state-independent) exponential server at each node and a total of K jobs circulating inside (a special case of the Gordon–Newell model). The steady-state distribution of the network state is given by

$$p(\mathbf{n}) = p(n_1, n_2, \ldots, n_N) = \frac{1}{G} \prod_{i=1}^{N} \rho_i^{n_i}; \quad n_1 + n_2 + \cdots + n_N = K \quad (3.31)$$

where $\rho_i = e_i/\mu_i$, $(e_1, e_2, \ldots, e_N)$ is any solution of the equations (3.7) and the normalising constant G is equal to

$$G = \sum_{n_1 + \cdots + n_N = K} \left(\prod_{i=1}^{N} \rho_i^{n_i} \right). \quad (3.32)$$

Even in this rather simple case the computational problem is non-trivial. There are $\binom{N+K-1}{N-1}$ terms in the summation on the right-hand side of (3.32), which means that the "brute force" approach for evaluating G is impractical for any but the smallest values of N and K. We shall use the "generating function method" of Williams and Bhandiwad [24] to develop an efficient algorithm (due originally to Buzen [7]) for computing G.

Consider the product of infinite power series

$$g(z) = \prod_{i=1}^{N} g_i(z) = \prod_{i=1}^{N} \left[\sum_{n_i=0}^{\infty} \rho_i^{n_i} z^{n_i} \right] \tag{3.33}$$

defined whenever the component series converge. $g(z)$ will be called the generating function of the network, and the factors $g_i(z)$ the generating functions of the individual nodes ($i = 1, 2, \ldots, N$). Clearly, the coefficient of z^K in $g(z)$ is precisely our normalising constant G: that coefficient, like G, is the sum of terms of the type $\rho_1^{n_1} \rho_2^{n_2} \cdots \rho_N^{n_N}$, one term for each composition $n_1 + n_2 + \cdots + n_N = K$.

Denote by $\gamma_i(z)$ the partial products in (3.33):

$$\gamma_1(z) = g_1(z), \quad \gamma_i(z) = \gamma_{i-1}(z) g_i(z), \quad i = 2, 3, \ldots, N \tag{3.34}$$

and let $G_i(j)$ be the coefficient of z^j in $\gamma_i(z)$. Our task is to compute $G = G_N(K)$. Using the fact that, in this case, $g_i(z)$ is a simple geometric series, $g_i(z) = 1/(1 - \rho_i z)$, we rewrite (3.34) as

$$\gamma_i(z) = \gamma_{i-1}(z) + \rho_i z \gamma_i(z)$$

which implies the following recurrence relation for the coefficients $G_i(j)$:

$$G_i(j) = G_{i-1}(j) + \rho_i G_i(j-1), \quad i = 2, 3, \ldots, \quad j = 1, 2, \ldots. \tag{3.35}$$

The algorithm suggested by (3.35) (together with $G_1(j) = \rho_1^j, j = 0, 1, \ldots$, and $G_i(0) = 1, i = 1, 2, \ldots$) computes $G_N(K)$ in $O(NK)$ steps.

Similar ideas allow us to compute various performance measures. If, in the product (3.33) defining $g(z)$, we replace $g_1(z)$ by $g_1(z) - 1$, and then take the coefficient of z^K, we would have a sum of terms of the type $\rho_1^{n_1} \rho_2^{n_2} \cdots \rho_N^{n_N}$, where $n_1 + \cdots + n_N = K$ and $n_1 \geq 1$. According to (3.31), that sum divided by G is equal to the probability $P(n_1 \geq 1)$ of having at least one job at node 1. A similar statement is true, of course, for any other node. Since we are dealing with geometric series,

$$g(z)\frac{g_i(z) - 1}{g_i(z)} = \rho_i z g(z)$$

and the coefficient of z^K on the right-hand side is $\rho_i G_N(K - 1)$. Thus we have, for the utilisation factor U_i of node i,

$$U_i = \rho_i G_N(K - 1)/G_N(K). \tag{3.36}$$

Note that $G_N(K - 1)$ will have been computed in the process of computing $G_N(K)$. Note also that $(U_i/U_j) = (\rho_i/\rho_j)$ regardless of the value of K: the utilisation factor of any one node determines the utilisation factors of all other nodes. This last result is important, it is sometimes referred to as "the work-rate theorem".

From the utilisation factor U_i we can find the throughput λ_i at node i:

$$\lambda_i = U_i \mu_i = e_i G_N(K - 1)/G_N(K). \tag{3.37}$$

To obtain the average number $E[n_i]$ of jobs at node i we write

$$E[n_i] = \sum_{j=1}^{k} j P(n_i = j) = \sum_{j=1}^{K} P(n_i \geq j)$$

and, by an argument similar to the one which led to (3.36),

$$P(n_i \geq j) = \rho_i^j G_N(K - j)/G_N(K).$$

Hence

$$E[n_i] = \frac{1}{G_N(K)} \sum_{j=1}^{K} \rho_i^j G_N(K - j). \tag{3.38}$$

The average sojourn time at node i, $E[T_i]$, is given by (according to Little's theorem)

$$E[T_i] = E[n_i]/\lambda_i = \frac{1}{e_i G_N(K - 1)} \sum_{j=1}^{K} \rho_i^j G_N(K - j).$$

Let us now generalise the model a little, by allowing the speed of the server at node i to depend on the number of jobs there, with the usual notation $C_i(j)$ expressing the dependency. This generalisation includes multiple-server nodes $(C_i(j) = \min(j, c_i))$ and server-per-job nodes $(C_i(j) = j)$. The steady-state distribution of the network state is given by

$$p(n_1, n_2, \ldots, n_N) = \frac{1}{G} \prod_{i=1}^{N} \alpha_i(n_i), \quad n_1 + n_2 + \cdots + n_N = K$$

where $\alpha_i(0) = 1$, $\alpha_i(j) = \rho_i^j / [C_i(1) C_i(2) \ldots C_i(j)]$, $j \geq 1$ with the previous notation for ρ_i. The network generating function is

$$g(z) = \prod_{i=1}^{N} g_i(z) = \prod_{i=1}^{N} \left[\sum_{j=0}^{\infty} \alpha_i(j) z^j \right]$$

and again G is the coefficient of z^K in $g(z)$. This time, however, the convolution (3.34) does not simplify; the coefficient of z^j in $\gamma_i(z)$ is given by

$$G_i(j) = \sum_{s=0}^{j} G_{i-1}(s) \alpha_i(j - s).$$

This recurrence relation, together with the initial conditions $G_1(j) = \alpha_1(j)$, $j = 0, 1, \ldots$, allow $G_N(K)$ to be computed in $O(NK^2)$ steps.

To find the utilisation of node i, U_i, we proceed as before: $G \cdot U_i$ is the coefficient of z^K in the series

$$h_i(z) = g(z) \frac{g_i(z) - 1}{g_i(z)} = g(z)[1 - d_i(z)] \tag{3.39}$$

where $d_i(z)$ is the inverse of $g_i(z)$. Denoting the coefficients of $h_i(z)$ and $d_i(z)$ by $H_i(j)$ and $D_i(j)$, respectively, the convolution (3.39) yields a recurrence relation

$$H_i(j) = G_N(j) - \sum_{s=0}^{j} G_N(s) D_i(j - s). \tag{3.40}$$

The coefficients $D_i(j)$ are determined from the condition

$$d_i(z) g_i(z) = 1$$

which yields

$$D_i(0) = 1, \quad \sum_{s=0}^{j} D_i(s) \alpha_i(j - s) = 0, \quad j \geq 1.$$

or

$$D_i(j) = -\sum_{s=0}^{j-1} D_i(s)\alpha_i(j-s), \quad j \geq 1. \tag{3.41}$$

Thus (3.41) can be used to compute $D_i(j)$ and then (3.40) to compute $H_i(j)$. The utilisation of the i-th node is given by

$$U_i = H_i(K)/G_N(K). \tag{3.42}$$

Two remarks should be made concerning (3.42): firstly, if node i happens to contain a single-state independent server, then (3.42) coincides with (3.36) even though other nodes may be more complicated; secondly, the definition of U_i as $P(n_i \geq 1)$ is correct for single-server nodes but may be inappropriate if a state-dependent server is used to model a multiple-server node (for example, the utilisation of a server-per-job node is sometimes defined as the average number of jobs there).

The average number of jobs at node i $(E[n_i])$ is, perhaps, best obtained by first finding the marginal distribution at node i: $p_i(j) = P(n_i = j), j = 0, 1, \ldots, K$. The probability $p_i(j)$ is equal to a sum of terms of the type $\alpha_1(n_1)\ldots\alpha_i(j)\ldots\alpha_N(n_N)$, with $n_1 + \cdots + n_{i-1} + n_{i+1} + \cdots + n_N = K - j$, divided by G. Apart from the factor $\alpha_i(j)$, the sum in the numerator is the normalising constant of a network from which node i is removed, with $K - j$ jobs circulating in it; we shall denote it $G_{N\backslash i}(K - j)$. Thus

$$p_i(j) = \alpha_i(j)[G_{N\backslash i}(K - j)]/G_N(K) \tag{3.43}$$

and

$$E[n_i] = \sum_{j=1}^{K} jp_i(j), \quad i = 1, 2, \ldots, N.$$

The throughput of node i is given by

$$\lambda_i = \sum_{j=1}^{K} p_i(j)C_i(j)\mu_i.$$

Substituting (3.43) in this last expression and remembering that $C_i(j)\mu_i\alpha_i(j) = e_i\alpha_i(j - 1)$ we obtain, surprisingly,

$$\lambda_i = e_iG_N(K - 1)/G_N(K)$$

i.e. the same expression as (3.37)!

The methods described so far generalise to networks with more than one job class. The generating functions of such networks are multi-variate (there is one variable for each job class if jobs do not change classes; one variable for each subchain if they do). The normalisation constant and various quantities of interest are obtained by multi-variate convolutions (Reiser [21]; Reiser and Kobayashi [22]; Wong [25]). Some results remain unchanged: for example, the throughput λ_{ir} of class r jobs through node i, in a closed network with K_r jobs of class r circulating inside ($r = 1, 2, \ldots, R$), is given by

$$\lambda_{ir} = e_{ir} G_N(K_1, \ldots, K_r - 1, \ldots, K_R)/G_N(K_1, \ldots, K_R) \qquad (3.44)$$

where $\{e_{ir}\}$ is any solution of equations (3.27). Expression (3.44) is a generalisation of (3.37). If node i has single-server of constant speed, then its utilisation due to class r jobs (the fraction of time it spends serving class r jobs) is

$$U_{ir} = \lambda_{ir}/\mu_{ir}, \quad r = 1, 2, \ldots, R. \qquad (3.45)$$

If the service rate is state-dependent, U_{ir} can be computed from

$$U_{ir} = \sum_{\mathbf{S}_i} p_i(\mathbf{S}_i)\frac{n_{ir}}{n_i}$$

where $\mathbf{S}_i$ is the state of node i, $p_i(\mathbf{S}_i)$ is the probability of that state and n_{ir}/n_i is the fraction of server capacity allocated to class r jobs (for type 2 nodes), or the probability of a class r job being in service (type 1 or 4 nodes). Such a procedure would involve the computation of the normalising constant and then of the marginal probabilities $p_i(\mathbf{S}_i)$.

When we talk about response times in the context of a closed network, we usually mean the time between leaving a certain node and returning to it. For example, in a terminal-driven system the collection of terminals is modelled by one node (of type server-per-job). Let that be node i and suppose that there are K_r terminals of class r, $r = 1, 2, \ldots, R$ (in a heavily loaded system, when the terminals are busy all the time, jobs can be identified with terminals). The response time for a class r job is defined as the interval between the job leaving its terminal (the user presses "carriage return") and returning to it (the keyboard unlocks). Denote the average response time for class r jobs by W_{ir}. Let λ_{ir} be the throughput of class r jobs at node i and let $E[n_{ir}]$ be the average number of class r jobs at node

i (users in "think state"). The average number of class r jobs in the rest of the system is $K_r - E[n_{ir}]$ and, by Little's theorem,

$$W_{ir} = (K_r - E[n_{ir}])/\lambda_{ir}.$$

On the other hand, node i being of type 3, jobs do not wait there; the average sojourn time for class r jobs is equal to their average service time (or "think time") $1/\mu_{ir}$; again by Little's theorem, $E[n_{ir}] = \lambda_{ir}/\mu_{ir}$. Hence

$$W_{ir} = K_r/\lambda_{ir} - 1/\mu_{ir} \qquad (3.46)$$

where λ_{ir} is given by (3.44). Note that, while (3.44) relies on the assumptions of the model and on the product-form solution, (3.46) does not; it is a completely general relation between response time, think time and throughput. Because of its importance, we shall rewrite it in another form, relating response time, utilisation and required service.

Let j be any node which class r jobs visit (in computer system models j is usually taken to be the CPU but it does not have to be). Suppose that the server speed at node j is state-independent so that its utilisation is given by (3.45). Since the absolute and relative s at nodes i and j are proportional to each other, $(\lambda_{ir}/e_{ir}) = (\lambda_{jr}/e_{jr})$, we can write

$$\lambda_{ir} = \lambda_{jr}\frac{e_{ir}}{e_{jr}} = \frac{\lambda_{jr}}{\mu_{jr}} \cdot \frac{\mu_{jr}e_{ir}}{e_{jr}} = \frac{U_{jr}}{(e_{jr}/e_{ir})(1/\mu_{jr})}.$$

Now, the ratio e_{jr}/e_{ir} represents the average number of visits class r jobs make to node j in between successive visits to node i; $1/\mu_{jr}$ is the average amount of service they require from node j on each visit; therefore, $(e_{jr}/e_{ir}) \cdot (1/\mu_{jr})$ is the average amount of service class r jobs require from node j in between successive visits to node i. Denote that quantity by $E[s_{jr,i}]$. Thus we have the relation

$$\lambda_{ir} = \frac{U_{jr}}{E[s_{jr,i}]}. \qquad (3.47)$$

Substituting (3.47) into (3.46) gives

$$W_{ir} = K_r\frac{E[s_{jr,i}]}{U_{jr}} - \frac{1}{\mu_{ir}}. \qquad (3.48)$$

Equation (3.48) is fundamental to terminal systems under heavy load. It implies that, given the average think times and the total average required service times from any node (these are job class characteristics), the utilisation of that node and the average response time (with respect to the particular job class) uniquely determine each other. Moreover, (3.48) and (3.47), like (3.46), are valid under much more general assumptions than those of the BCMP model.

Let us now take, as an example, the terminal system introduced at the beginning of this chapter (see Fig. 3.1) and obtain for it expressions for some performance measures of interest. The system consisted of M terminals (modelled by a node of type 3), one CPU (a type 2 node), one paging drum and one filing disk (type 1 nodes). Suppose that there is only one job class and that on leaving the CPU jobs go to the terminals, the drum and the disk with probabilities p_1, p_3 and p_4, respectively, $(p_1+p_3+p_4 = 1)$. On leaving the terminals, the drum and the disk, jobs go to the CPU with probability 1. Let $1/\mu_i$, $i = 1, 2, 3, 4$ be, respectively, the average think times, the average CPU intervals, the average drum transfer times and the average disk transfer times (the latter two include rotational and/or seek delays). The corresponding distributions may be arbitrary Coxian for $i = 1, 2$, but have to be assumed exponential for $i = 3, 4$ (see section 3.5).

The flow equations, (3.7) or (3.27), are

$$e_1 = p_1 e_2 \qquad e_3 = p_3 e_2$$

$$e_2 = e_1 + e_3 + e_4 \quad e_4 = p_4 e_2$$

and one solution can be obtained by setting $e_2 = 1$, which gives $e_1 = p_1$, $e_3 = p_3$, $e_4 = p_4$. The distribution of the aggregate system state $\mathbf{n} = (n_1, n_2, n_3, n_4)$, where n_i is the number of jobs at node i $(i = 1, 2, 3, 4)$ given by (3.29):

$$p(\mathbf{n}) = \frac{1}{G}(\rho_1^{n_1}/n_1!)\rho_2^{n_2}\rho_3^{n_3}\rho_4^{n_4},$$

where $\rho_i = e_i/\mu_i (i = 1, 2, 3, 4)$. The normalising constant, $G = G_4(M)$, can be computed by using the recurrence relations

$$
\begin{aligned}
G_1(j) &= \rho_1^j/j!, & j &= 0, 1, \ldots, M \\
G_i(0) &= 1, & i &= 1, 2, 3, 4 \\
G_i(j) &= G_{i-1}(j) + \rho_i G_i(j-1), & i &= 2, 3, 4; \ j = 1, 2, \ldots, M.
\end{aligned}
$$

The CPU utilisation factor is given by (3.36),

$$U_2 = \rho_2 G_4(M-1)/G_4(M),$$

and the of jobs at the CPU is

$$\lambda_2 = \mu_2 U_2 = G_4(M-1)/G_4(M).$$

The s at the other nodes are, respectively, $\lambda_1 = p_1\lambda_2$, $\lambda_3 = p_3\lambda_2$ and $\lambda_4 = p_4\lambda_2$. The average number of jobs in "think state" is λ_1/μ_1 and that in "compute state" is $M - (\lambda_1/\mu_1)$. The average response time W can be obtained either from (3.46) or from (3.48):

$$W = [MG_4(M)/(p_1G_4(M-1))] - (1/\mu_1).$$

If the set of terminals is split into several subsets (classes) with different characteristics, the only significant change in the analysis will be in the computation of the normalising constant which will require multivariate convolution. Formulae (3.44), (3.45) and (3.46) can still be used to determine s, utilisation factors and average response times.

References

1. Barbour, A. D. (1976). Networks of queues and the method of stages. *Adv. Appl. Prob.*, **8**(3), 584–591.
2. Baskett, F., Chandy, K. M., Muntz, R. R. and Palacios, F. G. (1975). Open, closed and mixed networks of queues with different classes of customers. *J.A.C.M.*, **22**(2), 248–260.
3. Baskett, F. and Palacios, F. G. (1972). "Processor Sharing in a Central Server Queueing Model of Multiprogramming with Applications." Proc. 6th Ann. Princeton Conf. on Information Science and Systems, pp. 598–603. Princeton, New Jersey.
4. Burke, P. J. (1958). The output process of a stationary $M/M/s$ queueing system. *Ann. of Math. Stat.*, **39**, 114–1152.
5. Burke, P. J. (1972). "Output Processes and Tandem Queues." Proc. Symp. Computer Communications Networks and Telecommunications, Brooklyn.
6. Burke, P. J. (1976). Proof of a conjecture on the interarrival-time distribution in an $M/M/1$ queue with feedback. *IEEE Trans. on Comm.*, **24**(5), 175–176.
7. Buzen, J. P. (1972). "Queueing Network Models of Multiprogramming." Ph.D. Thesis, Harvard University, Cambridge, Massachusetts.
8. Chandy, K. M. (1972). "The Analysis and Solutions for General Queueing Networks." Proc. 6th Ann. Princeton Conf. on Information Science and Systems, pp. 224–228. Princeton, New Jersey.
9. Chandy, K. M., Howard, J. H. and Towsley, D. F. (1977). Product form and local balance in queueing networks. *J.A.C.M.*, **24**(2), 250–263.
10. Cox, D. R. (1955). A use of complex probabilities in the theory of stochastic processes. *Proc., Cambridge Phil. Soc.*, **51**, 313–319.
11. Gordon, W. J. and Newell, G. F. (1967). Closed queueing systems with exponential servers. *Operations Research*, **15**, 254–265.
12. Jackson, J. R. (1957). Networks of waiting lines. *Operations Research*, **15**, 254–265.

13. Jackson, J. R. (1963). Jobshop-like queueing systems. *Man. Sci.*, **10**(1), 131–142.
14. Jackson, R. R. P. (1954). Queueing systems with phase type service. *Operations Research Quart.*, **5**, 109–120.
15. Kelly, F. P. (1976). Networks of queues. *Adv. Appl. Prob.*, **8**(2), 416–423.
16. Kleinrock, L. (1967). Time-shared systems: A theoretical treatment, *J.A.C.M.*, **14**(2), 242–261.
17. Lam, S. S. (1977). Queueing networks with population size constraints. *IBM J. Res. Dev.*, **21**(4), 370–378.
18. Melamed, B. (1976). "Analysis and Simplifications of Discrete Event Systems and Jackson Queueing Networks." Ph.D. Thesis, University of Michigan.
19. Muntz, R. R. (1972). "Poisson Departure Processes and Queueing Networks." IBM Research Report, RC 4145, IBM Thomas J. Watson Research Center, Yorktown Heights, New York.
20. Reich, E. (1957). Waiting times when queues are in tandem. *Ann. Math. Stat.*, **28**, 768–773.
21. Reiser, M. (1976). "Numerical Methods in Separable Queueing Networks." IBM Research Report, RC 5842, IBM Thomas J. Watson Research Center, Yorktown Heights, New York.
22. Reiser, M. and Kobayashi, H. (1975). Queueing networks with multiple closed chains: Theory and computational algorithms. *IBM J. Res. Dev.*, **19**, 283–294.
23. Sevcik, K. C. and Mitrani I. (1979). "The Distribution of Queueing Network States at Input and Output Instants." Proc. 4th Int. Symp. on Modelling and Perfecting Evaluations of Computer Systems, Vienna. North-Holland, Amsterdam.
24. Williams, A. C. and Bhandiwad, K. A. (1974). "Queueing Network Models of Computer Systems." Proc. 3rd Texas Conf. on Computer Systems.
25. Wong, J. W.-N. (1975). "Queueing Network Models for Computer Systems." Ph.D. Thesis, University of California at Los Angeles.

Chapter 4

Queueing Networks with Multiple Classes of Positive and Negative Customers and Product Form Solution

4.1. Introduction

In papers dating from the end of the 1980's and early 1990's [3, 6], new models of queueing networks were introduced, in which customers can be either "negative" or "positive". Positive customers are the ones that we are used to when we model service systems: they enter a queue, wait and then receive service, and then they move on to another queue and the same thing may happen until they finally leave the network (or continually cycling inside the network indefinitely). However in this new model called a "Gelenbe Network" or G-Network, a positive customer may mutate into a negative customer when it enters another queue. A negative customer vanishes if it arrives to an empty queue, and otherwise it reduces by one the number of positive customers in the queue it enters. Furthermore, negative customers do not receive service so that their only effect is to reduce the amount of work at the queue which they enter or to "destroy" other customers, hence the term "negative".

It has been shown [6] that networks of queues with a single class of positive and negative customers have a product form solution if the external positive or negative customer arrivals are Poisson, the service times of positive customers are exponential and independent, and if the movement of customers between queues is Markovian. This chapter will discuss the theory of G-networks as it applies to networks of queues with multiple classes of positive and negative customers, with direct relations of "destruction" among negative customers of certain classes and positive customers of certain other classes. We will also allow changes among customer classes, as is usual in such models. Of course, as indicated in previous chapters of this book, the classical reference for multiple class queueing network models is [2] and the related theory is discussed there, and in other sources. Multiple class queueing networks which include negative customers were first developed in [19] and generalised in [20]. The extension of the original model [6] to multiple classes has also been discussed in [12].

Some applications of G-networks are summarised in [18]. G-Networks can be used to represent a variety of systems. The initial model [6] was motivated by the analogy with neural networks [4,11]: each queue represents a neuron, and customers represent excitation (positive) or inhibition (negative) signals. Indeed, signals in biophysical neurons, for instance in the brain of mammals, also take the form of random trains of impulses of constant size, just like customers travelling through a queueing network. Results similar to the ones presented in this paper have been used in [9 and 25], where "signal classes" correspond to different colours in images. Other applications, including to networking problems [17] have also been developed.

Another application is to multiple resource systems: positive customers can be considered to be resource requests, while negative customers can correspond to decisions to cancel such requests. G-Networks have been applied to model systems where redundancy is used to protect the system's operation against failures: work is scheduled on two different processors and then cancelled at one of the two processors as soon as the work is successfully completed at the other, as detailed in [8].

The single server queue with negative and positive customers has been discussed in [7], while stability conditions for G-Networks were first obtained under general conditions in [10]. G-Networks with "triggers" which are specific customers which can re-route other customers [14], and batch removal of customers by negative customers, have been introduced in [15]. Additional primitives for these networks have also been introduced in [13]. The computation of numerical solutions to the non-linear traffic equations, which will be examined in detail below, has been discussed in [5].

In this chapter we focus on G-Networks with **multiple classes of positive customers and one or more classes of negative customers**, together three types of service centers and service disciplines:

- Type 1: first-in-first-out (FIFO),
- Type 2: processor sharing (PS),
- Type 4: last-in-first-out with preemptive resume priority (LIFO/PR).

With reference to the usual terminology related to the BCMP theorem [2], we exclude from the present model the Type 3 service centers with an infinite number of servers **since they will not be covered by our results**. Furthermore, in this paper we deal only with exponentially distributed service times.

In section 2 we will prove that these multiple class G-Networks, with Types 1, 2 and 4 service centers, have product form. Due to the non-linearity of the traffic equations for these models [6] the existence and uniqueness of their solutions have to be addressed with some care. This issue will be examined in section 4 with techniques similar to those developed in [10].

4.2. The model

We consider networks with an arbitrary number N of queues, an arbitrary number of positive customer classes K, and an arbitrary number of negative customer classes S. As in [6] we are only interested in open G-Networks. Indeed, if the system is closed, then the total number of customers will decrease as long as there are negative customers in the network.

External arrival streams to the network are independent Poisson processes concerning positive customers of some class k or negative customers of some class c. We denote by $\Lambda_{i,k}$ the external arrival rate of *positive* customers of class k to queue i and by $\lambda_{i,m}$ be the external arrival rate of *negative* customers of class m to queue i.

Only positive customers are served, and after service they may change class, service center and nature (positive to negative), or depart from the system. The movement of customers between queues, classes and nature (positive to negative) is represented by a Markov chain.

At its arrival in a non-empty queue, a negative customer selects a positive customer in the queue in accordance with the service discipline at this station. If the queue is empty, then the negative customer simply disappears. Once the target is selected, the negative customer tries to destroy the selected customer. A negative customer, of some class m, succeeds in destroying the selected positive customer of some class k, at service center i with probability $K_{i,m,k}$. With probability $(1-K_{i,m,k})$ it does not succeed. A negative customer disappears as soon as it tries to destroy its targeted customer. Recall that a negative customer is either exogenous, or is obtained by the transformation of a positive customer as it leaves a queue.

A positive customer of class k which leaves queue i (after finishing service) goes to queue j as a positive customer of class l with probability $P^+[i,j][k,l]$, or as a negative customer of class m with probability $P^-[i,j][k,m]$. It may also depart from the network with probability $d[i,k]$.

Obviously we have for all i, k

$$\sum_{j=1}^{N}\sum_{l=1}^{R} P^+[i,j][k,l] + \sum_{j=1}^{N}\sum_{m=1}^{S} P^-[i,j][k,m] + d[i,k] = 1. \qquad (1)$$

We assume that all service centers have exponential service time distributions. In the three types of service centers, each class of positive customers may have a distinct service rate $\mu_{i,k}$.

When the service center is of Type 1 (FIFO) we place the following constraint on the service rate and the destruction rate due to incoming negative customers:

$$\mu_{i,k} + \sum_{m=1}^{S} K_{i,m,k}\lambda_{i,m} = c_i. \qquad (2)$$

Note that this constraint, together with the constraint (3) given below, have the effect of producing a *single positive customer class equivalent* for service centers with FIFO discipline.

The following constraints on the deletion probability are assumed to exist. Note that because services are exponentially distributed, positive customers of a given class are indistinguishable for deletion because of the obvious property of the remaining service time.

- The following constraint must hold for all stations i of Type 1 and classes of negative customers m such that $\sum_{j=1}^{N}\sum_{l=1}^{R} P^-[j,i][l,m] > 0$

  for all classes of positive customers k and p, $K_{i,m,k} = K_{i,m,p}$. $\qquad (3)$

  This constraint implies that a negative customer of some class m arriving from the network does not "distinguish" between the positive customer classes it will try to delete, and that it will treat them all in the same manner.

- For a Type 2 server, the probability that any one positive customer of the queue is selected by the arriving negative customer is $1/c$ if c is the total number of customers in the queue.

For Type 1 service centers, one may consider the following conditions which are simpler than (2) and (3):

$$\begin{aligned} \mu_{ik} &= \mu_{ip} \\ K_{i,m,k} &= K_{i,m,p} \end{aligned} \qquad (4)$$

for all classes of positive customers k and p, and all classes of negative customers m. Note however that these new conditions are more restrictive, though they do imply that (2), (3) hold.

4.2.1. *State representation*

We denote the state at time t of the queueing network by a vector $x(t) = (x_1(t), \ldots, x_N(t))$. Here $x_i(t)$ represents the state of service center i. The vector $x = (x_1, \ldots, x_N)$ will denote a particular value of the state and $|x_i|$ will be the total number of customers in queue i for state x.

For Types 1 and 4 servers, the instantaneous value of the state x_i of queue i is represented by the vector $(r_{i,j})$ whose length is the number of customers in the queue and whose jth element is the class index of the jth customer in the queue. Furthermore, the customers are ordered according to the service order (FIFO or LIFO); it is always the customer at the head of the list which is in service. We denote by $r_{i,1}$ the class number of the customer in service and by $r_{i,\infty}$ the class number of the last customer in the queue.

For a PS (Type 2) service station, the instantaneous value of the state x_i is represented by the vector $(x_{i,k})$ which is the number of customers of class k in queue i.

4.3. **Main results**

Let $\Pi(x)$ denote the stationary probability distribution of the state of the network, if it exists. The following result establishes the product form solution of the network being considered.

Theorem 1. Consider a G-network with the restrictions indicated above. If the system of non-linear equations:

probability that queue i has at least 1 customer of class k

$$q_{i,k} = \frac{\Lambda_{i,k} + \Lambda_{i,k}^+}{\mu_{i,k} + \sum_{m=1}^{S} K_{i,m,k}[\lambda_{i,m} + \lambda_{i,m}^-]} \tag{5}$$

rate of incoming positive customers coming from inside the network

$$\Lambda_{i,k}^+ = \sum_{j=1}^{N} \sum_{l=1}^{R} P^+[j,i][l,k]\mu_{j,l}q_{j,l} \tag{6}$$

rate of incoming negative customers coming from inside the network

$$\lambda_{i,m}^- = \sum_{j=1}^{N} \sum_{l=1}^{R} P^-[j,i][l,m]\mu_{j,l}q_{j,l} \tag{7}$$

has a solution such that

for each pair $i, k : q_{i,k} > 0$ and for each station i: $\sum_{k=1}^{R} q_{i,k} < 1$

then the stationary distribution of the network state is

$$\Pi(x) = G \prod_{i=1}^{N} g_i(x_i) \tag{8}$$

where each $g_i(x_i)$ depends on the type of service center i. The $g_i(x_i)$ in (8) have the following forms:

FIFO. If the service center is of Type 1, then

$$g_i(x_i) = \prod_{n=1}^{|x_i|} q_{i,r_{i,n}} \tag{9}$$

PS. If the service center is of Type 2, then

$$g_i(x_i) = |x_i|! \prod_{k=1}^{R} \frac{(q_{i,k})^{x_{i,k}}}{x_{i,k}!} \tag{10}$$

LIFO/PR. If the service center is of Type 4, then

$$g_i(x_i) = \prod_{n=1}^{|x_i|} q_{i,r_{i,n}} \tag{11}$$

and G is the normalisation constant.

Note that the conditions requiring that $q_{i,k} > 0$ and on that their sum over all classes at each center be less than 1, simply ensure the existence of the normalising constant G in Eq. (8).

The proof is based on simple algebraic manipulations of global balance equations, since it is not possible to use the "local balance" equations for customer classes at stations because of the effect of negative customer arrivals. We begin with some technical lemmas.

Lemma 1. *The following flow equation is satisfied:*

$$\sum_{i=1}^{N} \sum_{k=1}^{R} q_{i,k} \mu_{i,k}(1 - d[i,k]) = \sum_{i=1}^{N} \sum_{k=1}^{R} \Lambda_{i,k}^{+} + \sum_{i=1}^{N} \sum_{m=1}^{S} \lambda_{i,m}^{-}. \tag{12}$$

Proof. Consider (6), then sum it for all the stations and all the classes and exchange the order of summations in the right-hand side of the equation:

$$\sum_{i=1}^{N}\sum_{k=1}^{R}\Lambda_{i,k}^{+} = \sum_{j=1}^{N}\sum_{l=1}^{R}\mu_{j,l}q_{j,l}\left(\sum_{i=1}^{N}\sum_{k=1}^{R}P^{+}[j,i][l,k]\right).$$

Similarly, using equation (7)

$$\sum_{i=1}^{N}\sum_{m=1}^{S}\lambda_{i,m}^{-} = \sum_{j=1}^{N}\sum_{l=1}^{R}\mu_{j,l}q_{j,l}\left(\sum_{i=1}^{N}\sum_{m=1}^{S}P^{-}[j,i][l,m]\right)$$

and,

$$\sum_{i=1}^{N}\sum_{k=1}^{R}\Lambda_{i,k}^{+} + \sum_{i=1}^{N}\sum_{m=1}^{S}\lambda_{i,m}^{-}$$
$$= \sum_{j=1}^{N}\sum_{l=1}^{R}\mu_{j,l}q_{j,l}\left(\sum_{i=1}^{N}\sum_{k=1}^{R}P^{+}[j,i][l,k] + \sum_{i=1}^{N}\sum_{m=1}^{S}P^{-}[j,i][l,m]\right).$$

According to the definition of the routing matrix P (equation (1)), we have

$$\sum_{i=1}^{N}\sum_{k=1}^{R}\Lambda_{i,k}^{+} + \sum_{i=1}^{N}\sum_{m=1}^{S}\lambda_{i,m}^{-} = \sum_{j=1}^{N}\sum_{l=1}^{R}\mu_{j,l}q_{j,l}(1 - d[j,l]).$$

Thus the proof of the lemma is complete. $\square$

In order to carry out algebraic manipulations of the stationary Chapman-Kolmogorov (global balance) equations, we introduce some notation and develop intermediate results:

- The state dependent service rates for customers at service center j will be denoted by $M_{j,l}(x_j)$ where x_j refers to the state of the service center and l is the class of the customer concerned. From the definition of the service rate $\mu_{j,l}$, we obtain for the three types of stations:

  FIFO and LIFO/PR. $M_{j,l}(x_j) = \mu_{j,l}1_{\{r_{j,1}=l\}}$,
  PS. $M_{j,l}(x_j) = \mu_{j,l}\frac{x_{j,l}}{|x_j|}$.

- $N_{j,l}(x_j)$ is the deletion rate of class l positive customers due to external arrivals of all the classes of negative customers

  FIFO and LIFO/PR. $N_{j,l}(x_j) = 1_{\{r_{j,1}=l\}}\sum_{m=1}^{S}K_{j,m,l}\lambda_{j,m}$
  PS. $N_{j,l}(x_j) = \frac{x_{j,l}}{|x_j|}\sum_{m=1}^{S}K_{j,m,l}\lambda_{j,m}$.

- $A_{j,l}(x_j)$ is the condition which establishes that it is possible to reach state x_j by an arrival of a positive customer of class l

  FIFO. $A_{j,l}(x_j) = 1_{\{r_{j,\infty}=l\}}$,
  LIFO/PR. $A_{j,l}(x_j) = 1_{\{r_{j,1}=l\}}$,
  PS. $A_{j,l}(x_j) = 1_{\{|x_{j,l}|>0\}}$.

- $Z_{j,l,m}(x_j)$ is the probability that a negative customer of class m, arriving from the network, will delete a positive customer of class l.

  FIFO and LIFO/PR. $Z_{j,l,m}(x_j) = 1_{\{r_{j,1}=l\}}K_{j,m,l}$
  PS. $Z_{j,l,m}(x_j) = \frac{x_{j,l}}{|x_j|}K_{j,m,l}$.

- $Y_{j,m}(x_j)$ is the probability that a negative customer of class m which enters a non empty queue, will not delete a positive customer.

  FIFO and LIFO/PR. $Y_{j,m}(x_j) = \sum_{l=1}^{R} 1_{\{r_{j,1}=l\}}(1 - K_{j,m,l})$
  PS. $Y_{j,m}(x_j) = \sum_{l=1}^{R}(1 - K_{j,m,l})\frac{x_{j,l}}{|x_j|}$.

Denote by $(x_j + e_{j,l})$ the state of station j obtained by **adding to the server a positive customer of class** l. Let $(x_i - e_{i,k})$ be the state obtained by removing from the end of the list a class k customer (if it exists, since otherwise $(x_i - e_{i,k})$ will not be defined).

Lemma 2. *For any Type 1, 2, or 4 service center, the following relations hold:*

$$M_{j,l}(x_j + e_{j,l})\frac{g_j(x_j + e_{j,l})}{g_j(x_j)} = \mu_{j,l}q_{j,l} \tag{13}$$

$$N_{j,l}(x_j + e_{j,l})\frac{g_j(x_j + e_{j,l})}{g_j(x_j)} = \sum_{m=1}^{S}(K_{j,m,l}\lambda_{j,m})q_{j,l} \tag{14}$$

$$Z_{j,l,m}(x_j + e_{j,l})\frac{g_j(x_j + e_{j,l})}{g_j(x_j)} = K_{j,m,l}q_{j,l}. \tag{15}$$

The proof is purely algebraic. $\qquad\square$

Remark 1. As a consequence, we have from equations (6), (7) and (13):

$$\Lambda_{i,k}^{+} = \sum_{j=1}^{N}\sum_{l=1}^{R}M_{j,l}(x_j + e_{j,l})\frac{g_j(x_j + e_{j,l})}{g_j(x_j)}P^{+}[j,i][l,k] \tag{16}$$

and

$$\lambda_{i,m}^{-} = \sum_{j=1}^{N}\sum_{l=1}^{R}M_{j,l}(x_j + e_{j,l})\frac{g_j(x_j + e_{j,l})}{g_j(x_j)}P^{-}[j,i][l,m]. \tag{17}$$

Lemma 3. *Let i be any Type 1, 2, or 4 station, and let $\Delta_i(x_i)$ be:*

$$\Delta_i(x_i) = \sum_{m=1}^{S} \lambda_{i,m}^- Y_{i,m}(x_i)$$

$$- \sum_{k=1}^{R} (M_{i,k}(x_i) + N_{i,k}(x_i))$$

$$+ \sum_{k=1}^{R} A_{i,k}(x_i)(\Lambda_{i,k} + \Lambda_{i,k}^+) \frac{g_i(x_i - e_{i,k})}{g_i(x_i)}.$$

Then for the three types of service centers, $1_{\{|x_i|>0\}}\Delta_i(x_i) = \sum_{m=1}^{S} \lambda_{i,m}^- 1_{\{|x_i|>0\}}.$

Proof of the Lemma. The proof consists in algebraic manipulations for the three types of stations.

LIFO/PR. First consider an arbitrary LIFO station and recall the definition of Δ_i:

$$1_{\{|x_i|>0\}}\Delta_i(x_i) = 1_{\{|x_i|>0\}} \sum_{k=1}^{R} A_{i,k}(x_i)(\Lambda_{i,k} + \Lambda_{i,k}^+) \frac{g_i(x_i - e_{i,k})}{g_i(x_i)}$$

$$- 1_{\{|x_i|>0\}} \sum_{k=1}^{R} M_{i,k}(x_i) - 1_{\{|x_i|>0\}} \sum_{k=1}^{R} N_{i,k}(x_i)$$

$$+ 1_{\{|x_i|>0\}} \sum_{m=1}^{S} \lambda_{i,m}^- Y_{i,m}(x_i).$$

Then, we substitute the values of $Y_{i,m}$, $M_{i,k}$, $N_{i,k}$ and $A_{i,k}$ for a LIFO station:

$$1_{\{|x_i|>0\}}\Delta_i(x_i) = 1_{\{|x_i|>0\}} \sum_{k=1}^{R} 1_{\{r_{i,1}=k\}}(\Lambda_{i,k} + \Lambda_{i,k}^+)/q_{i,k}$$

$$- 1_{\{|x_i|>0\}} \sum_{k=1}^{R} 1_{\{r_{i,1}=k\}}\mu_{i,k}$$

$$- 1_{\{|x_i|>0\}} \sum_{k=1}^{R} 1_{\{r_{i,1}=k\}} \sum_{m=1}^{S} K_{i,m,k}\lambda_{i,m}$$

$$+ 1_{\{|x_i|>0\}} \sum_{m=1}^{S} \lambda_{i,m}^- \sum_{k=1}^{R} 1_{\{r_{i,1}=k\}}(1 - K_{i,m,k}).$$

We use the value of $q_{i,k}$ from equation (5) to obtain after some cancellations of terms:

$$1_{\{|x_i|>0\}}\Delta_i(x_i) = 1_{\{|x_i|>0\}} \sum_{k=1}^{R} 1_{\{r_{i,1}=k\}}$$

$$\times \left(\sum_{m=1}^{S} K_{i,m,k}\lambda_{i,m}^{-} + \sum_{m=1}^{S} \lambda_{i,m}^{-}(1 - K_{i,m,k}) \right)$$

$$= 1_{\{|x_i|>0\}} \sum_{m=1}^{S} \lambda_{i,m}^{-} \sum_{k=1}^{R} 1_{\{r_{i,1}=k\}}$$

and as $1_{\{|x_i|>0\}} \sum_{k=1}^{R} 1_{\{r_{i,1}=k\}} = 1_{\{|x_i|>0\}}$, we finally get the result:

$$1_{\{|x_i|>0\}}\Delta_i(x_i) = 1_{\{|x_i|>0\}} \sum_{m=1}^{S} \lambda_{i,m}^{-}. \tag{18}$$

FIFO. Consider now an arbitrary FIFO station:

$$1_{\{|x_i|>0\}}\Delta_i(x_i) = 1_{\{|x_i|>0\}} \sum_{k=1}^{R} A_{i,k}(x_i)(\Lambda_{i,k} + \Lambda_{i,k}^{+})\frac{g_i(x_i - e_{i,k})}{g_i(x_i)}$$

$$- 1_{\{|x_i|>0\}} \sum_{k=1}^{R} M_{i,k}(x_i) - \sum_{k=1}^{R} 1_{\{|x_i|>0\}}N_{i,k}(x_i)$$

$$+ 1_{\{|x_i|>0\}} \sum_{m=1}^{S} \lambda_{i,m}^{-}Y_{i,m}(x_i).$$

Similarly, we substitute the values of $Y_{i,m}$, $M_{i,k}$, $N_{i,k}$, $A_{i,k}$ and $q_{i,k}$:

$$1_{\{|x_i|>0\}}\Delta_i(x_i) = 1_{\{|x_i|>0\}} \sum_{k=1}^{R} 1_{\{r_{i,\infty}=k\}}$$

$$\times \left(\mu_{i,k} + \sum_{m=1}^{S} K_{i,m,k}\lambda_{i,m} + \sum_{m=1}^{S} K_{i,m,k}\lambda_{i,m}^{-} \right)$$

$$- 1_{\{|x_i|>0\}} \sum_{k=1}^{R} 1_{\{r_{i,1}=k\}}\mu_{i,k} - 1_{\{|x_i|>0\}}$$

$$\times \sum_{k=1}^{R} 1_{\{r_{i,1}=k\}} \sum_{m=1}^{S} K_{i,m,k}\lambda_{i,m}$$

$$+ 1_{\{|x_i|>0\}} \sum_{m=1}^{S} \lambda_{i,m}^{-} \sum_{k=1}^{R} 1_{\{r_{i,1}=k\}}(1 - K_{i,m,k}).$$

We separate the last term into two parts, and regroup terms:

$$
1_{\{|x_i|>0\}}\Delta_i(x_i) = 1_{\{|x_i|>0\}} \sum_{k=1}^{R} 1_{\{r_{i,\infty}=k\}}
$$
$$
\times \left(\mu_{i,k} + \sum_{m=1}^{S} K_{i,m,k}\lambda_{i,m} + \sum_{m=1}^{S} K_{i,m,k}\lambda_{i,m}^- \right)
$$
$$
- 1_{\{|x_i|>0\}} \sum_{k=1}^{R} 1_{\{r_{i,1}=k\}}
$$
$$
\times \left(\mu_{i,k} + \sum_{m=1}^{S} K_{i,m,k}\lambda_{i,m} + \sum_{m=1}^{S} K_{i,m,k}\lambda_{i,m}^- \right)
$$
$$
+ 1_{\{|x_i|>0\}} \sum_{m=1}^{S} \lambda_{i,m}^- \sum_{k=1}^{R} 1_{\{r_{i,1}=k\}}.
$$

Conditions (2) and (3) imply that the following relation must hold:

$$
\sum_{k=1}^{R} 1_{\{r_{i,\infty}=k\}} \left(\mu_{i,k} + \sum_{m=1}^{S} K_{i,m,k}\lambda_{i,m} + \sum_{m=1}^{S} K_{i,m,k}\lambda_{i,m}^- \right)
$$
$$
= \sum_{k=1}^{R} 1_{\{r_{i,1}=k\}} \left(\mu_{i,k} + \sum_{m=1}^{S} K_{i,m,k}\lambda_{i,m} + \sum_{m=1}^{S} K_{i,m,k}\lambda_{i,m}^- \right).
$$

Thus, as $1_{\{|x_i|>0\}} \sum_{k=1}^{R} 1_{\{r_{i,1}=k\}} = 1_{\{|x_i|>0\}}$, we finally get the expected result:

$$
1_{\{|x_i|>0\}}\Delta_i(x_i) = 1_{\{|x_i|>0\}} \sum_{m=1}^{S} \lambda_{i,m}^-. \tag{19}
$$

PS. Consider now an arbitrary PS station:

$$
1_{\{|x_i|>0\}}\Delta_i(x_i) = 1_{\{|x_i|>0\}} \sum_{k=1}^{R} A_{i,k}(x_i)(\Lambda_{i,k} + \Lambda_{i,k}^+)\frac{g_i(x_i - e_{i,k})}{g_i(x_i)}
$$
$$
- 1_{\{|x_i|>0\}} \sum_{k=1}^{R} M_{i,k}(x_i) - \sum_{k=1}^{R} 1_{\{|x_i|>0\}} N_{i,k}(x_i)
$$
$$
+ 1_{\{|x_i|>0\}} \sum_{m=1}^{S} \lambda_{i,m}^- Y_{i,m}(x_i).
$$

As usual, we substitute the values of $Y_{i,m}$, $M_{i,k}$, $N_{i,k}$, $A_{i,k}$:

$$1_{\{|x_i|>0\}}\Delta_i(x_i) = 1_{\{|x_i|>0\}} \sum_{k=1}^{R} 1_{\{|x_{i,k}|>0\}} \frac{(\Lambda_{i,k} + \Lambda_{i,k}^+)}{q_{i,k}} \frac{x_{i,k}}{|x_i|}$$

$$- 1_{\{|x_i|>0\}} \sum_{k=1}^{R} \mu_{i,k} \frac{x_{i,k}}{|x_i|}$$

$$- 1_{\{|x_i|>0\}} \sum_{k=1}^{R} \frac{x_{i,k}}{|x_i|} \sum_{m=1}^{S} K_{i,m,k}\lambda_{i,m}$$

$$+ 1_{\{|x_i|>0\}} \sum_{m=1}^{S} \sum_{k=1}^{R} \lambda_{i,m}^{-} \frac{x_{i,k}}{|x_i|} (1 - K_{i,m,k}).$$

Then, we apply equation (5) to substitute $q_{i,k}$. After some cancellations of terms we obtain:

$$1_{\{|x_i|>0\}}\Delta_i(x_i) = 1_{\{|x_i|>0\}} \sum_{k=1}^{R} \frac{x_{i,k}}{|x_i|} \sum_{m=1}^{S} K_{i,m,k}\lambda_{i,m}^{-}$$

$$+ 1_{\{|x_i|>0\}} \sum_{m=1}^{S} \sum_{k=1}^{R} \lambda_{i,m}^{-} \frac{x_{i,k}}{|x_i|} (1 - K_{i,m,k}).$$

Finally we have:

$$1_{\{|x_i|>0\}}\Delta_i(x_i) = 1_{\{|x_i|>0\}} \sum_{k=1}^{R} \frac{x_{i,k}}{|x_i|} \sum_{m=1}^{S} \lambda_{i,m}^{-}. \tag{20}$$

As $1_{\{|x_i|>0\}} \sum_{k=1}^{R} \frac{x_{i,k}}{|x_i|} = 1_{\{|x_i|>0\}}$, once again, we establish the relation we need. This concludes the proof of Lemma 3. $\square$

Let us now turn to the proof of the Theorem 1. Consider the global balance equation the networks considered is:

$$\Pi(x) \left[\sum_{j=1}^{N} \sum_{l=1}^{R} \left(\Lambda_{j,l} + M_{j,l}(x_j)1_{\{|x_j|>0\}} + N_{j,l}(x_j)1_{\{|x_j|>0\}} \right) \right]$$

$$= \sum_{j=1}^{N} \sum_{l=1}^{R} \Pi(x - e_{j,l})\Lambda_{j,l}A_{j,l}(x_j)1_{\{|x_j|>0\}}$$

$$+ \sum_{j=1}^{N} \sum_{l=1}^{R} \Pi(x + e_{j,l})N_{j,l}(x_j + e_{j,l})$$

$$+ \sum_{j=1}^{N} \sum_{l=1}^{R} \Pi(x + e_{j,l}) M_{j,l}(x_j + e_{j,l}) d[j,l]$$

$$+ \sum_{i=1}^{N} \sum_{j=1}^{N} \sum_{k=1}^{R} \sum_{l=1}^{R} M_{j,l}(x_j + e_{j,l}) \Pi(x - e_{i,k} + e_{j,l})$$

$$\times P^+[j,i][l,k] A_{i,k}(x_i) 1_{\{|x_i|>0\}}$$

$$+ \sum_{i=1}^{N} \sum_{j=1}^{N} \sum_{k=1}^{R} \sum_{l=1}^{R} \sum_{m=1}^{S} M_{j,l}(x_j + e_{j,l}) \Pi(x + e_{i,k} + e_{j,l})$$

$$\times P^-[j,i][l,m] Z_{i,k,m}(x_i + e_{i,k})$$

$$+ \sum_{i=1}^{N} \sum_{j=1}^{N} \sum_{l=1}^{R} \sum_{m=1}^{S} M_{j,l}(x_j + e_{j,l}) \Pi(x + e_{j,l})$$

$$\times P^-[j,i][l,m] Y_{i,m}(x_i) 1_{\{|x_i|>0\}}$$

$$+ \sum_{i=1}^{N} \sum_{j=1}^{N} \sum_{l=1}^{R} \sum_{m=1}^{S} M_{j,l}(x_j + e_{j,l}) \Pi(x + e_{j,l}) P^-[j,i][l,m] 1_{\{|x_i|=0\}}.$$

We divide both sides by $\Pi(x)$ and we assume that there is a product form solution. Then, we apply Lemma 2.

$$\sum_{j=1}^{N} \sum_{l=1}^{R} (\Lambda_{j,l} + M_{j,l}(x_j) 1_{\{|x_j|>0\}} + N_{j,l}(x_j) 1_{\{|x_j|>0\}})$$

$$= \sum_{j=1}^{N} \sum_{l=1}^{R} \frac{g_j(x_j - e_{j,l})}{g_j(x_j)} \Lambda_{j,l} A_{j,l}(x_j) 1_{\{|x_j|>0\}}$$

$$+ \sum_{j=1}^{N} \sum_{l=1}^{R} \sum_{m=1}^{S} \lambda_{j,m} K_{j,m,l} q_{j,l} + \sum_{j=1}^{N} \sum_{l=1}^{R} \mu_{j,l} q_{j,l} d[j,l]$$

$$+ \sum_{i=1}^{N} \sum_{j=1}^{N} \sum_{k=1}^{R} \sum_{l=1}^{R} \mu_{j,l} q_{j,l} P^+[j,i][l,k] A_{i,k}(x_i) \frac{g_i(x_i - e_{i,k})}{g_i(x_i)} 1_{\{|x_i|>0\}}$$

$$+ \sum_{i=1}^{N} \sum_{j=1}^{N} \sum_{k=1}^{R} \sum_{l=1}^{R} \sum_{m=1}^{S} \mu_{j,l} q_{j,l} P^-[j,i][l,m] K_{i,m,k} q_{i,k}$$

$$+ \sum_{i=1}^{N}\sum_{j=1}^{N}\sum_{l=1}^{R}\sum_{m=1}^{S} \mu_{j,l}q_{j,l}P^-[j,i][l,m]Y_{i,m}(x_i)1_{\{|x_i|>0\}}$$

$$+ \sum_{i=1}^{N}\sum_{j=1}^{N}\sum_{l=1}^{R}\sum_{m=1}^{S} \mu_{j,l}q_{j,l}P^-[j,i][l,m]1_{\{|x_i|=0\}}.$$

After some substitution, we group the first and the fourth terms of the right side of the equation.

$$\sum_{j=1}^{N}\sum_{l=1}^{R}(\Lambda_{j,l} + M_{j,l}(x_j)1_{\{|x_j|>0\}} + N_{j,l}(x_j)1_{\{|x_j|>0\}})$$

$$= \sum_{j=1}^{N}\sum_{l=1}^{R}1_{\{|x_j|>0\}}\frac{g_j(x_j - e_{j,l})}{g_j(x_j)}A_{j,l}(x_j)(\Lambda_{j,l} + \Lambda_{j,l}^+)$$

$$+ \sum_{j=1}^{N}\sum_{l=1}^{R}\sum_{m=1}^{S}\lambda_{j,m}K_{j,m,l}q_{j,l} + \sum_{j=1}^{N}\sum_{l=1}^{R}\mu_{j,l}q_{j,l}d[j,l]$$

$$+ \sum_{i=1}^{N}\sum_{k=1}^{R}\sum_{m=1}^{S}\lambda_{i,m}^-K_{i,m,k}q_{i,k} + \sum_{i=1}^{N}\sum_{m=1}^{S}\lambda_{i,m}^-Y_{i,m}(x_i)1_{\{|x_i|>0\}}$$

$$+ \sum_{i=1}^{N}\sum_{m=1}^{S}\lambda_{i,m}^-1_{\{|x_i|=0\}}.$$

We add to both sides the quantity $\sum_{j=1}^{N}\sum_{l=1}^{R}\mu_{j,l}q_{j,l}(1 - d[j,l])$ and factorise three terms in the right side

$$\sum_{j=1}^{N}\sum_{l=1}^{R}(\Lambda_{j,l} + M_{j,l}(x_j)1_{\{|x_j|>0\}} + N_{j,l}(x_j)1_{\{|x_j|>0\}}) + \mu_{j,l}q_{j,l}(1 - d[j,l])$$

$$= \sum_{j=1}^{N}\sum_{l=1}^{R}1_{\{|x_j|>0\}}\frac{g_j(x_j - e_{j,l})}{g_j(x_j)}A_{j,l}(x_j)(\Lambda_{j,l} + \Lambda_{j,l}^+)$$

$$+ \sum_{j=1}^{N}\sum_{l=1}^{R}q_{j,l}\left(\mu_{j,l} + \sum_{m=1}^{S}\lambda_{j,m}K_{j,m,l} + \sum_{m=1}^{S}\lambda_{j,m}^-K_{j,m,l}\right)$$

$$+ \sum_{i=1}^{N}\sum_{m=1}^{S}\lambda_{i,m}^-Y_{i,m}(x_i)1_{\{|x_i|>0\}} + \sum_{i=1}^{N}\sum_{m=1}^{S}\lambda_{i,m}^-1_{\{|x_i|=0\}}.$$

We substitute on the r.h.s, the value of $q_{i,k}$ in the second term. Then, we cancel the term $\Lambda_{j,l}$ which appears on both sides and we group terms to obtain:

$$
\sum_{j=1}^{N}\sum_{l=1}^{R}\mu_{j,l}q_{j,l}(1-d[j,l])
$$
$$
=\sum_{j=1}^{N}\sum_{l=1}^{R}\Lambda_{j,l}^{+}+\sum_{i=1}^{N}1_{\{|x_i|>0\}}\Delta_i(x_i)+\sum_{i=1}^{N}\sum_{m=1}^{S}\lambda_{i,m}^{-}1_{\{|x_i|=0\}} \qquad (21)
$$

where

$$
\Delta_i(x_i)=\sum_{m=1}^{S}\lambda_{i,m}^{-}Y_{i,m}(x_i)-\sum_{k=1}^{R}M_{i,k}(x_i)-\sum_{k=1}^{R}N_{i,k}(x_i)
$$
$$
+\sum_{k=1}^{R}A_{i,k}(x_i)(\Lambda_{i,k}+\Lambda_{i,k}^{+})\frac{g_i(x_i-e_{i,k})}{g_i(x_i)}.
$$

In Lemma 3, we have shown that $1_{\{|x_i|>0\}}\Delta_i(x_i)$ is equal to $\sum_{m=1}^{S}\lambda_{i,m}^{-}1_{\{|x_i|>0\}}$ for the three types of service centers. Thus,

$$
\sum_{j=1}^{N}\sum_{l=1}^{R}\mu_{j,l}q_{j,l}(1-d[j,l])
$$
$$
=\sum_{j=1}^{N}\sum_{l=1}^{R}\Lambda_{j,l}^{+}+\sum_{i=1}^{N}\sum_{m=1}^{S}\lambda_{i,m}^{-}(1_{\{|x_i|=0\}}+1_{\{|x_i|>0\}}).
$$

Finally, Lemma 1 shows that this flow equation is satisfied. This concludes the proof. $\qquad \square$

As in the BCMP [2] theorem, we can also compute the steady state distribution of the number of customers of each class in each queue. Let y_i be the vector whose elements are $(y_{i,k})$ the number of customers of class k in station i. Let y be the vector of vectors (y_i). We omit the proof of the following result.

Theorem 2. If the system of equations (5), (6) and (7) has a solution then, the steady state distribution $\pi(y)$ is given by

$$
\pi(y)=\prod_{i=1}^{N}h_i(y_i) \qquad (22)
$$

where the marginal probabilities $h_i(y_i)$ have the following form:

$$h_i(y_i) = \left(1 - \sum_{k=1}^{R} q_{i,k}\right) |y_i|! \prod_{k=1}^{R} [(q_{i,k})^{y_{i,k}}/y_{i,k}!]. \tag{23}$$

4.4. Existence of the solution to the traffic equations

Unlike BCMP or Jackson networks [2], the customer flow equations (5), (6) and (7) of the model we consider are non-linear. Therefore issues of existence and uniqueness of their solutions have to be examined.

In particular, our key result depends on the existence of solutions to (5), (6), (7). Thus the existence and uniqueness of solutions to these traffic equations is central to our work.

Note that if existence is established, then uniqueness follows easily for a simple reason. We are dealing with the stationary solution of a system of Chapman-Kolmogorov equations, which is known to be unique if it exists [10].

Define the following vectors:

Λ^+ with elements $[\Lambda_{i,k}^+ + \Lambda_{i,k}]$
λ^- with elements $[\lambda_{i,k}^- + \lambda_{i,k}]$
Λ with elements $\Lambda_{i,k}$, and
λ with elements $\lambda_{i,k}$

Furthermore, denote by P^+ the matrix of elements $\{P^+[i,j][k,l]\}$, and by P^- the matrix whose elements are $\{P^-[i,j][k,m]\}$.

Let F be a diagonal matrix with elements $0 \leq F_{i,k} \leq 1$. Equations (6) and (7) inspire us to write the following equation:

$$\Lambda^+ = \Lambda^+ FP^+ + \Lambda, \quad \lambda^- = \Lambda^+ FP^- + \lambda \tag{24}$$

or, denoting the identity matrix $\mathbf{I}$, as

$$\Lambda^+(\mathbf{I} - FP^+) = \Lambda, \tag{25}$$

$$\lambda^- = \Lambda^+ FP^- + \lambda. \tag{26}$$

Proposition 1. *If P^+ is a substochastic matrix which does not contain ergodic classes, then equations (25) and (26) have a solution (Λ^+, λ^-).*

Proof. The series $\sum_{n=0}^{\infty}(FP^+)^n$ is geometrically convergent, since $F \leq \mathbf{I}$, and because — by assumption — P^+ is substochastic and does not contain any ergodic classes [1]. Therefore we can write (25) as

$$\Lambda^+ = \Lambda \sum_{n=0}^{\infty} (FP^+)^n, \tag{27}$$

so that (26) becomes

$$\lambda^- - \lambda = \Lambda \sum_{n=0}^{\infty} (FP^+)^n FP^-. \tag{28}$$

Now denote $z = \lambda^- - \lambda$, and call the vector function

$$G(z) = \Lambda \sum_{n=0}^{\infty} (F(z)P^+)^n F(z)P^-.$$

Note that the dependency of G on z comes from F, which depends on λ^-.

It can be seen that $G : [0, G(0)] \to [0, G(0)]$ and that it is continuous. Therefore, by Brouwer's fixed point theorem

$$z = G(z) \tag{29}$$

has a fixed point z^*. This fixed point will yield the solution of (25) and (26) as:

$$\lambda^-(z^*) = \lambda + z^*, \qquad \Lambda^+(z^*) = \Lambda \sum_{n=0}^{\infty} (F(z^*)P^+)^n, \tag{30}$$

completing the proof of Proposition 1. □

Proposition 2. *Equations* (6), (7) *have a solution.*

Proof. This result is a direct consequence of Proposition 1, since we can see that (5), (6) and (7) are a special instance of (21). Indeed, it suffices to set

$$F_{i,k} = \frac{\mu_{i,k}}{\mu_{i,k} + \sum_{m=1}^{S} K_{i,m,k}[\lambda_{i,m} + \lambda_{i,m}^-]} \tag{31}$$

and to notice that $0 \leq F_{i,k} \leq 1$, and that (6), (7) now have taken the form of the generalised traffic equations (21). This completes the proof of Proposition 2.

The above two propositions state that the traffic equations *always* have a solution. Of course, the product form (8) will only exist if the resulting network is stable. The stability condition is summarised below and the proof is identical to that of a similar result in [10]. □

Theorem 3. Let z^* be a solution of $z = G(z)$ obtained by setting F as in (27). Let $\lambda^-(z^*), \Lambda^+(z^*)$ be the corresponding traffic values, and let the $q_{i,k}(z^*)$ be obtained from (5) as a consequence. Then the G-network is stable if all of the $0 \leq q_{i,k}(z^*) < 1$ for all i, k. Otherwise it is unstable.

4.5. Conclusion

In this chapter we have studied G-Networks. However, rather than develop all of the theory, starting from networks with a single customer class, we have dealt directly with G-Networks with multiple classes of positive and negative customers. We have developed in detail both the existence and uniqueness results for the steady-state solution of the model, and the explicit product form solution. In the model considered, the service centers are identical to the service centers considered in the BCMP theorem [2], with the exception of the "infinite server" case which is not considered. However, all service times considered are exponentially distributed with different service rates for different classes of positive customers.

Beyond this model, and the results discussed in [20] where multiple classes of signals are allowed, where a signal is a generalisation of a negative customer which has the ability to either destroy another customer or move it to another queue, further extensions of these results can be expected to emerge from future research.

We have mentioned applications of some of these results to algorithms for colour texture generation [9, 25], using a neural network analogy where colours are represented by customers of different types. The model we have described, in a simpler "single class" version has also been applied to texture recognition in medical images [21], and to optimisation problems in computer-communication networks [22]. Other important characteristics of these networks include their ability to approximate continuous and bounded functions [23] which we think will lead to new developments in the field of stochastic networks and their applications.

References

1. Kemmeny, J. G. and Snell, J. L. (1965). *Finite Markov Chains*. Von Nostrand, Princeton.
2. Baskett, F., Chandy, K., Muntz, R. R. and Palacios, F. G. (1975). Open, closed and mixed networks of queues with different classes of customers. *Journal ACM*, **22**(2), 248–260.

3. Gelenbe, E. (1989). Rseaux stochastiques ouverts avec clients ngatifs et positifs, et rseaux neuronaux. *Comptes-Rendus Acad. Sciences de Paris*, t. 309, Srie II, pp. 979–982.
4. Gelenbe, E. (1989). Random neural networks with negative and positive signals and product form solution. *Neural Computation*, **1**(4), 502–510.
5. Fourneau, J. M. (1991). Computing the steady-state distribution of networks with positive and negative customers. *Proc. 13-th IMACS World Congress on Computation and Applied Mathematics*, Dublin.
6. Gelenbe, E. (1991). Product form queueing networks with negative and positive customers. *Journal of Applied Probability*, **28**, 656–663.
7. Gelenbe, E., Glynn P. and Sigman, K. (1991). Queues with negative customers. *Journal of Applied Probability*, **28**, 245–250.
8. Gelenbe, E. and Tucci, S. (1991). Performances d'un système informatique dupliqué. *Comptes-Rendus Acad. Sci.*, t 312, Série II, pp. 27–30.
9. Atalay, V. and Gelenbe, E. (1992). Parallel algorithm for colour texture generation using the random neural network. *International Journal of Pattern Recognition and Artificial Intelligence*, **6**(2&3), 437–446.
10. Gelenbe, E. and Schassberger, R. (1992). Stability of G-Networks. *Probability in the Engineering and Informational Sciences*, **6**, 271–276.
11. Gelenbe, E. (1993). Learning in the recurrent random neural network. *Neural Computation*, **5**, 154–164.
12. Miyazawa, M. (1993). Insensitivity and product form decomposability of reallocatable GSMP. *Advances in Applied Probability*, **25**(2), 415–437.
13. Henderson, W. (1993). Queueing networks with negative customers and negative queue lengths. *Journal of Applied Probability*, **30**(3).
14. Gelenbe, E. (1993). G-Networks with triggered customer movement. *Journal of Applied Probability*, **30**(3), 742–748.
15. Gelenbe, E. (1993). G-Networks with signals and batch removal. *Probability in the Engineering and Informational Sciences*, **7**, 335–342.
16. Henderson, W., Northcote, B. S. and Taylor, P. G. (1994). Geometric equilibrium distributions for queues with interactive batch departures. *Annals of Operations Research*, **48**(1–4).
17. Henderson, W., Northcote, B. S. and Taylor, P. G. (1994). Networks of customer queues and resource queues. *Proc. International Teletraffic Congress 14*, Labetoulle, J. and Roberts, J. (Eds.), pp. 853–864, Elsevier.
18. Gelenbe, E. (1994). G-networks: a unifying model for neural and queueing networks. *Annals of Operations Research*, **48**(1–4), 433–461.
19. Fourneau, J.-M., Gelenbe, E. and Suros, R. (1996). G-networks with multiple classes of positive and negative customers. *Theoretical Computer Science*, **155**, 141–156.
20. Gelenbe, E. and Labed, A. (1998). G-networks with multiple classes of signals and positive customers. *European Journal of Operations Research*, **108**(2), 293–305.
21. Gelenbe, T. Feng and Krishnan, K. R. R. (1996). Neural network methods for volumetric magnetic resonance imaging of the human brain. *Proceedings of the IEEE*, **84**(10) 1488–1496.

22. Gelenbe, E., Ghanwani, A. and Srinivasan, V. (1997). Improved neural heuristics for multicast routing. *IEEE Journal of Selected Areas of Communications*, **15**(2), 147–155.

23. Gelenbe, E., Mao, Z.-H. and Li, Y.-D. (1999). Function approximation with spiked random networks. *IEEE Trans. on Neural Networks*, **10**(1), 3–9.

24. Gelenbe, E. and Fourneau, J.-M. (2002). G-Networks with resets. *Performance Evaluation*, **49**, 179–192, also in *Proc. IFIP WG 7.3/ACM-SIGMETRICS Performance '02 Conf.*, Rome, Italy, October 2002.

25. Gelenbe, E. and Hussain, K. (2002). Learning in the multiple class random neural network. *IEEE Trans. on Neural Networks*, **13**(6), 1257–1267.

26. Fourneau, J.-M. and Gelenbe, E. (2004). Flow equivalence and stochastic equivalence in G-networks. *Computational Management Science*, **1**(2), 179–192.

Chapter 5

Markov-Modulated Queues

There are many computer, communication and manufacturing systems which give rise to queueing models where the arrival and/or service mechanisms are influenced by some external processes. In such models, a single unbounded queue evolves in an environment which changes state from time to time. The instantaneous arrival and service rates may depend on the state of the environment and also, to a limited extent, on the number of jobs present.

The system state at time t is described by a pair of integer random variables, (I_t, J_t), where I_t represents the state of the environment and J_t is the number of jobs present. The variable I_t takes a finite number of values, numbered $0, 1, \ldots, N$; these are also called the environmental *phases*. The possible values of J_t are $0, 1, \ldots$ Thus, the system is in state (i, j) when the environment is in phase i and there are j jobs waiting and/or being served.

The two-dimensional process $X = \{(I_t, J_t); t \geq 0\}$ is assumed to have the Markov property, i.e. given the current phase and number of jobs, the future behaviour of X is independent of its past history. Such a model is referred to as a *Markov-modulated queue*. The corresponding state space, $\{0, 1, \ldots, N\} \times \{0, 1, \ldots\}$ is known as a *lattice strip*.

A fully general Markov-modulated queue, with arbitrary state-dependent transitions, is not tractable. However, one can consider a sub-class of models which are sufficiently general to be useful, and yet can be solved efficiently. Those models satisfy the following restrictions:

(i) There is a threshold M, such that the instantaneous transition rates out of state (i, j) do not depend on j when $j \geq M$.

(ii) the jumps of the random variable J are bounded.

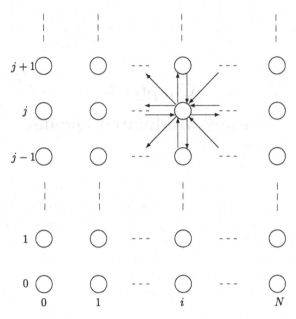

Fig. 5.1.   State diagram of a QBD process.

When the jumps of the random variable J are of size 1, i.e. when jobs arrive and depart one at a time, the process is said to be of the *Quasi-Birth-and-Death* type, or QBD (the term *skip-free* is also used (Latouche *et al.*, [7]). The state diagram for this common model, showing some transitions out of state (i, j), is illustrated in Fig. 5.1.

The requirement that all transition rates cease to depend on the size of the job queue beyond a certain threshold is not too restrictive. Note that there is no limit on the magnitude of the threshold M, although it must be pointed out that the larger M is, the greater the complexity of the solution. Similarly, although jobs may arrive and/or depart in fixed or variable (but bounded) batches, the larger the batch size, the more complex the solution.

The object of the analysis of a Markov-modulated queue is to determine the joint steady-state distribution of the environmental phase and the number of jobs in the system:

$$p_{i,j} = \lim_{t \to \infty} P(I_t = i, J_t = j); \quad i = 0, 1, \ldots, N; \quad j = 0, 1, \ldots. \qquad (5.1)$$

That distribution exists for an irreducible Markov process if, and only if, the corresponding set of balance equations has a positive solution that can be normalised.

The marginal distributions of the number of jobs in the system, and of the phase, can be obtained from the joint distribution:

$$p_{\cdot,j} = \sum_{i=0}^{N} p_{i,j} \tag{5.2}$$

$$p_{i,\cdot} = \sum_{j=0}^{\infty} p_{i,j}. \tag{5.3}$$

Various performance measures can then be computed in terms of these joint and marginal distributions.

The following are some examples of systems that are modelled as Markov-modulated queues.

5.1. A multiserver queue with breakdowns and repairs

A single, unbounded queue is served by N identical parallel servers (Mitrani and Avi-Itzhak, [9], Neuts and Lucantoni, [13]). Each server goes through alternating periods of being operative and inoperative, independently of the others and of the number of jobs in the system. The operative and inoperative periods are distributed exponentially with parameters ξ and η, respectively. Thus, the number of operative servers at time t, I_t, is a Markov process on the state space $\{0, 1, \ldots, N\}$. This is the environment in which the queue evolves: it is in phase i when there are i operative servers.

Jobs arrive according to a Poisson process, with a rate which may depend on the state of the environment, I_t. That is, when there are i operative servers, the instantaneous arrival rate is λ_i. Jobs are taken for service from the front of the queue, one at a time, by available operative servers. The required service times are distributed exponentially with parameter μ. An operative server cannot be idle if there are jobs waiting to be served. A job whose service is interrupted by a server breakdown is returned to the front of the queue. When an operative server becomes available, the service is resumed from the point of interruption, without any switching overheads. The flow of jobs is shown in Fig. 5.2.

The process $X = \{(I_t, J_t); t \geq 0\}$ is of the Quasi-Birth-and-Death type. The transitions out of state (i, j) are:

(a) to state $(i - 1, j)$ $(i > 0)$, with rate $i\xi$;
(b) to state $(i + 1, j)$ $(i < N)$, with rate $(N - i)\eta$;
(c) to state $(i, j + 1)$ with rate λ_i;
(d) to state $(i, j - 1)$ with rate $\min(i, j)\mu$.

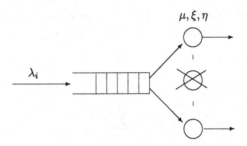

Fig. 5.2.   A multiserver queue with breakdowns and repairs.

Note that only transition (d) has a rate which depends on j, and that dependency vanishes when $j \geq N$.

Remark. The breakdown and repair processes could be generalised without destroying the QBD nature of the process. For example, the servers could break down and be repaired in batches, or a server breakdown could trigger a job departure. The environmental state transitions can be arbitrary, as long as the queue changes in steps of size 1.

In this example, as in all models where the environment state transitions do not depend on the number of jobs present, the marginal distribution of the number of operative servers can be determined without finding the joint distribution first. Moreover, since the servers break down and are repaired independently of each other, that distribution is binomial:

$$p_{i,\cdot} = \binom{N}{i} \left(\frac{\eta}{\xi+\eta}\right)^{i} \left(\frac{\xi}{\xi+\eta}\right)^{N-i} \; ; \; i = 0, 1, \ldots, N. \qquad (5.4)$$

Hence, the steady-state average number of operative servers is equal to

$$E(X_t) = \frac{N\eta}{\xi+\eta}. \qquad (5.5)$$

The overall average arrival rate is equal to

$$\lambda = \sum_{i=0}^{N} p_{i,\cdot} \lambda_i. \qquad (5.6)$$

This gives us an explicit condition for stability. The offered load must be less than the processing capacity:

$$\frac{\lambda}{\mu} < \frac{N\eta}{\xi+\eta}. \qquad (5.7)$$

Fig. 5.3. Two nodes with a finite intermediate buffer.

5.2. Manufacturing blocking

Consider a network of two nodes in tandem, such as the one in Fig. 5.3 (Buzacott and Shanthikumar, [1], Konheim and Reiser, [6]). Jobs arrive into the first node in a Poisson stream with rate λ, and join an unbounded queue. After completing service at node 1 (exponentially distributed with parameter μ), they attempt to go to node 2, where there is a finite buffer with room for a maximum of $N-1$ jobs (including the one in service). If that transfer is impossible because the buffer is full, the job remains at node 1, preventing its server from starting a new service, until the completion of the current service at node 2 (exponentially distributed with parameter ξ). In this last case, server 1 is said to be "blocked". Transfers from node 1 to node 2 are instantaneous.

The above type of blocking is referred to as "manufacturing blocking". (An alternative model, which also gives rise to a Markov-modulated queue, is the "communication blocking". There node 1 *does not start* a service if the node 2 buffer is full.)

In this system, the unbounded queue at node 1 is modulated by a finite-state environment defined by node 2. We say that the environment, I_t, is in state i if there are i jobs at node 2 and server 1 is not blocked ($i = 0, 1, \ldots, N - 1$). An extra state, $I_t = N$, is needed to describe the situation where there are $N - 1$ jobs at node 2 and server 1 is blocked.

The above assumptions imply that the pair $X = \{(I_t, J_t); t \geq 0\}$, where J_t is the number of jobs at node 1, is a QBD process. Note that the state $(N, 0)$ does not exist: node 1 may be blocked only if there are jobs present.

The transitions out of state (i, j) are:

(a) to state $(i - 1, j)$ $(0 < i < N)$, with rate ξ;
(b) to state $(N - 1, j - 1)$ $(i = N, j > 0)$, with rate ξ;
(c) to state $(i + 1, j - 1)$ $(0 \leq i < N - 1, j > 0)$, with rate μ;
(d) to state (N, j) $(i = N - 1, j > 0)$, with rate μ;
(e) to state $(i, j + 1)$ with rate λ.

The only dependency on j comes from the fact that transitions (b), (c) and (d) are not available when $j = 0$. In this example, the j-independency threshold is $M = 1$. Note that the state $(N, 0)$ is not reachable: node 1 may be blocked only if there are jobs present.

5.3. Phase-type distributions

There is a large and useful family of distributions that can be incorporated into queueing models by means of Markovian environments (Neuts, [12]). Those distributions are "almost" general, in the sense that any distribution function either belongs to this family or can be approximated as closely as desired by functions from it.

Let I_t be a Markov process with state space $\{0, 1, \dots, N\}$ and generator matrix $\tilde{A}$. States $0, 1, \dots, N - 1$ are transient, while state N, reachable from any of the other states, is absorbing (the last row of $\tilde{A}$ is 0). At time 0, the process starts in state i with probability α_i ($i = 0, 1, \dots, N - 1$; $\alpha_1 + \alpha_2 + \cdots + \alpha_{N-1} = 1$). Eventually, after an interval of length T, it is absorbed in state N. The random variable T is said to have a "phase-type" (PH) distribution with parameters $\tilde{A}$ and α_i.

The exponential distribution is obviously phase-type ($N = 1$). So is the Erlang distribution — the convolution of N exponentials. The corresponding generator matrix is

$$\tilde{A} = \begin{bmatrix} -\mu & \mu & & & \\ & -\mu & \mu & & \\ & & \ddots & \ddots & \\ & & & -\mu & \mu \\ & & & & 0 \end{bmatrix},$$

and the initial probabilities are $\alpha_0 = 1$, $\alpha_1 = \dots = \alpha_{N-1} = 0$.

Another common PH distribution is the "hyperexponential", where $I_0 = i$ with probability α_i, and absorbtion occurs at the first transition. The generator matrix of the hyperexponential distribution is

$$\tilde{A} = \begin{bmatrix} -\mu_0 & & & & \mu_0 \\ & -\mu_1 & & & \mu_1 \\ & & \ddots & & \vdots \\ & & & -\mu_{N-1} & \mu_{N-1} \\ & & & & 0 \end{bmatrix}.$$

The corresponding probability distribution function, $F(x)$, is a mixture of exponentials:

$$F(x) = 1 - \sum_{i=0}^{N-1} \alpha_i e^{-\mu_i x}.$$

The PH family is very versatile. It contains distributions with both low and high coefficients of variation. It is closed with respect to mixing and convolution: if X_1 and X_2 are two independent PH random variables with N_1 and N_2 (non-absorbing) phases respectively, and c_1 and c_2 are constants, then $c_1 X_1 + c_2 X_2$ has a PH distribution with $N_1 + N_2$ phases.

A model with a single unbounded queue, where either the interarrival intervals, or the service times, or both, have PH distributions, is easily cast in the framework of a queue in Markovian environment. Consider, for instance, the M/PH/1 queue. Its state at time t can be represented as a pair (I_t, J_t), where J_t is the number of jobs present and I_t is the phase of the current service (if $J_t > 0$). When I_t has a transition into the absorbing state, the current service completes and (if the queue is not empty) a new service starts immediately, entering phase i with probability α_i.

The PH/PH/n queue can also be represented as a QBD process. However, the state of the environmental variable, I_t, now has to indicate the phase of the current interarrival interval and the phases of the current services at all busy servers. If the interarrival interval has N_1 phases and the service has N_2 phases, the state space of I_t would be of size $N_1 N_2^n$.

5.4. Checkpointing and recovery in the presence of faults

The last example is not a QBD process. Consider a system where transactions, arriving according to a Poisson process with rate λ, are served in FIFO order by a single server. The service times are i.i.d. random variables distributed exponentially with parameter μ. After N consecutive transactions have been completed, the system performs a checkpoint operation whose duration is an i.i.d. random variable distributed exponentially with parameter β. Once a checkpoint is established, the N completed transactions are deemed to have departed. However, both transaction processing and checkpointing may be interrupted by the occurrence of a fault. The latter arrive according to an independent Poisson process with rate ξ. When a fault occurs, the system instantaneously rolls back to the last established checkpoint; all transactions which arrived since that moment either remain in the queue, if they have not been processed, or return to it, in order to be processed again (it is assumed that repeated service times are resampled independently).

This system can be modelled as an unbounded queue of (uncompleted) transactions, which is modulated by an environment consisting of completed transactions and checkpoints. More precisely, the two state variables, $I(t)$ and $J(t)$, are the number of transactions that have completed service since the last checkpoint, and the number of transactions present that have not completed service (including those requiring re-processing), respectively.

The Markov-modulated queueing process $X = \{[I(t), J(t)]; t \geq 0\}$, has the following transitions out of state (i, j):

(a) to state $(0, j + i)$, with rate ξ;
(b) to state $(0, j)(i = N)$, with rate β;
(c) to state $(i, j + 1)$, with rate λ;
(d) to state $(i + 1, j - 1)(0 \leq i < N, j > 0)$, with rate μ;

Because transitions (a), resulting from arrivals of faults, cause the queue size to jump by more than 1, this is not a QBD process.

5.5. Spectral expansion solution

Let us now turn to the problem of determining the steady-state joint distribution of the environmental phase and the number of jobs present, for a Markov-modulated queue. The solution method that we shall present is called "Spectral Expansion", for reasons that will become apparent.

We shall start with the most commonly encountered case, namely the QBD process, where jobs arrive and depart singly. The starting point is of course the set of balance equations which the probabilities $p_{i,j}$, defined in (5.1), must satisfy. In order to write them in general terms, the following notation for the instantaneous transition rates will be used.

(a) Phase transitions leaving the queue unchanged: from state (i, j) to state $(k, j)(0 \leq i, k \leq N; i \neq k)$, with rate $a_j(i, k)$;
(b) Transitions incrementing the queue: from state (i, j) to state $(k, j + 1)$ $(0 \leq i, k \leq N)$, with rate $b_j(i, k)$;
(c) Transitions decrementing the queue: from state (i, j) to state $(k, j - 1)$ $(0 \leq i, k \leq N; j > 0)$, with rate $c_j(i, k)$.

It is convenient to introduce the $(N + 1) \times (N + 1)$ matrices containing the rates of type (a), (b) and (c): $A_j = [a_j(i, k)]$, $B_j = [b_j(i, k)]$ and

$C_j = [c_j(i,k)]$, respectively (the main diagonal of A_j is zero by definition; also, $C_0 = 0$ by definition). According to the assumptions of the Markov-modulated queue, there is a threshold, $M(M \geq 1)$, such that those matrices do not depend on j when $j \geq M$. In other words,

$$A_j = A; \quad B_j = B; \quad C_j = C, \qquad j \geq M. \tag{5.8}$$

Note that transitions (b) may represent a job arrival coinciding with a change of phase. If arrivals are not accompanied by such changes, then the matrices B_j and B are diagonal. Similarly, a transition of type (c) may represent a job departure coinciding with a change of phase. Again, if such coincidences do not occur, then the matrices C_j and C are diagonal.

By way of illustration, here are the transition rate matrices for the model of the multiserver queue with breakdowns and repairs. In this case the phase transitions are independent of the queue size, so the matrices A_j are all equal:

$$A_j = A = \begin{bmatrix} 0 & N\eta & & & \\ \xi & 0 & (N-1)\eta & & \\ & 2\xi & 0 & \ddots & \\ & & \ddots & \ddots & \eta \\ & & & N\xi & 0 \end{bmatrix}.$$

Similarly, the matrices B_j do not depend on j:

$$B = \begin{bmatrix} \lambda_0 & & & \\ & \lambda_1 & & \\ & & \ddots & \\ & & & \lambda_N \end{bmatrix}.$$

Denoting

$$\mu_{i,j} = \min(i,j)\mu; \quad i = 0, 1, \ldots, N; \; j = 1, 2, \ldots,$$

the departure rate matrices, C_j, can thus be written as

$$C_j = \begin{bmatrix} 0 & & & \\ & \mu_{1,j} & & \\ & & \ddots & \\ & & & \mu_{N,j} \end{bmatrix}; \quad j = 1, 2, \ldots,$$

These matrices cease to depend on j when $j \geq N$. Thus, the threshold M is now equal to N, and

$$C = \begin{bmatrix} 0 & & & \\ & \mu & & \\ & & \ddots & \\ & & & N\mu \end{bmatrix}.$$

5.6. Balance equations

Using the instantaneous transition rates introduced above, the balance equations of a general QBD process can be written as

$$p_{i,j} \sum_{k=0}^{N} [a_j(i,k) + b_j(i,k) + c_j(i,k)]$$

$$= \sum_{k=0}^{N} [p_{k,j} a_j(k,i) + p_{k,j-1} b_{j-1}(k,i) + p_{k,j+1} c_{j+1}(k,i)], \quad (5.9)$$

where $p_{i,-1} = b_{-1}(k,i) = c_0(i,k) = 0$ by definition. The left-hand side of (5.9) gives the total average number of transitions out of state (i,j) per unit time (due to changes of phase, arrivals and departures), while the right-hand side expresses the total average number of transitions into state (i,j) (again due to changes of phase, arrivals and departures). These balance equations can be written more compactly by using vectors and matrices. Define the row vectors of probabilities corresponding to states with j jobs in the system:

$$\mathbf{v}_j = (p_{0,j}, p_{1,j}, \ldots, p_{N,j}); \quad j = 0, 1, \ldots. \quad (5.10)$$

Also, let D_j^A, D_j^B and D_j^C be the diagonal matrices whose ith diagonal element is equal to the ith row sum of A_j, B_j and C_j, respectively. Then equations (5.9), for $j = 0, 1, \ldots$, can be written as:

$$\mathbf{v}_j [D_j^A + D_j^B + D_j^C] = \mathbf{v}_{j-1} B_{j-1} + \mathbf{v}_j A_j + \mathbf{v}_{j+1} C_{j+1}, \quad (5.11)$$

where $\mathbf{v}_{-1} = \mathbf{0}$ and $D_0^C = B_{-1} = 0$ by definition.

When j is greater than the threshold M, the coefficients in (5.11) cease to depend on j:

$$\mathbf{v}_j [D^A + D^B + D^C] = \mathbf{v}_{j-1} B + \mathbf{v}_j A + \mathbf{v}_{j+1} C, \quad (5.12)$$

for $j = M + 1, M + 2, \ldots$.

In addition, all probabilities must sum up to 1:

$$\sum_{j=0}^{\infty} \mathbf{v}_j \mathbf{e} = 1, \tag{5.13}$$

where $\mathbf{e}$ is a column vector with $N+1$ elements, all of which are equal to 1.

The first step is to find the general solution of the infinite set of balance equations with constant coefficients, (5.12). The latter are normally written in the form of a homogeneous vector difference equation of order 2:

$$\mathbf{v}_j Q_0 + \mathbf{v}_{j+1} Q_1 + \mathbf{v}_{j+2} Q_2 = \mathbf{0}; \quad j = M, M+1, \ldots, \tag{5.14}$$

where $Q_0 = B$, $Q_1 = A - D^A - D^B - D^C$ and $Q_2 = C$.

Associated with equation (5.14) is the so-called "characteristic matrix polynomial", $Q(x)$, defined as

$$Q(x) = Q_0 + Q_1 x + Q_2 x^2. \tag{5.15}$$

Denote by x_k and $\mathbf{u}_k$ the "generalised eigenvalues", and corresponding "generalised left eigenvectors", of $Q(x)$. In other words, these are quantities which satisfy

$$\begin{aligned} \det[Q(x_k)] &= 0, \\ \mathbf{u}_k Q(x_k) &= \mathbf{0}; \quad k = 1, 2, \ldots, d, \end{aligned} \tag{5.16}$$

where $\det[Q(x)]$ is the determinant of $Q(x)$ and d is its degree. In what follows, the qualification *generalised* will be omitted.

The above eigenvalues do not have to be simple, but it is assumed that if one of them has multiplicity m, then it also has m linearly independent left eigenvectors. This tends to be the case in practice. So, the numbering in (5.16) is such that each eigenvalue is counted according to its multiplicity.

It is readily seen that if x_k and $\mathbf{u}_k$ are any eigenvalue and corresponding left eigenvector, then the sequence

$$\mathbf{v}_{k,j} = \mathbf{u}_k x_k^j; \quad j = M, M+1, \ldots, \tag{5.17}$$

is a solution of equation (5.14). Indeed, substituting (5.17) into (5.14) we get

$$\mathbf{v}_{k,j} Q_0 + \mathbf{v}_{k,j+1} Q_1 + \mathbf{v}_{k,j+2} Q_2 = x_k^j \mathbf{u}_k [Q_0 + Q_1 x_k + Q_2 x_k^2] = \mathbf{0}.$$

By combining any multiple eigenvalues with each of their independent eigenvectors, we thus obtain d linearly independent solutions of (5.14).

On the other hand, it is known that there cannot be more than d linearly independent solutions (Gohberg *et al.*, [4]). Therefore, any solution of (5.14) can be expressed as a linear combination of the d solutions (5.17):

$$\mathbf{v}_j = \sum_{k=1}^{d} \alpha_k \mathbf{u}_k x_k^j; \quad j = M, M+1, \ldots, \tag{5.18}$$

where α_k $(k = 1, 2, \ldots, d)$, are arbitrary (complex) constants.

However, the only solutions that are of interest in the present context are those which can be normalised to become probability distributions. Hence, it is necessary to select from the set (5.18), those sequences for which the series $\sum \mathbf{v}_j \mathbf{e}$ converges. This requirement implies that if $|x_k| \geq 1$ for some k, then the corresponding coefficient α_k must be 0.

So, suppose that c of the eigenvalues of $Q(x)$ are strictly inside the unit disk (each counted according to its multiplicity), while the others are on the circumference or outside. Order them so that $|x_k| < 1$ for $k = 1, 2, \ldots, c$. The corresponding independent eigenvectors are $\mathbf{u}_1, \mathbf{u}_2, \ldots, \mathbf{u}_c$. Then any normalisable solution of equation (5.14) can be expressed as

$$\mathbf{v}_j = \sum_{k=1}^{c} \alpha_k \mathbf{u}_k x_k^j; \quad j = M, M+1, \ldots, \tag{5.19}$$

where α_k $(k = 1, 2, \ldots, c)$, are some constants.

The set of eigenvalues of the matrix polynomial $Q(x)$ is called its "spectrum". Hence, expression (5.19) is referred to as the "spectral expansion" of the vectors $\mathbf{v}_j$. The coefficients of that expansion, α_k, are yet to be determined.

Note that if there are non-real eigenvalues in the unit disk, then they appear in complex-conjugate pairs. The corresponding eigenvectors are also complex-conjugate. The same must be true for the appropriate pairs of constants α_k, in order that the right-hand side of (5.19) be real. To ensure that it is also positive, the real parts of x_k, $\mathbf{u}_k$ and α_k should be positive.

So far, expressions have been obtained for the vectors $\mathbf{v}_M, \mathbf{v}_{M+1}, \ldots$; these contain c unknown constants. Now it is time to consider the balance equations (5.11), for $j = 0, 1, \ldots, M$. This is a set of $(M+1)(N+1)$ linear equations with $M(N+1)$ unknown probabilities (the vectors $\mathbf{v}_j$ for $j = 0, 1, \ldots, M-1$), plus the c constants α_k. However, only $(M+1)(N+1)-1$ of these equations are linearly independent, since the generator matrix of the Markov process is singular. On the other hand, an additional independent equation is provided by (5.13).

In order that this set of linearly independent equations has a unique solution, the number of unknowns must be equal to the number of equations, i.e. $(M + 1)(N + 1) = M(N + 1) + c$, or $c = N + 1$. This observation implies the following rather general result.

Proposition 5.1. *The QBD process has a steady-state distribution if, and only if, the number of eigenvalues of $Q(x)$ strictly inside the unit disk, each counted according to its multiplicity, is equal to the number of states of the Markovian environment, $N + 1$. Then, assuming that the eigenvectors of multiple eigenvalues are linearly independent, the spectral expansion solution of* (5.12) *has the form*

$$\mathbf{v}_j = \sum_{k=1}^{N+1} \alpha_k \mathbf{u}_k x_k^j; \quad j = M, M + 1, \dots. \tag{5.20}$$

In summary, the spectral expansion solution procedure consists of the following steps:

1. Compute the eigenvalues of $Q(x)$, x_k, inside the unit disk, and the corresponding left eigenvectors $\mathbf{u}_k$. If their number is other than $N + 1$, stop; a steady-state distribution does not exist.
2. Solve the finite set of linear equations (5.11), for $j = 0, 1, \dots, M$, and (5.13), with $\mathbf{v}_M$ and $\mathbf{v}_{M+1}$ given by (5.20), to determine the constants α_k and the vectors $\mathbf{v}_j$ for $j < M$.
3. Use the obtained solution in order to determine various moments, marginal probabilities, percentiles and other system performance measures that may be of interest.

Careful attention should be paid to step 1. The "brute force" approach which relies on first evaluating the scalar polynomial $\det[Q(x)]$, then finding its roots, may be very inefficient for large N. An alternative which is preferable in most cases is to reduce the quadratic eigenvalue-eigenvector problem

$$\mathbf{u}[Q_0 + Q_1 x + Q_2 x^2] = \mathbf{0}, \tag{5.21}$$

to a linear one of the form $\mathbf{u}Q = x\mathbf{u}$, where Q is a matrix whose dimensions are twice as large as those of Q_0, Q_1 and Q_2. The latter problem is normally solved by applying various transformation techniques. Efficient routines for that purpose are available in most numerical packages.

This linearisation can be achieved quite easily if the matrix $C = Q_2$ is non-singular (Jennings, [5]). Indeed, after multiplying (5.21) on the right by Q_2^{-1}, it becomes

$$\mathbf{u}[H_0 + H_1 x + I x^2] = \mathbf{0}, \tag{5.22}$$

where $H_0 = Q_0 C^{-1}$, $H_1 = Q_1 C^{-1}$, and I is the identity matrix. By introducing the vector $\mathbf{y} = x\mathbf{u}$, equation (5.22) can be rewritten in the equivalent linear form

$$[\mathbf{u}, \mathbf{y}] \begin{bmatrix} 0 & -H_0 \\ I & -H_1 \end{bmatrix} = x[\mathbf{u}, \mathbf{y}]. \tag{5.23}$$

If C is singular but B is not, a similar linearisation is achieved by multiplying (5.21) on the right by B^{-1} and making a change of variable $x \to 1/x$. Then the relevant eigenvalues are those outside the unit disk.

If both B and C are singular, then the desired result is achieved by first making a change of variable, $x \to (\gamma + x)/(\gamma - x)$, where the value of γ is chosen so that the matrix $S = \gamma^2 Q_2 + \gamma Q_1 + Q_0$ is non-singular. In other words, γ can have any value which is not an eigenvalue of $Q(x)$. Having made that change of variable, multiplying the resulting equation by S^{-1} on the right reduces it to the form (5.22).

The computational demands of step 2 may be high if the threshold M is large. However, if the matrices B_j $(j = 0, 1, \dots, M - 1)$ are non-singular (which is often the case in practice), then the vectors $\mathbf{v}_{M-1}, \mathbf{v}_{M-2}, \dots, \mathbf{v}_0$ can be expressed in terms of $\mathbf{v}_M$ and $\mathbf{v}_{M+1}$, with the aid of equations (5.11) for $j = M, M - 1, \dots, 1$. One is then left with equations (5.11) for $j = 0$, plus (5.13) (a total of $N + 1$ independent linear equations), for the $N + 1$ unknowns x_k.

Having determined the coefficients in the expansion (5.20) and the probabilities $p_{i,j}$ for $j < N$, it is easy to compute performance measures. The steady-state probability that the environment is in state i is given by

$$p_{i,\cdot} = \sum_{j=0}^{M-1} p_{i,j} + \sum_{k=1}^{N+1} \alpha_k u_{k,i} \frac{x_k^M}{1 - x_k}, \tag{5.24}$$

where $u_{k,i}$ is the ith element of $\mathbf{u}_k$.

The conditional average number of jobs in the system, L_i, given that the environment is in state i, is obtained from

$$L_i = \frac{1}{p_{i,\cdot}} \left[\sum_{j=1}^{M-1} j p_{i,j} + \sum_{k=1}^{N+1} \alpha_k u_{k,i} \frac{x_k^M (M - M x_k + x_k)}{(1 - x_k)^2} \right]. \tag{5.25}$$

The overall average number of jobs in the system, L, is equal to

$$L = \sum_{i=0}^{N} p_{i,\cdot} L_i. \tag{5.26}$$

5.7. Batch arrivals and/or departures

Consider now a Markov-modulated queue which is not a QBD process, i.e. one where the queue size jumps may be bigger than 1. As before, the state of the process at time t is described by the pair (I_t, J_t), where I_t is the state of the environment (the operational mode) and J_t is the number of jobs in the system. The state space is the lattice strip $\{0, 1, \ldots, N\} \times \{0, 1, \ldots\}$. The variable J_t may jump by arbitrary, but bounded amounts in either direction. In other words, the allowable transitions are:

(a) Phase transitions leaving the queue unchanged: from state (i, j) to state (k, j) $(0 \leq i, k \leq N; i \neq k)$, with rate $a_j(i, k)$;
(b) Transitions incrementing the queue by s: from state (i, j) to state $(k, j + s)$ $(0 \leq i, k \leq N; 1 \leq s \leq r_1; r_1 \geq 1)$, with rate $b_{j,s}(i, k)$;
(c) Transitions decrementing the queue by s: from state (i, j) to state $(k, j - s)$ $(0 \leq i, k \leq N; 1 \leq s \leq r_2; r_2 \geq 1)$, with rate $c_{j,s}(i, k)$,

provided of course that the source and destination states are valid.

Obviously, if $r_1 = r_2 = 1$ then this is a Quasi-Birth-and-Death process.

Denote by $A_j = [a_j(i, k)]$, $B_{j,s} = [b_{j,s}(i, k)]$ and $C_{j,s} = [c_{j,s}(i, k)]$, the transition rate matrices associated with (a), (b) and (c), respectively. There is a threshold M, such that

$$A_j = A; \quad B_{j,s} = B_s; \quad C_{j,s} = C_s; \qquad j \geq M. \tag{5.27}$$

Defining again the diagonal matrices D^A, D^{B_s} and D^{C_s}, whose ith diagonal element is equal to the ith row sum of A, B_s and C_s, respectively, the balance equations for $j > M + r_1$ can be written in a form analogous to (5.12):

$$\mathbf{v}_j \left[D^A + \sum_{s=1}^{r_1} D^{B_s} + \sum_{s=1}^{r_2} D^{C_s} \right] = \sum_{s=1}^{r_1} \mathbf{v}_{j-s} B_s + \mathbf{v}_j A + \sum_{s=1}^{r_2} \mathbf{v}_{j+s} C_s. \tag{5.28}$$

Similar equations, involving A_j, $B_{j,s}$ and $C_{j,s}$, together with the corresponding diagonal matrices, can be written for $j \leq M + r_1$.

As before, (5.28) can be rewritten as a vector difference equation, this time of order $r = r_1 + r_2$, with constant coefficients:

$$\sum_{\ell=0}^{r} \mathbf{v}_{j+\ell} Q_\ell = \mathbf{0}; \quad j \geq M. \tag{5.29}$$

Here, $Q_\ell = B_{r_1-\ell}$ for $\ell = 0, 1, \ldots r_1 - 1$,

$$Q_{r_1} = A - D^A - \sum_{s=1}^{r_1} D^{B_s} - \sum_{s=1}^{r_2} D^{C_s},$$

and $Q_\ell = C_{\ell-r_1}$ for $\ell = r_1 + 1, r_1 + 2, \ldots r_1 + r_2$.

The spectral expansion solution of this equation is obtained from the characteristic matrix polynomial

$$Q(x) = \sum_{\ell=0}^{r} Q_\ell x^\ell. \tag{5.30}$$

The solution is of the form

$$\mathbf{v}_j = \sum_{k=1}^{c} \alpha_k \mathbf{u}_k x_k^j; \quad j = M, M+1, \ldots, \tag{5.31}$$

where x_k are the eigenvalues of $Q(x)$ in the interior of the unit disk, $\mathbf{u}_k$ are the corresponding left eigenvectors, and α_k are constants ($k = 1, 2, \ldots, c$). These constants, together with the probability vectors $\mathbf{v}_j$ for $j < M$, are determined with the aid of the state-dependent balance equations and the normalising equation.

There are now $(M + r_1)(N + 1)$ so-far-unused balance equations (the ones where $j < M + r_1$), of which $(M + r_1)(N + 1) - 1$ are linearly independent, plus one normalising equation. The number of unknowns is $M(N + 1) + c$ (the vectors $\mathbf{v}_j$ for $j = 0, 1, \ldots, M - 1$), plus the c constants α_k. Hence, there is a unique solution when $c = r_1(N + 1)$.

Proposition 5.2. *The Markov-modulated queue has a steady-state distribution if, and only if, the number of eigenvalues of $Q(x)$ strictly inside the unit disk, each counted according to its multiplicity, is equal to the number of states of the Markovian environment, $N+1$, multiplied by the largest arrival batch, r_1. Then, assuming that the eigenvectors of multiple eigenvalues* *are linearly independent, the spectral expansion solution of* (5.28) *has the form*

$$\mathbf{v}_j = \sum_{k=1}^{r_1*(N+1)} \alpha_k \mathbf{u}_k x_k^j; \quad j = M, M+1, \ldots. \tag{5.32}$$

For computational purposes, the polynomial eigenvalue-eigenvector problem of degree r can be transformed into a linear one. For example, suppose that Q_r is non-singular and multiply (5.29) on the right by Q_r^{-1}. This leads to the problem

$$\mathbf{u} \left[\sum_{\ell=0}^{r-1} H_\ell x^\ell + I x^r \right] = \mathbf{0}, \tag{5.33}$$

where $H_\ell = Q_\ell Q_r^{-1}$. Introducing the vectors $\mathbf{y}_\ell = x^\ell \mathbf{u}$, $\ell = 1, 2, \ldots, r-1$, one obtains the equivalent linear form

$$[\mathbf{u}, \mathbf{y}_1, \ldots, \mathbf{y}_{r-1}] \begin{bmatrix} 0 & & & -H_0 \\ I & 0 & & -H_1 \\ & \ddots & \ddots & \\ & & I & -H_{r-1} \end{bmatrix} = x[\mathbf{u}, \mathbf{y}_1, \ldots, \mathbf{y}_{r-1}].$$

As in the quadratic case, if Q_r is singular then the linear form can be achieved by an appropriate change of variable.

5.8. A simple approximation

The spectral expansion solution can be computationally expensive. Its numerical complexity depends crucially on the number of environmental phases: that number determines the number of eigenvalues and eigenvectors that have to be evaluated, and influences the size of the set of simultaneous linear equations that have to be solved. Moreover, when N is large, there may be numerical problems concerned with ill-conditioned matrices. In some cases, both the complexity and the numerical stability of the solution are adversely affected when the system is heavily loaded.

For these reasons, it may be worth abandoning the exact solution, if one can develop a reasonable approximation which is simple, easy to implement, robust and computationally cheap. Such an approximation can be extracted from the spectral expansion solution. The idea is to use a "restricted" expansion, based on a single eigenvalue and its associated eigenvector. The eigenvalue provides a geometric approximation for the queue size distribution, while the eigenvector approximates the distribution of the environmental phase.

An attractive feature of the geometric approximation is that its accuracy improves when the offered load increases. In the heavy-traffic limit, i.e. when the system approaches saturation, the approximation becomes asymptotically exact.

In order to keep the presentation simple, the discussion will be restricted to QBD Markov-modulated queues whose solution is given by Proposition 5.1, with simple eigenvalues. However, the applicability of the proposed approximation is much more general.

A central role in the approximation is played by the largest eigenvalue that appears in (5.20), and its left eigenvector. Assume, without loss of generality, that the eigenvalues are numbered in increasing order of modulus, so that the largest is x_{N+1}. When the queue is stable, x_{N+1} is real and positive. Moreover, it has a positive eigenvector. From now on, x_{N+1} will be referred to as the "dominant eigenvalue", and will be denoted by γ.

The expression (5.20) implies that *the tail* of the joint distribution of the queue size and the environmental phase is approximately geometrically distributed, with parameter equal to the dominant eigenvalue, γ. To see that, divide both sides of (5.20) by γ^j and let $j \to \infty$. Since γ is strictly greater in modulus than all other eigenvalues, all terms in the summation vanish, except one:

$$\lim_{j \to \infty} \frac{\mathbf{v}_j}{\gamma^j} = \alpha_{N+1} \mathbf{u}_{N+1}. \tag{5.34}$$

In other words, when j is large,

$$\mathbf{v}_j \approx \alpha_{N+1} \mathbf{u}_{N+1} \gamma^j. \tag{5.35}$$

This product form implies that when the queue is large, its size is approximately independent of the environmental phase. The tail of the marginal distribution of the queue size is approximately geometric:

$$p_{\cdot,j} \approx \alpha_{N+1} (\mathbf{u}_{N+1} \cdot \mathbf{1}) \gamma^j, \tag{5.36}$$

where $\mathbf{1}$ is the column vector defined in (5.13).

These results suggest seeking an approximation of the form

$$\mathbf{v}_j = \alpha \mathbf{u}_{N+1} \gamma^j, \tag{5.37}$$

where α is some constant.

Note that γ and $\mathbf{u}_{N+1}$ can be computed without having to find *all* eigenvalues and eigenvectors. There are techniques for determining the eigenvalues that are near a given number. Here we are dealing with the eigenvalue that is nearest to but strictly less than 1.

If (5.37) is applied to all $\mathbf{v}_j$, for $j = 0, 1, \ldots$, then the approximation depends on just one unknown constant, α. Its value is determined by (5.13) alone, and the expressions for $\mathbf{v}_j$ become

$$\mathbf{v}_j = \frac{\mathbf{u}_{N+1}}{(\mathbf{u}_{N+1} \cdot \mathbf{1})}(1 - \gamma)\gamma^j; \quad j = 0, 1, \ldots. \tag{5.38}$$

This last approximation avoids completely the need to solve a set of linear equations. Hence, it also avoids all problems associated with ill-conditioned matrices. Moreover, it scales well. The complexity of computing γ and $\mathbf{u}_{N+1}$ grows roughly linearly with N when the matrices A, B and C are sparse. The price paid for that convenience is that the balance equations for $j \leq M$ are no longer satisfied.

Despite its apparent over-simplicity, the geometric approximation (5.38) can be shown to be asymptotically exact when the offered load increases.

5.9. The heavy traffic limit

Consider the case where a parameter associated with arrivals or services changes so that system becomes heavily loaded and approaches saturation. The parameters governing the evolution of the environment are assumed to remain fixed. Then the dominant eigenvalue, γ, is known to approach 1 (Gail *et al.*, [3]). When $\gamma = 1$ (i.e. there is a double eigenvalue at 1), the process $X = \{(I, J)\}$ is recurrent-null; when γ leaves the unit disc, the process is transient. Hence, instead of taking a limit involving a particular parameter, e.g. $\lambda \to \lambda_{\max}$ (where $\lambda_{\max}$ is the arrival rate that would saturate the system), we can equivalently treat the heavy-traffic regime in terms of the limit $\gamma \to 1$.

Since there is no equilibrium distribution when X is recurrent-null, we must have

$$\lim_{\gamma \to 1} \mathbf{v}_j = \mathbf{0}; \quad j = 0, 1, \ldots. \tag{5.39}$$

Hence, in order to talk sensibly about the "limiting distribution", some kind of normalisation must be applied. Multiply the queue size by $1 - \gamma$ and consider the process $Y = \{[I, J(1 - \gamma)]\}$. The limiting joint distribution of Y will be determined by means of the vector Laplace transform

$$\mathbf{h}(s) = [h_0(s), h_1(s), \ldots, h_N(s)], \tag{5.40}$$

where

$$h_i(s) = \lim_{\gamma \to 1} E[\delta(I = i)e^{-s(1-\gamma)J}]; \quad i = 0, 1, \ldots N, \qquad (5.41)$$

and $\delta(B)$ is the indicator of the boolean B: it is equal to 1 if B is true, 0 otherwise. In terms of the vectors $\mathbf{v}_j$, (5.40) is expressed as

$$\mathbf{h}(s) = \lim_{\gamma \to 1} \sum_{j=0}^{\infty} \mathbf{v}_j e^{-s(1-\gamma)j}. \qquad (5.42)$$

The objective will be to show that both the exact distribution, where the vectors $\mathbf{v}_j$ are given by (5.20), and the geometric approximation, where they are given by (5.38), have the same limiting distribution.

Consider first the exact distribution. When all eigenvalues are simple, the equations (5.20) and (5.39) imply that

$$\lim_{\gamma \to 1} \alpha_k \mathbf{u}_k = \mathbf{0}; \quad k = 1, 2, \ldots N + 1. \qquad (5.43)$$

This can be seen by taking $N + 1$ consecutive equations (5.20) and setting their left-hand sides to 0; the Vandermonde matrix involving powers of different eigenvalues is non-singular, and so the only solution is $\alpha_k \mathbf{u}_k = \mathbf{0}$.

On the other hand, since the environmental process has a finite number of states, and since the corresponding transition rates are fixed, the stationary marginal distribution of the environmental phase always exists and has a non-zero limit when $\gamma \to 1$. Denote that limit by the vector $\mathbf{q}$. This is the limiting eigenvector corresponding to the eigenvalue 1; it satisfies the equations

$$\mathbf{q}G = \mathbf{0}; \quad (\mathbf{q} \cdot \mathbf{1}) = 1, \qquad (5.44)$$

where G is the generator matrix of the environmental process. In terms of the matrix polynomial (5.15), G is the limiting matrix $Q(1) = Q_0 + Q_1 + Q_2$, obtained by replacing the changing traffic parameter with its limit. In particular, if the matrices B and C are diagonal, then $G = A - D^A$.

Hence, we can write

$$\lim_{\gamma \to 1} \sum_{j=0}^{\infty} \mathbf{v}_j = \mathbf{q}. \qquad (5.45)$$

Moreover, in view of (5.39), equation (5.45) holds if the lower index of the summation is $j = M$ (or any other non-negative integer), instead of $j = 0$.

Substituting (5.20) into (5.45) and changing the lower summation index to $j = M$ yields

$$\lim_{\gamma \to 1} \sum_{k=1}^{N+1} \alpha_k \mathbf{u}_k \frac{x_k^M}{1 - x_k} = \mathbf{q}. \tag{5.46}$$

However, the first N eigenvalues do not approach 1, while the last one, $x_{N+1} = \gamma$, does. Hence, according to (5.43), the first N terms in (5.46) vanish and leave

$$\lim_{\gamma \to 1} \frac{\alpha_{N+1} \mathbf{u}_{N+1}}{1 - \gamma} = \mathbf{q}. \tag{5.47}$$

Now, substituting (5.20) into (5.42), and arguing as for (5.47), we see that only the term involving the dominant eigenvalue survives:

$$\begin{aligned}
\mathbf{h}(s) &= \lim_{\gamma \to 1} \sum_{j=M}^{\infty} e^{-s(1-\gamma)j} \sum_{k=1}^{N+1} \alpha_k \mathbf{u}_k x_k^j \\
&= \lim_{\gamma \to 1} \sum_{k=1}^{N+1} \alpha_k \mathbf{u}_k \sum_{j=M}^{\infty} x_k^j e^{-s(1-\gamma)j} \\
&= \lim_{\gamma \to 1} \sum_{k=1}^{N+1} \alpha_k \mathbf{u}_k \frac{x_k^M e^{-s(1-\gamma)M}}{1 - x_k e^{-s(1-\gamma)}} \\
&= \lim_{\gamma \to 1} \frac{\alpha_{N+1} \mathbf{u}_{N+1}}{1 - \gamma e^{-s(1-\gamma)}}.
\end{aligned} \tag{5.48}$$

Combining this with (5.47) leads to

$$\mathbf{h}(s) = \mathbf{q} \lim_{\gamma \to 1} \frac{1 - \gamma}{1 - \gamma e^{-s(1-\gamma)}} = \mathbf{q} \frac{1}{1 + s}. \tag{5.49}$$

The last limit follows from L'Hospital's rule. The Laplace transform appearing in the right-hand side of (5.49) is that of the exponential distribution with mean 1. Thus we have established the following rather general result:

Proposition 5.3. *In any Markov-modulated queue, in the heavy-traffic limit $\gamma \to 1$, the environmental state I and the normalised queue size*

$(1 - \gamma)J$ are independent of each other. The first has distribution $\mathbf{q}$, while the second is distributed exponentially with mean 1.

It now remains to compare the limit (5.49) with the corresponding one for the geometric approximation, (5.38). Denote the approximate limiting vector Laplace transform by $\hat{\mathbf{h}}(s)$; it is given by (5.42), with $\mathbf{v}_j$ replaced by the approximations (5.38):

$$
\begin{aligned}
\hat{\mathbf{h}}(s) &= \lim_{\gamma \to 1} \frac{\mathbf{u}_{N+1}}{(\mathbf{u}_{N+1} \cdot \mathbf{1})} \sum_{j=0}^{\infty} (1 - \gamma)\gamma^j e^{-s(1-\gamma)j} \\
&= \lim_{\gamma \to 1} \frac{\mathbf{u}_{N+1}}{(\mathbf{u}_{N+1} \cdot \mathbf{1})} \lim_{\gamma \to 1} \frac{1 - \gamma}{1 - \gamma e^{-s(1-\gamma)}} \\
&= \frac{1}{1+s} \lim_{\gamma \to 1} \frac{\mathbf{u}_{N+1}}{(\mathbf{u}_{N+1} \cdot \mathbf{1})},
\end{aligned}
\tag{5.50}
$$

again using L'Hospital's rule.

The last limit in the right-hand side of (5.50) is simply the vector $\mathbf{q}$. This can be seen by arguing that the normalised left eigenvector of the eigenvalue γ must approach the normalised left eigenvector of the eigenvalue 1. Alternatively, multiply both sides of (5.47) by the column vector $\mathbf{1}$:

$$
\lim_{\gamma \to 1} \frac{\alpha_{N+1}(\mathbf{u}_{N+1} \cdot \mathbf{1})}{1 - \gamma} = 1.
\tag{5.51}
$$

Hence rewrite (5.47) as

$$
\lim_{\gamma \to 1} \frac{\mathbf{u}_{N+1}}{(\mathbf{u}_{N+1} \cdot \mathbf{1})} = \mathbf{q}.
\tag{5.52}
$$

Thus we have

$$
\hat{\mathbf{h}}(s) = \mathbf{q}\frac{1}{1+s} = \mathbf{h}(s).
\tag{5.53}
$$

So, in heavy traffic, the geometric approximation is asymptotically exact, in the sense that it yields the same limiting normalised distribution of environmental phase and queue size as the exact solution.

5.10. Applications and comparisons

It is instructive to present some numerical experiments aimed at evaluating the accuracy of the geometric approximation in the context of two different models of Markov-modulated queues. In all cases, the exact values of the performance measures are computed by applying the full spectral expansion solution (5.20).

The first system examined is the network of two nodes in tandem, with manufacturing blocking at node 1. The model is illustrated in Fig. 5.3. The parameters are λ (external arrival rate), μ (service rate at node 1), ξ (service rate at node 2) and N (the storage capacity at node 2 is $N - 1$).

In this system, the unbounded queue at node 1 is modulated by a finite-state environment defined by node 2. The environment, I, is in state i if there are i jobs at node 2 and server 1 is not blocked ($i = 0, 1, \ldots, N - 1$). An extra state, $I = N$, is needed to describe the situation where there are $N - 1$ jobs at node 2 and server 1 is blocked.

The pair $X = \{(I, J)\}$, where J is the number of jobs at node 1, is a QBD process. The transitions out of state (i, j) were given earlier.

Because the environmental process is coupled with the queueing process, the marginal distribution of the former (i.e. the number of jobs at node 2), cannot be determined without finding the joint distribution of I and J. There is no simple expression for the stability condition.

Figure 5.4 illustrates the close agreement between the exact solution of this model and the geometric approximation (5.38), when the system is heavily loaded. The performance measure is the average size of the unbounded queue; it is plotted against the arrival rate, λ. The service rates

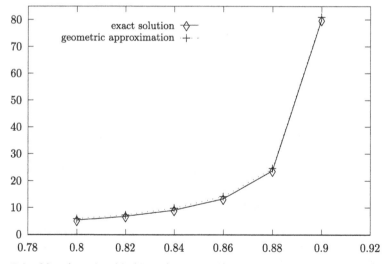

Fig. 5.4.   Manufacturing blocking: Average node 1 queue size against arrival rate, $N = 10$, $\mu = 1$, $\xi = 1$.

at nodes 1 and 2 are the same. Hence, the busier node 1, the higher the likelihood that the buffer will fill up and cause blocking. Because of that, the saturation point is not at $\lambda = 1$ (as it would be if node 1 was isolated), but at approximately $\lambda = 0.909$.

The geometric approximation for the marginal distribution of the environmental variable, I, indicating the number of jobs at node 2 and whether or not node 1 is blocked, is given by (5.38) as $\mathbf{q} \approx \mathbf{u}_{N+1}/(\mathbf{u}_{N+1} \cdot \mathbf{1})$. Since there are two environmental states, $I = N-1$ and $I = N$, representing $N-1$ jobs at node 2, the average length of the node 2 queue, L_2, is given by

$$L_2 = \sum_{i=1}^{N-1} iq_i + (N-1)q_N,$$

where q_i is the $i+1$st element of the vector $\mathbf{q}$. Figure 5.5 compares the exact value of L_2 with that provided by the geometric approximation, for the same parameters as in Fig. 5.4. It can be seen that this time the approximation is relatively less accurate, and converges to the exact solution more slowly. Intuitively, this is due to the fact that, in order to obtain an accurate value for L_2, *all* elements of $\mathbf{q}$ need to be accurate. Whereas, in a heavily loaded unbounded queue, only the tail of the distribution is important.

In Fig. 5.6, the average unbounded queue size is plotted against N. Increasing the size of the finite buffer enlarges the environmental state

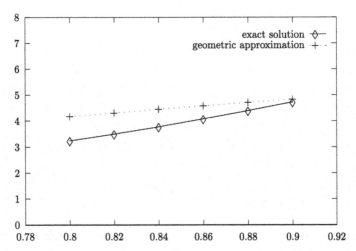

Fig. 5.5.   Manufacturing blocking: Average node 2 queue size against arrival rate, $N = 10$, $\mu = 1$, $\xi = 1$.

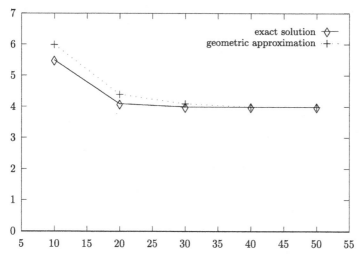

Fig. 5.6. Manufacturing blocking: Average node 1 queue size against N, $\lambda = 0.8$, $\mu = 1$, $\xi = 1$.

space. Consequently, the exact solution needs to compute more eigenvalues and eigenvectors, and solve larger sets of linear equations.

The accuracy of the geometric approximation is seen to increase with N. This is not really surprising, because enlarging the intermediate buffer reduces the coupling between the two nodes, making them behave more like independent queues. Nevertheless, the exact solution begins to experience numerical difficulties when $N > 35$. The software (Matlab) starts issuing warnings to the effect that the matrix is ill-conditioned, and the results may not be reliable (as it happens, the results returned seem fine). Of course the approximation displays no such symptoms, since it has no equations to solve.

The second model to be evaluated is that of the multiserver queue with breakdowns and repairs, described at the beginning of the chapter (Fig. 5.2). The parameters are λ (arrival rate; it will be assumed independent of the operative state of the servers), μ (service rate), ξ (breakdown rate), η (repair rate) and N (number of servers. The queue evolves in a Markovian environment which is in phase i ($i = 0, 1, \ldots, N$) when there are i operative servers.

In applying the geometric approximation to this model, there is a choice of approaches. One could use (5.37) for $j \geq N$, together with the balance equations for $j < N$. This will be referred to as the "partial geometric"

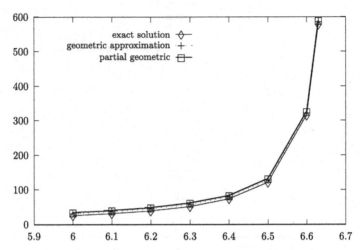

Fig. 5.7. Breakdowns and repairs: Average queue size against arrival rate, $N = 10$, $\mu = 1$, $\xi = 0.05$, $\eta = 0.1$.

approximation. Alternatively, the geometric approximation (5.38) can be used for all $j \geq 0$.

Intuitively, the partial geometric approximation can be expected to be more accurate, since it satisfies more of the balance equations. In fact, the results in Fig. 5.7 suggest that the opposite is true. The average queue size is plotted against the arrival rate, with parameters chosen so that the system is heavily loaded (the saturation point is $\lambda = 6.666\ldots$). It turns out that the simple geometric approximation is more accurate than the more complex partial geometric one. There seem to be two opposing effects here. On the one hand, relying only on the dominant eigenvalue tends to overestimate the average queue size; on the other hand, the additional approximation introduced by ignoring the boundary balance equations reduces that overestimation.

Since the marginal distribution of the environmental variable I is known to be given by (5.4), there is not much point in trying to approximate it. However, if the geometric approximation is nevertheless applied, e.g. to compute the average number of operative servers, then a similar picture to Fig. 5.5 emerges. The approximation improves when λ increases, even though the exact value of the average does not depend on λ.

In Fig. 5.8, the average queue size is evaluated for increasing number of servers, and hence decreasing load. This experiment disproves the conjecture that the geometric approximation always overestimates the exact

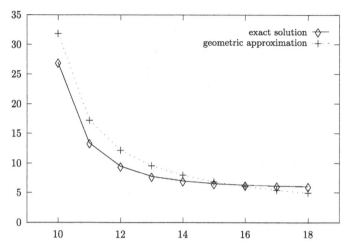

Fig. 5.8. Breakdowns and repairs: Average queue size against number of servers, $\lambda = 6$, $\mu = 1$, $\xi = 0.05$, $\eta = 0.1$.

values. Here the approximation starts off as an overestimate, but as N increases, it becomes an underestimate.

As in the previous model, when N becomes large (greater than about 30), the exact solution begins to warn of possible numerical problems due to ill-conditioned matrices; the geometric approximation does not display such symptoms.

5.11. Remarks

The presentation in this chapter is based on material from [8, 10, 11]. It is perhaps worth mentioning that there are two other solution techniques that can be used in the context of Markov-modulated queues. These are the matrix-geometric method (Neuts, [12]) and the generating functions method (as applied, for example, in [9]). However, we have chosen to concentrate on the spectral expansion solution method because it is versatile, readily implementable and efficient. A strong case can be made for using it, whenever possible, in preference to the other methods [10]. An additional point in its favour is that it provides the basis for a simple approximate solution.

The geometric approximation is valid for a large class of heavily loaded systems. The arguments presented here do not rely on any particular model structure. One could relax the QBD assumption and allow batch arrivals and departures. As long as there is a spectral expansion solution with finitely many eigenvalues, there would be a single dominant eigenvalue and therefore the geometric approximation would be asymptotically exact in heavy traffic. Moreover, it *may* also be reasonable for moderate and light loads, as the examples in Figs. 5.5 and 5.8 illustrate.

References

1. Buzacott, J. A. and Shanthikumar, J. G. (1993). *Stochastic Models of Manufacturing Systems*, Prentice-Hall.
2. Daigle, J. N. and Lucantoni, D. M. (1991). Queueing systems having phase-dependent arrival and service rates, in *Numerical Solutions of Markov Chains*, (ed. W. J. Stewart), Marcel Dekker.
3. Gail, H. R., Hantler, S. L. and Taylor, B. A. (1996). Spectral analysis of M/G/1 and G/M/1 type Markov chains, *Adv. in Appl. Prob.*, **28**, 114–165.
4. Gohberg, I., Lancaster, P. and Rodman, L. (1982). *Matrix Polynomials*, Academic Press.
5. Jennings, A. (1977). *Matrix Computations for Engineers and Scientists*, Wiley.
6. Konheim, A. G. and Reiser, M. (1976). A queueing model with finite waiting room and blocking, *JACM*, **23**(2), 328–341.
7. Latouche, G., Jacobs, P. A. and Gaver, D. P. (1984). Finite Markov chain models skip-free in one direction, *Naval Res. Log. Quart.*, **31**, 571–588.
8. Mitrani, I. (2005). Approximate Solutions for Heavily Loaded Markov Modulated Queues, *Performance Evaluation*, **62**, 117–131.
9. Mitrani, I. and Avi-Itzhak, B. (1968). A many-server queue with service interruptions, *Operations Research*, **16**(3), 628–638.
10. Mitrani, I. and Chakka, R. (1995). Spectral expansion solution for a class of Markov models: Application and comparison with the matrix-geometric method, *Performance Evaluation*.
11. Mitrani, I. and Mitra, D. (1991). A spectral expansion method for random walks on semi-infinite strips, *IMACS Symposium on Iterative Methods in Linear Algebra*, Brussels.
12. Neuts, M. F. (1981). *Matrix Geometric Solutions in Stochastic Models*, John Hopkins Press.
13. Neuts, M. F. and Lucantoni, D. M. (1979). A Markovian queue with N servers subject to breakdowns and repairs, *Management Science*, **25**, 849–861.

Chapter 6

Diffusion Approximation Methods
for General Queueing Networks

6.1. Introduction

Although considerable progress has been made in obtaining exact solutions
for large classes of queueing network models, one particularly simple type of
network, *an arbitrary network with first-come-first-served (FCFS) service
discipline and general distribution function of service time at the servers*,
has proved to be resilient to all approaches except for approximate solution
techniques. In this chapter our attention is limited to this type of queueing
network.

Several approximation methods have been suggested for its treatment.
On the one hand there are diffusion approximations [9, 10, 20] applicable
to two-station networks or to general queueing networks [11, 12, 13, 16, 22]
and on the other hand we have iterative techniques [5, 23]. The convergence
of the latter to the exact solution is not an established fact and we know
that the former tend, in certain simple cases, to the exact solution.

Most of the work published in the literature has concentrated on
evaluating the joint probability distribution of queue lengths for all the
queues in a network, but it is seldom possible to make use of this complete
information. In measurements on computer systems it is difficult enough to
collect data on the performance of a single resource, and the measurement
of joint data for several resources could become very time- and space-
consuming. The same can be said of simulation experiments where the task
of computing confidence intervals for estimated joint statistics becomes
impractical. Furthermore, when it comes to computing average response
times or queue lengths it suffices to know the average response time
encountered in each individual queue. Therefore it would suffice in many
cases to be able to compute with satisfactory accuracy the probability
distribution for the queue length at each individual resource.

The purpose of this chapter is to present an approximation method for general queueing networks: the diffusion approximations, which are particularly useful in treating open networks of queues. Both systems with single and with multiple classes will be considered.

We shall briefly review the approach based on the work of Kobayashi and Reiser [16, 22] using reflecting boundaries, but the bulk of the presentation will follow the work of Gelenbe and Pujolle [10, 11, 12, 13] which uses the instantaneous return model. We have two reasons for this: the latter approach, as we shall see below, leads to better models of the behaviour of system queues even when the traffic is light; furthermore, it has been shown in numerous cases that the results thus obtained are more accurate.

6.2. Diffusion approximation for a single queue

A promising method for the approximation of queueing systems with general service time distributions has originated with the work of Newell [20] and Gaver and Shedler [9] who suggested the use of a diffusion process to approximate the number in queue. The idea of the method is to replace the discrete number of jobs in the queue by a continuous variable which, according to the central limit theorem, will be approximately normally distributed under heavy traffic conditions. Consider for instance the $GI/G/1$ queue; basic to the diffusion approximation for this model is the assumption that as soon as a busy period begins (i.e. a customer arrives to a previously empty system) the stochastic process representing the number in queue is adequately approximated by the predictions of the central limit theorem which in reality are only valid asymptotically (as the duration of the busy period tends to infinity).

Several questions arise in the choice of the approximate diffusion process model:

(i) the choice of the appropriate boundary conditions;
(ii) the choice of the diffusion parameters b, α which characterise the drift and instantaneous variance of the process;
(iii) the selection of the discretisation step which may be used to work back to a discrete probability distribution from the continuous density of the diffusion process.

Before describing results for such general networks, we present two informal approaches to diffusion approximations of queue behaviour.

There are two ways in which we may intuitively understand the basis for diffusion approximations. The first uses a numerical analysis analogy, while the second calls upon the central limit theorem.

6.2.1. *Queues and the numerical discretisation of the diffusion equation*

Consider the following partial differential equation known as the "diffusion equation":

$$-\frac{\partial}{\partial t}f(x,t) - b\frac{\partial}{\partial x}f(x,t) + \frac{\alpha}{2}\frac{\partial^2}{\partial x^2}f(x,t) = 0 \tag{6.1}$$

where $f(x,t)$ is a function of space, the x variable, and of time t. $f(x,t)$ is chosen to be, for each t, the probability density function of a non-negative random variable $X(t)$:

$$Pr[x \leq X(t) < x + \mathrm{d}x] = f(x,t)\mathrm{d}x.$$

Equation (6.1) can be solved if an initial condition ($f(x,0)$ for all values of $x \geq 0$) and a boundary condition (conditions which must be satisfied by $f(0,t)$ and $\partial f(0,t)/\partial t$ are provided. We shall consider the following boundary condition given in terms of $P(t)$ a probability mass, function of time, located at the boundary point $x = 0$:

$$\frac{\mathrm{d}}{\mathrm{d}t}P(t) = -cP(t) + \lim_{x \to 0+}\left[-bf(x,t) + \frac{1}{2}\alpha\frac{\partial f(x,t)}{\partial x}\right] \tag{6.2}$$

$$f(0,t) = 0.$$

$P(t)$ and $f(x,t)$ are constrained so that

$$P(t) + \int_0^\infty f(x,t)\mathrm{d}x = 1$$

and $P(t)$ is interpreted as

$$P(t) = Pr[X(t) = 0].$$

Equations (6.1) and (6.2) are to be viewed, for the moment, simply as formal relations. The interpretation in terms of queueing phenomena can be obtained either in terms of their discretisation (as will be done here), or via the central limit theorem as in section 2.2.

Suppose that we discretise the x variable using the grid $x_0 = 0$, $x_i = i\Delta$, $i \geq 1$, with the constant discretisation step δ. Then, using standard numerical analysis techniques we can make the following approximations:

$$\frac{\partial}{\partial x} f(x_i, t) \approx \frac{f_{i+1}(t) - f_i(t)}{\delta}$$

$$\frac{\partial^2}{\partial x^2} f(x_i, t) \approx \frac{f_{i+1}(t) - 2f_i(t) + f_{i-1}(t)}{\delta^2}$$

where $f_i(t) \equiv f(x_i, t)$. The approximation to (6.1) and (6.2) is then for $i \geq 1$:

$$\frac{d}{dt} f_i(t) = \left(-\frac{b}{\delta} + \frac{\alpha}{2\delta^2}\right) f_{i+1} + \left(\frac{b}{\delta} - \frac{\alpha}{2\delta^2}\right) f_i + \frac{\alpha}{2\delta^2} f_{i-1} \qquad (6.3)$$

and

$$\frac{d}{dt} P(t) = -cP(t) + \frac{\alpha}{2\delta} f_1(t) \qquad (6.4)$$

where we have made use in (6.4) of the boundary condition (6.2).

Let us now call

$$p_0(t) \equiv P(t) \quad \text{and} \quad p_i(t) \equiv \Delta f_i(t)$$

so that

$$\sum_{i=0}^{M} p_i(t) \approx \int_0^{M\Delta} f(x, t) dx + P(t).$$

We can write (6.3), (6.4) as

$$\left.\begin{aligned}
\delta \frac{d}{dt} p_i(t) &= \left(\frac{\alpha}{2\delta} - b\right) p_{i+1} - \left(\frac{\alpha}{2\delta} - b\right) p_i + \frac{\alpha}{2\delta} p_{i-1}, \quad i \geq 1 \\
\frac{d}{dt} p_0(t) &= \frac{\alpha}{2\delta^2} p_1(t) - cp_0(t).
\end{aligned}\right\} \qquad (6.5)$$

Now, if we choose

$$c \equiv \lambda = \mu \equiv \alpha/2, \quad b = 0, \quad \delta = 1$$

we see that (6.5) are the Chapman–Kolmogorov equations for the $M/M/1$ queue with arrival rate λ equal to the service rate μ (see Chapter 1). Thus we can conclude that for this special case ($\lambda = \mu$), the diffusion equation is approximated by the equation for the $M/M/1$ queue and vice versa.

If we seek the *stationary solution* of (6.1), (6.2) or (6.5), then these equations are approximations of each other under general conditions.

Set $\partial f/\partial t = 0$, $\mathrm{d}P/\mathrm{d}t = 0$ in (6.3), (6.4) and $\mathrm{d}p_i(t) = 0$ in (6.5). Furthermore, let us use the notation:

$$\lambda' = \alpha/2\delta, \quad \mu = (\alpha/2\delta) - b, \quad \text{or} \quad b = \lambda - \mu$$

$$c = \lambda(1 + b/\mu) = \lambda^2/\mu.$$

Then, in steady-state (6.1), (6.2) become:

$$(\lambda - \mu)\frac{\partial f(x)}{\partial x} = \lambda\delta\frac{\partial^2 f(x)}{\partial x^2}, \quad f(0) = 0$$

$$(\lambda^2/\mu)P = \lambda\delta\left.\frac{\partial f(x)}{\partial x}\right|_{x=0}$$

where P and $f(x)$ denote the stationary solution. Similarly, for (6.5) we have

$$(\lambda + \mu)p_i = \mu p_{i+1} + \lambda p_{i-1}, \quad i \geq 1$$

$$\mu p_1 = \lambda p_0.$$

If $\lambda < \mu$, which is satisfied if $b < 0$, the stationary solution of the $M/M/1$ queue length equations have the well-known stationary solution

$$p_i = (\lambda/\mu)^i(1 - \lambda/\mu)$$

so that the diffusion equation has the approximate stationary solution

$$P \approx p_0; \quad f(i\delta) \approx p_i/\delta, \quad i \geq 1.$$

6.2.2. *An approach based on the central limit theorem*

Consider a single-server system and let $A(t)$ be the cumulative number of arrivals up to time t, and $D(t)$ be the cumulative number of departures up to time t. Suppose that the queue is initially empty. Then the number of units in queue (including the unit being serviced) at time t is given by

$$Q(t) = A(t) - D(t).$$

The change in the queue length between times t and $t + T$ is

$$Q(t + T) - Q(t) = [A(t + T) - A(t)] - [D(t + T) - D(t)],$$

or

$$\Delta Q(t) = \Delta A(t) - \Delta D(t).$$

Let the interarrival times and service times be sequences of independent and identically distributed random variables, with means and variances given by $(1/\lambda, V_a)$ and $(1/\mu, V_s)$, respectively. Then on the basis of the central limit theorem it can be shown that if T is sufficiently large so that many events take place between t and $t + T$ and if $Q(t)$ does not become zero in this interval, then $\Delta Q(t)$ should be approximately normally distributed with

$$E[\Delta Q(t)] = (\lambda - \mu)T = bT$$

and

$$\text{Var}[\Delta Q(t)] = (\lambda K_a^2 + \mu K_s^2)T = \alpha T$$

where $K_a^2 = V_a/(1/\lambda)^2$ is the square of the coefficient of variation of the interarrival times ($K_a^2 = 1$ for $M/G/1$ queues) and $K_s^2 = V_s/(1/\mu)^2$ is the square of the coefficient of variation of the service times. Hence, if the queue is not empty at time t, the number in it can be approximated by a continuous stochastic process $\{X(t), t \geq 0\}$ whose density function

$$f(x,t)\mathrm{d}x = Pr\{x \leq X(t) < x + \mathrm{d}x\}$$

satisfies the Kolmogorov forward diffusion equation (also known as the Fokker–Planck equation)(6.1):

$$-\frac{\partial}{\partial t}f(x,t) - b\frac{\partial}{\partial x}f(x,t) + \frac{\alpha}{2}\frac{\partial^2}{\partial x^2}f(x,t) = 0$$

where $\{X(t), t \geq 0\}$ is the continuous-path stochastic process approximating the number in queue.

Since the approach was initially intended for heavy traffic conditions it is also assumed that the lower boundary at $x = 0$ for the process $\{X(t), t \geq 0\}$ should act as a reflecting boundary. This last assumption implies that no probability mass can collect at $x = 0$.

From (6.1) we may write (for $f = f(x,t)$)

$$\int_{0+}^{\infty} \frac{\partial f}{\partial t}\mathrm{d}x = \int_{0+}^{\infty}\left[-b\frac{\partial}{\partial x}f + \frac{\alpha}{2}\frac{\partial^2 f}{\partial x^2}\right]\mathrm{d}x = \left[-bf + \frac{\alpha}{2}\frac{\partial f}{\partial x}\right]_{0+}^{\infty}.$$

The left-hand side must be zero because the total probability mass is one, and no probability mass collects at $x = 0$. Therefore, for all $t \geq 0$,

$$bf(0^+,t) = \frac{\alpha}{2}\frac{\partial f}{\partial x}(0^+,t)$$

since at $x = +\infty$ both $f(x,t)$ and $(\partial f/\partial x)$ must vanish if f is a probability density.

The steady-state distribution of $X(t)$ can be obtained from (6.1) by eliminating the dependence on t: replacing $f(x,t)$ by $f(x)$ and equating $\partial f/\partial t$ to zero, together with the requirement that

$$\int_0^\infty f(x)\mathrm{d}x = 1$$

leads to the unique steady-state solution

$$f(x) = -\gamma \mathrm{e}^{\gamma x}, \quad x \geq 0$$

$$= 0, \qquad x < 0$$

where $\gamma = 2b/\alpha = -2(1-\rho)/(\rho K_a^2 + K_s^2)$, provided that $\gamma < 0$, or $\rho = \lambda/\mu < 1$. This expression has an important shortcoming: the probability that the queue is empty, which should be $(1-\rho)$, is not available. Therefore the following heuristic modification has been suggested [16, 22]. Let $\hat{p}(i)$ denote the diffusion approximation to the probability that the queue is of length i in stationary state. Then take

$$\hat{p}(0) = 1 - \rho$$

$$\hat{p}(i) = \rho(1-\hat{\rho})\hat{\rho}^{i-1}, \quad i \geq 1$$

for $\hat{\rho} = \mathrm{e}^\gamma$.

6.2.3. *The instantaneous return process [10, 11]*

The diffusion process we shall present in this section is a generalisation of standard diffusion processes. To simplify and motivate the description of our model we shall imagine that the stochastic process $\{X(t), t \geq 0\}$ (which will be used to approximate the number in queue) represents the position of a particle moving on the closed interval $[0, M]$ of the real line. When the particle is in the open interval $]0, M[$ its motion is described by a diffusion process, where b and α, the mean and variance of the instantaneous rate of change of $X(t)$, are given by

$$b = \lim_{\Delta t \to 0} \frac{E[X(t+\Delta t) - X(t)]}{\Delta t}$$

$$\alpha = \lim_{\Delta t \to 0} \frac{E[(X(t+\Delta t) - X(t))^2] - (E[X(t+\Delta t) - X(t)])^2}{\Delta t}.$$

For our present purposes it is not necessary that b and α be functions of x, t; this restriction can be relaxed, however.

When the particle reaches the lower boundary of the interval $[0, M[$ it remains there for a period of time h which is a random variable, at the end of which it "jumps" instantaneously back into the open interval $]0, M]$ to a random point whose position is defined by the probability density function $f_1(x)$. Let us denote by $f_h(r)$ the probability density function of h. Let $f_h^*(s)$ be the Laplace transform of $f_h(r)$ and suppose that it has the form

$$f_h^*(s) = \int_0^\infty e^{-sr} f_h(r) dr = \sum_{i=1}^n (1 - b_i) a_i \prod_{j=1}^i \frac{\lambda_j}{(s + \lambda_j)}$$

where

$$a_i = \begin{cases} 1 & \text{if } i = 1 \\ b_1 \ldots b_{i-1} & \text{if } i > 1, \ 0 < b_i \le 1. \end{cases}$$

This is the Coxian, or method of stages, representation of a Laplace transform. We saw in Chapter 3 that it approximates almost general density functions.

When the particle hits the upper boundary at $x = M$ it remains there for a random holding time H whose probability density function $f_H(r)$ is also Coxian and its Laplace transform is

$$f_H^*(s) = \int_0^\infty e^{-sr} f_H(r) dr = \sum_{i=1}^m (1 - B_i) A_i \prod_{j=1}^i \frac{\mu_j}{(s + \mu_j)}$$

where

$$A_i = \begin{cases} 1 & \text{if } i = 1 \\ B_1 \ldots B_{i-1} & \text{if } i > 1, \ 0 < B_i \le 1. \end{cases}$$

At the end of the holding time at the upper boundary the particle jumps back instantaneously to a random point in $]0, M[$ whose position is determined by the probability density function $f_2(x).f_1(x)$ and $f_2(x)$ may be taken to be functions of the instant at which the jumps occur.

Notice that

$$E[h] = \sum_{i=1}^n \frac{a_i}{\lambda_i};$$

similarly,

$$E[H] = \sum_{i=1}^{m} \frac{A_i}{\mu_i}.$$

Let us introduce the notation

$$\lambda = (E[h])^{-1}, \quad \mu = (E[H])^{-1}.$$

For the variances of h and H we have, from Chapter 3,

$$\mathrm{Var}(h) = \sum_{i=1}^{n} \frac{a_i}{\lambda_i^2}, \quad \mathrm{Var}(H) = \sum_{i=1}^{n} \frac{A_i}{\mu_i^2}.$$

It is easy to see that the process $\{X(t), t \geq 0\}$ defined in this section is non-Markovian: once the particle is at any one of the boundaries the additional time it will remain there is not independent of the amount of time it has resided at the boundary up to the present instant.

Let $f = f(x, t)$ denote the probability density function of the stochastic process $\{X(t), t \geq 0\}$ in the open interval $]0, M[$ and let $A_{x,t}$ and $C_{x,t}$ be operators defined by

$$A_{x,t}f = -\frac{\partial}{\partial t}f - \frac{\partial}{\partial x}bf + \frac{1}{2}\frac{\partial^2}{\partial x^2}\alpha f$$

$$C_{x,t}f = -bf + \frac{1}{2}\frac{\partial}{\partial x}\alpha f.$$

Also, let $P_i(t)$, $1 \leq i \leq n$, be the probability that the particle is in the i-th stage of the holding time at the lower boundary at time t while $Q_i(t)$, $1 \leq i \leq m$, is the probability that it is in the i-th stage of the holding time at the upper boundary at time t. The equations describing the evolution of the particle are

$$A_{x,t}f + \sum_{i=1}^{n} \lambda_i(1 - b_i)P_i(t)f_1(x) + \sum_{i=1}^{m} \mu_i(1 - B_i)Q_i(t)f_2(x) = 0 \quad (6.6)$$

$$\frac{\mathrm{d}}{\mathrm{d}t}P_i(t) = \begin{cases} -\lambda_1 P_1(t) + C_{0,t}f & \text{if } i = 1 \\ -\lambda_i P_i(t) + \lambda_{i-1}b_{i-1}P_{i-1}(t) & \text{if } 1 < i \leq n \end{cases} \quad (6.7)$$

$$\frac{\mathrm{d}}{\mathrm{d}t}Q_i(t) = \begin{cases} -\mu_1 Q_1(t) - C_{M,t}f & \text{if } i = 1 \\ -\mu_i Q_i(t) + \mu_{i-1}B_{i-1}Q_{i-1}(t) & \text{if } 1 < i \leq m \end{cases} \quad (6.8)$$

where

$$C_{0,t}f = \lim_{x \to 0} \left[-bf + \frac{1}{2}\frac{\partial}{\partial x}\alpha f \right]$$

$$C_{M,t}f = \lim_{x \to M} \left[-bf + \frac{1}{2}\frac{\partial}{\partial x}\alpha f \right]$$

$$\lambda = (E[h])^{-1}, \quad \mu = (E[H])^{-1}.$$

Define $P(t)$ as the probability that the particle is at the lower boundary at time t, and let $Q(t)$ be the corresponding quantity for the upper boundary:

$$P(t) = \sum_{i=1}^{n} P_i(t), \quad Q(t) = \sum_{i=1}^{m} Q_i(t).$$

From (6.7), (6.8) we obtain

$$\frac{\mathrm{d}}{\mathrm{d}t}P(t) = -\sum_{i=1}^{n} \lambda_i(1 - b_i)P_i(t) + C_{0,t}f \tag{6.9}$$

$$\frac{\mathrm{d}}{\mathrm{d}t}Q(t) = -\sum_{i=1}^{m} \mu_i(1 - B_i)Q_i(t) - C_{M,t}f. \tag{6.10}$$

Equations (6.6), (6.7), (6.8) are simple to interpret. Suppose Ω is a subinterval of $]0, M[$. Then (6.6) can be deduced from

$$\frac{\partial}{\partial t}\int_{\Omega} f\mathrm{d}x = \int_{\Omega} \left[-\frac{\partial}{\partial x}bf + \frac{1}{2}\frac{\partial^2}{\partial x^2}\alpha f \right] \mathrm{d}x + \sum_{i=1}^{n} \lambda_i(1 - b_i)P_i(t)\int_{\Omega} f_1(x)\mathrm{d}x$$

$$+ \sum_{i=1}^{m} \mu_i(1 - B_i)Q_i(t)\int_{\Omega} f_2(x)\mathrm{d}x \tag{6.11}$$

which states that the rate of change of the probability mass in Ω is equal to the rate of flow of the probability mass out of Ω (the first term on the right-hand side of (6.11)) plus the rate of flow into Ω from $x = 0$ and from $x = M$ (the second and third terms, respectively, on the right-hand side). In order to deduce (6.7), notice that for $1 < i \le n$ we may write for any $t \ge 0$,

$$P_i(t + \Delta t) = (1 - \lambda_i\Delta t)P_i(t) + \lambda_{i-1}b_{i-1}\Delta t P_{i-1}(t)$$

since the time the particle spends in any one of the stages of the Cox distribution is exponentially distributed; by collecting terms, dividing both sides by Δt and taking $\Delta t \to 0$, this yields (6.7) for $1 < i \le n$ in the usual way. To obtain (6.7) with $i = 1$ a similar procedure is applied if one notices that $C_{0,t}f$ is the flow of probability mass *out* of $]0, M[$ from the lower boundary and, of course, into the first stage of the holding time at $x = 0$. A similar interpretation can be given for (6.8); notice now that $-C_{M,t}f$ is the flow of probability mass away from $]0, M[$ via the upper boundary.

In addition to (6.6), (6.7), (6.8) appropriate boundary conditions for $f(x,t)$ must be specified and initial conditions (at $t = 0$) must be given for the stochastic process. Since the boundaries at $x = 0$ and $x = M$ behave as absorbing boundaries during their respective holding times we set $\lim_{x \to 0} f(x,t) = \lim_{x \to M} f(x,t) = 0$ for all $t \geq 0$. Of course, we set

$$\int_0^M f\,\mathrm{d}x + P(t) + Q(t) = 1.$$

We shall now prove that the stationary solution P, Q, f of (6.6), (6.9), (6.10) depends only on the average holding time λ^{-1}, μ^{-1} on the boundaries $x = 0$, $x = M$ and not on the complete density functions $f_h(r)$, $f_H(r)$. We set

$$\frac{\mathrm{d}P_i(t)}{\mathrm{d}t} = 0, \quad \frac{\mathrm{d}Q_i(t)}{\mathrm{d}t} = 0, \quad \frac{\partial t(x,t)}{\partial t} = 0$$

in (6.6), (6.7), (6.8) to obtain the relationships

$$P_1 = \lambda_1^{-1}C_0 f, \quad P_i = (\lambda_{i-1}b_{i-1}/\lambda_i)P_{i-1}, \quad 1 < i \leq n$$

so that

$$P_i = \lambda_i b_1 \ldots b_{i-1}C_0 f = \frac{a_i}{\lambda_i}C_0 f, \quad 1 < i \leq n.$$

Therefore,

$$P = \sum_1^n P_i = \lambda^{-1}C_0 f;$$

similarly, we can show that

$$Q = -\mu^{-1}C_M f.$$

But

$$\sum_{i=1}^n \lambda_i(1 - b_i)P_i = \sum_{i=1}^n a_i(1 - b_i)C_0 f = C_0 f$$

and similarly

$$\sum_{i=1}^{m} \mu_i(1 - B_i)Q_i = -C_M f.$$

Therefore (6.6), (6.9), (6.10) become in stationary state

$$A_x f + \lambda P f_1(x) + \mu Q f_2(x) = 0 \qquad (6.12)$$

$$\lambda P = C_0 f \qquad (6.13)$$

$$\mu Q = -C_M f. \qquad (6.14)$$

Since these equations depend on $E[h]$ and $E[H]$ only we have proved that the stationary probabilities $f(x), P, Q$ are independent of the higher moments of h and H.

This result shows that if we are interested in approximating the stationary queue length probability distribution using the instantaneous return process, it suffices to use a model where h and H are *exponential* This is the assumption we will make in the sequel.

6.2.4. *Application to the GI/G/1 queue: stationary solution*

In this section we propose an approximation to the number of customers in a single-server queue with general service time distribution of mean $1/\mu$ and variance V_s independent of the interarrival times or of queue length, and with independent interarrival times having a general distribution function with mean $1/\lambda$ and variance V_a. The stochastic process $\{X(t), t \geq 0\}$ approximating the number in queue at time t takes values on the non-negative real line $[0, \infty[$; it will be an instantaneous return process. In this model the case $X(t) = 0$ refers to the empty queue; an arrival at time t to the empty queue corresponds to an instantaneous jump of $X(t)$ from 0 to 1, hence we take in (6.6), $f_1(x) = \delta(x - 1)$. For a finite value of t there can be no probability mass at infinity hence we only have a probability mass $P(t)$ at the origin. The parameters b and α in the operators $A_{x,t}$ and $C_{x,t}$ are chosen from the predictions of the central limit theorem as in section 2.1:

$$b = \lambda - \mu$$

$$\alpha = \lambda^3 V_a + \mu^3 V_s = \lambda K_a^2 + \mu K_s^2.$$

It is important to note that in our approximation method the random variable h refers to the time interval between the last departure from the queue in a busy period to the first arrival of the next busy period. If the arrival process is Poisson it is natural to take $\lambda = (E[h])^{-1}$. However, if the arrival process is not Poisson then the interarrival time distribution and the distribution of h need not be the same. Let us consider the case where $(E[h])^{-1} = \lambda' \neq \lambda$.

The instantaneous return process approximation in stationary state for the $GI/G/1$ queue is represented by the equations obtained from (6.12), (6.13):

$$-b\frac{\partial f}{\partial x} + \frac{1}{2}\alpha\frac{\partial^2 t}{\partial x^2} + \lambda' P \delta(x-1) = 0 \tag{6.15}$$

$$\lambda' P = C_0 f. \tag{6.16}$$

Notice that the term $f_1(x)$ in (6.12) has been replaced by the Dirac density function concentrated at $x = 1, \delta(x-1)$. This represents the fact that when an arrival occurs, the queue length jumps instantaneously from $x = 0$ to $x = 1$. In addition to (6.15) and (6.16) we also use $f(0) = 0$ and

$$P + \int_{0+}^{\infty} f(x)\mathrm{d}x = 1.$$

The solution to (6.15), (6.16) is

$$f = \begin{cases} R[e^{-\gamma} - 1]e^{\gamma x}, & x \geq 1 \\ R[1 - e^{\gamma x}], & 0 \leq x \leq 1 \end{cases} \tag{6.17}$$

$$P = 1 - R \tag{6.18}$$

where $\gamma = -2(1-\rho)/(\rho K_a^2 + K_s^2)$, $\rho = \lambda/\mu$, and

$$R = \lambda'/(\lambda' + \mu - \lambda). \tag{6.19}$$

The condition for existence of the stationary solution is $\rho = \lambda/\mu < 1$ since it results from the condition $\gamma < 1$. We see, however, that the usual queueing theory result $P = 1 - \rho$ will only be obtained if we set $\lambda' = \lambda$. Therefore we shall adopt this value of λ' so that $R = \lambda/\mu = \rho$, which is exact for the case of Poisson arrivals (i.e. the $M/G/1$ queue). The computations in the present section are made with this assumption.

The approximate expected queue length at stationary state is then given by

$$L = \int_0^{\infty} xf \, \mathrm{d}x = \rho\left[\frac{1}{2} + \frac{\rho K_a^2 + K_s^2}{2(1-\rho)}\right] = \rho\left[\frac{1}{2} - \frac{\alpha}{2b}\right]. \tag{6.20}$$

L has a form similar to the Pollaczek–Khintchine formula for the $M/G/1$ queue which is

$$\hat{L} = \rho \left[1 + \frac{\rho(1 + K_s^2)}{2(1 - \rho)} \right].$$

In fact, if we set $K_a = 1$ in (6.20) in order to represent a Poisson arrival process we obtain that the error in the formula (6.20) is:

$$\hat{L} - L = \frac{1}{2}\rho(1 - K_s^2)$$

so that the relative error $(\hat{L} - L)/\hat{L}$ tends to zero as $\rho \to 1$.

6.2.5. *Application to a closed two-server system with general service time distributions*

A special case of the model presented in section 6.2.3 will be proposed here as an approximation to a queueing system containing a finite number of customers and two servers.

The system whose behaviour we wish to approximate is shown in Fig. 6.1. It consists of a central processing unit (CPU) and an input-output device (IOD); a finite and fixed number M of programs are being executed in the system. We shall assume that service times at the CPU are independent and identically distributed (i.i.d.) random variables with distribution function with mean μ^{-1} and variance V_s; they are independent of the service times at the IOD which are also i.i.d. random variables of mean λ^{-1} and variance V_a. In general we do not exclude the possibility that λ, V_a, μ and V_s be functions of the total number of programs in the system.

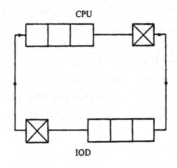

Fig. 6.1.

Again, we use the results obtained in section 6.2.3, which allow us to assume exponentially distributed holding times at the boundaries for the instantaneous process model.

Let $\{X(t), t \geq 0\}$ be the stochastic process approximating the number of programs in the CPU queue of the multiprogramming system described in Fig. 6.1. We shall approximate it by a diffusion process represented the probability density $f(x, t)$ for $0 < X(t) < M$, and the probability masses $P(t)$ and $Q(t)$ for $X(t) = 0$ and $X(t) = M$, respectively. The equations are

$$A_{x,t}f(x,t) + \lambda'P(t)\delta(x-1) + \mu'Q(t)\delta(x-M+1) = 0 \qquad (6.21)$$

$$\frac{\mathrm{d}}{\mathrm{d}t}P(t) = -\lambda'P(t) + C_{0,t}f(x,t) \qquad (6.22)$$

$$\frac{\mathrm{d}}{\mathrm{d}t}Q(t) = -\mu'Q(t) - C_{M,t}f(x,t) \qquad (6.23)$$

where $1/\lambda' = E[h]$ and $1/\mu' = E[H]$ are the average holding times at the lower and upper boundaries, respectively. Of course, the lower boundary $x = 0$ represents the state in which the CPU queue is empty while the boundary $x = M$ is the state in which all of the programs are in the CPU queue. We choose again $b = \lambda - \mu$ and $\alpha = \lambda^3 V_a + \mu^3 V_s$ as in the previous sections. In general it is possible to choose λ' and μ' in order to obtain the best possible approximation to the system being modelled.

Here we shall see that the choice of $\lambda = \lambda'$, $\mu = \mu'$ yields satisfactory numerical results. Solving (6.21), (6.22), (6.23) in stationary state with these parameters we readily obtain:

$$f = \begin{cases} K[1 - \mathrm{e}^{\gamma x}], & 0 < x \leq 1 \\ K[\mathrm{e}^{-\gamma} - 1]\mathrm{e}^{\gamma x}, & 1 \leq x \leq M-1 \\ K[\mathrm{e}^{\gamma(x-M)} - 1]\mathrm{e}^{\gamma(M-1)}, & M-1 \leq x < M \end{cases} \qquad (6.24)$$

with P and Q the probability masses at 0 and at M, respectively, at stationary state being

$$P = K(1 - \rho)/\rho, \quad Q = K(1 - \rho)\mathrm{e}^{\gamma(M-1)}$$

where $\rho = \lambda/\mu$, and

$$K = \rho(1 - \rho^2\mathrm{e}^{\gamma(M-1)})^{-1}.$$

This result can be either verified by substitution in (6.21), (6.22), (6.23) with the appropriate boundary conditions and setting partial derivatives

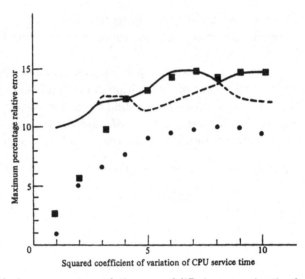

Fig. 6.2.   Maximum percentage relative error of diffusion approximation for closed two-server system. ● ● ●, exponential IOD; ■■■, constant IOD; ---, confidence interval for exponential IOD; —, confidence interval for constant IOD.

with respect to time equal to zero or obtained by solving the differential equations directly.

In Fig. 6.2 we summarise the result of simulation experiments [2] concerning the predictions for the multiprogramming system model. The quantity plotted is the absolute value of the error term relative to the quantity obtained by simulation, for the stationary probability $(1 - P)$ that the CPU is active. That is, if $\eta = (1 - P)$ obtained from the diffusion model and β is the corresponding CPU utilisation obtained by the simulation experiments, then the quantity plotted is $|\eta - \beta|/\beta$. Two sets of simulation results, one with constant service time at the IOD and the other with exponentially distributed service time at the IOD are given. In each case we have also plotted the estimated confidence intervals for a 95% confidence level. The value of ρ has been varied between 0.25 and 0.9 and M has been varied between 1 and 10; the relative error plotted for each value of K_s is the *maximum* absolute relative error over all these values of ρ and M for a given value of K_s. This error remains relatively low, and in any case is smaller than the width of the confidence interval.

A comprehensive accuracy study of the model presented in this section can be found in [2]. The analysis we present here is from [10], although a different study of the same model can be found in [9].

6.2.6. *The discretisation problem*

The diffusion approximation yields a continuous state space approximation to a discrete process. Thus, one is tempted to work back to a discrete probability distribution from the continuous density. This is done, for instance, in the derivation of (6.5) for the reflecting boundary model.

Consider (6.17), (6.18) with $R = \rho$, giving the instantaneous return process approximation to the $GI/G/1$ queue:

$$f(x) = \begin{cases} \rho[e^{-\gamma} - 1]e^{\gamma x}, & x \geq 1 \\ \rho[1 - e^{\gamma x}], & 0 \leq x \leq 1 \end{cases} \tag{6.25}$$

where $\gamma = -2(1 - \rho)/(\rho K_a^2 + K_s^2)$, and

$$P = 1 - \rho.$$

It can be discretised in several different ways. First consider the discretisation $p_1(i), i = 0, 1, \ldots$ suggested in [6]:

$$p_1(i) = f(i) \quad \text{for } i \geq 1$$
$$p_1(0) = P$$

which is

$$p_1(i) = \rho[\hat{\rho} - 1]\hat{\rho}^i = \rho[1 - \hat{\rho}]\hat{\rho}^{i-1}$$
$$p_1(0) = 1 - \rho$$

where $\hat{\rho} = e^{\gamma}$; notice that this is identical to (6.5). The average queue length obtained is then

$$L_1 = \sum_{i=1}^{\infty} i p_1(i) = \rho/(1 - \hat{\rho})$$

Another discretisation $p_2(i), i = 0, 1, \ldots$ developed in [10] is

$$p_2(i) = \int_{i-1}^{i} f(x)\mathrm{d}x = \frac{\rho}{\gamma \hat{\rho}^2}(1 - \hat{\rho})^2 \hat{\rho}^i, \quad i \geq 2$$
$$p_2(1) = \rho\left[1 - \frac{1}{\gamma}(\hat{\rho} - 1)\right] \tag{6.26a}$$
$$p_2(0) = 1 - \rho$$

and the average queue length is

$$L_2 = \rho\left[1 - \frac{1}{\gamma}\right] = \rho\left[1 + \frac{\rho K_a^2 + K_s^2}{2(1-\rho)}\right].$$

These approximate formulae can be compared when $K_a^2 = 1$ to the Pollaczek–Khintchine formula (1.68) for the average length of the $M/G/1$ queue, which is

$$L_{PK} = \rho\left[1 + \frac{\rho(1 + K_s^2)}{2(1-\rho)}\right].$$

In order to examine the difference between L_1, L_2 and L_{PK} for $K_a^2 = 1$, first notice that

$$L_2 - L_{PK} = \frac{1}{2}\rho K_s^2$$

so that the error increases with ρ and K_s^2. But the relative error $(L_2 - L_{PK})/L_{PK}$ has the following properties:

(i) $\lim_{\rho \to 1}(L_2 - L_{PK})/L_{PK} = 0$;

(ii) $\lim_{K_s^2 \to \infty}(L_2 - L_{PK})/L_{PK} = 2(1 - \rho)$.

Property (ii) is important since it states that as K_s^2 increases, the relative error depends only on ρ; but the factor $2(1 - \rho)$ will be unacceptably high for small values of ρ. Property (i) is a general property of diffusion approximations: the relative error tends to zero under heavy traffic conditions.

Let us examine how L_1 behaves when K_s^2 is large and ρ small, i.e. when L_2 is a poor approximation. With $K_a^2 = 1$, we have

$$\hat{\rho} = \exp(-2(1 - \rho)/(\rho + K_s^2))$$

which is

$$\hat{\rho} \cong \exp[(-2/K_s^2) \cdot (1 - \rho/K_s^2)(1 - \rho)]$$

for $K_s^2 \gg 1 \gg \rho$, or

$$\hat{\rho} \cong 1 - 2(1 - \rho)/K_s^2$$

so that

$$L_1 \cong \frac{\rho}{2(1-\rho)}K_s^2.$$

Therefore, for $K_s^2 \gg 1 \gg \rho$, we have

$$L_1 - L_{PK} \cong \frac{\rho}{2(1-\rho)}[K_s^2(1-\rho) - 2 + \rho]$$

$$\cong \frac{\rho}{2}K_s^2 + \frac{\rho(\rho-2)}{2(1-\rho)}.$$

Thus, for $\rho \ll 1$,

$$\lim_{K_s^2 \to \infty} (L_1 - L_{PK})/L_{PK} = 2(1-\rho)$$

just as for L_2.

Consider now the case where $\varepsilon = (1-\rho) \ll 1$. This analysis has been carried out in [25]. We will have

$$\hat{\rho} \cong 1 - \frac{2\varepsilon}{\rho + K_s^2} + \frac{1}{2}\left(\frac{2\varepsilon}{\rho + K_s^2}\right)^2 + O(\varepsilon^3)$$

so that

$$L_1 \cong \frac{\rho(\rho + K_s^2)}{2(1-\rho)}\left[1 + \frac{(1-\rho)}{\rho + K_s^2} + O(\varepsilon^2)\right]$$

and

$$L_1 - L_{PK} \cong \frac{\rho}{2}\left[K_s^2 + \frac{1}{\rho + K_s^2} + O(\varepsilon^2)\right].$$

Therefore:

(iii) $\lim_{\rho \to 1}(L_1 - L_{PK})/L_{PK} = 0$, and for $\varepsilon = (1-\rho) \ll 1$, we have

(iv) $\lim_{K_s^2 \to \infty} (L_1 - L_{PK})/L_{PK} = \frac{1-\rho}{\rho} + O(\varepsilon^2)$

while for L_2, we have (ii); thus we see that for ρ close to 1, L_1 has a relative accuracy which is twice as good as that of L_2.

In fact, the form of the Pollaczek–Khintchine formula suggests a new approximation which was noticed in [10] and further developed in [6]. Instead of choosing γ as has been done above, suppose that we take

$$\gamma' = \frac{-2(1-\rho)}{\rho(K_a^2 + K_s^2)}.$$

We may then derive

$$L_2' = \rho\left[1 - \frac{1}{\gamma'}\right] = \rho\left[1 + \frac{\rho(K_a^2 + K_s^2)}{2(1-\rho)}\right]$$

using the same form for the probabilities as given in (6.25) except that we replace γ by γ' and $\hat{\rho}$ by $\hat{\rho}'$:

$$\hat{\rho}' = e^{\gamma'}.$$

Of course, L_2' is the Pollaczek–Khintchine formula when $K_a^2 = 1$.

Further analysis of this type can be found in [6], from which we take the numerical results of Tables 6.1, 6.2 and 6.3.

Table 6.1. Exact and approximate average queue lengths of the $M/G/1$ queue for $\rho = 0.8$

K_s^2	L_2' (exact result)	L_2	L_1
128.00	207.20	258.40	258.00
64.00	104.80	130.40	130.00
32.00	53.60	66.40	66.00
16.00	28.00	34.40	34.00
8.00	15.20	18.40	18.00
4.00	8.80	10.40	10.00
2.00	5.60	6.40	6.00
1.00	4.00	4.40	4.01
0.50	3.20	3.40	3.02
0.33	2.93	3.07	2.69
0.25	2.80	2.90	2.53
0.20	2.72	2.80	2.43
0.00	2.40	2.40	2.03

Table 6.2. Approximate average queue length for the $E_2/H_2/1$ system compared with simulation results (95% confidence intervals) for $K_a^2 = 0.5$

ρ	K_s^2	Simulation	L_2'	L_2	L_1
$\rho = 0.75$	2	3.44 ± 0.05	3.56	4.31	3.95
	4	5.67 ± 0.12	5.81	7.31	6.94
	8	10.08 ± 0.32	10.31	13.31	12.94
	16	19.27 ± 0.83	19.31	25.31	24.94
	32	37.39 ± 1.92	37.31	49.31	48.94
	64	73.02 ± 4.73	73.31	97.31	96.94
	128	146 ± 14.00	145.3	193.30	192.90
$\rho = 0.8$	2	4.67 ± 0.09	4.80	5.60	5.21
	4	7.83 ± 0.22	8.00	9.60	9.21
	8	14.11 ± 0.53	14.40	17.60	17.20
	16	27.24 ± 1.39	27.20	33.60	33.20
	32	52.95 ± 3.02	52.80	65.60	65.20
	64	102.40 ± 8.00	104.00	129.60	129.20
	128	203.70 ± 21.00	206.40	257.60	257.20

Table 6.3. Comparison of diffusion approximations and exact results for the average queue length of an $E_2/M/1$ queue ($K_a^2 = 0.5$)

ρ	Exact result	L_2'	L_2	L_1
0.95	14.331	14.487	14.962	14.492
0.90	6.829	6.974	7.425	6.985
0.85	4.327	4.463	4.887	4.477
0.80	3.075	3.200	3.600	3.219
0.75	2.323	2.438	2.813	2.460
0.70	1.820	1.925	2.275	1.950

The results of Table 6.3 use the well-known fact that in general the stationary solution of the $GI/M/1$ queue is given by (see, for instance, [14]):

$$p_0 = 1 - \rho$$

$$p_i = \rho(1 - \alpha)\alpha^{i-1}, \quad i \geq 1$$

where α is the solution of

$$\alpha = A^*(\mu - \mu\alpha)$$

and $A^*(s) = \int_0^\infty e^{-sx} dA(x)$, where $A(x)$ is the interarrival time distribution. Therefore, the average stationary queue length of the $G1/M/1$ queue is $\rho/(1 - \alpha)$.

The various analytical results and numerical examples are evidence to the effect that the heuristic modification γ' should be chosen. The corresponding diffusion parameters are $b = \lambda - \mu$ and $\alpha' = \lambda K_a^2 + \mu\rho K_s^2$. These will be the values retained in the following sections, so that the discretised approximation which we shall use is

$$p_0 = 1 - \rho$$

$$p_1 = \rho\left[1 - \frac{1}{\gamma'}(\hat{\rho} - 1)\right],$$

$$p_i = \frac{\rho}{\gamma'\rho}(1 - \hat{\rho})^2 \hat{\rho}^{i-1}, \quad i \geq 2 \tag{6.26b}$$

with $\hat{\rho} = e^{\gamma'}$.

6.3. Diffusion approximations for general networks of queues with one customer class

In this section we present an approximation method using a diffusion model to obtain the stationary probability of queue length for any given queue

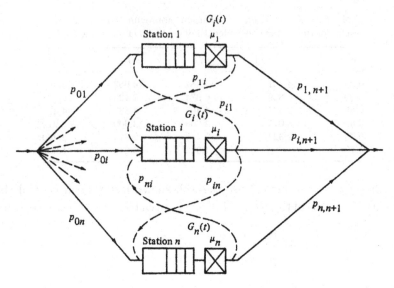

Fig. 6.3.   General open queueing network with first-in-first-out service discipline.

in an open or closed queueing network composed of FCFS service stations, each composed of a single server with general service time distribution. The method is applied to some examples of interest and the model predictions are compared with simulation results. First consider the general network of Fig. 6.3 in which:

(i) External arrivals constitute a renewal process of rate λ_0; the variance of the interarrival time is V_0, and its squared coefficient of variation is $K_0^2 = \lambda_0^2 V_0$.

(ii) The transition of customers from one station to another is defined by a first-order Markov chain with transition matrix $\mathbf{P} = (p_{ij})$, $1 \leq i$, $j \leq n + 1$, is the probability that a customer having terminated its service at station i then enters station j, or leaves the system when $j = n+1$; $\mathbf{P}$ is assumed to have a single absorbing state $n+1$, and no closed subchains.

(iii) The service times for successive customers at station i are independent and identically distributed with common distribution function $F_i(t)$: service times are also independent from one station to another.

(iv) Customers first entering the network are directed to station i with fixed probability p_{0i}.

Let e_i, $1 \leq i \leq n$, be the solution to the system of equations

$$e_i = p_{0i} + \sum_{j=1}^{n} e_j p_{ji}$$

which is unique under these assumptions (see Chapter 3). Then e_i is the expected number of visits which a customer of the network will make to station i. The arrival rate of customers to station i is $\lambda_i = \lambda_0 e_i$ at steady-state; also the steady-state probability ρ_i that station i contains at least one customer is given by

$$\rho_i = \frac{\lambda_0 e_i}{\mu_i} \quad \text{if } \lambda e_i < \mu_i$$

where

$$\mu_i^{-1} = \int_0^{\infty} t \, dF_i(t)$$

is the average service time for a customer at station i. This fact can be easily established rigorously; one way is to treat an open network of this kind as a limiting case of a closed network when one station is saturated and to apply the work-rate theorem (see Chapter 3).

The approach we develop in this section is based on the following assumption, which in general is unjustified: the departure process from any station in the open network is a renewal process, i.e. times between successive departures are independent and identically distributed. We shall make use of this assumption in order to compute the first two moments of the interdeparture time distribution, although it is in general not satisfied. This assumption is valid in the open network with Poisson arrivals and exponentially distributed service times. It is also valid for the output of station i when $\lambda_0 e_i / \mu_i \geq 1$, or when all $\rho_j \cong 0$. Let C_i, $1 \geq i \geq n$, be the squared coefficient of variation of the *interdepartures* times at station i, and denote by A_i the interarrival time, S_i the service time, A_i' the idle time, and by τ_i the interdeparture time. We shall define $C_0 = K_0^2$ in order to maintain a uniform presentation.

For t large enough, and assuming that the output processes from each individual queue are independent, the total number of arrivals to station i in the interval $[0, t]$ will be normally distributed with mean $\lambda_i t$ and variance

$$\sum_{j=0}^{n} [(C_j - 1)p_{ji} + 1]\lambda_j p_{ji} t.$$

Here we have used the fact that the sum of independent normal random variables is normal with variance being the sum of individual variances. In the usual diffusion equations for approximating the length of each queue (6.15), (6.16), the following parameters will be chosen, following (6.26) (see section 6.2.6):

$$
\left.
\begin{aligned}
b_i &= \lambda_i - \mu_i, \quad \lambda_i' = \lambda_i, \quad \rho_i = \lambda_i/\mu_i \\
\alpha_i &= \rho_i\mu_i K_i^2 + \sum_{j=0}^{n}[(C_j - 1)p_{ji} + 1]\lambda_j p_{ji}
\end{aligned}
\right\} \tag{6.27}
$$

where the subscript i refers to the parameters of the equations of the i-th queue, and K_i^2 is the squared coefficient of variation of service time at the i-th queue.

In order to complete the development we must obtain $C_i, 1 \leq i \leq n$. We shall assume that τ_i is a service time S_i with probability ρ_i or an interarrival time plus a service time $A_i + S_i$ with probability $(1 - \rho_i)$. We then have

$$
E[\tau_i] = \rho_i\mu_i^{-1} + (1 - \rho_i)(\lambda_i^{-1} + \mu_i^{-1}) = \lambda_i^{-1}
$$

as would be expected, and

$$
E[\tau_i^2] = (\lambda_i^{-1})^2(1 + C_i) = E[S_i^2] + (1 - \rho_i)(E[A_i^2] + 2E[A_i]E[S_i])
$$

so that

$$
C_i + 1 = \rho_i^2(K_i^2 + 1) + (1 - \rho_i)(\lambda_i^2 E[A_i^2] + 2\rho_i).
$$

Finally, it is the

$$
\sum_{j=0}^{n}[(C_j - 1)p_{ji} + 1]\lambda_j p_{ji} = \lambda_i^3(E[A_i^2] - (\lambda_i^{-1})^2).
$$

This yields, for $1 \leq i \leq n$,

$$
(C_i - 1) - \frac{(1 - \rho_i)}{\lambda_i - \lambda_i p_{ii}^2(1 - \rho_i)} \sum_{\substack{j=0 \\ j \neq i}}^{n}(C_j - 1)\lambda_j p_{ji}^2 = \frac{\rho_i(K_i^2 - 1)}{1 - (1 - \rho_i)p_{ii}^2} \tag{6.28}
$$

which is a convenient form for numerical solution. An approximation to this system of equations is obtained if we can neglect the second term on the left-hand side:

$$
C_i \cong \frac{\rho_i^2(K_i^2 - 1)}{1 - (1 - \rho_i)p_{ii}^2} + 1. \tag{6.29}
$$

We now use these parameters to construct the diffusion approximation to the length of each individual queue. The instantaneous process model for queue i will use the equations (see (6.15), (6.16))

$$-\frac{\partial f_i}{\partial t} - b_i \frac{\partial f_i}{\partial x_i} + \frac{1}{2}\alpha_i \frac{\partial^2 f_i}{\partial x_i^2} + \lambda_i P_i(t)\delta(x_i - 1) = 0$$

$$\frac{d}{dt}P_i(t) = -\lambda_i P_i(t) + \lim_{x_i \to 0^+}\left[-b_i f_i + \frac{1}{2}\alpha_i \frac{\partial f_i}{\partial x_i}\right]$$

$$f_i(0, t) = 0 \text{ (absorbing boundary).}$$

$f_i(x_i, t)$ is the density function approximating the length of the i-th queue and $P_i(t)$ is the probability that the i-th queue is empty. The stationary solution will be obtained as

$$f_i(x_i) = \begin{cases} \rho_i(e^{-\gamma_i} - 1)e^{\gamma_i x_i}, & x_i \geq 1 \\ \rho_i(1 - e^{\gamma_i x_i}), & 0 \leq x_i \leq 1 \end{cases}$$

$$P_i = 1 - \rho_i$$

where $\gamma_i = -2b_i/\alpha_i$, $\rho_i = \lambda_i/\mu_i$, and the approximate average queue length is

$$L_i = \rho_i[1 - \alpha_i/2b_i]$$

where b_i and α_i are defined in (6.27).

This approach can be improved in the case of self-loops in queues where a customer leaving a queue may immediately return to the same queue. Suppose that for some i, $p_{ii} \neq 0$. In this case the assumption of having a renewal process of arrivals to the i-th queue independent of queue length is obviously too strong, especially if p_{ii} is relatively large. Whenever $p_{ii} \neq 0$ we suggest the following modification to the diffusion model [17]. Modify the parameters of the i-th queue so that

(i) p_{ij}, $1 \leq j \leq n + 1$, is replaced by $\bar{p}_{ij} = \begin{cases} 0 & \text{if } j = 1 \\ p_{ij}/(1 - p_{ii}) & \text{if } j \neq 1; \end{cases}$

(ii) μ_i is replaced by $\bar{\mu}_i = \mu_i(1 - p_{ii})$, and K_i^2 is replaced by $\bar{K}_i^2 = (1 - p_{ii})K_i^2 + p_{ii}$.

The system of equations (6.28) is then solved with the modified values $\bar{p}_{ij}$ and $\bar{K}_i^2$. Notice that the arrival rate to a queue is modified only if $p_{ii} \neq 0$ in the original network; however, the value of the load factor $\rho_i = \lambda_i/\mu_i$ is unchanged since λ_i becomes $\lambda_i(1 - p_{ii})$ and μ_i becomes $\mu_i(1 - p_{ii})$.

The queue length is also preserved, since service times are being replaced by longer service times (see (ii)) which are the sum of a geometrically distributed number of service times corresponding to the feedback of customers to the queue. That is, S_i is being replaced by

$$\bar{S}_i = \sum_{k=1}^{l} S_i^k$$

with probability $p_{ii}^{l-1}(1 - p_{ii})$, where $S_i^1, \ldots, S_i^l$ are independent and distributed identically to S_i.

Since there is no exact method of solution for the type of network considered here, most of the material on validation of our approximations will be based on simulation results.

As mentioned above, in the case of Poisson external arrivals and exponential service times at all stations our predictions for the C_i, $1 \leq i \leq n$, from (6.29) are exact. It has been shown in Chapter 3 that for FCFS service, interdeparture times are exponentially distributed only if arrivals are Poisson and service times are exponential.

The output of an $M/D/1$ queue has been examined in considerable detail [21] so that all moments of the interdeparture time distribution are available. We may apply this information to the system shown in Fig. 6.4, when arrivals to the first queue are Poisson and its service times are constant. For that case equation (6.18) predicts $C_1 = 1 - \mu_1^2$ for the departures from the first queue; the value obtained by Pack [21] is exactly the same. Thus, the squared coefficient of variation or interarrival times to the second queue is $1 - \mu_1^2$.

The output process of an $M/G/1$ queue has been studied [19] by means of a Wiener–Hopf factorisation to obtain the Laplace transform of the interdeparture time distribution. In [8] the variance of interdeparture times has been computed explicitly for the system $M/G/1/N$, i.e. with finite population N; the results of interest to us are obtained by setting $N \to \infty$. In this case, too, we see that our predictions are exact. The variance of interdeparture times from the first queue of the system in Fig. 6.2 if service time is general and external arrivals are Poisson is computed from [8] as

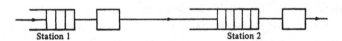

Fig. 6.4.

being $[(1 - \mu_1^2)/\lambda^2 + K_1^2/\mu_1^2]$; the value of C_1/λ^2 obtained from equation (6.28) is exactly this value.

Example 6.1

In order to illustrate the degree of accuracy which can be obtained from the approximation techniques for open single-customer class queueing networks which we have presented in this section, we shall apply the preceding results to the system model presented on Fig. 6.5. The model which is shown was introduced in [1] in order to evaluate the performance of an interactive system. In this model, jobs arrive at the system in a Poisson stream of rate λ_0; after passing through server 1 (which represents a central processing unit) they either leave the system with probability $(1 - \theta_1)$ or enter the queue of server 2 (representing an input-output device). A customer will either enter once again the queue of server 2, with probability θ_2, or proceed to server 1 after finishing its service at server 2. The following simulations and numerical results have been obtained by Dinh [7]. The results shown in Table 6.5 provide a comparison, with respect to simulation results, of the accuracy of the method developed earlier in this section as well as of the approach of Reiser and Kobayashi which we have summarised in section 6.3.2. Confidence intervals for the values estimated from the simulation experiments have not been provided. However, the precise conditions under which the simulations were carried out are shown in Table 6.4 for the five simulation runs. These data indicate that it was impossible in any of the simulations to obtain the same arrival

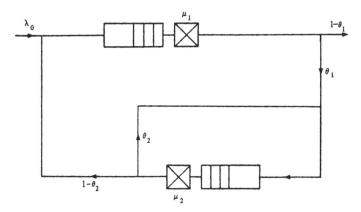

Fig. 6.5.   System model analysed in Example 6.1.

Table 6.4. Parameters for the experiments described in Example 6.1

Experiment No.	θ_1	θ_2	λ_0	K_0	Queue No.	μ_i^{-1}	K_i	λ_i Simulated	λ_i Computed	μ_i Simulated	μ_i Computed
1	0.510	0.503	0.512	0.941	1	0.91123	0.427	1.0489	1.045	0.957	0.953
					2	0.84000	0	1.078	1.073	0.905	0.901
2	0.509	0.499	0.410	0.944	1	0.91591	0.423	0.835	0.836	0.764	0.766
					2	0.84000	0	0.848	0.849	0.712	0.713
3	0.516	0.506	0.342	0.945	1	0.91443	0.414	0.707	0.706	0.646	0.646
					2	0.84000	0	0.738	0.738	0.620	0.620
4	0.512	0.502	0.293	0.967	1	0.90436	0.432	0.601	0.602	0.544	0.544
					2	0.84000	0	0.619	0.619	0.520	0.520
5	0.504	0.507	0.257	0.952	1	0.91094	0.422	0.519	0.519	0.472	0.473
					2	0.84000	0	0.530	0.531	0.444	0.446

rates, probabilities or service time distributions which were assumed in the diffusion model.

The results shown in Table 6.5 are the values of the squared coefficients of variation of interdeparture times C_1, C_2 and of interarrival times K^1, K^2 from or to the two servers, as well as the average queue lengths for each of the five experiments indicated in Table 6.4. These quantities are estimated from the simulation results and also computed using the Gelenbe–Pujolle diffusion approximation (denoted by GP) which we have already described in this section, as well as by the approach of Reiser and Kobayashi (denoted by R/K) which we have reported in section 6.3.2. The values of C_1, C_2 for the Reiser–Kobayashi method are not tabulated since they are identical to the squared coefficients of variation for the service times which are already given in Table 6.4 (K_1 and K_2): notice that these are considerably different from those obtained by simulation. In the case of average queue lengths, we show the result without ("No mod.") and with ("With mod.") the modification suggested for handling self-loops or feedback of customers as we have in server 1 of Fig. 6.5. We notice that the accuracy of the diffusion approximation is consistently worse in the case of server 2, although the self-loop modification does improve matters.

6.3.1. *Application to packet-switching computer-communication networks*

The diffusion approximation method developed in this section is particularly suited for the analysis of packet-switching computer-communication networks [14]. Consider the packet-switching network shown in Fig. 6.6. It is composed of *nodes* 1 to 5. The physical *links* carrying data between nodes are numbered 1 to 12. Data are transported through the network in the form of packets of variable length, which can be viewed as the customers of the network, while the transmission time of the packets along a link can be viewed as service times. Therefore each link behaves as a server, and the packets waiting for transmission along a link form a queue within the node which precedes the link (e.g. node 2 precedes link 5 in Fig. 6.6). Most analyses of such networks have assumed that buffer space at each node is infinite and that the packet sizes are exponentially distributed [15] so that Jackson's theorem may be used. Here we shall show that diffusion approximations can yield more accurate predictions for such systems when a more accurate representation of packet length is necessary.

Table 6.5.　Comparison of the Gelenbe–Pujolle and Reiser–Kobayashi diffusion approximations for single-customer class queueing networks with simulations

Experiment No.	Queue No.	C_i		K^i			Average queue length			
		Simulation	G/P	Simulation	G/P	R/K	Simulation	R/K	G/P No mod.	G/P with mod.
1	1	0.466	0.469	0.738	0.757	0.718	13.821	11.648	12.013	11.966
	2	0.329	0.153	0.859	0.651	0.602	7.831	2.949	3.124	5.735
2	1	0.653	0.621	0.860	0.825	0.717	2.359	2.002	2.106	2.093
	2	1.478	0.422	1.765	0.759	0.604	1.871	0.970	1.031	1.694
3	1	0.944	0.707	1.055	0.862	0.723	1.603	1.168	1.207	1.200
	2	2.533	0.543	2.754	0.808	0.595	1.467	0.709	0.718	1.149
4	1	1.070	0.785	1.189	0.898	0.729	1.046	0.815	0.821	0.818
	2	2.858	0.663	3.008	0.860	0.603	1.005	0.545	0.502	0.781
5	1	1.184	0.824	1.284	0.912	0.728	0.758	0.632	0.619	0.617
	2	3.341	0.740	3.438	0.890	0.599	0.731	0.453	0.382	0.589

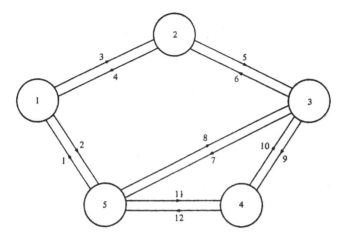

Fig. 6.6.   Model of a packet-switching network.

The traffic in the packet-switching network wil be specified by (i) the input traffic; (ii) the final destination matrix $\mathbf{D}$; and (iii) the routing matrix $\mathbf{R}$. We shall denote by $\bar{\lambda}_i$ (in packets per second) the arrival rate of packets which *enter* the network at node i.

$\mathbf{D} \equiv (d_{ij})$ is an $n \times n$ matrix where n is the number of nodes; d_{ij} is the proportion of packets entering the network at node i whose final destination is node j. The routing matrix $\mathbf{R} \equiv (r_{ij})$ is also $n \times n$; r_{ij} is the number of the next link which will be traversed by a packet which is currently at node i and whose final destination is node j. Clearly, r_{ij} must be an output link of node i. Notice that $\mathbf{R}$ defines a static, i.e. pre-determined, routing policy in the network. Dynamic policies can also be defined and have been discussed in [4, 15]. We must also specify the distribution of packet length; this distribution will immediately give us the distribution of transit times (or service times) for each link, since link speed (in bits per second) is known. In such analyses propagation times (which are usually short since the link lengths are short compared to the distance travelled by light in one second) in the links, and switching times inside the nodes are neglected [4, 15]. It is also assumed that a packet arriving at its final destination is instantaneously "consumed": this implies that we do not analyse the queues which form for the output of packets from the destination node towards some output device or computer.

This representation must now be transformed into a queueing network model. The model will have as many servers and queues as there are links in the packet-switching network. We must therefore determine the arrival rate of packets λ_k to the k-th link as well as the transition probabilities p_{kl} from link k to link l.

Each non-zero element of $\mathbf{D}$, say d_{ij}, defines a source-destination pair (i, j) which will be used to construct a *path* from node i to node i using the routing matrix $\mathbf{R}$. A path will be a vector $\boldsymbol{\pi} = (\pi_1, \dots, \pi_L)$ where L is the path length ($L \leq n$ since the network cannot contain cycles) or number of links traversed by a packet whose source-destination pair is (i, j). First number each link as a pair (c, d) if the link connects node c to node d. This will yield a new routing matrix $\mathbf{R}'$ (notice that $\mathbf{R}'$ is not necessarily isomorphic to $\mathbf{R}$ since there may be several distinct links connecting node c to node d). Then create a vector $\boldsymbol{\pi}' = (\pi_1', \dots, \pi_L')$ as follows:

$$\pi_1' = r_{ij}' = (c_1, d_1)$$

$$\begin{cases} \pi_{k+1}' = (c_{k+1}', d_{k+1}') = r_{d_k, j}', & \text{if } d_k' \neq j \\ L = k, & \text{if } d_k' = m. \end{cases}$$

From $\boldsymbol{\pi}'$ and $\mathbf{R}$ it is simple to return to the vector $\boldsymbol{\pi}$. The *path traffic* λ_π is simply

$$\lambda_\pi = \bar{\lambda}_i d_{ij}$$

where $\bar{\lambda}_i$ (defined above) is the traffic entering the network at node i. Finally, we obtain the *link traffic* λ_k as follows. Let $\mathcal{P}_k$ be the set of all paths containing link k. Then

$$\lambda_k = \sum_{\pi \in \mathcal{P}_k} \lambda_\pi. \tag{6.30}$$

Clearly, λ_k is the number of packets per second which will be carried by link k, and is the arrival rate of packets to the queue, or buffer, of packets which are waiting to enter the link. Let $\mathcal{P}_{kl}$ be the set of all paths of the form $\boldsymbol{\pi} = (\pi_1, \dots, \pi_x, k, l, \pi_{x+2}, \dots, \pi_L)$; i.e. $\boldsymbol{\pi}$ is a path in which link k is followed by link l. Then we shall take p_{kl} to be

$$p_{kl} = \sum_{\pi \in \mathcal{P}_{kl}} \lambda_\pi / \lambda_k \tag{6.31}$$

or the proportion of packets which enter link l after having entered link k. The λ_k and p_{kl} obtained from (6.30) and (6.31) can now be used in (6.28) to compute the C_k, which approximate the squared coefficients of variation of interarrival times to the buffer queue for link k. Since the K_k^2 are known from the distribution of packet lengths we now have all the data necessary for the computation of the approximate queue length distribution and, in particular, the average buffer queue lengths L_k from (6.20), using (6.27), (6.28),

$$L_k = \rho_k \left[\frac{1}{2} - \frac{\alpha_k}{2b_k} \right], \quad b_k = \lambda_k - \mu_k \qquad (6.32)$$

where $\rho_k = \lambda_k/\mu_k$, μ_k^{-1} is the average transit time of a packet along link k. If the usual formula [15] using Jackson's theorem had been used, we would have had (see Chapter 3):

$$L_k' = \rho_k/(1 - \rho_k). \qquad (6.33)$$

Example 6.2

Let us now apply these results to a numerical example given in [4]. The network is shown in Fig. 6.6 and the external arrival process is Poisson with rates:

$$\bar{\lambda}_1 = 6; \quad \bar{\lambda}_2 = 8.25; \quad \bar{\lambda}_3 = 7.5; \quad \bar{\lambda}_4 = 6.75; \quad \bar{\lambda}_5 = 1.5.$$

Packet lengths are assumed to be constants so that $K_k^2 = 0$ for all links $1 \le k \le 12$, and the packet length is 1000 bits. Links 1, 2, 7, 8, 11, 12 have a data-transmission capacity of 4800 bits/second, while links 3, 4, 5, 6, 9, 10 have a capacity of 48,000 bits/second. Therefore

$$\mu_1 = \mu_2 = \mu_7 = \mu_8 = \mu_{11} = \mu_{12} = 4.8$$

$$\mu_3 = \mu_4 = \mu_5 = \mu_6 = \mu_9 = \mu_{10} = 48.$$

The distribution matrix is

$$\mathbf{D} = \begin{bmatrix} 0.0 & 0.10 & 0.2 & 0.10 & 0.60 \\ 0.4 & 0.00 & 0.4 & 0.15 & 0.05 \\ 0.1 & 0.20 & 0.0 & 0.60 & 0.10 \\ 0.3 & 0.30 & 0.3 & 0.00 & 0.10 \\ 0.1 & 0.25 & 0.3 & 0.35 & 0.00 \end{bmatrix},$$

while the routing matrix is

$$\mathbf{R} = \begin{bmatrix} 0 & 3 & 3 & 3 & 2 \\ 4 & 0 & 5 & 5 & 4 \\ 6 & 6 & 0 & 9 & 8 \\ 10 & 10 & 10 & 0 & 12 \\ 1 & 1 & 7 & 11 & 0 \end{bmatrix}.$$

The system as described was simulated until 6000 packets were received at their destinations. Although the simulation results have not been analysed in order to compute statistical confidence intervals, this simulation experiment is comparable in duration to a measurement session on a real computer network, the main point being that the diffusion approximation is capable of making predictions which are as accurate as simulation of such systems. The results obtained are given in Table 6.6.

We see that for buffer queues which are lightly loaded, Jackson's formula (6.33) yields results which are of the same degree of accuracy as the diffusion approximation. However for link 2, which is heavily loaded, the diffusion approximation is considerably more accurate.

Let us complete this section by deriving another formula which is of interest in the analysis of packet-switching networks. A useful performance measure is the average source-destination *transit delay* $T_{(i,j)}$ for the source-destination pair (i,j). For fixed routing this corresponds simply to the

Table 6.6. Average buffer queue lengths for the packet-switching network of Fig. 6.6

Average queue length	Jackson	Diffusion approximation	Simulation
L_1	0.123	0.116	0.117
L_2	3.000	1.875	1.920
L_3	0.139	0.131	0.132
L_4	0.170	0.157	0.163
L_5	0.127	0.125	0.105
L_6	0.157	0.146	0.173
L_7	0.104	0.099	0.087
L_8	0.185	0.171	0.208
L_9	0.162	0.147	0.155
L_{10}	0.145	0.136	0.129
L_{11}	0.123	0.116	0.106
L_{12}	0.164	0.152	0.154

average time to traverse the path $\pi(i,j)$ which corresponds to (l,m). Therefore

$$T_{(i,j)} = \sum_{k \in \pi(i,j)} L_k / \lambda_k. \tag{6.34}$$

The important case of networks with finite storage capacity will not be analysed here, and the interested reader is referred to [3] for results on this subject.

6.3.2. The approach of Kobayashi and Reiser to the approximation of queueing networks

In [16], Kobayashi proposes a generalisation to an open or closed queueing network of arbitrary topology of the results of Gaver and Shedler [9]. Kobayashi imposes reflecting boundaries to the n-dimensional diffusion process and arrives at an equilibrium joint distribution of queue lengths which is in product form. He introduces from queueing theory the known probability of an empty queue at each node to modify the solution of the diffusion equation so as to obtain a more accurate representation of queue length distribution. Reiser and Kobayashi [22] have presented a simplified diffusion model derived from that approach, and we will briefly review their results.

The squared coefficient of variation of the interarrival time to queue i is chosen to be

$$K^{(i)} = (\lambda_i)^{-1} \sum_{j=0}^{n} [(K_j^2 - 1)p_{ji} + 1] \lambda_j p_{ji} \tag{6.35}$$

where $\lambda_j = \lambda_0 e_j$, $1 \le j \le n$, and K_j^2 is the squared coefficient of variation of the service time at queue j if $j \ne 0$; $K_0 = \lambda_0^2 V_0$. An equilibrium queue size distribution

$$\hat{p}_i(m_i) = \begin{cases} 1 - \rho_1, & \text{if } m_i = 0 \\ \rho_i(1 - \hat{\rho}_i)\hat{\rho}_i m_i^{-1}, & \text{if } m_i \ge 1 \end{cases} \tag{6.36}$$

is proposed for queue i where m_i is the i-th queue's length, and

$$\hat{\rho}_i = e^{\gamma i}$$

where

$$\gamma_i = \frac{2(\lambda_i - \mu_i)}{\lambda_i K^{(i)} + \mu_i K_i}. \tag{6.37}$$

The approximation proposed for the joint probability distribution is

$$p(m_1, \ldots, m_n) = \prod_{i=1}^{n} \hat{p}_i(m_i) \tag{6.38}$$

for the n queues in an open network. Obviously the result holds only if $\lambda_i \leq \mu_i$, $1 \leq i \leq n$, which is the usual stability condition.

For a closed network, the following treatment has been suggested. Suppose $\hat{\rho}_i$ is the utilisation of server i; the joint probability distribution is taken to be (for M customers in the network):

$$\hat{p}(m_1, \ldots, m_n) = G' \prod_{i=1}^{n} \hat{p}_i(m_i) \tag{6.39}$$

where

$$\hat{p}_i(m_i) = \begin{cases} 1 - \hat{\rho}_i, & m_i = 0 \\ \hat{\rho}_i(1 - \hat{\rho}_i)\hat{\rho}_i^{m_i-1}, & m_i = 1, 2, \ldots, M \end{cases} \tag{6.40}$$

and G' is a normalising constant. Several methods are suggested for choosing ρ_i. The simplest seems to be to assume that M is sufficiently large so that there exists a "bottle-neck" queue (say k) whose utilisation is 1. Then, by application of the work-rate theorem (see Chapter 3),

$$\hat{\rho}_i = X_i \mu_K / X_k \mu_i \tag{6.41}$$

where X_i, X_k are the equilibrium probabilities that a customer will be at station i, k, respectively, which is the solution to (see Chapter 3)

$$X_i = \sum_{i=1}^{n} X_j p_{ji} \quad \text{and} \quad \sum_{i=1}^{n} X_i = 1.$$

The Reiser–Kobayashi approach yields less accurate results in certain cases. For instance, consider once again the network of Fig. 6.4; their approach yields $K^{(2)} = 1$ for the squared coefficient of variation of interarrivals to queue 2, while the correct result is $1 - \mu_i^2$ which is obtained in [21] and also by the approach developed above. In many cases, however, its accuracy is comparable to that of the method we have described in this section.

6.4. Approximate behaviour of a single queue in a network with multiple customer classes

In this section we are concerned with an open network containing n stations. Each station contains one server. Customers of the network belong to R classes. At each station service is rendered in strict FIFO order with *no* priorities between classes. The solution method we develop is closely related to the approach of the previous section.

The r-th class of customers, $1 \leq r \leq R$, is characterised by:

(i) a stream of arrivals to the network which is a renewal process: its rate is $\lambda_{0,r}$ and the squared coefficient of variation of interarrival times is $K_{0,r}$;

(ii) a general service time distribution function $F_r^i(x)$ at the i-th service station, $1 \leq i \leq n$. $\mu_{i,r}^{-1}$ will be its average and $K_{i,r}$ its squared coefficient of variation.

Furthermore, transitions of customers through the network are described by a Markov chain $(p_{i,r;j,r'})$ where $1 \leq i \leq n$, $1 \leq r$, $r' \leq R$, $1 \leq j \leq n+1$. $p_{i,r;j,r'}$ is the probability that a class r customer leaving station i enters station j in class r'. The fictitious station $(n+1)$ denotes a departure from the network. We shall call $q_{i,r}$ the probability that an arriving customer of class r enters station i of the network.

The reader will notice that the queueing network we have thus defined cannot be solved by any of the available exact solution methods. Such models are of particular interest in performance evaluation studies of computer systems which take into account the existence of multiple job classes. In the area of computer networks they reflect well the presence of "short" and "long" packets: the former can represent interactive processing while the latter can represent the transfer of files.

As in the approach taken in section 6.3, the analysis proceeds in two parts: the first concerns the computation of the parameters of the arrival process to each queue while the second part uses the results of the first part in the queue-length computations using diffusion approximations.

6.4.1. *Computation of the approximate interarrival statistics for each queue*

We shall first derive the equations which will allow us to compute the interarrival statistics; the algorithm used for computing these statistics will then be given in compact form. We shall first need $\lambda_{i,r}$, the arrival rate of class r customers to queue i, obtained by solving

$$\lambda_{i,r} = \lambda_{0,r} q_{i,r} + \sum_{j=1}^{n} \sum_{r'=1}^{R} \lambda_{j,r}, \ p_{j,r';i,r}. \tag{6.42}$$

Let us denote $\rho_{i,r} = \lambda_{i,r}/\mu_{i,r}$: it can be viewed as the load imposed by class r customers on station i. We shall define

$$\rho_i = \sum_{r=1}^{R} \rho_{i,r} \tag{6.43}$$

and

$$\lambda_i = \sum_{r=1}^{R} \lambda_{i,r}, \ \pi_{i,r} = \lambda_{i,r}/\lambda_i \quad \text{for } 1 \le i \le n, \ 1 \le r \le R,$$
$$\lambda_0 = \sum_{r=1}^{R} \lambda_{0,r}, \tag{6.44}$$

where ρ_i is the *utilisation* (steady-state probability that the queue is busy), and λ_i is the total arrival rate, associated with station i.

Having obtained the $\lambda_{i,r}$, from (6.37) we need to compute the squared coefficients of variation of the interarrival times of class r customers at station i. These are obtained by *assuming* that the arrival and departure processes of class r customers to and from each queue are renewal processes. Let τ_i be the time separating two successive departures from station i. We shall write the following heuristic relation:

$$\tau_i = \begin{cases} S_i & \text{with probability } u_i \\ S_i + A_i & \text{with probability } (1 - u_i) \end{cases} \tag{6.45}$$

where A_i is an interarrival time to queue i, and S_i is $S_{i,r}$ with probability $\pi_{i,r}$, $S_{i,r}$ being the service time of class r customer at station i. Therefore, from (6.45)

$$E[\tau_i] = E[S_i] + E[A_i](1 - u_i)$$
$$= \sum_{r=1}^{R} \mu_{i,r}^{-1} \pi_{i,r} + \lambda_i^{-1}(1 - u_i)$$
$$= \lambda_i^{-1} = \left(\sum_{i=1}^{R} \lambda_{i,r} \right)^{-1}.$$

We also obtain:

$$E[\tau_i^2] = u_i E[S_i^2] + (1 - u_i)E[S_i^2 + 2A_i S_i + A_i^2]$$

$$= E[S_i^2] + 2(1 - u_i)\lambda_i^{-1} \sum_{r=1}^{R} \mu_{i,r}^{-1} \pi_{i,r} + (1 - u_i)E[A_i^2].$$

Denote by $C_i = \lambda_i^2\{E[\tau_i^2] - (E[\tau_i])^2\}$ the squared coefficient of variation of *interdeparture times* at the i-th queue, and let G_i be the squared coefficient of variation of *interarrival times* to the i-th queue. We then have

$$C_i + 1 = \lambda_i^2 E[S_i^2] + (1 - \rho_i)(G_i + 1) + 2\rho_i(1 - \rho_i).$$

The service time S_i is $S_{i,r}$ if it is the service of a class r customer (i.e. with probability $\pi_{i,r} = \lambda_{i,r}/\lambda_i$). Therefore

$$E[S_i^2] = \sum_{r=1}^{R} E[S_{i,r}^2]\pi_{i,r}$$

$$= \sum_{r=1}^{R} (K_{i,r}^2 + 1)(\mu_{i,r}^{-1})^2 \lambda_{i,r}/\lambda_i$$

so that

$$C_i + 1 = \lambda_i \sum_{i=r}^{R} \rho_{i,r}\mu_{i,r}^{-1}(K_{i,r}^2 + 1) + (1 - \rho_i)(G_i + 1 + 2\rho_i). \qquad (6.46)$$

Using an argument similar to the one used in section 6.3, assuming that the output processes of the n queues are mutually independent renewal processes, we can write that the variance of the number of arrivals at the i-th queue in a long interval $(0, t)$ will be

$$\lambda_i^3\{E[A_i^2] - (E[A_i])^2\}t = \lambda_i G_i t \cong \sum_{j=0}^{n}[(C_j - 1)p_{ji} + 1]\lambda_j p_{ji}t$$

so that we take, for $1 \le i \le n$

$$G_i = \lambda_i^{-1} \sum_{j=0}^{n}[(C_j - 1)p_{ji} + 1]\lambda_j p_{ji} \qquad (6.47)$$

where p_{ji} is the probability that a job leaving station j enters station i, or

$$p_{ji} = \sum_{r=1}^{R} \sum_{r'=1}^{R} \pi_{j,r} p_{j,r;i,r'} \qquad (6.48)$$

for $0 \leq j \leq n$, $1 \leq i \leq n$. In (6.47) C_0 is the squared coefficient of variation of external interarrival times. Notice that the variance of the number of arrivals in $(0, t)$ is, asymptotically for large t,

$$\left(\sum_{r=1}^{R} \lambda_{0,r} \right) C_0 t = \sum_{r=1}^{R} \lambda_{0,r} K_{0r}^{2t}$$

so that we compute C_0 from this relation:

$$C_0 = \sum_{r=1}^{R} \lambda_{0,r} K_{0,r}^2 / \lambda_0. \tag{6.49}$$

Using (6.46) and (6.47) we now obtain the system of n linear equations for the C_i, $1 \leq i \leq n$:

$$C_i = \lambda_i \sum_{i=1}^{R} \rho_{i,r} \mu_{i,r}^{-1} (K_{i,r}^2 + 1) + \sum_{j=0}^{n} (1 - p_{ji}) \frac{\lambda_j}{\lambda_i} p_{ji} - 2\rho_i^2 + \sum_{j=0}^{n} \frac{\lambda_j}{\lambda_i} p_{ji}^2 C_j. \tag{6.50}$$

Finally, notice that $G_{i,r}$ (the squared coefficient of variation of interarrival times of class r to queue i) will be given by

$$G_{i,r} = (G_i - 1)\pi_{i,r} + 1. \tag{6.51}$$

This completes the computation of the interarrival statistics to each queue of the network which we can summarise as follows:

Begin

Step 1 Obtain the $\lambda_{i,r}$, $1 \leq i \leq n$, $1 \leq r \leq R$ from the linear system of nR equations (6.42).

Step 2 Compute ρ_i, λ_i, $\pi_{i,r}$ from (6.43), (6.44).

Step 3 Use (6.48) to obtain the p_{ji}, $0 \leq j \leq n$, $1 \leq i \leq n$.

Step 4 Obtain the C_i, $1 \leq i \leq n$, by solving the n linear equations (6.50) using C_0 from (6.49).

Step 5 Compute G_i, and $G_{1,r}$, $1 \leq i \leq n$, $1 \leq r \leq R$, from (6.47) using the result of Step 4, and using (6.51).

End.

6.4.2. *Diffusion approximation to the queue length process*

We now consider the behaviour of any queue, say the i-th, in the network and approximate the queue length process by a diffusion process.

The queue length probability density function $f_i(x, t)$ is assumed to satisfy the diffusion equations

$$-\frac{\partial f_i}{\partial t} - b_i \frac{\partial f_i}{\partial x_i} + \frac{1}{2}\alpha_i \frac{\partial^2 f_i}{\partial x_i^2} + \lambda_i P_i(t)\delta(x_i - 1) = 0$$

$$\frac{\mathrm{d}}{\mathrm{d}t}P_i(t) = -\lambda_i P_i(t) + \lim_{x_i \to 0^+}\left[-b_i f_i + \frac{1}{2}\alpha_i \frac{\partial f_i}{\partial x_i}\right]$$

with $\lim_{x_i \to 0^+} f_i(x_i, t) = 0$, and where $P_i(t)$ is the probability that the queue length is $x_i = 0$ at time t. The parameters for the diffusion process are chosen to be

$$b_i = \lambda_i - \mu_i, \quad \alpha_i = \rho_i \lambda_i G_i + \mu_i^3 V_i \tag{6.52}$$

where V_i is an equivalent variance of service time at queue i:

$$V_i = E[S_i^2] - (E[S_i])^2$$

$$= \sum_{i=1}^{R}(K_{i,r}^2 + 1)(\mu_{i,r}^{-1})^2 \lambda_{i,r}/\lambda_i - \left(\sum_{i=1}^{R}\mu_{i,r}^{-1}\lambda_{i,r}/\lambda_i\right)^2. \tag{6.53}$$

Writing $\gamma_i = 2b_i/\alpha_i$ we obtain the stationary solution, which exists for $\gamma_i < 0$ or $\rho_i < 1$:

$$P_i = 1 - \lambda_i/\mu_i = 1 - \rho_i \tag{6.54}$$

$$f_i(x) = \begin{cases} \rho_i[1 - e^{\gamma_i x_i}], & 0 \le x_i \le 1 \\ \rho_i[1 - e^{-\gamma_i}]e^{\gamma_i x_i}, & x_i \ge 1 \end{cases} \tag{6.55}$$

which, when discretised using (6.26b), yields the diffusion approximation to the average queue length given by

$$L_i = \rho_i \left[1 + \frac{\rho_i(G_i + K_i^2)}{2(1 - \rho_i)}\right]. \tag{6.56}$$

From the distribution for the total number in queue we will now work back to the distribution of the number of customers of each class in queue. We proceed as follows. Discretise the probability density function $f_i(x)$ by using (6.26b). $p_i(n_i)$ will be the discrete approximation to the stationary queue length distribution at station i. Let $p_{i,r}(l_i)$ be the probability of finding

l_i customers of class r at station i; we take

$$p_{i,r}(l_i) = \sum_{n \geq l} \binom{n}{l_i} \pi_{i,r}^{l_i}(1 - \pi_{i,r})^{n-l_i} p_i(n_i) \qquad (6.57)$$

since each customer in queue i belongs to class r with probability $\pi_{i,r}$.

A quantity of interest is the average response (or transit) time through the network for customers of each class. Denote this quantity by T_r for class r: T_r is the average time spent by a customer of class r between the instant at which it enters the network and the instant at which it departs. Clearly, a customer's waiting time at each queue does not depend on its class; let $T_{i,r}$ be the response (or transit) time of a class r customer through station i and $W_{i,r}$ the waiting time. We have (using Little's formula)

$$W_{i,r} = L_i/\lambda_i - \mu_i^{-1}$$

and

$$T_{i,r} = L_i/\lambda_i - \mu_i^{-1} + \mu_{i,r}^{-1}. \qquad (6.58)$$

Therefore

$$T_r = \sum_{i=1}^{n} T_{i,r}\lambda_{i,r}/\lambda_{0,r} \qquad (6.59)$$

since a class r customer will visit station i on average $\lambda_{i,r}/\lambda_{0,r}$ times.

A detailed validation of this model's predictions is given in [7] for a computer system with two job classes. The accuracy seems to be very good. Comparisons with simulation results reported in [7] yield a relative error of less than 10% in average queue lengths for each class.

6.5. Conclusion

Many important practical cases of large-scale computer systems are too complex to be represented exactly by a mathematical model. Even when a precise mathematical model can be constructed, the analyst is faced with a problem of dimension. Models with a number of states proportional to 10^6 are easy to obtain, but program packages capable of solving Markov chains of this dimension are not yet available. Often the mathematical models which arise from computer systems have properties which make them particularly difficult to handle numerically; for instance, the time constants related to various parts of the system will vary widely leading to "stiff" systems of equations. Such properties also make simulation modelling particularly difficult. If a system is composed of parts with very small and very large time constants, it will be necessary to simulate it at the time scale which corresponds to the rapidly varying portions in order to preserve the desired accuracy; yet the total simulation time will have to be large compared to the slowly varying parts in order for the simulation to reach steady-state. Furthermore, the probabilistic or statistical tools available at present do not allow us to estimate accurately the confidence intervals of simulation results except for the simplest models which have a regenerative structure or other simplifying properties.

All these considerations make it particularly desirable to have computationally tractable and relatively accurate approximate mathematical models for computer systems. We have seen that diffusion approximations satisfy these two criteria. If they are used carefully, under relatively heavy load conditions and when traffic and service times do not have excessively high coefficients of variation, their accuracy is comparable to that of simulation models. The computational effort involved in solving them is negligible by comparison; it will usually involve the solution of a system of linear equations whose size is the product of the number of stations and of customer classes, and the computation of moments from a continuous or discretised density function.

The open problems in this area are of both a mathematical and a practical nature. The convergence of the queueing models to the diffusion approximations has been established only for the simplest and the least interesting cases — which is hardly surprising since the mathematical tools for this are still rudimentary. From a more practical point of view we need to extend further our understanding of "good" diffusion models for various cases of interest, such as queue-dependent arrival or service times, which are not yet properly handled. Also, further practical and theoretical understanding of the properties of the flow of customers in a queueing network will improve the accuracy of diffusion approximations. Many more validations and applications to real systems are also needed in this area.

References

1. Anderson, H. A. and Sargent, R. (1972). The statistical evaluation of the performance of an experimental APL/360 system. *In* Statistical Computer Performance Evaluation (W. Freiberger, Ed.), pp. 73–98. Academic Press, London.

2. Badel, M. (1975). "Quelques Problèmes liés à la Simulation de Modèls de Systèmes Informatiques." Ph.D. Thesis, Université Paris VI.
3. Badel, M. and Zonzon, M. (1976). "Validation d'un modèle à processus de diffusion pour un réseau de files d'attente général." IRIA Research Report, No. 209.
4. Banh-Tri-An, (1978). "Reseaux d'Ordinateurs à Commutation de Paquets." Ph.D. Thesis, Université de Liège.
5. Chandy, M. Herzog, U. and Woo, L. (1975). Parametric analysis of queueing networks. *IBM J. Res. and Dev.*, **19**, 36–42.
6. Chiamsiri, S. and Craig-Moore, S. (1977). "Accuracy Comparisons between Two Diffusion Approximations for $M^x/G/1$ Queues, Instantaneous Return versus Reflecting Boundary." Paper presented at the *Joint Meeting of ORSA and TIMS*, Atlanta.
7. Dinh, V. (1978). "Application of a Diffusion Model to Computer Performance Evaluation." Report of IBM-France Field Systems Center.
8. Disney, R. L. and Cherry, W. P. (1974). Some topics in queueing network theory. *In* "Mathematical Methods in Queueing Theory" (A. B. Clarke, Ed.). Springer, Berlin.
9. Gaver, D. P. and G: S. Shedler, G. S. (1971). "Multiprogramming System Performance via Diffusion Approximations." IBM Research Report, RJ-938, Yorktown Heights, New York.
10. Gelenbe, E. (1975). On approximate computer system models. *J.A.C.M.*, **22**, 261–263.
11. Gelenbe, E. (1976). "A Non-Markovian Diffusion Model and its Application to the Approximation of Queueing System Behaviour." IRIA Research Report, No. 158, Rocquencourt, France.
12. Gelenbe, E. and Pujolle, G. (1976). The behaviour of a single queue in a general queueing network. *Acta Informatica*, **7**, 123–160.
13. Gelenbe, E. and Pujolle, G. (1977). "A Diffusion Model for Multiple Class Queueing Networks." IRIA Research Report, No. 242, Rocquencourt, France.
14. Kleinrock, L. (1976). "Queueing Systems. Vol. I: Theory." John Wiley.
15. Kleinrock, L. (1976). "Queueing Systems. Vol. II: Computer Applications." John Wiley.
16. Kobayashi, H. (1974). Application of the diffusion approximation to queueing networks: Parts I and II. *J.A.C.M.*, **21**, 316–328; 459–469.
17. Kühn, P. (1976). "Analysis of Complex Queueing Networks by Decomposition." Proc. of International Teletraffic Congress, Melbourne.
18. Labetoulle, J. and Pujolle, G. (1978). Modelling of packet switching communication networks with finite buffer size at each node. *In* "Computer Performance" (K. M. Chandy and M. Reiser, Eds), pp. 515–536. North-Holland, Amsterdam.
19. Marshall, K. T. (1968). Some relationships between the distributions of waiting time, idle time, and inter-output time in $GI/G/1$ queue. *SIAM J. Appl. Math.*, **16**, 324–327.
20. Newell, G. F. (1971). "Applications of Queueing Theory" ch. 6. Chapman and Hall, London.

21. Pack, C. D. (1975). The output of an $M/D/1$ queue. *Operations Research*, **23**, 750–760.

22. Reiser, M. and Kobayashi, H. (1974). Accuracy of the diffusion approximation for some queueing systems. *IBM J. Res. and Dev.*, **18**, 110–124.

23. Shum, A. and Buzen, J. (1978). A method for obtaining approximate solutions to closed queueing networks with general service times. *In* Modelling and Performance Evaluation of Computer Systems" (H. Beilner and E. Gelenbe, Eds). North-Holland, Amsterdam.

24. Vicard, J. (1977). Exactitude de modèles mathématiques de l'unité de pagination d'un ordinateur. *RAIRO Informatique*, **11**, 287–299.

25. Yu, P. S. (1977). "On Accuracy Improvement and Applicability Conditions of Diffusion Approximation with Application to Modelling of Computer Systems." Technical Report, No. 129, Digital Systems Laboratory, Stanford University.

Chapter 7

Approximate Decomposition and Iterative Techniques for Closed Model Solution

7.1. Introduction

In general, the computer system analyst has to adapt the panoply of tools at his disposal to the specific problem at hand, and often his problem will not fit exactly into any available framework. If the analyst has a mathematical orientation, and enough time available, he may attempt an original solution method. If he is pressed for time, or if he is not mathematically inclined, he will tend to program a simulation of the system he has to analyse if the programming and computer time can be afforded.

There is, however, a third approach he might take: the use of numerical approximation which in some cases provides only a first-order approximation, and which in others provides highly accurate results. The diffusion approximation developed in Chapter 4 is an example of this approach. In this chapter we will examine a set of approximations which retain, contrary to diffusion approximations, the discrete nature of the model. They will all be based on a similar approach to a heuristic iterative solution of the steady-state "Birth and Death" equations. However, in certain cases, a formal justification will be available on the basis of problem structure while in other cases the only justification will be the intuitive appeal of the approach and its similarity with techniques used in other areas of applied science.

7.2. Subsystem isolation

The set of numerical solution procedures we present in this chapter has been designed for the approximate analysis of *closed* networks of queues. All the procedures call upon the concept of an *isolated* subsystem composed of one or more queues in the network. This isolated subsystem is examined in *detail*

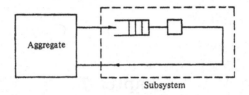

Fig. 7.1.   Simple aggregate/subsystem decomposition of a queueing network.

under the effect of the rest of the system viewed as an *aggregate*. In certain
cases, we consider several subsystems interacting with each other and with
the rest of the model. The simplest such structure is shown in Fig. 7.1,
where the subsystem is a single queue while the aggregate contains the
remaining queues of the system. An iterative solution technique based on
an aggregate/subsystem decomposition will often iterate between several
different decompositions of the type shown in Fig. 7.1 in order to reach an
approximate solution. The stationary solution will then be framed either in
terms of marginal distributions for each subsystem or as a product of the
marginal distributions when the stationary distribution for global network
state is desired.

In order to illustrate this common heuristic approach, we will first apply
it to a class of queueing networks for which it yields an *exact* result: a closed
network of exponential queues with FIFO service discipline and a single
class of customers.

7.2.1. *Aggregate/subsystem decomposition for a closed Jackson network*

Consider a closed Jackson network (see Chapter 3) with K customers, N
service centres with state-dependent service rates $\mu_i(n_i)$ where

$$\mathbf{n} = (n_1, \ldots, n_N)$$

is the occupancy vector (number of customers in queue) at each station.
The $N \times N$ stochastic matrix $\mathbf{P} = (p_{ij})$ represents the routing probabilities.

Let us now apply the decomposition of Fig. 7.1 where the subsystem
is queue 1. Its interaction with the rest of the system is achieved via
the steady-state flow λ_1 of customers per unit time to queue 1, and the
same flow (since the system is closed) back to the aggregate. We solve
the subsystem as an $M/M/1$ queue with state-dependent service and

call $p_1(n_1)$ its steady-state distribution:

$$p_1(n_1) = p_1(0) \left[\lambda_1^{n_1} \bigg/ \prod_{j=1}^{n_1} \mu_1(j) \right]$$

for $0 \leq n_1 \leq K$. The same is done for all of the remaining queues:

$$p_i(n_i) = p_i(0) \left[\lambda_i^{n_i} \bigg/ \prod_{j=1}^{n_i} \mu_i(j) \right] .$$

Finally, we relate the input flow to any queue to the output flows from all the queues:

$$\lambda_i = \sum_{j=1}^{N} \lambda_j P_{ji}$$

and postulate a product-form solution

$$p(\mathbf{n}) = G \prod_{i=1}^{N} p_i(n_i)$$

which, of course, yields the exact result in this particular case.

7.2.2. *Solution with one single aggregate/subsystem decomposition*

In the example of section 7.2.1 the aggregate/subsystem decomposition was carried out for *each* of the queues in the network. In certain cases the special structure of the aggregate leads one to attempt a solution using only a single specific aggregate/subsystem decomposition. This will be especially the case if, for instance, only the marginal distribution associated with the aggregate or the subsystem are required, or if the aggregate and subsystem can each be analysed separately using known analytical results.

Proceeding again via a simple example, let us examine a closed Jackson network. For further simplicity assume that service rates are *independent* of queue length. Let $(N-1)$ queues be in the aggregate and let queue number N be the subsystem.

We shall *imagine* that the aggregate interacts infrequently with the subsystem so that for long periods of time the aggregate itself behaves as a closed system: i.e. the transition rates $\mu_j p_{jN}$ of a customer going from queue j, $j \neq N$, to queue N are much smaller than the other non-zero transition rates. Furthermore, we suppose that the aggregate is strongly connected, i.e. that a customer can move with non-zero probability from any queue to any other one in the aggregate (but not necessarily in one step).

The quantity we wish to compute is $p_N(n_N)$, the marginal probability distribution of the N-th queue. The arrival rate to the N-th queue is

$$\lambda_N(n_N) = \sum_{i=1}^{N-1} p_{iN} \sum_{\substack{n_i>0 \\ \sum^{N-1} n_j=K-n_N}} \mu_i p(n_1, \ldots, n_{N-1}, n_N).$$

Now, assuming that the aggregate and the subsystem (the N-th queue) interact very infrequently, we can write using (3.37)

$$\sum_{\substack{n_i>0 \\ \sum^{N-1} n_j=K-n_N}} p(n_1, \ldots, n_{N-1}, n_N) \cong \left(\frac{e_i}{\mu_i}\right) \frac{G_{N-1}(K-n_N-1)}{G_{N-1}(K-n_N)}$$

which means that we suppose that the queues $1, \ldots, N-1$ behave as a *closed system* for any given value of n_N. Thus

$$\lambda_N(n_N) \cong \sum_{1=1}^{N-1} e_i p_{iN} \frac{G_{N-1}(K-n_N-1)}{G_{N-1}(K-n_N)} \cong e_N \frac{G_{N-1}(K-n_N-1)}{G_{N-1}(K-n_N)}.$$

$$(7.1)$$

We now solve for $p_N(n_N)$ in isolation, assuming a Poisson arrival rate $\lambda_N(j)$ when the N-th queue contains j customers:

$$p_N(n_N) \cong C \prod_{i=1}^{n_N} \left(\frac{\lambda(i-1)}{\mu_N}\right) \tag{7.2}$$

or using (7.1):

$$\frac{p_N(n_N)}{p_N(n_N-1)} \cong \left(\frac{e_N}{\mu_N}\right) \frac{G_{N-1}(K-n_N)}{G_{N-1}(K-n_N+1)}. \tag{7.3}$$

This procedure yields in fact the exact result for a Jackson network. Using (3.37) and the argument leading to (3.38) we can see that

$$p_N(n_N) = \frac{(e_N/\mu_N)^{n_N} G_N(K-n_N) - (e_N/\mu_N)^{n_N+1} G_N(K-n_N-1)}{G_N(K)}.$$

But using (3.35) we obtain

$$p_N(n_N) = \left(\frac{e_N}{\mu_N}\right)^{n_N} \frac{G_{N-1}(K-n_N)}{G_N(K)}$$

which obviously satisfies (7.3). Therefore (7.2) is in fact the *exact* form of the solution.

7.3. Decomposition as an approximate solution method

In the previous sections we considered decompositions of the Jackson network leading to exact solutions for marginal distributions. Such decomposition techniques are mainly used, however, in order to obtain *approximate* solutions to networks for which exact solutions are *unavailable* in closed form. In this section we shall describe an approach which originated with the work of Courtois [3, 4]. Our presentation will only be an introduction because a more complete presentation of the method is available elsewhere [4] in book-form and with many examples of applications.

Although the approach is applicable to open systems as well, we shall concentrate our attention on closed systems. We assume that the system we consider consists of N service centres and that its behaviour is Markovian so that it may be described by a *discrete time* Markov chain $\mathbf{Q} = (q(\mathbf{n}, \mathbf{n}'))$:

$$p(\mathbf{n}, t + \Delta t) = \sum_{\mathbf{n}'} p(\mathbf{n}', t) q(\mathbf{n}', \mathbf{n}) \tag{7.4}$$

where $\mathbf{n}$, $\mathbf{n}'$ are state vectors:

$$\mathbf{n} = (\mathbf{n}_1, \ldots, \mathbf{n}_N), \quad \mathbf{n}' = (\mathbf{n}'_1, \ldots, \mathbf{n}'_N)$$

and the vector

$$\mathbf{n}_i = (n_{i1}, \ldots, n_{ia_i}), \quad 1 \leq i \leq N$$

is the complete state representation associated with service centre i: we do not specify exactly what it is, but (as in Chapter 3) it may include a "method of stages" or "Coxian" representation of a general service distribution and of a multiple server with a complex service discipline. The only restrictions are that:

(i) each of the n_{ij}, $1 \leq i \leq N$, $1 \leq j \leq a_i$ are non-negative integers; and
(ii) the number n_i of customers present at station i can be directly deduced from $\mathbf{n}_i$: let us write this relation as $n_i = f(\mathbf{n}_i)$.

Since the system is closed we have, for some finite K, $K = \sum_1^N n_i$.

Of course, the passage from (7.4) to the Chapman–Kolmogorov differential equations can be carried out by taking the limit as $\Delta t \to 0$ of $[p(\mathbf{n}, t + \Delta t) - p(\mathbf{n}, t)]/\Delta t$, but it will be more convenient to work with (7.4) instead. We maintain the usual assumption that the system is strongly connected (irreducible and aperiodic), i.e. each state can be reached from any other state with non-zero probability in a finite amount of time.

Let τ be a partition of the set of service centres $\{1, \ldots, N\}$: $\tau = \{\tau_1, \ldots, \tau_l\}$. We shall say that *two state vectors* $\mathbf{n}$ *and* $\mathbf{n}'$ *are* τ-*equivalent* if and only if

$$(\forall j) \sum_{i \in \tau_j} n_i = \sum_{i \in \tau_j} n_i'.$$

Thus τ-equivalence of two state vectors $\mathbf{n}$ and $\mathbf{n}'$, denoted $\mathbf{n}$-τ-$\mathbf{n}'$, simply means that the number of customers in the group of service centres corresponding to each element τ_i of τ is the same for $\mathbf{n}$ and $\mathbf{n}'$.

The τ-equivalence relation induces a partition on the set of states of the Markov chain $\mathbf{Q}$. Let π denote the partition of the set of states $\mathbf{n}$ of $\mathbf{Q}$ induced by τ:

$$\pi = \{\pi_1, \ldots, \pi_k\}.$$

We now introduce the concept of a *nearly completely decomposable* (NCD) queueing network on a partition τ of the set of service centres. We shall say that the queueing network is NCD on τ if for each state vector $\mathbf{n}$, and each $\mathbf{n}'$-τ-$\mathbf{n}$,

$$q(\mathbf{n}, \mathbf{n}') \gg \sum_{\substack{\mathbf{n}'' \\ \mathbf{n}'' \not\tau - \mathbf{n}}} q(\mathbf{n}, \mathbf{n}'') \tag{7.5}$$

where $\mathbf{n}''$-$\not\tau$-$\mathbf{n}$ means that $\mathbf{n}''$ and $\mathbf{n}$ are *not* τ-equivalent. Inequality (7.5) stipulates that the transitions between states which are τ-equivalent are far more likely than others, and hence far more frequent. Thus, if a queueing network is NCD on a partition τ of its service centres, changes in the number of customers in each element of τ will be relatively infrequent with respect to state transitions which do not modify that number.

We shall say that a partition $\tau = \{\tau_1, \ldots, \tau_l\}$ is *non-trivial* if $1 < l < N$. An *element* of a non-trivial partition will be *non-trivial* if it contains more than one service centre. Henceforth we will consider a non-trivial partition; let τ_k be one of its non-trivial elements, and each element π_i of π corresponds to a set of τ-equivalent states:

$$\mathbf{n}, \mathbf{n}' \in \pi_i \quad \textit{if and only if} \quad \mathbf{n}\text{-}\tau\text{-}\mathbf{n}'.$$

We require that each element $\boldsymbol{\pi}_i$ of $\boldsymbol{\pi}$ be strongly connected: that is, for each $\mathbf{n}$, $\mathbf{n}' \in \boldsymbol{\pi}_i$ the probability of transition from $\mathbf{n}$ to $\mathbf{n}'$ in a finite number of steps *without passing through some state* $\mathbf{n}'' \notin \boldsymbol{\pi}_i$ is positive.

Let $\mathbf{D}$ be a stochastic matrix of the same dimension as $\mathbf{Q}$ (the matrix whose elements are the $q(\mathbf{n}, \mathbf{n}')$) such that its elements $d(\mathbf{n}, \mathbf{n}')$ have the property

$$d(\mathbf{n}, \mathbf{n}') \neq 0 \ \textit{only if} \ \mathbf{n}\text{-}\boldsymbol{\tau}\text{-}\mathbf{n}'.$$

$\mathbf{Q}$ may be written as

$$\mathbf{Q} = \mathbf{D} + \varepsilon\mathbf{E} \tag{7.6}$$

where $\mathbf{D}$, ε, $\mathbf{E}$ are determined as follows:

$$d(\mathbf{n}, \mathbf{n}') = \begin{cases} \left(q(\mathbf{n}, \mathbf{n}') \Big/ \displaystyle\sum_{n-\tau-n''} q(\mathbf{n}, \mathbf{n}'') \right) & \text{if } \mathbf{n}\text{-}\boldsymbol{\tau}\text{-}\mathbf{n}' \\ 0 & \text{otherwise} \end{cases} \tag{7.7}$$

$$\varepsilon = \max_{\mathbf{n},\mathbf{n}'} |q(\mathbf{n}, \mathbf{n}') - d(\mathbf{n}, \mathbf{n}')|. \tag{7.8}$$

$\mathbf{E}$ is a matrix, of same dimension as $\mathbf{Q}$ and $\mathbf{D}$, such that its elements $e(\mathbf{n}, \mathbf{n}')$ are given by

$$e(\mathbf{n}, \mathbf{n}') = [q(\mathbf{n}, \mathbf{n}') - d(\mathbf{n}, \mathbf{n}')]/\varepsilon.$$

Since both $\mathbf{Q}$ and $\mathbf{D}$ are stochastic matrices, it follows that row sums of $\mathbf{E}$ will be zero. Furthermore, $|e(\mathbf{n}, \mathbf{n}')| \leq 1$.

It is clear from (7.7) that by a permutation of rows and columns, $\mathbf{D}$ may be rewritten in block diagonal form as:

$$\mathbf{D} = \begin{bmatrix} \boxed{\mathbf{D}_1} & & & \mathbf{0} \\ & \boxed{\mathbf{D}_2} & & \\ & & \ddots & \\ \mathbf{0} & & & \boxed{\mathbf{D}_k} \end{bmatrix} \tag{7.9}$$

where each $\mathbf{D}_i$ corresponds to the element $\boldsymbol{\pi}_i$ of the partition $\boldsymbol{\pi}$. Without loss of generality we shall assume that this has been done, and that $\mathbf{Q}$ and $\mathbf{E}$ are also written so that their rows and columns coincide with those of $\mathbf{D}$.

7.3.1. *Approximate stationary solution of the system Q*

Our purpose is to exploit the NCD of $\mathbf{Q}$ in order to obtain an approximate solution to the system of equations (7.4) in stationary state. That is, we seek the solution $\mathbf{q}$ to the equation

$$\mathbf{q} = \mathbf{qQ} \qquad (7.10)$$

with

$$\sum_{\mathbf{n}} q(\mathbf{n}) = 1$$

where $q(\mathbf{n})$ is the element of the row vector $\mathbf{q}$ corresponding to $\mathbf{n}$.

A vector $\mathbf{d}$, satisfying the equation

$$\mathbf{d} = \mathbf{dD} \qquad (7.11)$$

will be used to approximate $\mathbf{q}$. In fact (7.11) does not have a unique solution, even when the condition

$$\sum_{\mathbf{n}} d(\mathbf{n}) = 1$$

is used ($d(\mathbf{n})$ is the element of $\mathbf{d}$ corresponding to $\mathbf{n}$) because of the block diagonal structure of $\mathbf{D}$: from (7.9) we see that k additional equations have to be provided. We shall presently examine how these conditions may be chosen in order to obtain a "good" approximation $\mathbf{d}$ of the vector of equilibrium probabilities $\mathbf{q}$. We write

$$\mathbf{q} = \mathbf{qQ} = \mathbf{qD} + \varepsilon\mathbf{qE} \qquad (7.12)$$

and we may express $\mathbf{q}$ as

$$\mathbf{q} = \mathbf{d} + \boldsymbol{\delta} \qquad (7.13)$$

where $\boldsymbol{\delta}$ is the "error" vector. Then (7.12) becomes

$$\mathbf{d} + \boldsymbol{\delta} = (\mathbf{d} + \boldsymbol{\delta})\mathbf{D} + \varepsilon\mathbf{qE}$$

or

$$\boldsymbol{\delta}(\mathbf{I} - \mathbf{D}) = \varepsilon\mathbf{qE}. \qquad (7.14)$$

Our problem is now to choose the k additional relations to be satisfied by the $d(\mathbf{n})$, so that the elements $\delta(\mathbf{n})$ of the error vector will be small. A natural choice of these conditions results from concepts related to the *lumpability* of stochastic matrices which will be examined below.

Let $\mathbf{A} = (a(\mathbf{n}, \mathbf{n}'))$ be a stochastic matrix (of same dimension as $\mathbf{Q}$). We shall say that $\mathbf{A}$ *is lumpable on* $\boldsymbol{\pi}$ if for each $\mathbf{n}$ (used to denote a row or column of $\mathbf{A}$)

$$\sum_{\mathbf{n}' \in \pi_i} a(\mathbf{n}, \mathbf{n}') = \sum_{\mathbf{n}' \in \pi_i} a(\mathbf{n}'', \mathbf{n}')$$

for each $\mathbf{n}''$, $\mathbf{n} \in \boldsymbol{\pi}_j$, and for all $\boldsymbol{\pi}_i$, $\boldsymbol{\pi}_j$. If $\mathbf{A}$ is lumpable on $\boldsymbol{\pi}$, we can then construct the *lumped matrix* $\mathbf{A}_{\boldsymbol{\pi}}$ from $\mathbf{A}$: $\mathbf{A}_{\boldsymbol{\pi}}$ is a $k \times k$ stochastic matrix ($\boldsymbol{\pi} = \{\boldsymbol{\pi}_1, \ldots, \boldsymbol{\pi}_k\}$) such that $\mathbf{A}_{\boldsymbol{\pi}} = (\alpha(i, j))$ and

$$\alpha(i, j) = \sum_{\mathbf{n}' \in \pi_j} a(\mathbf{n}, \mathbf{n}'), \quad \text{for any} \quad \mathbf{n} \in \boldsymbol{\pi}_i.$$

Clearly, $\mathbf{A}_{\boldsymbol{\pi}}$ is a stochastic matrix.

Example 7.1

Let

$$\mathbf{A} = \begin{bmatrix} \dfrac{1}{8} & \dfrac{3}{8} & \dfrac{1}{2} \\[2mm] \dfrac{1}{4} & \dfrac{1}{4} & \dfrac{1}{2} \\[2mm] \dfrac{1}{3} & \dfrac{1}{3} & \dfrac{1}{3} \end{bmatrix}.$$

$\mathbf{A}$ is lumpable on the partition $\boldsymbol{\pi} = \{(1, 2), (3)\}$ and

$$\mathbf{A}_{\boldsymbol{\pi}} = \begin{bmatrix} \dfrac{1}{2} & \dfrac{1}{2} \\[2mm] \dfrac{2}{3} & \dfrac{1}{3} \end{bmatrix}.$$

Example 7.2

The matrix $\mathbf{D}$ defined by (7.4) and shown in (7.9) is lumpable on $\boldsymbol{\pi} = \{\boldsymbol{\pi}_1, \ldots, \boldsymbol{\pi}_k\}$ and

$$\mathbf{D}_{\boldsymbol{\pi}} = \begin{bmatrix} 1 & & & 0 \\ & 1 & & \\ & & \ddots & \\ 0 & & & 1 \end{bmatrix}.$$

is the $k \times k$ unit matrix.

(a) *The case when* $\mathbf{Q}$ *is lumpable on* $\boldsymbol{\pi}$: Suppose that $\mathbf{Q}$ is lumpable on $\boldsymbol{\pi}$. $\mathbf{Q}_{\boldsymbol{\pi}}$ is the $k \times k$ stochastic matrix obtained by lumping $\mathbf{Q}$ on $\boldsymbol{\pi}$, and let $\mathbf{q}^{\boldsymbol{\pi}}$ be the stochastic row vector satisfying

$$\mathbf{q}^{\boldsymbol{\pi}} \mathbf{Q}_{\boldsymbol{\pi}} = \mathbf{q}^{\boldsymbol{\pi}}, \quad \sum_{i=1}^{k} q_i^{\boldsymbol{\pi}} = 1.$$

Clearly, the i-th element $q_i^{\boldsymbol{\pi}}$ of $\mathbf{q}^{\boldsymbol{\pi}}$ is the stationary probability of finding $\mathbf{Q}$ in any of the states $\mathbf{n} \in \pi_i$, $1 \leq i \leq k$.

We shall then use the k additional conditions

$$q_i^{\boldsymbol{\pi}} = \sum_{\mathbf{n} \in \pi_i} \mathbf{d}(\mathbf{n}), \quad 1 \leq i \leq k \qquad (7.15)$$

in order to solve the system

$$\mathbf{d} = \mathbf{d}\mathbf{D}.$$

Because $\mathbf{Q}$ is lumpable on $\boldsymbol{\pi}$, it can be easily seen that $\mathbf{q}$, its stationary probability distribution vector, has the property

$$\sum_{\mathbf{n} \in \pi_i} q(\mathbf{n}) = q_i^{\boldsymbol{\pi}}, \quad 1 \leq i \leq k.$$

Thus for the error vector, for all $1 \leq i \leq k$,

$$\sum_{\mathbf{n} \in \pi_i} \boldsymbol{\delta}(\mathbf{n}) = 0. \qquad (7.16)$$

and the approximate solution $\mathbf{d}$ is now *exact* on the lumped states.

(b) *Error analysis when* $\mathbf{Q}$ *is lumpable*: Approximating $\mathbf{q}$ by $\mathbf{d}$, obtained by using the k conditions (7.15), leads to a particular error vector: an estimation of its magnitude, which we shall presently derive, will also provide a quantitative meaning for the decomposition method.

In order to evaluate the nature of the approximation, it is necessary to let either $\mathbf{D} \to \mathbf{Q}$ or $\mathbf{Q} \to \mathbf{D}$, and to examine the effect of this limiting effect on the manner in which $\mathbf{d} \to \mathbf{q}$ or $\mathbf{q} \to \mathbf{d}$. The analysis here will be based on the following premises:

(i) $\mathbf{Q}$ is *fixed*, $\mathbf{D} = \mathbf{Q} - \varepsilon \mathbf{E}$ and $\mathbf{D} \to \mathbf{Q}$ as $\varepsilon \to 0$;

(ii) the matrix $\mathbf{E}$, of relative differences with respect to the maximum difference ε, is also *fixed* as ε varies. This determines the manner in which $\mathbf{D} \to \mathbf{Q}$ as $\varepsilon \to 0$.

We may write (7.14) as

$$\boldsymbol{\delta}_\varepsilon = \boldsymbol{\delta}_\varepsilon[\mathbf{Q} - \varepsilon\mathbf{E}] + \varepsilon\mathbf{q}\mathbf{E}. \tag{7.17}$$

Clearly, for each $\varepsilon \geq 0$ this system of equations has a unique solution since both $\mathbf{q}$ and $\mathbf{d}$ exist and are unique (if the conditions of (a) are used). We can verify that the solution may be written in the following form

$$\boldsymbol{\delta}_\varepsilon = \sum_{i=1}^\infty \mathbf{a}_i \varepsilon^i$$

where the $\mathbf{a}_i$ are vectors satisfying:

$$\mathbf{a}_1 = \mathbf{a}_1\mathbf{Q} = \mathbf{q}\mathbf{E}$$
$$\mathbf{a}_{i+1} = \mathbf{a}_{i+1}\mathbf{Q} - \mathbf{a}_i\mathbf{E}, \quad i \geq 1. \tag{7.18}$$

Clearly, $\boldsymbol{\delta}_0 = \mathbf{O}$ so that the above summation must indeed begin with $i = 1$. Furthermore, (7.18) can be verified by substitution in (7.17). Clearly, the vectors $\mathbf{a}_i$ are independent of ε so that for very small ε,

$$\boldsymbol{\delta}_\varepsilon \approx \boldsymbol{a}_1\varepsilon.$$

Thus we can provide, by computing $\mathbf{a}_1$, a first-order estimate of the error made in approximating $\mathbf{q}$ by $\mathbf{d}$, and (7.18) provides a precise meaning for the approximation involved in this method.

(c) *The general case*: Suppose now that $\mathbf{Q}$ is not lumpable on $\boldsymbol{\pi}$. We shall write $\mathbf{Q}$ as

$$\mathbf{Q} = \hat{\mathbf{Q}} + \mu\mathbf{U} \tag{7.19}$$

where $\hat{\mathbf{Q}}$, $\mathbf{U}$ are matrices of the same dimension as $\mathbf{Q}$; $\hat{\mathbf{Q}}$ is stochastic and lumpable on $\boldsymbol{\pi}$ and μ is a real number.

Let us define, for $i \neq j$,

$$\mu_{ij} = \max_{\mathbf{n}\in\pi_i}\left[\sum_{\mathbf{n}'\in\pi_j} q(\mathbf{n},\mathbf{n}')\right] \tag{7.20}$$

and designate by $\mathbf{c}_i$ any single vector element of $\boldsymbol{\pi}_i$. For $\mathbf{n} \in \boldsymbol{\pi}_i$ and $j \neq 1$, let

$$\mu_{ij}(\mathbf{n}) = \mu_{ij} - \sum_{\mathbf{n}'\in\pi_i} q(\mathbf{n},\mathbf{n}'). \tag{7.21}$$

$\hat{\mathbf{Q}} = (\hat{q}(\mathbf{n}, \mathbf{n}'))$, μ and $\mathbf{U}$ are constructed as follows. For some $1 \leq i \leq k$, let $\mathbf{n} \in \pi_i$ (without loss of generality):

$$
\hat{q}(\mathbf{n}, \mathbf{n}') = \begin{cases} q(\mathbf{n}, \mathbf{n}') + \mu_{ij}(\mathbf{n}), & \text{if } \mathbf{n}' = \mathbf{c}_i \text{ and } i \neq j \\[2mm] q(\mathbf{n}, \mathbf{n}) - \displaystyle\sum_{\substack{j=1 \\ j\neq i}}^{k} \mu_{ij}(\mathbf{n}), & \text{if } \mathbf{n}' = \mathbf{n} \\[2mm] q(\mathbf{n}, \mathbf{n}'), & \text{otherwise.} \end{cases} \tag{7.22}
$$

Thus $\hat{\mathbf{Q}}$ is obtained by adding to exactly *one* element $q(\mathbf{n}, \mathbf{c}_i)$ of each row the quantity $\mu_{ij}(\mathbf{n})$ which will ensure that for each $\mathbf{n}$, $\mathbf{n}'' \in \pi_i$

$$
\sum_{\mathbf{n}' \in \pi_j} \hat{q}(\mathbf{n}, \mathbf{n}') = \sum_{\mathbf{n}' \in \pi_j} \hat{q}(\mathbf{n}'', \mathbf{n}'), \quad 1 \leq j \leq k,
$$

and by subtracting the sum of the quantities added from the diagonal elements; μ is taken to be

$$
\mu = \max_i \sum_{\substack{j=1 \\ j\neq i}}^{k} \mu_{ij}. \tag{7.23}
$$

This guarantees that all elements of $\mathbf{U}$ will be less than one in absolute value. The following points should be noticed:

(i) $\mu \leq \varepsilon$ (see (7.8));
(ii) the diagonal elements $\hat{q}(\mathbf{n}, \mathbf{n})$ are *positive* because $\mathbf{Q}$ is NCD (see (7.5));
(iii) as a consequence $\hat{\mathbf{Q}}$ is irreducible and aperiodic if $\mathbf{Q}$ is.

Let $\hat{\mathbf{q}}$ be the vector of stationary probabilities associated with $\hat{\mathbf{Q}}$:

$$
\hat{\mathbf{q}} = \hat{\mathbf{q}}\hat{\mathbf{Q}}.
$$

The procedure for obtaining an approximate solution to the vector $\mathbf{q}$ could be the following.

Procedure: If μ is "small enough", and if $\hat{\mathbf{Q}}$ is NCD, the problem reduces to that of (b) since one will now construct a decomposable matrix $\mathbf{D}$ and solve $\mathbf{dD} = \mathbf{d}$ using $\mathbf{d}$ as an approximation to $\mathbf{q}$ solution of $\mathbf{qQ} = \mathbf{q}$.

Of course, since $\hat{\mathbf{Q}}$ is lumpable on $\boldsymbol{\pi}$, we shall use the $\hat{q}_i^\pi$, $1 \leq i \leq k$, as the k additional conditions

$$\hat{q}_i^\pi = \sum_{\mathbf{n} \in \pi_i} d(\mathbf{n}) \quad \text{where } \hat{q}_i^\pi = \sum_{\mathbf{n} \in \pi_i} \hat{q}(\mathbf{n})$$

in order to solve $\mathbf{dD} = \mathbf{d}$. It will now be necessary to evaluate the error with respect to μ in addition to the error with respect to ε (as in (b)).

(d) *Error analysis in the general case*: We shall first consider the error resulting from the approximation of $\mathbf{q}$ by $\hat{\mathbf{q}}$. As in (b) we shall assume that:

  (i) $\mathbf{Q}$ is fixed (given);
 (ii) the relative error matrix $\mathbf{U}$ remains constant as μ varies ($\mu > 0$);
(iii) $\hat{\mathbf{Q}} \rightarrow \mathbf{Q}$ as $\mu \rightarrow 0$.

Write

$$\mathbf{q} = \hat{\mathbf{q}} + \boldsymbol{\alpha}$$

where $\boldsymbol{\alpha}$ is the error vector obtained when approximating $\mathbf{q}$ by $\hat{\mathbf{q}}$. From (7.19) we can write

$$\hat{\mathbf{q}} + \boldsymbol{\alpha} = \hat{\mathbf{q}} + \boldsymbol{\alpha}\hat{\mathbf{Q}} + \mu\mathbf{q}\mathbf{U}$$

or

$$\boldsymbol{\alpha} = \boldsymbol{\alpha}\hat{\mathbf{Q}} + \mu\mathbf{q}\mathbf{U} = \boldsymbol{\alpha}[\mathbf{Q} - \mu\mathbf{U}] + \mu\mathbf{q}\mathbf{U}. \tag{7.24}$$

We write

$$\boldsymbol{\alpha} = \sum_{i=1}^{\infty} \mathbf{b}_i \mu^i \tag{7.25}$$

where the vectors $\mathbf{b}_i$, by substitution in (7.24), must satisfy

$$\mathbf{b}_1 = \mathbf{b}_1\hat{\mathbf{Q}} + \mathbf{q}\mathbf{U}$$
$$\mathbf{b}_{i+1} = \mathbf{b}_{i+1}\hat{\mathbf{Q}} - \mathbf{b}_i\mathbf{U}, \quad i \leq 1 \tag{7.26}$$

so that, for small μ,

$$\boldsymbol{\alpha} \cong \boldsymbol{b}_1\mu \tag{7.27}$$

which gives us the first-order approximation to the error vector. Therefore

$$\mathbf{q} \cong \mathbf{d} + \mu\mathbf{b}_1 + \varepsilon\mathbf{a}_1 \tag{7.28}$$

if we write

$$(\hat{\mathbf{q}} - \mathbf{d}) = \sum_{i=1}^{\infty} \mathbf{a}_i \varepsilon^i$$

where the $\mathbf{a}_i$ are determined as in (b).

Decomposition methods will be used in the study of multiprogramming virtual memory systems in Chapter 7.

7.4. An electric circuit analogy for queueing network solution

A technique which is very closely related to decomposition, inspired by electric network equivalents, was developed by Chandy, Herzog and Woo [1]. In electric networks, a complex portion of the network can be simplified by replacing it by an equivalent current source and parallel impedance, or by a voltage source and series impedance (Norton or Thévenin equivalent circuits). These equivalent circuits are exact equivalences for electric systems, and they suggest a heuristic equivalence for queueing networks. The approach developed in [1] is in fact a special form of decomposition, as seen in section 7.3, but it has been applied with success also to systems which are not decomposable.

Suppose that we decompose a queueing network containing K customers into two disjoint subnetworks, as shown in Fig. 7.2. Assume that the quantities of interest are the marginal probabilities $p_1(K_1)$, $p_2(K_2)$, of the number of customers in SUBNET 1 and SUBNET 2, respectively. Here K_1, K_2 represent the number of customers in SUBNET 1 and SUBNET 2, respectively. The heuristic application of Norton's theorem proceeds as follows:

(i) Remove the connection between the two subnetworks, so that a customer leaving SUBNET 1 at A_1 immediately returns to SUBNET 1 through B_1; a customer leaving SUBNET 2 from B_2 will immediately return to it through A_2.

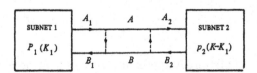

Fig. 7.2.   Norton's equivalent applied to a queueing network.

(ii) For *fixed* values of $K_1 = 0, 1, \ldots, K$ compute the flow of customers from A_1 to B_1 in stationary state for the isolated SUBNET 1. Call it $\lambda_1(K_1)$. Do the same thing for $\lambda_2(K_2)$, which is the flow of customers in the isolated SUBNET 2. Notice that it is possible that $\lambda_1(0) \neq 0$ or $\lambda_2(0) \neq 0$ if external arrivals can occur.

(iii) Now replace the system of Fig. 7.2 by that of Fig. 7.3 in which SUBNET 1 and SUBNET 2 have been replaced by equivalent servers of rates $\lambda_1(\cdot)$ and $\lambda_2(\cdot)$, respectively.

(iv) In order to obtain the marginal distributions $p_1(K_1) = p_2(K - K_1)$ treat the system of Fig. 7.3 as two $M/M/1$ state-dependent systems or, equivalently, as a finite-capacity $M/M/1$ state-dependent system so that (see Chapter 1)

$$p_1(K_1) = p_2(K - K_1) = p_1(0) \prod_{i=1}^{K_1} \frac{\lambda_2(K - i + 1)}{\lambda_1(i)}$$

where

$$p_1(0) = \left[1 + \sum_{K_1=1}^{K} \prod_{i=1}^{K_1} \frac{\lambda_2(K - i)}{\lambda_1(i)} \right]^{-1} .$$

It is clear that this heuristic, very similar in spirit to the approaches presented in the previous sections of this chapter, can be applied at various levels of detail (i.e. for different numbers of queues or service stations in SUBNET 1 or SUBNET 2). It may also be refined so as to consider more

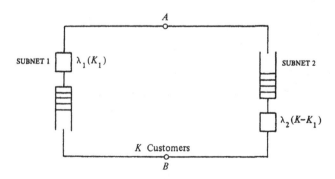

Fig. 7.3. The equivalent simplified queueing network.

complex statistics of the flow of customers, as done in Chapter 4 for diffusion approximations.

More complex approximation techniques similar to this one have been developed by Marie [5], where numerous examples and evaluations of the accuracy of these techniques may be found.

Chandy, Herzog and Woo [1] have shown that "Norton's theorem" holds for networks which satisfy local balance: we exhibit a special instance of this in section 7.2.2. In [2] they show how this concept can be applied to the computation of an approximate solution for closed networks of queues for which an exact solution is not known. We shall outline their method here.

Let us consider here a closed network with K customers and N service centres. Let p_{ij}, $1 \leq i, j \leq N$, denote as usual the transition probabilities and $F_i(t)$ the service time distribution at centre i which is allowed to be general; let μ_i^{-1} denote the average service time at centre i, and let the service discipline be first-come-first-served.

Denote by e_i, $1 \leq i \leq N$, a solution of the system of equations

$$\sum_1^N e_j p_{ji} = e_i$$

so that e_i is the average number, relative with respect to some station, of visits that a customer makes to centre i.

We shall construct a sequence of queueing networks, called $R_0, R_1, \ldots,$ $R_m, \ldots$ which will be used to approximate the queueing network R defined above. R_0 is obtained from R by replacing all of the $F_i(t)$ by exponential distributions having the same average μ_i^{-1}. R_m, $m \geq 1$, may differ from R_0 *only* in the average service times at its servers, which we shall call $\mu_{i,m}^{-1}$. Thus the quantities e_i, $1 \leq i \leq N$, are the same for each R_m and preserve the same physical meaning.

Let $\hat{U}_{i,m}$ be an estimate of the , or number of customers served per unit time, at centre i of network R_m; $\hat{U}_{i,m}$ is merely an estimate since (as seen below) it will be computed approximately.

Similarly, let $\hat{Q}_{i,m}$ be an estimate of average queue length at centre i in R_m.

Notice that the $U_{i,m}$, the true s for R_m, must satisfy

$$\sum_{j=1}^N U_{j,m} p_{ji} = U_{i,m}$$

and the normalised $\theta_{i,m} = U_{i,m}/e_i$ satisfies the system

$$\sum_{j=1}^{N} \theta_{j,m} e_j p_{ji} = \theta_{i,m} e_i, \quad 1 \le i \le N$$

whose solutions must necessarily satisfy

$$\theta_{i,m} = \theta_{j,m} \quad \text{for all } i, j.$$

Again, we shall make use of $\hat{\theta}_{i,m} = \hat{U}_{i,m}/e_i$ rather than of $\theta_{i,m}$.

We now present the construction of R_{m+1} from R_m.

Step (1): R_m is a closed network of exponential servers of rates $\mu_{i,m}$, $1 \le i \le N$, with K customers.

Step (1.1): For each fixed i, construct the equivalent subnetwork containing all service centres *except* i; call this subnetwork $C_{i,m}$. Compute the output rate from $C_{i,m}$ towards centre i, considering $C_{i,m}$ as a *closed* network with $1, \dots, K$ customers and call it $\lambda_{i,m}(l)$, $l = 1, \dots, K$.

Step (1.2): Solve the two-queue network of Fig. 7.4 using an appropriate method (exact, numerical, etc). Notice that the service time distribution of centre i is the general distribution given in the initial network R, for this step.

Step (1.3): Compute $\hat{Q}_{i,m}$ and $\hat{U}_{i,m}$ from the results of step (1.2).

Step (1.4): If, for some small positive constant ε,

$$(i) \qquad (1 - \varepsilon)K \le \sum_{i=1}^{N} \hat{Q}_{i,m} \le (1 + \varepsilon)K, \quad \text{and}$$

$$(ii) \qquad (1 - \varepsilon)\frac{1}{N}\sum_{j=1}^{N} \hat{\theta}_{j,m} \le \hat{\theta}_{i,m} \le (1 + \varepsilon)\frac{1}{N}\sum_{j=1}^{N} \hat{\theta}_{j,m},$$

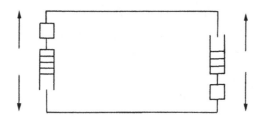

Fig. 7.4.

for all i, then proceed to step (1.5); otherwise go to step (2).

Step (1.5): Compute, for $1 \le i \le N$,

$$\mu_{i,m+1} = \mu_{i,m} \hat{\theta}_{i,m} N \left/ \sum_{j=1}^{N} \hat{\theta}_{j,m} \right. .$$

If

$$|\mu_{i,m+1} - \mu_{i,m}| \le \mu_{i,m} \varepsilon$$

then the procedure stops at the m-th iteration: the quantities computed in step (1.2) are considered to be a satisfactory approximation to R. Otherwise start at step (1) with m replaced by $m+1$ and $\mu_{i,m+1}$ computed in step (1.5).

Step (2): If (i) is *not* satisfied but (ii) is satisfied, go to step (2.2); otherwise proceed to step (2.1).

Step (2.1): Compute, for $1 \le i \le N$,

$$\mu_{i,m+1} = \mu_{i,m} \hat{\theta}_{i,m} N \left/ \sum_{j=1}^{N} \hat{\theta}_{j,m} \right. .$$

If

$$|\mu_{i,m+1} - \mu_{i,m}| \le \mu_{i,m} \varepsilon$$

go to step (2.2); otherwise start the $(m + 1)$-th step of the iteration by returning to step (1) with the values $\mu_{i,m+1}$ computed above.

Step (2.2): Compute

$$\mu_{i,m+1} = \mu_{i,m} N \left/ \sum_{j=1}^{N} \hat{Q}_{i,m} \right.$$

for all $1 \le i \le M$. The effect is to increase the service rates if queue lengths are too large, and to decrease them if they are too small. Now return to step (1), to begin the $(m + 1)$-th step of the iteration.

The role of the steps of this iterative technique merits some explanation. All parts of steps (1) are used to compute an approximation from R_m to the related quantities of the original network R. Step (2) constructs modifications to R_m which will be incorporated in R_{m+1}.

Step (1.1) applies Norton's theorem to each complementary network $C_{i,m}$ of the queue i, for each i; step (1.2) solves the pair (queue i equivalent queue of $C_{i,m}$) using some appropriate technique. Step (1.4) verifies that the solutions thus obtained are within reasonable bounds to conditions which the exact solution must satisfy. Step (1.5) checks whether an improvement in the $\mu_{i,m}$ will be significant, and does "fine tuning" to obtain R_{m+1} from R_m. Step (2) modifies R_m if the conditions checked in step (1.4) are not satisfied.

This completes the description of the iterative method of [2]: the reader is referred to the reference for some partial results concerning its accuracy and to [5] for related results and examples. Another technique for solving similar models can be found in [6].

References

1. Chandy, K. M., Herzog, U. and Woo, L. (1975). Parametric analysis of general queueing networks. *IBM Res. and Dev.*, **19**, 36–42.
2. Chandy, K. M., Herzog, U. and Woo, L. (1975). Approximate analysis of general queueing networks. *IBM J. Res. and Dev.*, **19**, 43–49.
3. Courtois, P. J. (1972). "On the Near-Complete Decomposability of Networks of Queues and of Stochastic Models of Multiprogramming Computer Systems." Computer Science Report, CMU-CS-72, III, Carnegie-Mellon University, Pittsburgh, Pennsylvania.
4. Courtois, P. J. (1977). "Decomposability: Queueing and Computer System Applications." Academic Press, New York.
5. Marie, R. (1978). "Méthodes itératives de Résolution de Réseaux de files d'Attente", Doctoral Thesis, Université de Rennes.
6. Shum, A. V. and Buzen, J. P. (1977). A method for obtaining approximate solutions to closed queueing networks with general service times. *In* "Modelling and Performance Evaluation of Computer Systems" (H. Beilner and E. Gelenbe, Eds), pp. 201–220. North-Holland, Amsterdam.

Chapter 8

Synthesis Problems in Single-Resource Systems: Characterisation and Control of Achievable Performance

8.1. Problem formulation

So far, we have taken an analytic approach to performance evaluation: for a given system we have tried (by analysing an appropriate mathematical model) to obtain the values of certain performance measures of interest. Suppose, however, that the manager of a computer installation is given a performance objective to be achieved and that he has a certain freedom in deciding how the system should be organised and operated. That manager will then wish to know not what the system performance will be for a particular mode of operation but what mode of operation, if any, should be chosen in order to meet the performance objective. The latter type of question gives rise to what we call problems of synthesis.

The factors which influence the performance of a computer system can be grouped into three broad categories: physical characteristics (processor speed, memory capacity, etc.); demand characteristics (number and nature of different job types, arrival patterns, etc.); and scheduling strategies (admission procedures, order in which jobs are executed by processors, memory allocation procedures, etc.). Having once acquired the hardware and allowed a population of users access to the facilities, the installation management has usually little or no further control over the first two categories; the physical and demand parameters can therefore be regarded as given and fixed. The freedom of choice, and hence the possibilities for control, are provided by the scheduling strategies. In the following, we shall devote our attention to several important synthesis problems stated in terms of designing scheduling strategies to meet performance objectives.

This chapter is concerned with single-resource systems where the demand comprises different job types and where the performance objectives discriminate between them. The basic model employed is a single-server queue with a finite number, R, of customer classes arriving in independent streams. As a measure of system performance we take the vector (to be called "performance vector")

$$\mathbf{W} = (W_1, W_2, \ldots, W_R)$$

where W_r is the steady-state average response time (time spent in the system) for jobs of class r ($r = 1, 2, \ldots, R$). Clearly, given the physical and demand characteristics (i.e. the speed of the server and the arrival and job length distribution parameters for the different job classes), the performance vector vector depends only on the algorithm that selects jobs for service — the scheduling strategy. If to a scheduling strategy S there corresponds a performance vector $\mathbf{W}$ we say that S achieves $\mathbf{W}$ and denote it by

$$S \to \mathbf{W}.$$

A given performance vector $\mathbf{W}$ is said to be achievable if there exists a scheduling strategy S such that $S \to \mathbf{W}$; there may, of course, be many scheduling strategies which achieve the same performance vector.

The first and most basic problem to be considered is one of characterisation: What is the set of the achievable performance vectors? How can one tell whether or not a given performance vector belongs to that set? Next, there come problems of design and optimisation: for a given performance objective, determine a suitable scheduling strategy to meet it. The answers to these questions depend on the precise definition of "scheduling strategy"; they depend on the degree of complexity that is allowed in the servicing disciplines and on the amount of information supplied about the jobs. For example, both the set of the achievable performance vectors and various "best" scheduling strategies depend on whether pre-emption of jobs in service is allowed or not, whether exact jobs lengths or only their distributions are known in advance, etc.

Just as, in physical systems, there are certain invariants governed by the fundamental laws of nature and governing the behaviour of physical phenomena, so in the servicing systems that concern us there are certain invariants and laws governing their performance. These laws are basic to the study of synthesis problems and we shall now proceed to derive them.

8.2. Conservation laws and inequalities

Let us introduce the notion of "virtual load". For a particular realisation of the queueing process under scheduling strategy S, the virtual load at time $t, V_S(t)$, is defined as the total amount of work in the system at time t, i.e. the sum of the remaining required service times for all jobs that are in the system at time t. If the speed of the server is 1 (which we may, and do, assume without loss of generality), "required service times" can be replaced by "service times" in this definition. A typical realisation of $V_S(t)$ is illustrated in Fig. 8.1.

At the instants of job arrivals $V_S(t)$ jumps upwards by an amount equal to the required service time of the incoming job; while a job is being served (any job), it decreases linearly with slope -1 (or $-C$ if C is the server speed); while the server is idle it remains constant (non-zero if there are jobs in the system, zero otherwise); it jumps downwards whenever a job departs before the end of its service (the amount of such a jump being the remaining service time of the departing job). It should be obvious from the definition that, given the sequence of job arrival instants and required service times, the only way in which the scheduling strategy S can influence $V_S(t)$ is by forcing the server to be idle when there are jobs in the system and by making jobs leave before their service is completed (we assume that jobs do not leave unfinished of their own free will). If these two actions are disallowed (and they are indeed alien to most computer operating systems) then $V_S(t)$ would be independent of S.

A scheduling strategy which does not allow the server to be idle when there is work to be done and does not cause jobs to depart before they are

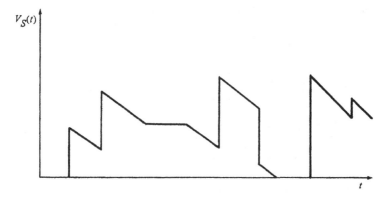

Fig. 8.1.

finished is called "work-conserving". From now on, even if we do not say so explicitly, all scheduling strategies will be presumed work-conserving.

We shall assume now that the stochastic process $V_S(t)$ has an equilibrium distribution and denote its steady-state average by V_S:

$$V_S = \lim_{t \to \infty} E[V_S(t)].$$

Since $V_S(t)$, and hence $E[V_S(t)]$, is independent of S for every t, we have the following basic result.

Theorem 8.1 (General Conservation Law). *For any single-server queueing system in equilibrium there exists a constant V, determined only by the parameters of the arrival and required service times processes, such that*

$$V_S = V \tag{8.1}$$

for all work-conserving scheduling strategies S.

Let us examine the implications of this result. We can rewrite (8.1) as

$$\sum_{r=1}^{R} V_S(r) = V \tag{8.2}$$

where $V_S(r)$ is the expected steady-state virtual load due to jobs of class r (the sum of the average remaining service times of all class r jobs in the system at a random point in the steady-state) under scheduling strategy S. For a given r, the value of $V_S(r)$ depends on S in general (e.g. if the priority of class r jobs is increased, $V_S(r)$ is likely to decrease). Theorem 8.1 asserts that the vector $(V_S(1), V_S(2), \ldots, V_S(R))$ always varies with S in such a way that the sum of its elements remains constant. Note that the truth of this statement does not rely on any assumptions about interarrival times, service times or independency between them.

Intuitively, the average virtual load due to class r is related to the average number of class r jobs in the system, and hence to the average response time for class r jobs. The general conservation law (8.2) should therefore imply a relation among the elements of the response time vector **W**. However, in order to render such a relation explicit we have to make more restrictive assumptions regarding the nature of the demand processes and the complexity of the scheduling strategies.

A scheduling strategy is a procedure for deciding which job, if any, should be in service at any moment of time. It takes as input any information that is available (the time of day, the types of job in the system, their arrival instants, the amounts of service they have received, etc.) and returns the identifier of the job to be served, or zero if the server is to be idle. The only restriction imposed so far has been that the procedure returns zero if, and only if, there are no jobs in the system. Now we add two more restrictions:

(i) every time the server becomes idle the procedure's memory is cleared; the scheduling decisions made during one busy period are not based on information about previous busy periods;

(ii) only information about the current state and the past of the queueing process is used in making scheduling decisions; thus, it is possible to discriminate among jobs on the basis of their expected remaining service times (since their types and attained service are known), but not on the basis of exact remaining service times.

The reason for condition (i) is that, if different scheduling strategies are operated during different busy periods, there will be no interference among them. This property will be useful later. Restriction (ii) is necessary in order that the distribution of a class r job service time, given that the job is in the system, is the same as the unconditional class r service time distribution, $r = 1, 2, \ldots, R$. (For example, if the exact service times for class r jobs were known in advance, and the strategy were to serve shorter jobs first, then the class r jobs found in the system by a random observer would tend to be the longer ones; their service time distribution would be different from the *a priori* one.) Most scheduling strategies used in practice satisfy these two conditions.

The interarrival and required service times are assumed independent of each other and of the system state. Denote, as usual, the arrival rate, average service time and traffic intensity for class r jobs by λ_r, $1/\mu_r$ and $\rho_r = \lambda_r/\mu_r$ respectively ($r = 1, 2, \ldots, R$). Also let $\rho = \rho_1 + \rho_2 + \cdots + \rho_R$ be the total traffic intensity. The system is non-saturated if $\rho < 1$.

Consider first the case when the required service times for all job classes are distributed exponentially. The memoryless property of the exponential distribution plus condition (ii) imply that the average remaining service time of any class r job in the system is $1/\mu_r$, regardless of how much service that job has already received. Therefore, the average steady-state virtual load due to class r, under scheduling strategy S, is given by

$$V_S(r) = N_r/\mu_r, \quad r = 1, 2, \ldots, R,$$

where N_r is the steady-state average number of class r jobs in the system, under strategy S. On the other hand, $N_r = \lambda_r W_r$, according to Little's theorem (W_r is the average response time for jobs of class r, under scheduling strategy S). Hence,

$$V_S(r) = \rho_r W_r, \quad r = 1, 2, \ldots, R \qquad (8.3)$$

where W_r depends on S. Substituting these values into (8.2), we obtain a special conservation law (Kleinrock [4]):

Theorem 8.2. *When the required service times are distributed exponentially, there exists a constant V determined only by the interarrival time distributions and by the parameters μ_r, such that*

$$\sum_{r=1}^{R} \rho_r W_r = V, \qquad (8.4)$$

for all work-conserving scheduling strategies satisfying condition (ii).

Thus, in the context of this conservation law all achievable performance vectors $\mathbf{W}$ lie on the hyperplane defined by (8.4). Any decrease in one of the components of $\mathbf{W}$ must be compensated by a proportional increase in one or more of the other components. If a scheduling strategy achieves $R-1$ of the components of an achievable performance vector, it also achieves the R-th component. In the special case of $R = 1$, all scheduling strategies yield the same average response time.

The restriction on exponentially distributed service times can be removed at the expense of narrowing further the class of admissible scheduling strategies. Consider the case when the required service times for class r jobs have general distribution (with mean $1/\mu_r, r = 1, 2, \ldots, R$) and the scheduling strategies are non-pre-emptive (i.e. once a job has entered service, it is served to completion). Denote by n_r the average number of class r jobs in the queue (none of them have started service yet) and by w_r the average time that class r jobs spend in the queue (both these quantities depend on the scheduling strategy).

From Little's theorem $n_r = \lambda_r w_r$ and $N_r = \lambda_r W_r$; these relations, together with $W_r = w_r + (1/\mu_r)$, imply $N_r = n_r + \rho_r, r = 1, 2, \ldots, R$. Hence, the average number of class r jobs being served is equal to ρ_r and, since there can be at most one job being served, the probability that a class r job is being served is equal to ρ_r. Because the scheduling strategy is non-pre-emptive, the steady-state average remaining service time of the job in service, given that it is of class r, is equal to the average residual life γ_r of the class r service time. γ_r is given by

$$\gamma_r = \frac{1}{2} M_{2r} \mu_r, \quad r = 1, 2, \ldots, R, \tag{8.5}$$

where M_{2r} is the second moment of the class r service time distribution (see (1.66), Chapter 1).

We can now write, for the average virtual load due to class r jobs, $r = 1, 2, \ldots, R$,

$$V_S(r) = n_r \frac{1}{\mu_r} + \rho_r \gamma_r = \rho_r w_r + \rho_r \gamma_r = \rho_r W_r - \rho_r \left(\frac{1}{\mu_r} - \gamma_r \right). \tag{8.6}$$

Substitution of (8.6) into (8.2) yields what is usually known as Kleinrock's conservation law:

Theorem 8.3 (Kleinrock [4], Schrage [11]). *For any multiclass $GI/G/1$ queueing system in the steady-state, there exists a constant V, determined only by the interarrival and service time distributions, such that*

$$\sum_{r=1}^{R} \rho_r W_r = V + \sum_{r=1}^{R} \rho_r \left(\frac{1}{\mu_r} - \gamma_r \right) \tag{8.7}$$

regardless of the scheduling strategy, as long as the latter is work-conserving, non-pre-emptive and satisfies condition (ii).

Again, we have a hyperplane on which all achievable performance vectors must lie. However, the linear combination $\sum_{r=1}^{R} \rho_r W_r$ can now be larger, or smaller, than the average virtual load V, depending on the shape of the service time distributions. The two coincide, of course, when all service time distributions are exponential ($\gamma_r = 1/\mu_r$).

What is the value of the constant V? In order to determine this we have to analyse the model under some particular scheduling strategy (any strategy satisfying the restrictions will do) and obtain an expression for the steady-state virtual load. A closed-form solution exists only when the arrival streams for all job classes are Poisson. Then, it suffices to consider the FCFS scheduling strategy (serving jobs in order of arrival, without distinction of class and without pre-emption). All job classes can be lumped together and the model treated as an $M/G/1$ queue with arrival rate

$$\lambda = \lambda_1 + \lambda_2 + \cdots + \lambda_R,$$

average service time

$$\frac{1}{\mu} = \sum_{r=1}^{R} \frac{\lambda_r}{\lambda} \cdot \frac{1}{\mu_r},$$

second moment of the service time

$$M_2 = \sum_{r=1}^{R} \frac{\lambda_r}{\lambda} M_{2r}$$

and traffic intensity $\rho = \lambda/\mu = \rho_1 + \rho_2 + \cdots + \rho_R$. The average virtual load in this system is equal to the average time a new arrival would have to wait before beginning service; that average waiting time is given by Pollaczek–Khintchine's formula (see Chapter 1). We can write, therefore,

$$V = \frac{\lambda M_2}{2(1 - \rho)} = \frac{\sum_{r=1}^{R} \lambda_r M_{2r}}{2(1 - \rho)} = \frac{w_0}{1 - \rho} \qquad (8.8)$$

where

$$w_0 = \sum_{r=1}^{R} \rho_r \gamma_r \qquad (8.9)$$

is the average residual service time of the job in service.

Thus, when all arrival streams are Poisson, our two special conservation laws (8.4) and (8.7) become:

Law 1. Valid under exponential service times assumptions ($M_{2r} = 2/\mu_r^2, r = 1, 2, \ldots, R$). Scheduling strategies must be work-conserving and satisfy condition (ii) but are otherwise unrestricted:

$$\sum_{r=1}^{R} \rho_r W_r = \frac{1}{1 - \rho} \sum_{r=1}^{R} \frac{\rho_r}{\mu_r}. \qquad (8.10)$$

Law 2. Valid under general service times assumptions. Scheduling strategies must be work-conserving, satisfy condition (ii) and not use pre-emptions:

$$\sum_{r=1}^{R} \rho_r W_r = \frac{w_0}{1 - \rho} + \sum_{r=1}^{R} \rho_r \left(\frac{1}{\mu_r} - \gamma_r \right) = \frac{w_0 \rho}{1 - \rho} + \sum_{r=1}^{R} \frac{\rho_r}{\mu_r} \qquad (8.11)$$

where γ_r is given by (8.5) and w_0 by (8.9).

So far, we have established that the elements of any achievable (within a certain class of strategies) performance vector $\mathbf{W}$ must satisfy an equality constraint of the type (8.4) or (8.7). We shall now demonstrate that there is a set of inequality constraints which must be satisfied as well.

Let $g \subset \{1, 2, \ldots, R\}$ be any non-empty subset of job class indices. We shall refer to the jobs whose classes are in g as "g-jobs". Consider the virtual load $V_S^g(t)$ due to g-jobs, the sum of the remaining service times of all g-jobs in the system at time t. A typical realisation of $V_S^g(t)$ would look like the plot in Fig. 8.1, except that there would be no downward jumps. The horizontal segments of $V_S^g(t)$ at non-zero level correspond to intervals when there are g-jobs in the system but when jobs of other classes are being served. We shall refer to them as "$\hat{g}$-intervals". The $\hat{g}$-intervals, and hence $V_S^g(t)$, depend in general on the scheduling strategy S: for a given realisation of the demand processes, the smaller the $\hat{g}$-intervals, the lower the value of $V_S^g(t)$. Therefore, if S^* is a strategy which minimises the $\hat{g}$-intervals for every realisation of the demand processes, then every realisation of $V_{S^*}^g(t)$ is minimal. Taking expectations, we would obtain

$$E[V_S^g(t)] \geq E[V_{S^*}^g(t)], \quad t \geq 0$$

for all S. Next, if a steady-state exists, we can write

$$V_S^g \geq V_{S^*}^g, \quad \text{for all } S \tag{8.12}$$

where

$$V_S^g = \lim_{t \to \infty} E[V_S^g(t)] \quad \text{and} \quad V_{S^*}^g = \lim_{t \to \infty} E[V_{S^*}^g(t)].$$

Does such a minimising strategy S^* exist? If pre-emptions are allowed, the answer is clearly yes: any strategy which gives pre-emptive priority to g-jobs over non-g-jobs can be taken as S^*, since all these strategies eliminate the $\hat{g}$-intervals completely. (8.12) can then be rewritten as

$$\sum_{r \in g} V_S(r) \geq V^g, \quad \text{for all } S \tag{8.13}$$

where V^g is the (strategy-independent) steady-state average virtual load in a system where the demand consists only of g-jobs. Thus, the sum of the average virtual loads due to the job classes in g is bounded from below by a constant independent of the scheduling strategy. Furthermore, that bound cannot be improved because there are scheduling strategies, (the ones giving pre-emptive priority to g-jobs) for which it is reached.

Now, if we make the assumptions that ensure the validity of (8.10) we can go through steps (8.3) and (8.8) and obtain from (8.13) a generalisation of conservation law 1 (Coffman and Mitrani [1]).

Theorem 8.4. *In any multiclass $M/M/1$ queueing system in equilibrium, for every non-empty subset g of job class indices, the corresponding elements of the response time vector* **W** *satisfy the inequality*

$$\sum_{r \in g} \rho_r W_r \geq \left[1 - \sum_{r \in g} \rho_r \right]^{-1} \sum_{r \in g} (\rho_r / \mu_r) \qquad (8.14)$$

regardless of the scheduling strategy, as long as the latter is work-conserving and satisfies condition (ii). Moreover, (8.14) becomes an equality if the strategy gives pre-emptive priority to g-jobs (e.g. if $g = \{1, 2, \ldots, R\}$).

Note that the Poisson input assumptions were used only in order to write a closed-form expression for the right-hand side of (8.13); if we leave it as V^g, Theorem 8.4 will continue to hold.

The situation is less straightforward if one is restricted to non-pre-emptive scheduling strategies only. Now, if g is a proper and non-empty subset of $\{1, 2, \ldots, R\}$, the influence of the jobs whose classes are in $\{1, 2, \ldots, R\}$-g cannot be eliminated completely. There is no scheduling strategy which minimises the $\hat{g}$-intervals for every realisation of the demand processes. However, for a given realisation, the strategy which minimises the $\hat{g}$-intervals has to be one that gives head-of-the-line priority to g-jobs (eliminating all $\hat{g}$-intervals except, perhaps, those at the start of g-jobs busy periods). Therefore, only such a priority strategy can minimise the steady-state average virtual load due to g-jobs, V_S^g. Making the appropriate assumptions and using (8.6) we can rephrase the above statement thus: in order to minimise the linear combination $\sum_{r \in g} \rho_r W_r$ it is necessary to give non-pre-emptive priority to g-jobs.

Now suppose that the input streams are Poisson. If the g-jobs have non-pre-emptive priority, the only way their average response time can be influenced by the non-g-job is through the probability that an incoming g-jobs finds a non-g-jobs in service. But with Poisson arrivals, that probability is independent of the scheduling strategy (see Chapter 1). Hence, if g-jobs have non-pre-emptive priority, V_S^g is independent of the order of service among the non-g-jobs. It is also independent of the order of service among the g-jobs because, once the g-jobs have started being served, there are no $\hat{g}$-intervals until the end of the busy period. Thus, the minimal value of $\sum_{r \in g} \rho_r W_r$ can be obtained by lumping all g-jobs in one class, all non-g-jobs in another class, and giving head-of-the-line priority to the g-jobs. Performing these calculations yields a generalisation of conservation law 2:

Theorem 8.5. *In any multiclass $M/G/1$ queueing system in equilibrium, for every non-empty subset g of job class indices, the corresponding elements of the response time vector* **W** *satisfy*

$$\sum_{r \in g} \rho_r W_r \geq w_0 \left(\sum_{r \in g} \rho_r \right) \left[1 - \sum_{r \in g} \rho_r \right]^{-1} + \sum_{r \in g} (\rho_r / \mu_r) \qquad (8.15)$$

(where w_0 is given by (8.9)), regardless of the scheduling strategy, as long as the latter is work-conserving, satisfies condition (ii) and does not use pre-emptions. Moreover, (8.15) becomes an equality if the strategy gives non-pre-emptive priority to g-jobs.

In the next section, the relations derived here will lead to a characterisation of the sets of achievable performance vectors. Before proceeding, however, we should take another look at the assumptions that have been made and at the possibilities for relaxing them.

First, we shall consider the scheduling strategies. It is evident that if the strategies are not required to be work-conserving, Theorem 8.1 and all that follows from it will hold no more. The necessity of condition (ii) for the special conservation laws is less obvious (that condition is very rarely mentioned in the literature) but it, too, turns out to be unavoidable. We shall give examples of both pre-emptive and non-pre-emptive scheduling strategies where exact service times are known in advance and where (8.10) and (8.11) do not hold.

Could we drop the exponential service times assumption and still allow pre-emptions? The answer is again, alas, no. Neither (8.10) nor (8.11) are satisfied in the case of the classic pre-emptive priority disciplines with general service times.

Finally, we know that the Poisson inputs assumption is not necessary for the validity of Theorem 8.4. What is not known is whether Theorem 8.5 continues to hold (perhaps with different constants on the right-hand side of the inequalities) if that assumption is relaxed.

8.3. Characterisation theorems

We have obtained several results which can be interpreted as necessary conditions for achievability. The special conservation laws state that if a performance vector is achievable, then it must lie in a certain hyperplane. The inequality constraints narrow the possibilities further by specifying that if a performance vector is achievable, then it must belong to a certain polytope (a set bounded by planes) in that hyperplane. Now we shall demonstrate that these necessary conditions are also sufficient: every performance vector which belongs to the relevant polytope is achievable. This will give us a complete analytical characterisation of the achievable performance vectors.

We continue to consider two distinct cases. Denote by H_1 the set of performance vectors that are achievable in multiclass $M/M/1$ systems. In the notation of section 8.1,

$$H_1 = \{\mathbf{W} = (W_1, W_2, \ldots, W_R) \mid M/M/1 \text{ system}; \ \exists S : S \to \mathbf{W}\}.$$

Similarly, let H_2 be the set of performance vectors that are achievable in multiclass $M/G/1$ systems by non-pre-emptive scheduling strategies:

$$H_2 = \{\mathbf{W} = (W_1, W_2, \ldots, W_R) \mid M/G/1 \text{ system};$$
$$\exists \text{ non-pre-emptive } S : S \to \mathbf{W}\}.$$

In both cases, the scheduling strategies have to satisfy the restrictions of the last section. Next, denote by H_1^* the set of performance vectors $\mathbf{W}$ that satisfy equation (8.10) and the 2^R-2 inequalities (8.14), where g runs through all the proper and non-empty subsets of $\{1, 2, \ldots, R\}$. Let H_2^* be the set of performance vectors $\mathbf{W}$ that satisfy equation (8.11) and the 2^R-2 inequalities (8.15), where g runs through all the proper and non-empty subsets of $\{1, 2, \ldots, R\}$. These definitions are illustrated in Fig. 8.2, for the special case of two job classes. When $R = 2$, the performance vectors, are points in the two-dimensional plane, the conservation law defines a line and the two inequalities define half-planes; the set H_1^* (also H_2^*) is a line segment. Note that the defining inequalities, together with the conservation laws, imply that H_1^* and H_2^* are always bounded.

Theorem 8.4 asserts that every element of H_1 is an element of H_1^*, i.e.

$$H_1 \subset H_1^*. \tag{8.16}$$

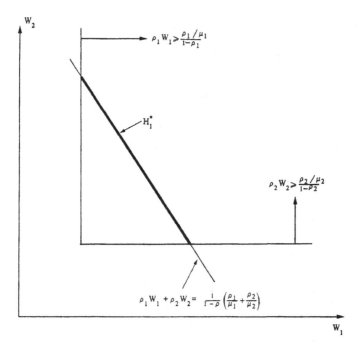

Fig. 8.2.

Similarly, Theorem 8.5 implies

$$H_2 \subset H_2^*. \tag{8.17}$$

Our aim will be to prove the opposite inclusions.

We shall begin by showing that all vertices of H_1^* are achievable (belong to H_1), and that all vertices of H_2^* are achievable by non-pre-emptive scheduling strategies (belong to H_2). More precisely, the vertices of H_1^* are achievable by pre-emptive priority disciplines and the vertices of H_2^* are achievable by head-of-the-line priority disciplines.

Let $(1, 2, \ldots, R), \ldots, (R, R-1, \ldots, 1)$ be the $R!$ possible permutations of job class indices. To each permutation there corresponds one pre-emptive priority discipline and one head-of-the-line priority discipline (see Chapter 1). Denote by $\mathbf{W}_1(i_1, i_2, \ldots, i_R)$ the response time vector of the pre-emptive priority discipline $(i_1, i_2, \ldots, i_R)$ in an $M/M/1$ system, and by $\mathbf{W}_2(i_1, i_2, \ldots, i_R)$ the response time vector of the head-of-the-line priority discipline $(i_1, i_2, \ldots, i_R)$ in an $M/G/1$ system. The elements of these vectors are given by (1.81) and (1.78), respectively.

The following results were established in [1].

Lemma 8.1. *For every vertex* $\mathbf{W}_1^*$ *of* H_1^* *there exists a pre-emptive priority discipline* $(i_1, i_2, \ldots, i_R)$ *such that*

$$\mathbf{W}_1^* = \mathbf{W}_1(i_1, i_2, \ldots, i_R).$$

Lemma 8.2. *For every vertex* $\mathbf{W}_2^*$ *of* H_2^* *there exists a head-of-the-line priority discipline* $(i_1, i_2, \ldots, i_R)$ *such that*

$$\mathbf{W}_2^* = W_2(i_1, i_2, \ldots, i_R).$$

Proof of Lemma 8.1. Let $\mathbf{W}_1^* = (W_1^*, W_2^*, \ldots, W_R^*)$ be a vertex of H_1^*. According to the definition of H_1^*, $\mathbf{W}_1^*$ must lie at the intersection of R hyperplanes, one of which is (8.10) and the others of which are some of the bounds in (8.14). Therefore, the elements of $\mathbf{W}_1^*$ satisfy R simultaneous linear equations

$$\sum_{r \in g_j} \rho_r W_r^* = \left(\sum_{r \in g_j} \rho_r / \mu_r \right) \bigg/ \left(1 - \sum_{r \in g_j} \rho_r \right) \quad j = 1, 2, \ldots, R$$

where one of the g_j is the set $\{1, 2, \ldots, R\}$ and the others are proper, non-empty and different subsets. Using the notation $a_r = \rho_r / \mu_r$, $a_g = \sum_{r \in g} a_r$ and $\rho_g = \sum_{r \in g} \rho_r$, we rewrite these equations as

$$\sum_{r \in g_j} \rho_r W_r^* = a_{g_j} / (1 - \rho_{g_j}); \quad j = 1, 2, \ldots, R. \tag{8.18}$$

We shall demonstrate that all the subsets g_j are strictly included in each other. Suppose that this is not so, and that there are two subsets g_j and g_k such that both $h_{jk} = g_j - (g_j \wedge g_k)$ and $h_{kj} = g_k - (g_j \wedge g_k)$ are non-empty. Consider the union $G_{jk} = g_j \vee g_k$. From (8.18) it follows that

$$\sum_{r \in G_{jk}} \rho_r W_r^* = [a_{g_j} / (1 - \rho_{g_j})] + [a_{g_k} / (1 - \rho_{g_k})] - \sum_{r \in g_{jk}} \rho_r W_r^*$$

where $g_{jk} = g_j \wedge g_k$; the last term is zero by definition if g_{jk} is empty. Since (8.14) must hold for $g = g_{jk}$ (if non-empty), we can write

$$\sum_{r \in G_{jk}} \rho_r W_r^* \leq [a_{g_j} / (1 - \rho_{g_j})] + [a_{g_k} / (1 - \rho_{g_k})] - [a_{g_{jk}} / (1 - \rho_{g_{jk}})]. \tag{8.19}$$

Next, it is not difficult to see that

$$(1 - \rho_{g_j})(1 - \rho_{g_k}) > (1 - \rho_{g_{jk}})(1 - \rho_{G_{jk}})$$

when h_{jk} and h_{kj} are non-empty. Also,

$$[a_{g_j}(1 - \rho_{g_k})] + [a_{g_k}(1 - \rho_{g_j})] - [a_{g_{jk}}(1 - \rho_{G_{jk}})] < a_{G_{jk}}(1 - \rho_{g_{jk}})$$

when h_{jk} and h_{kj} are non-empty. (8.19) then implies

$$\sum_{r \in G_{jk}} \rho_r W_r^* < a_{G_{jk}}/(1 - \rho_{G_{jk}})$$

which violates (8.14) for $g = G_{jk}$. Thus we must have (perhaps after renumbering)

$$g_1 = \{i_1\}$$
$$g_2 = \{i_1, i_2\}$$
$$g_{R-1} = \{i_1, i_2, \ldots, i_{R-1}\}$$
$$g_R = \{i_1, i_2, \ldots, i_R\} = \{1, 2, \ldots, R\}$$

for some $i_1, i_2, \ldots, i_R \in \{1, 2, \ldots, R\}$ such that $i_j \neq i_k$, $j \neq k$. The system of equations (8.18) is triangular; its solution is readily obtained as

$$W_r^* = (1 - \rho_{g_{r-1}})^{-1}[1/\mu_r + a_{g_r}/(1 - \rho_{g_r})]; \quad r = 1, 2, \ldots, R,$$

where $\rho_{g_0} = 0$ by definition. But those are precisely the elements of the response time vector of the pre-emptive priority discipline $(i_1, i_2, \ldots, i_R)$. □

Proof of Lemma 8.2. This proof is almost identical to the above and need not be given in full. It suffices to note that the right-hand side of (8.15) is also of the form

$$\left(\sum_{r \in g} b_r\right) \bigg/ \left(1 - \sum_{r \in g} \rho_r\right)$$

with $b_r > 0$ $(r = 1, 2, \ldots, R)$. Again, the system of equations defining a vertex is triangular; its solution turns out to be the response time vector of a head-of-the-line priority discipline. □

Another way of interpreting Lemmas 8.1 and 8.2 is the following. Let H_1^{**} be the convex hull defined by the $R!$ response time vectors

$\mathbf{W}_1^*(1, 2, \ldots, R), \ldots, \mathbf{W}_1^*(R, R - 1, \ldots, 1)$; i.e. $\mathbf{W} \in H_1^{**}$ if and only if $\mathbf{W}$ can be represented as a convex combination

$$\mathbf{W} = \alpha_1 \mathbf{W}_1^*(1, 2, \ldots, R) + \cdots + \alpha_{R!} \mathbf{W}_1^*(R, R - 1, \ldots, 1) \qquad (8.20)$$

where $\alpha_1, \ldots, \alpha_{R!} \geq 0$ and $\alpha_1 + \cdots + \alpha_{R!} = 1$. Similarly, let H_2^{**} be the convex hull defined by $\mathbf{W}_2^*(1, 2, \ldots, R), \ldots, \mathbf{W}_2^*(R, R - 1, \ldots, 1)$. Since H_1^* and H_2^* are bounded polytopes, Lemmas 8.1 and 8.2 imply that

$$H_1^* \subset H_1^{**} \qquad (8.21)$$

and

$$H_2^* \subset H_2^{**}. \qquad (8.22)$$

Now, we know that all vertices of H_1^{**} are achievable in an $M/M/1$ system, i.e. they belong to the set H_1. If it can be shown that H_1 is convex (a set in a vector space is called convex if, together with any two elements x_1 and x_2, it contains all elements of the form $\alpha x_1 + (1 - \alpha) x_2, 0 \leq \alpha \leq 1$), then it would follow that the whole of H_1^{**} is included in H_1. We would have, from (8.16) and (8.21), $H_1 \subset H_1^* \subset H_1^{**} \subset H_1$, and therefore

$$H_1 = H_1^* = H_1^{**}. \qquad (8.23)$$

Similarly, if it can be shown that the set H_2 is convex, it would follow that

$$H_2 = H_2^* = H_2^{**}. \qquad (8.24)$$

To prove the convexity of H_1 and H_2 we introduce, following [1], the notion of "mixing scheduling strategies". Given two scheduling strategies S_1 and S_2, a mixing strategy is obtained by making a random choice between S_1 and S_2 every time the system becomes idle: with probability α all scheduling decisions during the next busy period are made according to S_1 and with probability $1 - \alpha$ they are made according to $S_2 (0 \leq \alpha \leq 1)$. The random choices are independent of each other and of everything else in the system. Thus a mixing strategy is determined by a triple (S_1, S_2, α). Note that if S_1 and S_2 are work-conserving and satisfy conditions (i) and (ii), so does (S_1, S_2, α) for every $0 \leq \alpha \leq 1$; in other words, the class of strategies with which we are dealing is closed with respect to the mixing operation. Moreover, the subclass of the non-pre-emptive scheduling strategies is also closed with respect to mixing (since no pre-emption is involved in that operation).

An almost obvious relationship exists between the performance vectors of the constituent strategies and that of the mixing strategy.

Theorem 8.6. *If* $\mathbf{W}_1$ *and* $\mathbf{W}_2$ *are the response time vectors of* S_1 *and* S_2 *respectively, then the response time vector* $\mathbf{W}$ *of* (S_1, S_2, α) *is given by*

$$\mathbf{W} = \alpha \mathbf{W}_1 + (1 - \alpha)\mathbf{W}_2; \quad 0 \leq \alpha \leq 1. \tag{8.25}$$

The convexity of H_1 *and* H_2 *follows immediately from this theorem and the remarks above. Every performance vector which lies on the line segment between two achievable performance vectors is also achievable; it suffices to construct an appropriate mixing strategy in order to achieve it.*

Proof of Theorem 8.6. The busy periods in a single-server system are completely determined by the virtual load function $V(t)$: they begin when $V(t)$ jumps up from zero and end when $V(t)$ touches zero again. Since $V(t)$ is independent of the scheduling strategy, so also are the busy periods. Furthermore, the beginnings of busy periods are regeneration points for the queueing process (because interarrival and service times are mutually independent). It follows that the lengths of consecutive busy periods are independent and identically distributed, regardless of the scheduling strategy. The same can be said about the numbers of jobs of various classes that are served during different busy periods.

Consider the n-th arriving job of class r, J_n^r ($n = 1, 2, \ldots; r = 1, 2, \ldots, R$), under the mixing strategy (S_1, S_2, α). The above arguments imply two things. Firstly, J_n^r arrives in (or commences) a busy period of type 1 (respectively of type 2) with probability α (respectively $1 - \alpha$). Secondly, if J_n^r arrives in (or commences) a busy period of type j ($j = 1, 2$), then it experiences exactly the same delay as it would have done had it been the n-th class r job under S_j operating from the beginning with the same initial state. (Recall that according to assumption (i) of section 8.2, the scheduling decisions in one busy period are independent of those in previous busy periods.)

Therefore, not only the steady-state expectations but also the transient distribution functions of the response times under S_1, S_2 and (S_1, S_2, α) are related as in (8.25), provided that the three strategies are started with the same initial conditions. $\qquad\square$

Remark. The notion of mixing scheduling strategies, and Theorem 8.6, can be extended in an obvious way to more than two constituents. If we are given m strategies $S_1, S_2, \ldots, S_m$ with performance vectors $\mathbf{W}_1, \mathbf{W}_2, \ldots, \mathbf{W}_m$, and m positive fractions $\alpha_1, \alpha_2, \ldots, \alpha_m$ such that $\alpha_1 + \alpha_2 + \cdots + \alpha_m = 1$, we can construct a mixing strategy $(S_1, S_2, \ldots, S_m; \alpha_1, \alpha_2, \ldots, \alpha_m)$ whose performance vector $\mathbf{W}$ is given by

$$\mathbf{W} = \sum_{j=1}^{m} \alpha_j \mathbf{W}_j. \tag{8.26}$$

Equations (8.23) and (8.24) are now established; these are important results which will be referred to as "characterisation theorems".

The identities $H_1 = H_1^*$ and $H_2 = H_2^*$ can be termed "analytical characterisations". They supply us with simple means for checking whether or not a pre-specified performance vector is achievable. For example, to determine whether a performance vector $\tilde{\mathbf{W}}$ is achievable in an $M/G/1$ system by a non-pre-emptive scheduling strategy it suffices to verify equation (8.11) and the 2^R-2 inequalities (8.15). This task can be accomplished without too much difficulty for values of R as high as 12 or 13. Note that if $\tilde{\mathbf{W}}$ satisfies the inequalities (8.15) but a substitution into (8.11) yields a strict inequality

$$\sum_{r=1}^{R} \rho_r \tilde{W}_r > w_0 \rho / (1 - \rho) + \sum_{r=1}^{R} (\rho_r / \mu_r),$$

then, while $\tilde{\mathbf{W}}$ is not achievable, there exists a vector dominated by $\tilde{\mathbf{W}}$ (one whose elements are all smaller than or equal to those of $\tilde{\mathbf{W}}$) which is achievable. This situation is illustrated in Fig. 8.2 for the case $R = 2$ ($M/M/1$ system).

On the other hand, the identities $H_1 = H_1^{**}$ and $H_2 = H_2^{**}$ can be regarded as "geometrical characterisations". They specify the vertices (the extremes) of the sets of achievable performance vectors and point the way for designing scheduling strategies to meet performance objectives. Suppose, for example, that we are given in an $M/M/1$ system a performance vector $\tilde{\mathbf{W}}$ and have already shown it to be achievable; the problem now is to find a scheduling strategy which achieves it. One solution is provided by the mixing strategies: since there exists for $\tilde{\mathbf{W}}$ a representation of the type (8.20) $\tilde{\mathbf{W}}$ can be achieved by mixing the $R!$ pre-emptive priority strategies with probabilities $\alpha_1, \ldots, \alpha_{R!}$. Such a solution certainly looks unappealing ($R!$ grows rather rapidly), but it is not quite as bad as it appears. All except R of the coefficients in the representation (8.20) can be made zeros (this is because the set H_1^{**} belongs to an R-dimensional hyperplane).

The R pre-emptive priority disciplines to be mixed and the parameters of the mix can be determined using standard linear programming methods.

This, and other problems concerned with the design of scheduling strategies will be addressed in the following sections.

8.4. The realisation of pre-specified performance vectors. Complete families of scheduling strategies

We have solved the first of the synthesis problems outlined at the beginning of this chapter. If asked whether a performance vector $\tilde{\mathbf{W}}$ is achievable (in an arbitrary $M/M/1$ system or in an $M/G/1$ system without pre-emption), we can give a clear "yes" or "no" answer by a rather simpler algorithm. Let us now approach the next immediate problem. Having determined that $\tilde{\mathbf{W}}$ is achievable (or, better still, that a vector dominated by $\tilde{\mathbf{W}}$ is achievable), find a scheduling strategy which achieves $\tilde{\mathbf{W}}$ (or achieves a vector dominated by $\tilde{\mathbf{W}}$).

As a general principle, it is easier to find something if one knows where to look for it. So the search for a scheduling strategy would be easier if one could narrow it down to some well-defined "simple" family of strategies. In order not to miss the target, however, the narrower family has to be as rich (as far as the achievable performance vectors are concerned) as the set of all scheduling strategies. We are thus led to the notion of "completeness" (Mitrani and Hine [8]).

Let φ be a family of scheduling strategies (satisfying conditions (i) and (ii) of section 8.2). Denote by H_φ the set of performance vectors which are achievable by strategies from φ:

$$H_\varphi = \{\mathbf{W} \mid \exists S \in \varphi; \ S \to \mathbf{W}\}.$$

We say that φ is $M/M/1$-complete if $H_\varphi = H_1$, i.e. if an $M/M/1$ system any achievable performance vector can be achieved by a strategy from φ. Similarly, we say that φ is $M/G/1$-complete if all strategies in φ are non-pre-emptive and $H_\varphi = H_2$. It is obvious from these definitions that if we have a complete family φ of scheduling strategies and wish to achieve a pre-specified performance vector, we can limit our search only to the strategies in φ. If, in addition, the family φ is parametrised (i.e. all the strategies in it have the same general form and are determined by the values of a few parameters), then our task is reduced to finding an appropriate point in the parameter space.

As a first application of these ideas consider, in an $M/M/1$ system the family Φ_1 of scheduling strategies formed by mixing up to R of the $R!$ pre-emptive priority disciplines. To simplify the notation a little, let $\mathbf{Q}_1, \mathbf{Q}_2, \ldots, \mathbf{Q}_{R!}$ be the performance vectors of the pre-emptive priority disciplines. According to (8.26), the performance vectors of the strategies in Φ_1 can be expressed as convex combinations

$$\mathbf{W} = \alpha_1 \mathbf{Q}_{i_1} + \alpha_2 \mathbf{Q}_{i_2} + \cdots + \alpha_R \mathbf{Q}_{i_R}, \tag{8.27}$$

where $\alpha_j \geq 0$ $(j = 1, 2, \ldots, R)$, $\alpha_1 + \alpha_2 + \cdots + \alpha_R = 1$ and $\mathbf{Q}_{i_1}, \mathbf{Q}_{i_2}, \ldots, \mathbf{Q}_{i_R}$ are R of the vectors $\mathbf{Q}_1, \ldots, \mathbf{Q}_{R!}$. On the other hand, the characterisation theorem $H_1 = H_1^{**}$ asserts that every achievable performance vector is of the form (8.20). Moreover, since the dimensionality of H_1 is $R - 1$ (because of the conservation law), at most R of the coefficients in (8.20) need to be non-zero (e.g. every point inside a planar polygon can be expressed as a convex combination of three of the vertices). Thus every achievable performance vector is of the form (8.27), i.e. Φ_1 is $M/M/1$-complete.

The problem of finding a strategy from Φ_1 which achieves a pre-specified (and achievable) performance vector $\tilde{\mathbf{W}}$ can now be stated as follows: find $R!$ non-negative numbers $\alpha_1, \alpha_2, \ldots, \alpha_{R!}$, all but R of which are equal to zero, such that

$$\sum_{j=1}^{R!} \alpha_j = 1 \quad \text{and} \quad \sum_{j=1}^{R!} \alpha_j \mathbf{Q}_j = \tilde{\mathbf{W}}.$$

We have here $R + 1$ linear constraints, R of which are independent (the vectors $\mathbf{Q}_j$ and $\tilde{\mathbf{W}}$ have only $R - 1$ independent elements), to which we wish to find a non-negative solution such that at most R of the variables are non-zero. This is the well-known "initial basis" problem in linear programming. It can be solved by introducing R artificial variables β_0 and $\boldsymbol{\beta} = (\beta_1, \beta_2, \ldots, \beta_{R-1})$ and solving the linear program

$$\max \sum_{j=1}^{R!} \alpha_j \tag{8.28}$$

subject to the constraints

$$\alpha_j \geq 0 \ (j = 1, 2, \ldots, R!), \quad \beta_j \geq 0 \ (j = 0, 1, \ldots, R),$$

$$\beta_0 + \sum_{j=1}^{R!} \alpha_j = 1 \quad \text{and} \quad \boldsymbol{\beta} + \sum_{j=1}^{R!} \alpha_j \mathbf{Q}_j = \tilde{\mathbf{W}}$$

(using only the first $R-1$ elements of $\mathbf{Q}_j$ and $\tilde{\mathbf{W}}$). An initial basis for (8.28) is obtained by setting $\alpha_j = 0$ $(j = 1, 2, \ldots, R!)$, $\beta_0 = 1$, $\boldsymbol{\beta} = \tilde{\mathbf{W}}$. When an objective value of 1 is reached (as we know it will be if $\tilde{\mathbf{W}}$ is achievable), the corresponding α_jS and $\mathbf{Q}_j$S define a mixing strategy $S \in \Phi_1$ which achieves $\tilde{\mathbf{W}}$.

Note that there may be (and probably are) many solutions to this problem. Figure 8.3 shows an example of the set H_1 for $R = 3$ (the priority ordering at each vertex is indicated in brackets) and a target vector $\tilde{\mathbf{W}}$ in the interior of H_1. This particular target vector can be achieved by mixing the priority disciplines (123), (321) and (213); or by mixing the disciplines (213), (132) and (231), etc. The figure suggests that there are eight mixing strategies which achieve $\tilde{\mathbf{W}}$.

The other case of interest is when the target $\tilde{\mathbf{W}}$ is not achievable but dominates an achievable performance vector (i.e. it satisfies the inequalities (8.14) but lies above the conservation law hyperplane). Then, before solving the linear program (8.28), we have to find an achievable performance vector $\hat{\mathbf{W}}$ dominated by $\tilde{\mathbf{W}}$. This is another initial basis problem: $\hat{\mathbf{W}}$ has to satisfy the inequalities (8.14) plus the conservation law equality, plus the inequality $\hat{\mathbf{W}} \leq \tilde{\mathbf{W}}$. Again one can introduce artificial variables

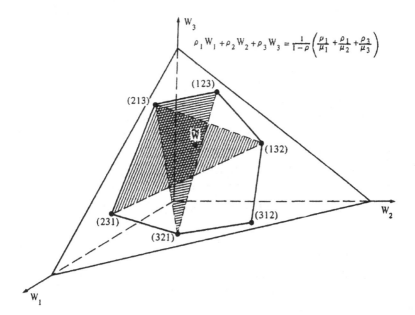

Fig. 8.3.

and solve an auxiliary linear program. Since the solution of that program is a vertex of the set of feasible vectors, the vector $\hat{\mathbf{W}}$ thus obtained is either one of the vectors $\mathbf{Q}_j$ $(j = 1, 2, \ldots, R!)$, or it satisfies $\hat{W}_r = \tilde{W}_r$ for some $r = 1, 2, \ldots, R$. This suggests the following alternative algorithm for finding $\hat{\mathbf{W}}$.

For $r = 1, 2, \ldots, R$ check whether the projection of $\tilde{\mathbf{W}}$ along the r-th coordinate axis into the conservation law hyperplane is achievable; if yes, then take that projection as $\hat{\mathbf{W}}$ and stop. For $j = 1, 2, \ldots, R!$ check whether $\mathbf{Q}_j$ is dominated by $\tilde{\mathbf{W}}$; if yes, take $\mathbf{Q}_j$ as $\hat{\mathbf{W}}$ and stop.

That algorithm may, in some cases, be more efficient than the linear programming one. For example, if one of the elements of $\tilde{\mathbf{W}}$ is obviously too large, a projection along the corresponding coordinate axis is likely to yield the result.

The above results apply, with straightforward modifications, to $M/G/1$ systems where pre-emptions are disallowed. The family Φ_2 of scheduling strategies formed by mixing up to R of the $R!$ head-of-the-line priority disciplines, is $M/G/1$-complete. To find a strategy from Φ_2 which achieves a pre-specified (and achievable) performance vector $\tilde{\mathbf{W}}$, one solves a linear program similar to (8.28); the vectors $\mathbf{Q}_j$ $(j = 1, 2, \ldots, R!)$ are replaced by the performance vectors of the head-of-the-line priority disciplines. If the target $\tilde{\mathbf{W}}$ is not achievable but dominates an achievable performance vector, one such vector can be obtained either by solving an initial basis problem or by a vertex searching algorithm.

So, the families Φ_1 and Φ_2 have several attractive features: they are conceptually simple, easily implementable, parametrised, complete; there are algorithms for selecting a strategy that achieves (or improves upon) a given performance vector. We should point out, however, that these mixing strategies have one important disadvantage: the variances in response times which they introduce may be unacceptable large, especially in heavily loaded systems. Suppose, for example, that in an $M/M/1$ system with two job classes, the pre-emptive priority disciplines $(1, 2)$ and $(2, 1)$ are mixed in the proportion $\alpha = 0.9$. Suppose, further, that the system is heavily loaded, most of the load being contributed by class 2 (say $\rho_1 = 0.15, \rho_2 = 0.8$). Then, while most of the class 1 jobs have very short waiting times, a significant proportion (approximately 10%) will have to wait much longer; the over-all mean response time may be as required, but the variance will be rather large. Managers of computer installations usually avoid such strategies because the unlucky 10% of the users tend to be more vociferous than the satisfied 90%.

It is desirable, therefore, to try to find families of scheduling strategies which are not only complete and parametrised, but are also better suited for practical applications.

We shall begin by deriving a set of sufficient conditions for a parametrised family of scheduling strategies to be complete. Take, as an illustration, the case of an $M/M/1$ system with two job classes. The set of achievable performance vectors, H_1, is now a line segment (see Fig. 8.2) at the two extremes of which are the performance vectors $\mathbf{W}_1(1,2)$ and $\mathbf{W}_1(2,1)$ of the two pre-emptive priority disciplines. Suppose that we have a family φ of scheduling strategies which depend on a single parameter α; to a given value of α there corresponds a strategy in φ and hence a performance vector $\mathbf{W}(\alpha)$ in H_1. In this case one can easily see a set of conditions that would ensure the completeness of φ. It is sufficient that there exist two parameter values α_1 and α_2 such that $\mathbf{W}(\alpha_1) = \mathbf{W}_1(1,2)$ and $\mathbf{W}(\alpha_2) = \mathbf{W}_1(2,1)$, and that when α varies between α_1 and α_2, $\mathbf{W}(\alpha)$ varies continuously. $\mathbf{W}(\alpha)$ would then be certain to sweep the entire segment H_1, i.e. φ would be complete.

These intuitive ideas can be generalised and made more precise. Suppose that in a system with R job classes we have a family φ of scheduling strategies depending on m continuous parameters $\alpha_1, \alpha_2, \ldots, \alpha_m$. In other words, there is a set A in the m-dimensional space $\alpha_1 \times \alpha_2 \times \cdots \times \alpha_m$ such that every point $\boldsymbol{\alpha} \in A$ corresponds uniquely to a strategy $S \in \varphi$ and vice versa. Hence, to every point $\boldsymbol{\alpha} \in A$ corresponds (via the strategy) a performance vector $\mathbf{W} \in H_\varphi$ and all performance vectors in H_φ have inverse images in A, although not necessarily unique.

The following theorem (Mitrani and Hine [8]) is useful in establishing the completeness of parametrised families of scheduling strategies:

Theorem 8.7. *If A is $(R-1)$-dimensional (i.e. $m = R - 1$) and compact, and if the mapping of A on to H_φ is one-to-one and continuous, and if the boundary of A is mapped on to the boundary of some $(R-1)$-dimensional set H in the $\mathbf{W}$-space, then $H_\varphi = H$. In particular, if the boundary of A is mapped on to the boundary of H_1, then φ is $M/M/1$-complete; if the boundary of A is mapped on to the boundary of H_2 (and the strategies in φ are non-pre-emptive), then φ is $M/G/1$-complete.*

This theorem has a simple intuitive meaning. Its main assertion is that if the strategies in φ can achieve the boundary (the extremes) of a given set of performance vectors, then they can achieve the whole set. The analogy with the case $R = 2$ can be seen easily. Note that the requirement concerning the dimensionality of A (and hence of φ) is important. For example, in the case of $R = 3$ (see Fig. 8.3), the boundary of H_1 can be achieved by mixing pre-emptive priority disciplines two at a time (1-dimensional parameter set); that family cannot achieve all points in the interior of H_1.

We shall prove the theorem at the end of this section; let us now turn to some applications.

8.4.1. *Generalised processor-sharing strategies*

In section 3.4 we defined a processor-sharing strategy whereby the available processing capacity is divided equally among the jobs in the system. That strategy can be generalised (Kleinrock [5]) by allowing jobs of different classes to receive different fractions of the processing capacity. The division is controlled by a vector of positive "weights" $(\alpha_1, \alpha_2, \ldots, \alpha_R)$: if the processor speed is C instructions per unit time and there are n_r jobs of class r in the system ($r = 1, 2, \ldots, R$), then all jobs proceed in parallel, each class r job being served at rate

$$f_r(n_1, n_2, \ldots, n_R) = C\alpha_r \left/ \left(\sum_{j=1}^{R} \alpha_j n_j \right) \right. \tag{8.29}$$

instructions per unit time.

It is clear from (8.29) that if all α_rs are multiplied by the same constant the strategy will not change. One of the parameters can therefore be fixed arbitrarily; let $\alpha_R = 1$.

We now have an $(R - 1)$-dimensional parameter set A:

$$A = \{(\alpha_1, \alpha_2, \ldots, \alpha_{R-1}) \mid \alpha_r > 0,\, r = 1, 2, \ldots, R - 1\}. \tag{8.30}$$

Each point $\boldsymbol{\alpha} \in A$ determines uniquely a processor-sharing strategy and hence a performance vector $\mathbf{W}$. Moreover, the correspondence is one-to-one and continuous; we shall establish this later by finding $\mathbf{W}$ explicitly as a function of $\boldsymbol{\alpha}$. We are thus almost in the domain of applicability of Theorem 8.7 and are tempted to claim that the family of generalised processor-sharing strategies (denote that family by Ψ) is $M/M/1$-complete.

Unfortunately, the parameter set is not compact. For compactness it is necessary that the set includes its boundary, and our A is open (and unbounded). Also, the boundary of H_1 cannot be achieved by strategies from Ψ. Take, for example, the bounding plane B_1 defined by

$W_1 = 1/[\mu_1(1 - p_1)]$ (see (8.14), with $g = \{1\}$). According to Theorem 8.4, it is necessary to give pre-emptive priority to class 1 in order to achieve any performance vector $\mathbf{W} \in B_1$; the strategies in Ψ are unable to do this because they allow all jobs in the system to proceed in parallel.

Nevertheless, it can be shown that Ψ is "nearly $M/M/1$-complete":

Lemma 8.3. *Every performance vector $\mathbf{W}$ in the interior of H_1 can be achieved by a scheduling strategy from the family Ψ. If $\mathbf{W}$ is on the boundary of H_1, then it can be approximated as closely as desired by strategies from Ψ.*

Proof. We have to show that H_Ψ is equal to H_1 without its boundary. Consider the parameter regions

$$A_{\varepsilon,E} = \{(\alpha_1, \alpha_2, \ldots, \alpha_{R-1}) \mid \varepsilon \le \alpha_r \le E, \ r = 1, 2, \ldots, R - 1; \varepsilon < E\}$$

and let $\Psi_{\varepsilon,E}$ be the family of processor-sharing strategies defined over $A_{\varepsilon,E}$. We have

$$A = \lim_{\substack{\varepsilon \to 0 \\ E \to \infty}} A_{\varepsilon,E}$$

and therefore

$$H_\Psi = \lim_{\substack{\varepsilon \to 0 \\ E \to \infty}} H_{\Psi_{\varepsilon,E}}.$$

Each of the regions $A_{\varepsilon,E}$ is compact. Its boundary consists of those points $\boldsymbol{\alpha}$ for which $\alpha_i = \varepsilon$ for at least one i and/or $\alpha_j = E$ for at least one j $(i, j = 1, 2, \ldots, R - 1)$. Denote by $B_{\varepsilon,E}$ the set of performance vectors which correspond to these boundary points. According to Theorem 8.7, $H_{\Psi_{\varepsilon,E}}$ consists of $B_{\varepsilon,E}$ and all performance vectors inside it.

Let B be the limiting surface

$$B = \lim_{\substack{\varepsilon \to 0 \\ E \to \infty}} B_{\varepsilon,E}.$$

The performance vectors in B are obtained by letting $\alpha_i \to 0$ for at least one i and/or $\alpha_j \to \infty$ for at least one j $(i, j = 1, 2, \ldots, R - 1)$. Taking a closer look at (8.29) and remembering that α_R is fixed, we see that such a limiting process always results in effectively giving pre-emptive priority to one or more job classes over the remaining job classes. Therefore (see Theorem 8.4), B is part of the boundary of H_1. However, both these surfaces are closed and continuous (topologically equivalent to a sphere); if one of them is part of the other they must coincide.

The proof can now be completed by remarking that, since the surfaces $B_{\varepsilon,E}$ approach the boundary of H_1, every performance vector $\mathbf{W}$ in the interior of H_1 is in the interior of some $B_{\varepsilon,E}$. As we have seen, this implies that $\mathbf{W} \in H_{\Psi_{\varepsilon,E}}$ and hence $\mathbf{W} \in H_\Psi$. Thus H_Ψ contains all points in H_1 except its boundary. □

Here we have a family of scheduling strategies which is (to all practical purposes) complete, and which does not produce high variances in the response times. An implementation of a processor-sharing strategy would involve an approximation by a Round-Robin discipline: if processor time is allocated in quanta of size Q and Q is small, the effect of processor-sharing with fractions (8.29) can be achieved by giving α_r quanta of service to the job at the head of the queue if that job is of class r $(r = 1, 2, \ldots, R)$.

It remains to provide an algorithm which, given a performance vector $\hat{\mathbf{W}}$, would find a processor-sharing strategy (or rather a set of values for $\alpha_1, \alpha_2, \ldots, \alpha_R$) that achieves $\hat{\mathbf{W}}$. We shall approach this problem from the opposite direction, i.e. we shall analyse the system in order to find the performance vector $\mathbf{W}$ that corresponds to a given set of parameter values $\alpha_1, \alpha_2, \ldots, \alpha_R$. The analysis is a special case of that presented in [2], where processor-sharing strategies are studied under more general assumptions.

Let $W_r(t)$ be the steady-state average response time of a class r job whose required service is t. $W_r(t)$ can also be interpreted as the average time necessary for a class r job whose service requirement is greater than t to attain service t. Hence, $\mathrm{d}W_r(t) = W_r(t+\mathrm{d}t) - W_r(t)$ is the average time necessary for a class r job to increase its attained service from t to $t + \mathrm{d}t$.

Another expression for this last quantity can be obtained from the definition of processor-sharing. Let J_r be a job of class r whose required service is greater than t. Denote by $n_j(t)$ the average number of class j jobs in the system (excluding J_r) at the moment when J_r attains service t $(j = 1, 2, \ldots, R)$. Then the average time necessary for J_r to increase its service from t to $t + \mathrm{d}t$ is equal to

$$\mathrm{d}t/f_r(n_1(t), \ldots, n_r(t) + 1, \ldots, n_R(t))$$

where $f_r(\cdot, \cdot, \ldots, \cdot)$ is given by (8.29). Assuming, without loss of generality, that the processor speed C is 1, we obtain

$$W_r'(t) = 1 + \sum_{j=1}^{R} \frac{\alpha_j}{\alpha_r} n_j(t), \quad r = 1, 2, \ldots, R. \tag{8.31}$$

To find $n_j(t)$, note that this quantity has two components: n', the average number of class j jobs which were in the system when J_r arrived and are still there when J_r attains service t; n'', the average number of class j jobs which arrived after J_r and are still in the system when J_r attains service t. Note, further, that while J_r receives one unit of service any class j job which is together with it in the system receives α_j/α_r units of service.

Suppose that a class j job had attained service u when J_r arrived. For that class j job to be still in the system when J_r attains service t, its service requirement has to be greater than $u + (\alpha_j t/\alpha_r)$; the probability of that event, given that the requirement is greater than u, is $\exp[-\mu_j(\alpha_j t/\alpha_r)]$. Next, consider the subsystem of class j jobs whose attained service is between u and $u + du$: jobs arrive in it at rate $\lambda_j e^{-\mu_j u}$ (since every class j arrival with service requirement greater than u is bound to join the subsystem); the average time jobs spend in that subsystem is $dW_j(u) = W'_j(u)du$. Therefore, from Little's theorem, the steady-state average number of class j jobs with attained service u is equal to $\lambda_j e^{-\mu_j u} W'_j(u)du$ (see also [7], [9]). Integrating over all possible values of u, we obtain the first component of $n_j(t)$:

$$n' = \lambda_j e^{-\mu_j(\alpha_j t/\alpha_r)} \int_0^\infty e^{-\mu_j u} W'_j(u)du.$$

Turning to the second component, we remark that while J_r increases its attained service from u to $u + du$, an average of $\lambda_j dW_r(u)$ class j jobs arrive. Each of those arrivals is still in the system when J_r attains service t with probability $\exp[-\mu_j \alpha_j(t-u)/\alpha_r]$. Integrating over $u \in (0,t)$ we obtain

$$n'' = \lambda_j \int_0^t e^{-\mu_j \alpha_j(t-u)/\alpha_r} W'_r(u)du.$$

Finally, substituting the sums of n' and n'' into (8.31) yields a system of integrodifferential equations:

$$W'_r(t) = 1 + \sum_{j=1}^R \frac{\lambda_j \alpha_j}{\alpha_r} \left\{ e^{-\mu_j \alpha_j t/\alpha_r} \int_0^\infty e^{-\mu_j u} W'_j(u)du \right.$$

$$\left. + \int_0^t e^{-\mu_j \alpha_j(t-u)/\alpha_r} W'_r(u)du \right\} \quad r = 1, 2, \ldots, R. \qquad (8.32)$$

The boundary conditions are obvious: $W_r(0) = 0$, $r = 1, 2, \ldots, R$.

This system of equations can be solved for $W_r(t)$, $r = 1, 2, \ldots, R$ (see [2]). However, that is not our aim here; we are interested only in the unconditional average response times

$$W_r = \int_0^\infty \mu_r e^{-\mu_r t} W_r(t) dt = \int_0^\infty e^{-\mu_r t} W_r'(t) dt, \quad r = 1, 2, \ldots, R.$$

Accordingly, we multiply both sides of (8.32) by $e^{-\mu_r t}$ and integrate over $t \in (0, \infty)$. This yields, after some arithmetic,

$$W_r = \frac{1}{\mu_r} + \sum_{j=1}^R \left[\frac{\alpha_j \lambda_j}{\alpha_j \mu_j + \alpha_r \mu_r} (W_j + W_r) \right], \quad r = 1, 2, \ldots, R. \qquad (8.33)$$

We are now in a position to tackle either the analysis or the synthesis problem. For a given processor-sharing strategy, i.e. a given parameter vector $\boldsymbol{\alpha}$, the corresponding performance vector $\mathbf{W}$ can be found by solving the (linear) system of equations (8.33) for W_r ($r = 1, 2, \ldots, R$). If, on the other hand, we are given an achievable performance vector $\mathbf{W}$, we can find a processor-sharing strategy which achieves $\mathbf{W}$ by setting $\alpha_R = 1$ and solving the (non-linear) system of equations (8.33) for α_r ($r = 1, 2, \ldots, R-1$). In the second case one would probably have to employ a numerical iteration procedure.

It is not difficult to conceive of other families of scheduling strategies which are $M/M/1$-complete (see [8]). For example, rather than sharing the processor among all jobs in the system one could share it among the top jobs in each job class queue (according to a vector of weights). That family has similar properties to the one we have considered but seems to be more difficult to analyse. No result like (8.33) is available for it.

Let us also give, without proof, another example of a family of non-pre-emptive scheduling strategies which is $M/G/1$-complete. Take the case of $R = 2$. Consider the strategy which, after each service completion, selects for service a class 1 or a class 2 job with probabilities α and $(1 - \alpha)$, respectively (if only one class is present then a job of that class is chosen with probability 1). The family of these strategies, when α varies in the interval $[0, 1]$, is $M/G/1$-complete. This is because the extreme points of H_2 are achieved for $\alpha = 0$ and $\alpha = 1$, and the mapping $\alpha \rightarrow \mathbf{W}$ is obviously continuous. Moreover, since the "mixing" decisions are made after each service completion rather than at the end of each busy period, the response time variances are not as large as under the earlier mixing strategies. Generalising these ideas to the case $R > 2$ would produce an $(R - 1)$-dimensional family of scheduling strategies which is $M/G/1$-complete. At present there are no analytical results concerning that family. There are, however, some operating systems which use similar "proportional admission" strategies; the choice of parameters is usually made by experimentation.

We shall now give the proof of Theorem 8.7.

Proof of Theorem 8.7. Since H_φ is the image of a compact set by a continuous mapping, and since H_φ is bounded (it is contained in the set of achievable vectors) it must also be compact. Suppose that $H_\varphi \neq H$. This means that there are points on the boundary of H_φ which are not on the boundary of H (a point belongs to the boundary of a set if, and only if, every open sphere containing it also contains points not of the set). Let $\mathbf{W}_0$ be one such point and let $\boldsymbol{\alpha}_0$ be the inverse image of $\mathbf{W}_0$ in A. Since the boundary of A is mapped on to the boundary of $H, \boldsymbol{\alpha}_0$ must be an inner point of A. There exists, therefore, an open sphere A_0 such that $\boldsymbol{\alpha}_0 \in A_0$ and $A_0 \subset A$. Let H_0 be the image of A_0 in H_φ. It is known that under the conditions of the theorem the image of an open set is open. Therefore, H_0 is an open set contained in H_φ and containing $\mathbf{W}_0$. That, however, is impossible because $\mathbf{W}_0$ was a boundary point of H_φ. □

8.5. Optimal scheduling strategies

We have studied several problems which had to do with achieving specific performance vector targets. Now let us consider the question of how to choose an appropriate target. What is "the best" response time vector to aim for? Clearly, the answer to that question depends on the criterion that is being used to evaluate and compare different choices. We shall examine some frequently used criteria and the "best" scheduling strategies corresponding to them.

The general formulation of an optimisation problem is in terms of a cost function. We assume that with every response time vector $\mathbf{W}$ is associated with a cost $C(\mathbf{W})$; the problem is to minimise $C(\mathbf{W})$ over the set of achievable response time vectors. Consider the case when $C(\mathbf{W})$ is linear in the elements of $\mathbf{W}$:

$$C(\mathbf{W}) = \sum_{r=1}^{R} c_r W_r, \quad c_r \geq 0; \quad r = 1, 2, \ldots, R. \qquad (8.34)$$

From the characterisation theorems of section 8.3 we know that the set of achievable performance vectors is a polytope (H_1^* in the case of $M/M/1$ systems, H_2^* for $M/G/1$ systems). Moreover, we know exactly what are the vertices of that polytope (Lemmas 8.1 and 8.2). Since the minimum of a linear function over a polytope is always reached at one of the vertices, we immediately obtain the following results.

Lemma 8.4. *In an $M/M/1$ system any cost function of the type* (8.34) *is minimised by one of the $R!$ pre-emptive priority disciplines.*

Lemma 8.5. *In a non-pre-emptive $M/G/1$ system any cost function of the type* (8.34) *is minimised by one of the $R!$ head-of-the-line priority disciplines.*

We have thus come to the rather remarkable conclusion that, with a linear cost function, no amount of sophistication in a scheduling strategy can do better than a simple priority discipline which bases its decisions only on the presence or absence of jobs of various types in the system. It is still presumed, of course, that the strategies under consideration satisfy condition (ii) of section 8.2.

It is not difficult now to determine exactly which priority discipline is the optimal one. Take any priority ordering, say $(1, 2, \ldots, R)$, and consider the effect of interchanging the priorities of two adjacent job classes, j and $j + 1$. Let $\mathbf{W}$ and $\tilde{\mathbf{W}}$ be the response time vectors before and after the interchange. From the nature of priority disciplines (both pre-emptive and non-pre-emptive), it follows that

$$W_j < \tilde{W}_j; \quad W_{j+1} > \tilde{W}_{j+1};$$
$$W_r = \tilde{W}_r \quad \text{for } r < j \text{ or } r > j + 1.$$

The last equalities, together with the conservation laws, imply

$$\rho_j W_j + \rho_{j+1} W_{j+1} = \rho_j \tilde{W}_j + \rho_{j+1} \tilde{W}_{j+1}. \tag{8.35}$$

Consider the difference in the cost functions which can be written as

$$
\begin{aligned}
C(\mathbf{W}) - C(\tilde{\mathbf{W}}) &= c_j W_j + c_{j+1} W_{j+1} - (c_j \tilde{W}_j + c_{j+1} \tilde{W}_{j+1}) \\
&= \frac{c_j}{\rho_j}(\rho_j W_j - \rho_j \tilde{W}_j) + \frac{c_{j+1}}{\rho_{j+1}}(\rho_{j+1} W_{j+1} - \rho_{j+1} \tilde{W}_{j+1}).
\end{aligned}
$$

Suppose that $(c_{j+1}/\rho_{j+1}) > (c_j/\rho_j)$. Then, since the bracketed term which multiplies (c_{j+1}/ρ_{j+1}) is positive,

$$C(\mathbf{W}) - C(\tilde{\mathbf{W}}) > \frac{c_j}{\rho_j} \left(\rho_j W_j - \rho_j \tilde{W}_j + \rho_{j+1} W_{j+1} - \rho_{j+1} \tilde{W}_{j+1}\right) = 0$$

on account of (8.35). Similarly, if $(c_{j+1}/\rho_{j+1}) \leq (c_j/\rho_j)$, then $C(\mathbf{W}) - C(\tilde{\mathbf{W}}) \leq 0$.

Thus, the cost function can be reduced by giving higher priority to a job class for which the ratio "cost coefficient/traffic intensity" is larger. An optimal scheduling strategy is obtained as follows:

(i) find an index ordering $(r_1, r_2, \ldots, r_R)$ such that

$$(c_{r_1}/\rho_{r_1}) \geq (c_{r_2}/\rho_{r_2}) \geq \cdots \geq (c_{r_R}/\rho_{r_R}); \qquad (8.36)$$

(ii) choose the discipline which gives highest priority to class r_1, second highest priority to class $r_2, \ldots$, lowest priority to class r_R.

The above prescription applies to both $M/M/1$ and $M/G/1$ systems, with the proviso that in the first case the priorities should be pre-emptive and in the second non-pre-emptive. In the case of non-pre-emptive $M/G/1$ systems this is a classic result (Fife [3], Smith [14]; see also Kleinrock [6]).

Let us examine some special cases. Suppose that our objective is to minimise the over-all average response time. The corresponding cost function is

$$C(\mathbf{W}) = \sum_{r=1}^{R} \frac{\lambda_r}{\lambda} W_r,$$

where $\lambda = \lambda_1 + \lambda_2 + \cdots + \lambda_R$ is the total arrival rate. To obtain the optimal strategy we rank the quantities $\lambda_r/\rho_t = \mu_r$ in descending order, or the average service times $1/\mu_r$ in ascending order. The result is the Shortest-Expected-Processing-Time-first discipline (SEPT), in either pre-emptive or non-pre-emptive version.

Consider now a single-class $M/G/1$ system where the exact service time of every incoming job is known. As matters stand, this information cannot be used in scheduling the jobs because of condition (ii) of section 8.2; all admissible non-pre-emptive scheduling strategies yield the same average response time as, for example, the FIFO discipline:

$$W_{\text{FIFO}} = \frac{1}{\mu} + \frac{\lambda M_2}{2(1 - \rho)} \tag{8.37}$$

where M_2 is the second moment of the service time distribution (see (8.11)).

The restriction on scheduling strategies can be avoided by introducing "artificial" job classes. Assume first that the service times can take only a finite number of values: they are equal to x_j with probability p_j, $j = 1, 2, \ldots, J$; $p_1 + p_2 + \cdots + p_J = 1$. The system can be treated as an $M/G/1$ queue with J job classes, class j having arrival rate $\lambda_j = \lambda p_j$, mean service time $(1/\mu_j) = x_j$, traffic intensity $\rho_j = \lambda p_j x_j$ and second moment of service time distribution $M_{2j} = x_j^2$. Scheduling strategies which use information about exact service times are now admissible because that information is contained in the class identifiers. To minimise the over-all average response time one has to give class j non-pre-emptive priority over class k if $x_j < x_k$. This is the Shortest-Processing-Time-first discipline (SPT): when the server is ready to begin a new service it selects the shortest job of those present in the system.

The above argument generalises easily to an arbitrary service time distribution. Thus, in any non-pre-emptive $M/G/1$ system the average response time is minimised by the SPT discipline.

We see that the optimal strategy to be followed depends on the amount of information available. If only the distribution of service times is known then the best strategy is SEPT which, in the case of one job class, reduces to serving jobs in order of arrival; the resulting average response time is given by (8.37). If individual service times are known then the optimal strategy is SPT; the corresponding average response time is (see expression (1.79), Chapter 1)

$$W_{\text{SPT}} = \frac{1}{\mu} + \frac{\lambda M_2}{2} \int_0^\infty \frac{\mathrm{d}F(x)}{[1 - G(x^-)][1 - G(x^+)]} \tag{8.38}$$

where $F(x)$ is the service time distribution function and

$$G(x) = \int_0^x y \, \mathrm{d}F(y)$$

(the notation x^- and x^+ means, respectively, left-hand and right-hand limit).

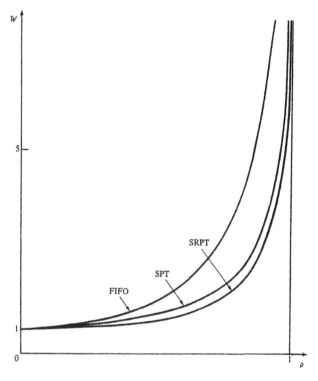

Fig. 8.4.

Since (8.38) represents a minimum over a wider domain of strategies, it is clear that $W_{\text{SPT}} \leq W_{\text{FIFO}}$. Moreover, we conjecture that the inequality is strict as long as the service time distribution is not degenerate. Two of the graphs in Fig. 8.4 show W_{FIFO} and W_{SPT} as functions of the traffic intensity, ρ, for a fixed value of μ (exponentially distributed service times).

The STP discipline is an example of a non-pre-emptive scheduling strategy for which the $M/G/1$ conservation law (Theorem 8.3) does not hold. Condition (ii) of section 8.2 is violated.

At this point, one naturally asks the question "can the average response time be reduced still further by allowing interruptions of service?". In other words, if individual service times are known in advance, is there a better way of using that information than by serving the shortest job first? Intuitively the answer is positive. If, for example, a newly arriving job with service time x finds a job in service with remaining service time $y > x$, it seems better to start the new job immediately rather than wait until the current service is completed.

These considerations lead to the Shortest-Remaining-Processing-Time-first discipline (SRPT), whereby at any moment in time the job with the least remaining service time of those present in the system is being served. The following result, due to Schrage [10], establishes the optimality of that discipline.

Lemma 8.6. *The SRPT scheduling strategy achieves the lowest possible value of the over-all average response time in a $G/G/1$ queueing system.*

Proof. A stronger assertion can be demonstrated: for every realisation of the interarrival and service time processes, SRPT minimises the number of jobs in the system at any point in time. Indeed, consider a particular sequence of arrival instants and job service times and suppose that the scheduling strategy is not SRPT. Then at some point t there must be two jobs in the system, j and k, with remaining service times x_j and x_k respectively, such that (i) $x_j > x_k$ and (ii) j is in service at t and remains in service for some interval $(t, t+v)$. Denote by σ the set of intervals following t during which either job j or job k is being served. The total length of the intervals in σ is $x_j + x_k$ and is independent of the scheduling strategy. Let us now modify the scheduling strategy by giving pre-emptive priority to job k over job j during σ; at all other instants the strategy remains unchanged. Clearly, this modification affects only jobs j and k. Its effect is to bring forward the earlier of the two departure instants (because of $x_k < x_j$), without changing the later one. Hence, there will be an interval of time during which the number of jobs in the system under the modified strategy is one less than under the original one; at all other times the two are the same.

Thus, every non-SRPT scheduling strategy can be improved with respect to the number of jobs in the system. It follows, therefore, that the smallest number of jobs is achieved under the SRPT discipline. This completes the proof of the lemma since, according to Little's theorem, minimising the average number of jobs in the system is equivalent to minimising the average response time.   □

The $M/G/1$ queueing system under SRPT scheduling was analysed by Schrage and Miller [12]; the average response time is given by

$$W_{\mathrm{SRPT}} = \int_0^\infty \frac{1 - F(x)}{1 - \lambda G(x)}\, \mathrm{d}x + \frac{\lambda}{2} \int_0^\infty \frac{G_2(x) + x^2[1 - F(x)]}{[1 - \lambda G(x^-)][1 - \lambda G(x^+)]}\, \mathrm{d}F(x)$$

$$(8.39)$$

where $G(x)$ has the same meaning as in (8.38) and

$$G_2(x) = \int_0^x y^2 \mathrm{d}F(y).$$

Since W_{SRPT} is a minimum over all scheduling strategies, it must be that $W_{\text{SRPT}} \leq W_{\text{SPT}}$. Moreover, it seems again that the inequality is strict except when the service times are constant. The dependency of W_{SRPT} on ρ for a fixed value of μ and for exponentially distributed service times is illustrated in Fig. 8.4. The SRPT discipline is an example of a pre-emptive strategy for which the $M/M/1$ conservation law does not hold (because condition (ii) of section 8.2 is not satisfied).

Let us recapitulate the results obtained so far in this section, for cost functions of the type (8.34).

(i) $M/G/1$ *systems, pre-emption of service disallowed.* If only the distributions of service times are known, then the optimal scheduling strategy is obtained by ranking the ratios c_r/ρ_r and applying non-pre-emptive priorities. This reduces to SEPT when the objective is to minimise the overall average response time ($c_r = \lambda_r/\lambda$). If individual service times are known, and if $c_r = \lambda_r/\lambda$, then the optimal strategy is SPT.

(ii) $M/M/1$ *systems, pre-emption of service allowed.* If only the distributions of service times are known, then the optimal strategy is obtained by ranking the ratios c_r/ρ_r and applying pre-emptive priorities. In view of the remark following Theorem 8.4, this result holds also for $G/M/1$ systems. If individual service times are known, and if $c_r = \lambda_r/\lambda$, then SRPT is optimal in arbitrary $G/G/1$ systems.

There is an obvious gap in the above: an $M/G/1$ (non-exponential service times) system where only the distributions of service times are known and where pre-emptions are allowed. The optimal scheduling strategy in this case is still an open problem. If, however, all jobs to be executed are assumed to be in the system at time zero (no further arrivals), then the problem has been solved by Sevcik [13]. He has defined a strategy called Smallest-Rank-first (SR) and proved its optimality. Moreover, Sevcik has put forward the conjecture (supported by an intuitive argument) that SR is optimal in the $M/G/1$ case, too.

The Smallest-Rank strategy works as follows: suppose that the processor is assigned for an interval y to a job of class r with attained service time t. The average amount of processor time that the job will actually use is equal to

$$Q_r(t, y) = \left\{ \int_0^y [1 - F_r(t + x)] \mathrm{d}x \right\} \Big/ [1 - F_r(t)],$$

where $F_r(x)$ is the required service time distribution function for class r. The probability that the job will complete within the allocated time y is equal to

$$S_r(t, y) = [F_r(t + y) - F_r(t)]/[1 - F_r(t)].$$

These two quantities are used to define the rank $v_r(t)$ of a class r job with attained service t:

$$v_r(t) = \min_y \frac{Q_r(t, y)}{c_r S_r(t, y)},$$

where c_r is the cost coefficient associated with class r. The minimum is taken over the set of permissible allocations y (if jobs can be interrupted at any point, all $y \geq 0$ are permissible). The smallest value of y for which the minimum is reached is called the "rank quantum". At each scheduling decision point, the processor is assigned to the job with the smallest rank for the duration of the corresponding rank quantum.

When $v_r(t)$ is a non-increasing function of the attained service t for every $r = 1, 2, \ldots, R$, the *SR* strategy behaves like a pre-emptive priority discipline based on the ordering (8.36), except that the average service times are replaced by the average remaining service times. This tends to happen when the service time distributions have coefficients of variation not greater than 1 (e.g. uniform, Erlang or exponential distributions). If, on the other hand, $v_r(t)$ is an increasing function of t for every r, then SR behaves like a Processor-Sharing discipline (e.g. for hyperexponential distributions). This confirms the intuitive idea that when the variations in service times are small, jobs should not be interrupted too much, and when the variations are large, it is better to interrupt them often.

The optimality of the SR discipline for the case of no arrivals is proved by induction on the number of jobs present. We shall omit that proof here; the interested reader is referred to [13].

A few words should be said about minimising cost functions which are non-linear in the elements of $\mathbf{W}$. The general problem (min $C(\mathbf{W})$, subject to the constraints $\mathbf{W} \in H_1$, or $\mathbf{W} \in H_2$, depending on whether the system is $M/M/1$ or $M/G/1$) can be tackled by classic mathematical programming methods. The fact that the constraints are always linear — they are given by Theorems 8.4 and 8.5 — may facilitate the solution. Take, as an example, a two-class $M/M/1$ system and consider the problem

$$\min(W_1^2 + W_2^2)$$

(find the point (W_1, W_2) which is closest to the origin). The constraints are

$$\rho_1 W_1 + \rho_2 W_2 = (\rho_1/\mu_1 + \rho_2/\mu_2)/(1 - \rho_1 - \rho_2) \quad \text{(conservation law)}$$
$$W_1 \geq 1/[\mu_1(1 - \rho_1)]$$
$$W_2 \geq 1/[\mu_2(1 - \rho_2)].$$

Using only the first constraint, by means of a Lagrange multiplier, we find a possible solution

$$\hat{W}_1 = (K/2)\rho_1; \quad \hat{W}_2 = (K/2)\rho_2,$$

where the Lagrange multiplier K is determined from the equality constraint:

$$K = 2(\rho_1/\mu_1 + \rho_2/\mu_2)/[(1 - \rho_1 - \rho_2)(\rho_1^2 + \rho_2^2)].$$

There are now three possibilities: if the vector $(\hat{W}_1, \hat{W}_2)$ satisfies both inequality constraints, then it is achievable and is, therefore, the solution of the problem. A scheduling strategy to achieve it can be found by using one of the parameterised families of section 8.4. If $\hat{\mathbf{W}}$ violates one of the inequality constraints (it cannot violate them both because of the conservation law), then the solution is at the corresponding extreme point of H_1. The optimal scheduling strategy will be the pre-emptive priority discipline associated with that extreme point.

We have obtained in this chapter some rather general results concerning the characterisation, control and optimisation of performance in single-resource systems. We have also seen that there are many problems still unsolved. Other ways of measuring performance form a large area to be explored. For instance, among the scheduling strategies that achieve a given performance vector, is there a strategy that minimises the vector of variances of response times and, if so, how can it be found?

In the next chapter, we shall consider some synthesis problems in multiple-resource systems. As can be expected, the situation there is much more complicated. Several methods of control will be examined, using various models of multiprogrammed computer systems.

References

1. Coffman, E. G., Jr. and Mitrani, I. (1980). A characterisation of waiting time performance realisable by single-server queues. *Operations Research*.

2. Fayolle, G., Iasnogorodski, R. and Mitrani, I. (1978). On the sharing of a processor among many job classes. Research Report, No. 275, IRIA-Laboria; also to appear (1980), *JACM*.

3. Fife, D. W. (1965). Scheduling with random arrivals and linear loss functions. *Man. Sci.*, **11**(3), 429–437.

4. Kleinrock, L. (1965). A conservation law for a wide class of queueing disciplines. *Nav. Res. Log. Quart.*, **12**, 181–192.

5. Kleinrock, L. (1967). Time-shared systems: A theoretical treatment. *J.A.C.M.*, **14**(2), 242–261.

6. Kleinrock, L. (1976). "Queueing Systems." Vol. 2. John Wiley, New York.

7. Kleinrock, L. and Coffman, E. G., Jr. (1967). Distribution of attained service in time-shared systems. *J. Comp. Sys. Sci.*, 287–298.

8. Mitrani, I. and Hine, J. H. (1977). Complete parameterised families of job scheduling strategies. *Acta Informatica*, **8**, 61–73.

9. O'Donovan, T. M. (1974). Distribution of attained and residual service in general queueing systems. *Operations Research*, **22**, 570–575.

10. Schrage, L. E. (1968). A proof of the optimality of the SRPT discipline. *Operations Research*, **16**(3), 687–690.

11. Schrage, L. (1970). An alternative proof of a conservation law for the queue $G/G/1$. *Operations Research*, **18**, 185–187.

12. Schrage, L. E. and Miller, L. W. (1966). The queue $M/G/1$ with the shortest remaining processing time discipline. *Operations Research*, **14**, 670–683.

13. Sevcik, K. C. (1974). A proof of the optimality of "smallest rank" scheduling. *J.A.C.M.*, **21**, 66–75.

14. Smith, W. E. (1956). Various optimisers for single-stage production. *Nav. Res. Log. Quart.*, **3**, 59–66.

Chapter 9

Control of Performance
in Multiple-Resource Systems

9.1. Some problems arising in multiprogrammed computer systems

Large computer systems contain, as a rule, several processors: some of these perform arithmetic and logical operations, others transfer information between primary and secondary memory, still others control various communication lines, etc. In order to ensure the efficient use of the resources, and to allow a number of users simultaneous access to the facilities, such systems are usually multiprogrammed. A number of jobs are admitted into main memory; these jobs are called "active". Several processors may thus serve several of the active jobs at the same time.

The first and most pressing problem arising in this connection is that of the degree of multiprogramming (the number of jobs that are active at any one time). If the degree of multiprogramming is too low then the processors are underutilised. If, on the other hand, it is too high then each active job can be allocated only a small portion of main memory; consequently, a heavy traffic of information to and from secondary memory is generated (paging); as a result, very little useful work is done. This latter phenomenon is called "thrashing". The problem is, therefore, to maintain a degree of multiprogramming such that processor utilisation is high and thrashing does not occur. Moreover, one should be able to do this dynamically, under changing load conditions.

There is more freedom of choice when the demand consists of several job classes. Differences in program behaviour can be exploited in order to produce a better mix of active jobs. For example, jobs whose "locality of reference" is good (such jobs acquire their working set of pages quickly and then cease to contribute to the paging traffic), can be admitted in greater numbers to the active set.

Apart from seeking the best degree of multiprogramming and the best mix of active jobs, there are usually some pre-specified performance objectives which have to be satisfied by the scheduling algorithm. These are often stated in terms of average response times (the performance vector introduced in Chapter 6). For instance, in a system where the demand arriving per unit time consists of many short, I/O-bound jobs and a few long CPU-bound jobs, the objective might be to guarantee a certain maximum average response time for the short jobs.

All these problems are of the same type as the synthesis problems discussed in Chapter 6: for a given set of system parameters (describing the hardware configuration and the behaviour of various job classes) and for a given performance objective, find a scheduling strategy to achieve that objective. However, the scheduling decisions involved in multiprogrammed, multiple-resource systems are more complex; they are also more interrelated. One has to decide how many jobs, and of what classes, should be admitted into the active set: this part of the scheduling strategy will be called "admission control policy". Another set of decisions concern the scheduling of active jobs among the system resources (how much main memory to allocate to each active job, what queueing discipline to use at various processors, etc.): these will be referred to as "resource allocation policy". Clearly, the admission policy and the resource allocation policy influence each other.

The results which allowed us to characterise the achievable performance vectors in single-server systems do not carry over to multiple-resource systems. We do not know what is the set of performance vectors that can be achieved by varying the scheduling strategy. Neither do we know, in general, what is "the best" scheduling strategy corresponding to a given performance objective function. Existing studies have concentrated on evaluating particular admission and resource allocation policies, or families of such policies.

There is one general result which is still valid, and it concerns the convexity of the set of achievable performance vectors: if two performance vectors $\mathbf{W}_1$ and $\mathbf{W}_2$ are achievable by scheduling strategies S_1 and S_2, then all performance vectors on the line segment between $\mathbf{W}_1$ and $\mathbf{W}_2$ are also achievable, by mixing scheduling strategies (S_1, S_2, α) (see section 8.3).

In this chapter we shall present a general model for multiprogrammed, multiple-resource systems and shall consider several control policies. These will be directed at optimising the degree of multiprogramming in single-class systems, as well as at controlling the performance vector in systems with many job classes.

9.2. The modelling of system resources and program behaviour

A group of system resources — to be called "the inner system" — is involved in the execution of active jobs: this group comprises the CPU, the main memory, disk and drum processors, etc. Another group — "the outer system" — is concerned with getting jobs into and out of the inner system: terminals and batch entry stations are of that type. This distinction is sometimes conceptual rather than physical, e.g. a disk unit may contain files referred to by the active jobs (inner system) and, at the same time, be used for spooling or roll-in-roll-out operations (outer system). The determining characteristic of resources in the inner system is that any job using them occupies a certain amount of main memory. The system structure is illustrated in Fig. 9.1. The inner system is modelled by a queueing network: node 0 represents the CPU (assuming a single CPU), node 1 represents the "paging device" (usually a drum) and nodes $2, 3, \ldots, K$ represent other I/O devices. We can think of the admission control policy as a node, too, since it may delay jobs coming from the outside and may also remove active jobs from the inner system, hold them and reintroduce them at a later stage.

Main memory is allocated to the active jobs in units of fixed size called "page frames"; their total number is M. The information that can be stored in a page frame is a "page". Every job requires a certain set of pages in

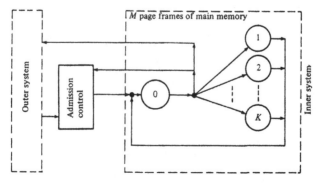

Fig. 9.1.

order to complete execution: that set is its "virtual memory". Typically, only a fraction of a job's virtual memory can be contained in the page frames allocated on that job, the rest is stored in secondary memory (on the paging device). When an active job requires a page from its virtual memory which is not already in main memory (i.e. when a "page fault" occurs) a new page frame has to be allocated and the page brought in before the job can continue execution. This, in turn, may necessitate the freeing (perhaps by removing a page) of another page frame from the memory allocation for that or for another job.

Thus, the finiteness of main memory influences system performance through the page faults, the traffic of pages to and from the paging device, and the ensuing delays. These effects can be incorporated into the model in a convenient way by associating with each active job a "lifetime function", $e(m)$ (Belady and Kuehner [2]). For a job which is executing in m page frames of main memory, $e(m)$ is the average amount of CPU service received by the job between two consecutive page faults (not necessarily a continuous CPU interval; it may be interrupted by visits to other I/O devices). Alternatively, $1/e(m)$ is the rate at which a job whose current memory allocation is m pages frames interrupts its CPU service to go to the paging device.

Intuitively, $e(m)$ should be an increasing function of m: the more page frames a job has, the less often it is likely to have page faults. There are also reasons to believe that $e(m)$ is convex, at least for small values of m (this is the case, for instance, when pages are referenced independently of each other). Two analytic (as distinct from empirically derived) forms of $e(m)$ have been used frequently. These are

$$e(m) = am^k; \quad a > 0, \; k > 1 \tag{9.1}$$

(Belady and Kuehner [2]), and

$$e(m) = \frac{2b}{1 + (c/m)^2}; \quad b, c > 0 \tag{9.2}$$

(Chamberlin, Fuller and Lin [4]). The two functions are shown in Fig. 9.2.

When a new job is admitted into the inner system, i.e. becomes active, it is allocated a certain number of page frames. This implies, in general, that the allocation of one or more other jobs is reduced; they begin, therefore, to operate at a different point on their lifetime curves — closer to the origin — and start visiting node 1 more often. Similarly, when a job departs from

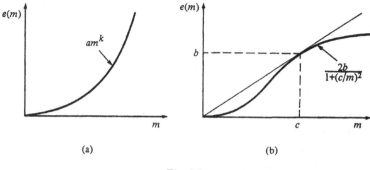

Fig. 9.2.

the inner system, one or more other jobs start visiting node 1 less often. Thus, not only the service times at node 0 but also the probability that a job goes to node j after leaving node 0 depend on the number and types of active jobs.

This behaviour of the inner system means, unfortunately, that the results of Chapter 3 are not directly applicable to the present model. No matter what assumptions we make about queueing disciplines, required service time distributions, etc., a queueing network model of a multi-programmed system such as the one in Fig. 9.1 will not have a product-form solution; and without a product-form solution we cannot hope to have efficient methods for the exact evaluation of performance measures. It is almost imperative, therefore, to look for approximate solutions.

The parameters of most real-life systems are such that the corresponding models lend themselves easily to decomposition. The interactions between the inner and the outer systems are weak compared to those within the inner systems: jobs are admitted into, and depart from, the inner system at a much lower rate than that at which they circulate inside it. This allows one to assume that the inner system reaches equilibrium in between consecutive changes in the degree of multiprogramming. For a given set of active jobs, the inner system can be treated as a closed queueing network; that network can be analysed in the steady-state to obtain the rates at which jobs of various classes obtain CPU service; those rates can be used to replace the whole inner system by a single server whose rate of service depends on the system state (via the set of active jobs).

We shall elaborate further on this approach when we apply it to specific synthesis problems. Our interest will be directed primarily towards the design of admission and memory allocation policies.

9.3. Control of the degree of multiprogramming

It is intuitively obvious that the efficiency of a system should depend on the degree of multiprogramming. To render that intuition quantitative, let us introduce as a measure of efficiency the over-all T: the average number of jobs that are completed per unit time. In terms of the model in Fig. 9.1 this is the average number of jobs taking the path from node 0 to the outer system per unit time. The differences between job types are thus removed from consideration; if there are several job classes they are all lumped together.

Suppose that the inner system is multiprogrammed at a constant degree n: there are n jobs circulating in it at all times and as soon as one of them leaves a new one is admitted immediately. Let the steady-state under these conditions be $T(n)$, and the steady-state CPU utilisation (the probability that node 0 is busy) be $U_0(n)$. Denote, further, the average CPU time required per job by $1/\mu$ (this is a job characteristic and is independent of n). Then, since jobs are completed at rate μ while the CPU is busy, we have

$$T(n) = \mu U_0(n). \tag{9.3}$$

The is directly related to the CPU utilisation.

If we plot $T(n)$ or $U_0(n)$ against n, we obtain typically a graph that looks like that in Fig. 9.3 (see, for example, Denning *et al.* [6]). We can distinguish three broad regions on the graph of $T(n)$. (i) When $n < n_1$, the system is underloaded; CPU utilisation and are low because there are not enough active jobs to make efficient use of the resources. (ii) When $n > n_2$, the system is thrashing; CPU utilisation and are low because there are too many active jobs, each is allocated only a few page frames in main memory, the page fault rate is very high and most of the jobs spend most of their

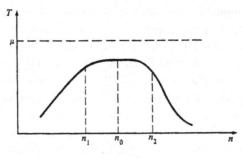

Fig. 9.3.

time at the paging drum. The task of a control algorithm is therefore to ensure that the degree of multiprogramming is maintained dynamically in the region of efficient operation (iii) $n_1 \leq n \leq n_2$, and preferably close to the optimum n_0.

We shall discuss three methods of control, all of which have intuitive justifications and have been shown empirically to perform well (to a greater or lesser extent) under various conditions. However, at present there is no formal proof for either of them. The "knee" and the "$L = S$" criteria were studied by Denning and Kahn [5, 6]; the "50% drum utilisation" method was proposed by Leroudier and Potier [11].

9.3.1. The knee criterion

This control procedure works by monitoring the inter-page-fault intervals for all active jobs and allocating memory in such a way that each job operates at, or near, a certain point on its lifetime curve called the "knee". The knee m^* of a lifetime function $e(m)$ is defined as the point maximising the ratio $e(m)/m$, when that maximum exists:

$$e(m^*)/m^* \geq e(m)/m \quad \text{for all } m > 0. \tag{9.4}$$

Geometrically, m^* is such that the ray from the origin passing through the point $(m^*, e(m^*))$, dominates the entire curve $\{e(m), m \geq 0\}$. For example, the knee of the lifetime function defined by (9.2) is at $m^* = c$ (see Fig. 9.2).

In order to give the intuitive justification for the knee criterion we need to introduce a quantity called "space-time product", and establish a relation between it and the . The space-time product, Y, for a job whose execution time is D (this is total real time spent in the inner system, not virtual CPU time), is defined as

$$Y = \int_0^D m(t)\mathrm{d}t \tag{9.5}$$

where $m(t)$ is the number of page frames that the job holds at time t of its execution. If $\bar{m}$ is the average number of page frames held by the job, then

$$Y = \bar{m}D. \tag{9.6}$$

Now consider a large period of time, V, during which all M memory frames are in use. The total space-time in the system over that period is

MV. On the other hand, the average number of jobs executed during the period is $T(n)V$ (since an average of $T(n)$ jobs depart per unit time). Hence, the average space-time product per job is

$$Y = \frac{MV}{T(n)V} = \frac{M}{T(n)}. \tag{9.7}$$

Thus Y and $T(n)$ are inversely proportional to each other; minimising the space-time product per job leads to maximising the and vice versa (this fact was also pointed out by Buzen [3] in an operational analysis context).

Let us derive a rough estimate of Y, for a job running in m page frames of memory and with a lifetime function $e(m)$. Since the average CPU requirement is $1/\mu$ and the average inter-page-fault interval is $e(m)$, the job has an average of $1/[\mu e(m)]$ page faults. Let τ be the average delay incurred as a consequence of a page fault (this includes page transport time plus waiting at drum and CPU). Denote by σ the average delay, per unit of CPU time, caused by visits to the other I/O devices (the number of those visits does not depend on m). Then the average time the job spends in the inner system is equal to

$$D = \frac{1}{\mu} + \frac{\tau}{\mu e(m)} + \frac{\sigma}{\mu} \tag{9.8}$$

and, from (9.6), the space-time product is

$$Y = \frac{1}{\mu} \left[m(\sigma + 1) + \frac{m\tau}{e(m)} \right]. \tag{9.9}$$

Bearing in mind that the knee m^* of the lifetime function maximises the ratio $e(m)/m$, we see from (9.9) that m^* minimises the component of the space-time product due to paging. Since the I/O device speeds are unaffected by the allocation of memory, letting each active job operate at the knee of its lifetime function tends to minimise the space-time product per job. Such an allocation tends, therefore, to maximise the $T(n)$.

This intuitive argument can be carried a step further by taking the lifetime function defined by (9.2), substituting it in (9.9) and finding the optimal memory allocation m_{opt} explicitly. Assuming, as a rough approximation, that τ and σ are independent of m, and solving the equation

$dY/dm = 0$, we obtain

$$m_{\text{opt}} = c/(1 + 2b(\sigma + 1)/\tau)^{\frac{1}{2}}.$$

Hence if $2b(\sigma + 1)/\tau$ is not large (usually it is less than 1), $m_{\text{opt}} \sim c = m^*$; the optimal allocation is indeed close to the knee of the lifetime function.

An implementation of the knee criterion would involve, for each active job, a continuing monitoring of its paging activity, an estimation of its lifetime function and an allocation of memory corresponding to the knee point. The degree of multiprogramming is thus controlled indirectly via the memory allocation. Such a control policy can be expected to be expensive, both in instrumentation and in overheads. On the other hand, as Denning and Kahn's experiments suggest (see [6]), the knee criterion is robust and yields near-optimal degrees of multiprogramming over a wide range of loading conditions. One cannot, of course, apply the knee criterion if jobs behave according to a lifetime function that has no knee, such as the one defined by (9.1). A finite value for m_{opt} may still exist, as we shall see shortly, and it may be possible to obtain an estimate for it. The memory allocation controller can then use that estimate.

9.3.2. The $L = S$ criterion

This is a control policy that acts directly on the degree of multiprogramming. It uses a single control variable — the average (taken over all active jobs) inter-page-fault interval $L(n)$; the "system lifetime". At any moment in time, $L(n)$ can be estimated by the mean of the last k inter-page-fault intervals:

$$L(n) \sim \frac{1}{k} \sum_{j=1}^{k} e_j, \tag{9.10}$$

where e_j is the j-th most recent interval, regardless of which job generated it.

The $L = S$ control policy attempts to balance the system lifetime and the paging drum average service time S: it maintains the degree of multiprogramming n at such a level that

$$L(n) \geq cS, \tag{9.11}$$

where c is a constant not much greater than 1. The intuition behind this criterion derives from the bounds that device service times place on .

Let $1/b_i$ and U_i be, respectively, the mean service time and the utilisation of node i in the inner system ($i = 0, 1, \ldots, K; 1/b_1 = S$). The parameters $b_1, b_2, \ldots, b_k$ are independent of n but b_0 depends on it via the memory allocation and lifetime functions. The utilisations U_i depend, of course, on n. Denote further by $1/a_i$ the mean CPU interval (not necessarily continuous) between consecutive requests for device i; $i = 1, 2, \ldots, K$. These are averages over all active jobs. $1/a_1$ is the system lifetime $L(n)$; all other a_is are program characteristics and are independent of n.

While the CPU is busy, jobs depart from it in the direction of node i at rate a_i ($i = 1, 2, \ldots, K$); the probability that the CPU is busy is U_0; therefore, the rate at which jobs arrive into device i is equal to $U_0 a_i$. Similarly, the rate at which jobs leave device i is equal to $U_i b_i$ ($i = 1, 2, \ldots, K$). Since these two rates are equal in the steady-state, we have

$$U_0 a_i = U_i b_i \quad i = 1, 2, \ldots, K. \tag{9.12}$$

These equations, combined with relation (9.3), allow us to write $K + 1$ expressions for the system :

$$T(n) = \begin{cases} U_0 \mu \\ U_i \mu b_i / a_i, & i = 1, 2, \ldots, K. \end{cases} \tag{9.13}$$

Now, the utilisations U_i, being probabilities, must satisfy the inequalities $U_i \leq 1$, $i = 0, 1, \ldots, K$. Therefore,

$$T(n) \leq \begin{cases} \mu \\ \mu b_i / a_i, & i = 1, 2, \ldots, K. \end{cases} \tag{9.14}$$

Of these $K + 1$ bounds, only $b_1/a_1 = L(n)/S$ depends on n.

By introducing the "I/O constant"

$$I = \min\{1, b_2/a_2, \ldots, b_K/a_K\} \tag{9.15}$$

we can rewrite (9.14) as

$$T(n) \leq \mu \min\{I, L(n)/S\}. \tag{9.16}$$

From the above, the is bound by two functions. One of them is constant and the other is decreasing with n (the more active jobs, the less memory per job and hence the smaller CPU intervals between page faults). These bounds are illustrated in Fig. 9.4. If the two bounds intersect, they do so at point $\tilde{n}$ which satisfies $L(\tilde{n}) = IS$. Intuitively, the should start decreasing for $n > \tilde{n}$, i.e. $\tilde{n}$ is slightly larger but close to the optimal value of n.

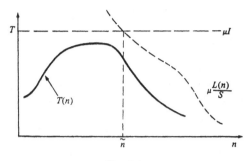

Fig. 9.4.

The control policy indicated by this intuition is to maintain the degree of multiprogramming so that $L(n) \geq cIS$, for some small constant $c > 1$. When $I = 1$, i.e. when $a_i \leq b_i$ $(i = 2, 3, \ldots, K)$, or the system is not "I/O-bound", that is the policy (9.11).

The $L = S$ criterion is not inconsistent with minimising the space-time product per job. If we take the lifetime function (9.1), $e(m) = am^k$, substitute it in (9.9) and solve the equation $dY/dm = 0$ (with τ and σ independent of n), we see that a solution m_{opt} exists and satisfies

$$am_{\text{opt}}^k = \frac{(k-1)\tau}{\sigma + 1}.$$

If the system is not I/O-bound, the constant σ (the average I/O delay per unit of CPU time) is small; the constant k of the Belady lifetime function is usually less than 2. Assuming that τ (the average delay per page fault) is not much greater than the drum service time S, we conclude that $e(m_{\text{opt}})$ is near S: we arrive again at the $L = S$ criterion.

A controller based on the $L = S$ rule is simpler and easier to implement than one based on the knee criterion. All that is required is an estimate of the current system lifetime $L(n)$, obtained as in (9.10). However, this policy appears to be less robust and in some cases (especially in I/O-bound systems) leads to a degree of multiprogramming which is significantly lower than the optimal (see [6]).

9.3.3. *The 50% criterion*

This rule states, very simply, that the degree of multiprogramming should be maintained at a level such that the utilisation of the paging drum is approximately $0.5 + d$, where d is a constant less than 0.1.

The supporting argument for the 50% criterion is equally simple. It proceeds as follows.

One of the manifestations of thrashing is a high rate of page faults, hence a high rate of requests for the paging drum. A high rate of requests implies a long queue; thus, a queue at the paging drum is symptomatic of a thrashing system and, to prevent thrashing, queues should not be allowed to develop. An average of one request at the paging drum is a good target to aim for. If we treat that device as an independent $M/M/1$ queue we can write for the average number $\bar{n}$ of requests there (see Chapter 1)

$$\bar{n} = U_1/(1 - U_1),$$

where U_1 is the traffic intensity, or the probability that the drum is busy. If we wish that average to be $\bar{n} = 1$ we should keep the utilisation at $U_1 = 0.5$.

Tenuous though the above argument may appear, the 50% rule seems to perform reasonably well, especially in systems where the average drum service time S is lower than the knee lifetime $e(m^*)$ (see [6]). In other cases this criterion tends to be less reliable than the other two and to underestimate the optimal degree of multiprogramming. On the other hand, it is the simplest of the three and the most straightforward to implement.

To summarise, we have described here three heuristic control rules for maintaining the degree of multiprogramming at, or near, its optimal level. We say that they are heuristic because there are no mathematical proofs establishing their validity, only intuitive arguments. There is, however, a certain amount of empirical and numerical evidence [1, 12, 13] which suggests that these rules can be applied successfully in practical systems.

It should be emphasised that any dynamic control is necessarily involved with transient phenomena whereas the theoretical support for the proposed control procedures is based on steady-state analysis. The degree of multiprogramming is assumed to remain constant long enough for the inner system to reach steady-state. If the loading conditions change rapidly in relation to the control actions (or, alternatively, if the control procedure reacts slowly to changes in the load conditions) then this assumption is violated and the control, if it works at all, will be unstable. There are no general assertions that can be made in this connection; much depends on implementation and instrumentation, as well as on the control algorithm. For example, some experiments (Leroudier and Potier [11]) indicate that the 50% rule responds rapidly to load fluctuations.

In the following sections we shall present some control algorithms which take into account, and exploit, the differences in behaviour patterns that exist in systems with several job classes.

9.4. The page fault rate control policy (RCP)

We have seen that there are certain trade-offs that govern the choice of a control algorithm. Program-driven algorithms (ones that collect and use information about individual programs in the active set) tend to perform better but are more expensive in terms of implementation and overheads. On the other hand, load-driven algorithms (based on global system behaviour) tend to be less robust but are easier to implement and have lower overheads. The page fault rate control policy (Gelenbe, Kurinckx and Mitrani [8]) combines the two principles by doing a small amount of program monitoring (counting page faults for each active job) and some load monitoring (estimating).

Control is exercised by forcing active jobs into a special, "impeded", state from time to time (see Fig. 9.5) and keeping them there for random periods. A job is removed from the inner system and put into the impeded set (freeing all its pages in main memory) as soon as it has had $J + 1$, consecutive page faults; J is a parameter of the policy. Thus, some "well-behaved" jobs complete their execution without ever entering the impeded set while others, with heavy paging demands, may pass through it several times before completing. The parameter J plays a role analogous to that of the CPU quantum in a conventional time-sharing scheduler, since it forces a job to relinquish its resources if it requires more than J accesses to the paging drum.

The periods that jobs spend in the impeded set should depend on the over-all system behaviour: when the system is thrashing, i.e. when is low,

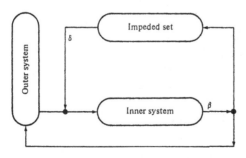

Fig. 9.5.

jobs should remain impeded longer; when the improves, impeded jobs can be reintroduced into the active set at a higher rate. Under the page fault rate control policy, the average time $1/\delta$ that jobs remain in the impeded set is proportional to the average interval $1/\beta$ between departures from the active set. We set

$$\delta = h\beta \qquad (9.17)$$

where h is a small constant (in the numerical evaluations of the policy its value was chosen as $h = 0.01$).

Thus, an implementation of the policy would involve two types of monitoring: (i) counting page faults for each active job in order to decide when to remove jobs to the impeded set, and (ii) estimating the total rate of departures from the inner system in order to regulate the average times that jobs spend in the impeded set. This compromise between program-driven and load-driven control allows the policy to prevent thrashing by discriminating against the jobs which contribute to it most — the jobs with most page faults.

An exact analysis of the system performance under RCP is not feasible for the reasons mentioned in the last section: the behaviour of active jobs depends on their number. However, an approximate evaluation can be obtained by applying decomposition. First, we consider the inner system as a closed network with a fixed number n_r of class r jobs circulating inside ($r = 1, 2, \ldots, R$). An analysis of the closed network will enable us to replace the whole inner system by a single aggregate server which gives simultaneous service to all active jobs, at rates depending on the state $\mathbf{n} = (n_1, n_2, \ldots, n_R)$. To do this we need the steady-state probability $\pi_r(n_1, n_2, \ldots, n_R)$ that, in the closed network, a class r job is in service at the CPU: that probability determines the for class r jobs in state $\mathbf{n}$. Also necessary is the steady-state probability $\pi_r^J(n_1, n_2, \ldots, n_R)$ that a class r job which has already had J page faults is in service at the CPU: it determines the rate at which jobs leave the inner system to join the impeded set.

An important distinguishing feature of the jobs of a given job class is their paging behaviour. In the model, a different lifetime function $e_r(m)$ is associated with each job class ($r = 1, 2, \ldots, R$). The "counting" of page faults in the closed network is modelled by splitting class r into $J + 1$ "artificial" job classes $(r, 0), (r, 1), \ldots, (r, J)$. At each visit to the paging drum, a job of class (r, j) becomes a job of class $(r, j+1)$ if $j = 0, 1, \ldots, J-1$ and it becomes a job of class $(r, 0)$ if $j = J$.

Exact expressions for $\pi_r(\mathbf{n})$ and $\pi_r^J(\mathbf{n})$ can be obtained, under a suitable set of assumptions, by applying the BCMP theorem of Chapter 3 (the formulae for a special case can be found in [8]). However, the computational effort associated with the solution of a multiclass network (calculation of normalisation constant, aggregation of states to find marginal distributions, etc.) is considerable. What is more, that effort grows rather rapidly with the size of the model, in particular with the number of artificial job classes resulting from a large value of J. On the other hand, an exact solution is rarely necessary, especially in view of the fact that the whole model is approximate (because of the decomposition and because parameters have to be estimated). Good approximations for the probabilities $\pi_r(\mathbf{n})$ and $\pi_r^J(\mathbf{n})$ can be obtained rather easily as follows.

Solve a single-class closed network with $n = n_1 + n_2 + \cdots + n_R$ jobs circulating inside. As a lifetime function, use the linear combination

$$e = \sum_{r=1}^{R} (n_r/n) e_r.$$

If other parameters vary across job classes, they are also averaged in a similar fashion. That single-class solution yields the over-all CPU utilisation $U_0(\mathbf{n})$.

Now return for a moment to the full model (including the outer system and the impeded set) and let $1/\mu_r$ be the average total CPU time required by a class r job; assume that the distribution of that time is exponential. Then, while a class r job is being served by the CPU, it leaves for the outer system at rate μ_r. Similarly, while a class r job is in service at the CPU it leaves for the impeded set at rate $1/[(J+1)e_r]$ (it is ejected at the $J + 1$st page fault). Therefore, in the virtual CPU time of a class r job the average interval between consecutive departures from the inner system is equal to

$$Q_r = \left[\mu_r + \frac{1}{(J+1)e_r} \right]^{-1} = \frac{(J+1)e_r}{1 + (J+1)e_r\mu_r}; \quad r = 1, 2, \ldots, R. \quad (9.18)$$

Intuitively, the proportion of all CPU busy time which is devoted to class r jobs can be approximated by

$$q_r = n_r Q_r \Big/ \sum_{s=1}^{R} n_s Q_s; \quad r = 1, 2, \ldots, R. \quad (9.19)$$

Furthermore, the class r jobs which have had J page faults (these are the class (r, J) jobs) occupy approximately a fraction $1/(J+1)$ of that proportion. We therefore set

$$\pi_r(n_1, n_2, \ldots, n_R) = q_r U_0(n_1, n_2, \ldots, n_R)$$
$$\pi_r^J(n_1, n_2, \ldots, n_R) = [q_r/(J+1)]U_0(n_1, n_2, \ldots, n_R); \quad r = 1, 2, \ldots, R.$$
$$\text{(9.20)}$$

Remark. If we were dealing with a generalised Round–Robin server which gives Q_r quanta of service to each class r job every time its turn comes, then (9.19) would be exactly the fraction of the server busy time devoted to class r jobs (see section 8.4). We are, in effect, assuming here that the inner system behaves approximately like a Round–Robin server. A limited validation of expressions (9.20), performed by simulation, showed good agreement with observed values ([8]).

The inner system can now be replaced by a single aggregate server. When the state of its queue is $\mathbf{n} = (n_1, n_2, \ldots, n_R)$, that server returns class r jobs to the outer system at rate

$$\xi_r(\mathbf{n}) = \mu_r \pi_r(\mathbf{n}); \quad r = 1, 2, \ldots, R \tag{9.21}$$

and it sends class r jobs to the impeded set at rate

$$\vartheta_r(\mathbf{n}) = (1/e_r)\pi_r^J(\mathbf{n}); \quad r = 1, 2, \ldots, R. \tag{9.22}$$

The total rate at which class r jobs depart from the aggregate server is $\beta_r(\mathbf{n}) = \xi_r(\mathbf{n}) + \vartheta_r(\mathbf{n})$. The rate at which each impeded job returns to the aggregate server is given by (9.17), with $\beta = \beta_1 + \beta_2 + \cdots + \beta_R$.

The model has thus been reduced to a queueing network with three nodes: the outer system, the aggregate server and the impeded set. The state of the network (under exponential assumptions) is a 2R-dimensional Markov process $(\mathbf{n}; \mathbf{k}) = (n_1, n_2, \ldots, n_R; k_1, k_2, \ldots, k_R)$, where n_r and k_r are the numbers of class r jobs at the aggregate server and in the impeded set, respectively ($r = 1, 2, \ldots, R$). While it is easy to write the steady-state balance equations for that process, solving them is by no means easy: there is no product-form solution because the behaviour of the aggregate server depends on the vector $\mathbf{n}$ and not just on the total number of jobs there. However, in some cases another level of decomposition may simplify matters considerably.

Consider the case of two job classes and suppose that the outer system consists of two finite sources: N_1 terminals of class 1 and N_2 terminals of class 2. There are thus N_1 and N_2 class 1 and class 2 jobs circulating endlessly among the three nodes; the system state is $(n_1, n_2; k_1, k_2)$, where $n_1 + k_1 \leq N_1$, $n_2 + k_2 \leq N_2$. The number of states, and hence the number of balance equations, is $\binom{N_1 + 2}{2} \binom{N_2 + 2}{2}$.

If the two job classes have very different lifetime function characteristics, we can attempt another decomposition. Suppose that the ejection threshold J can be chosen in such a way that jobs of one class, say class 2, are ejected from the inner system much more often than the others (the choice of J will be examined later). Then, if the aggregate server and the impeded set are considered in isolation, with I_1 and I_2 class 1 and class 2 jobs circulating among them, it can be assumed that all I_1 jobs are at the aggregate server. The probabilities $P(I_1, n_2 \mid I_1, I_2)$ that there are n_2 class 2 jobs at the aggregate server, given I_1 and I_2 ($n_2 = 0, 1, \ldots, I_2$) can be obtained by solving a simple $I_2 + 1$ state Markov process.

As the next step, the aggregate server and the impeded set are replaced by a single server which, when in state I_1, I_2, sends class r jobs to the terminals at rate

$$\zeta_r(I_1, I_2) = \sum_{n_2=0}^{I_2} \xi_r(I_1, n_2) P(I_1, n_2 \mid I_1, I_2), \quad r = 1, 2,$$

where $\xi_r(n_1, n_2)$ is given by (9.21).

The system state is now determined by the vector (I_1, I_2), $I_1 = 0, 1, \ldots, N_1$; $I_2 = 0, 1, \ldots, N_2$. The steady-state distribution of that vector is obtained (assuming exponentially distributed think times) by solving a system of $(N_1 + 1)(N_2 + 1)$ linear equations. From the joint distribution of I_1 and I_2 one can compute the marginal distribution I_r ($r = 1, 2$) and hence the average number $E[I_r]$ of class r jobs in execution (inner system and impeded set). The average number of class r jobs at the terminals is $N_r - E[I_r]$ and therefore the rate at which class r jobs are submitted for execution is $\lambda_r(N_r - E[I_r])$, where $1/\lambda_r$ is the mean think time at class r terminals. Little's theorem now yields the average response time W_r of class r jobs:

$$W_r = E[I_r] / [\lambda_r(N_r - E[I_r])], \quad r = 1, 2. \tag{9.23}$$

Figure 9.6 shows W_1 as a function of N_1 (for a fixed value of N_2) and W_2 as a function of N_2 (for a fixed value of N_1). The corresponding response time curves in an uncontrolled system are also illustrated; the difference is very striking. The Belady lifetime function (9.1) was assumed for this example. The two job classes differed in the value of the locality

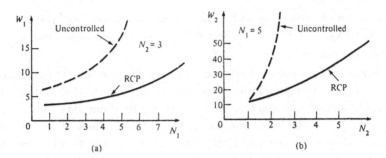

Fig. 9.6.

parameter k of the lifetime function: $k = 1.8$ for the "good" class 1 jobs and $k = 1.5$ for the "bad" class 2 jobs. Main memory was divided equally among the active jobs and an ejection threshold $J = 30$ was used.

On the basis of some numerical comparisons (see [7] and [8]) it appears that if the load characteristics do not vary rapidly with time, the control exercised by the page fault rate control policy is close to optimal. Those evaluations, however, ignored the overheads associated with the policy and, in particular, the times taken to move jobs between the active and impeded sets. The ability of the policy to react quickly to variations in program behaviour is also open to investigation.

The choice of J: The function of the control parameter J is twofold: first, to prevent thrashing effectively and second, to ensure that the "good" jobs — those that do not have page faults often — are not ejected from the active set often. To fulfil the first objective J should not be too large (otherwise there would be no control), and to fulfil the second it should not be too small. This trade-off can be assessed by evaluating the probability p_r that a class r job is ejected from the active set before it is completed. Under exponential assumptions about total execution and inter-page fault times we can write (see Chapter 1)

$$p_r = \left[\frac{1/e_r}{\mu_r + (1/e_r)} \right]^J = \left[\frac{1}{e_r \mu_r + 1} \right]^J, \quad r = 1, 2, \ldots, R.$$

In the case of two job classes suppose that class 1 is much "better" than class 2 (i.e. $e_1 \gg e_2$) and that it is possible to choose J so that $Je_1\mu_1 \gg 1$ and $Je_2\mu_2 \ll 1$. Then we would have $p_1 \sim 0$, $p_2 \sim 1$ and both objectives would be satisfied. If the difference between the two classes is not so extreme and it is not possible to achieve $p_1 \sim 0$ without at the same time having $p_2 \sim 0$, then the decision is much less clear-cut. One could proceed by experimentation. Another possibility is to choose (if possible) the smallest J such that $(p_1/p_2) > c$, for some $c > 1$. Note that thrashing can always be prevented even if there is no discrimination between the job classes.

9.5. Control of performance by selective memory allocation

Let us now return to the synthesis problem considered in Chapter 6: given a computer system with an input composed of R job classes, and the freedom to vary the scheduling strategy, what vectors of average response times $\mathbf{W} = (W_1, W_2, \ldots, W_R)$ can be achieved? Posed in that generality (even assuming Poisson inputs and exponential service times) the problem is still open for multiple-resource systems. The conservation laws which allowed us to obtain the characterisation theorems of section 6.3 are no longer valid. We shall therefore pursue a more modest aim: that of defining and studying a family of scheduling strategies which achieve, if not all achievable performance vectors, at least a large subset of them.

In the single-processor systems of Chapter 6, the idea behind the complete families of scheduling strategies (section 6.4) was to divide the processing capacity in unequal fractions among the different job classes. The same idea can be applied to the multiprogrammed system that we are considering here (Hine, Mitrani and Tsur [10]). This time, the resource to be divided will be the main memory.

We shall define a memory allocation strategy controlled by a vector of positive real "weights" $\boldsymbol{\alpha} = (\alpha_1, \alpha_2, \ldots, \alpha_R)$, whose elements correspond to the job classes. If the number of class r jobs submitted for execution is N_r $(r = 1, 2, \ldots, R)$, then the fraction of main memory allocated to class r is equal to

$$\gamma_r = \alpha_r I_{(N_r > 0)} \Big/ \sum_{s=1}^{R} \alpha_s I_{(N_s > 0)}; \quad r = 1, 2, \ldots, R, \tag{9.24}$$

where I_B is the indicator function

$$I_B = \begin{cases} 1 & \text{if } B \text{ is true} \\ 0 & \text{otherwise.} \end{cases}$$

The memory allocated to class r is divided equally among the active class r jobs. This memory allocation strategy must be accompanied by a job admission strategy, in order to avoid thrashing.

Of the N_r jobs of class r present, a certain number n_r will be admitted into the active set; $N_r - n_r$ jobs wait in an external queue $(r = 1, 2, \ldots, R)$. Each active class r job thus runs in $\gamma_r M/n_r$ pages of main memory (those amounts may have to be adjusted slightly to make them integers), where M is the number of pages available and γ_r is given by (9.24); $r = 1, 2, \ldots, R$. There are several possibilities for the admission strategy. Suppose, for example, that the lifetime function for class r is of type (9.2)

$$e_r(m) = 2b_r/[1 + (c_r/m)^2], \quad r = 1, 2, \ldots, R.$$

One could then decide to admit a class r job into the active set if there are c_r free pages in the allocation for class r (the knee criterion, section 9.3). In this last case, the number of class r jobs in the active set would be

$$n_r = \min(N_r, \lfloor \gamma_r M/c_r \rfloor), \quad r = 1, 2, \ldots, R. \tag{9.25}$$

where $\lfloor x \rfloor$ denotes the integer part of x.

Note that the division of memory resulting from the rule (9.24) is state-dependent, but it is state-dependent in a very special way. Only the presence or absence of jobs of a given class matter, not their number. It is thus possible for a single job to cause an entire partition of memory to be allocated to it, while jobs of another class have to wait outside because their partition is full. This policy will be referred to as "static partitioning". Later we shall compare it to a "dynamic partitioning" policy which takes congestion into account.

The static partitioning strategies defined by (9.24) achieve a wide range of performance vectors. If we let, for instance, $\alpha_1 \to \infty$, keeping α_r $(r = 2, 3, \ldots, R)$ finite, the resulting policy is to allocate the whole memory to class 1 as soon as there are class 1 jobs present. In other words, the result is to give pre-emptive priority to class 1. Similarly, if $\alpha_1 \to 0$, the result is to give pre-emptive priority to all other classes over class 1. Thus the average response time for any job class can be made to range from the best to the worst achievable. Any of the $R!$ pre-emptive priority orderings can be approximated as closely as desired by strategies from the family.

In the single-server case these properties would have ensured that the family is complete, i.e. that all achievable performance vectors can be achieved by strategies from it. Now, we cannot assert this for we do not know what is the set of achievable performance vectors. It is clear, however, that static partitioning strategies can achieve a large subset of the achievable vectors. Moreover, these strategies are easy to implement and would not involve significant operational overheads (in addition to those associated with whatever load control policy is employed).

To evaluate the performance of the static partitioning strategies we apply the familiar decomposition approach. The inner system is considered in isolation with a fixed population of $\mathbf{n} = (n_1, n_2, \ldots, n_R)$ active jobs circulating inside. An analysis of that closed network, using the BCMP theorem of section 3.5, yields the probabilities $\pi_r(n_1, n_2, \ldots, n_R)$ that a class r job is in service at the CPU (the formulae for a special case can be found in [10]). The inner system is then replaced by a single aggregate server which, when in state $\mathbf{n} = (n_1, n_2, \ldots, n_R)$, services class r jobs at rate

$$\xi_r(\mathbf{n}) = \mu_r \pi_r(\mathbf{n}), \quad r = 1, 2, \ldots, R. \tag{9.26}$$

Here, as before, $1/\mu_r$ is the average CPU time required by a class r job; the distribution of that time is assumed to be exponential.

The global system state is now described by the vector $\mathbf{N} = (N_1, N_2, \ldots, N_R)$, where N_r is the number of class r jobs submitted for execution. Using the appropriate mapping $\mathbf{N} \to \mathbf{n}$ (equation (9.25) is an example) in conjunction with (9.26), one can write balance equations for the steady-state distribution of $\mathbf{N}$. These equations have to be solved numerically (perhaps using an approximation technique: see [10]), since there are no closed-form solutions for R-dimensional Markov processes. From the distribution of $\mathbf{N}$ one can find the mean number of class r jobs submitted and hence, by Little's theorem, the average response time W_r $(r = 1, 2, \ldots, R)$.

Some results for the case of two-job classes are illustrated in Fig. 9.7. The outer system in that example consisted of two independent Poisson streams of jobs, with rates λ_1 and λ_2 for class 1 and class 2, respectively. The inner system comprised a CPU, a paging drum and a filing disk;

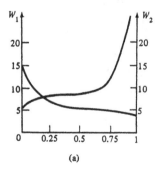
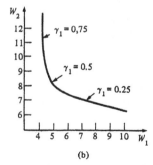

Fig. 9.7.

Chamberlin's lifetime functions were assumed and admissions into the active set were controlled by (9.25). With two-job classes, the static partitioning strategies depend on one parameter only: if, in (9.24), α_1 and α_2 are multiplied by the same constant, the strategy does not change. Part (a) of the figure shows W_1 and W_2 as functions of γ_1, the fraction of main memory allocated to class 1 ($0 \leq \gamma_1 \leq 1$). The response time vectors $\mathbf{W} = (W_1, W_2)$ achieved by strategies from the static partitioning family are shown in part (b). Note the marked difference between this and the single-server case (Fig. 8.2): there the achievable performance vectors formed a straight-line segment.

Let us now tackle the "static" nature of these scheduling strategies. Intuitively, it seems a good idea to allow jobs whose partition is temporarily overloaded to "spill over" into a partition which is temporarily underloaded (if one exists). To this end, we propose a family of strategies depending on $2R$ parameters: a vector of positive real weights $\boldsymbol{\alpha} = (\alpha_1, \alpha_2, \ldots, \alpha_R)$ and a vector of positive integers $\mathbf{m} = (m_1, m_2, \ldots, m_R)$. The α's play the same role as before, they define a partitioning of main memory according to (9.24). The way that partitioning is used, however, depends on the vector $\mathbf{m}$ and on the state of the system $\mathbf{N} = (N_1, N_2, \ldots, N_R)$. The number m_r is the minimum number of pages that a job of class r may be allocated; in the case of Chamberlin's lifetime functions, $m_r = c_r$ is a good choice ($r = 1, 2, \ldots, R$).

There are three possibilities:

(i) If $N_r m_r < \gamma_r M$ for all $r = 1, 2, \ldots, R$, then all partitions are underloaded; all jobs present are admitted into the active set and each class r job is allocated $\gamma_r M / N_r$ pages of main memory ($r = 1, 2, \ldots, R$).

(ii) If $N_r m_r \geq \gamma_r M$ for all $r = 1, 2, \ldots, R$, then all partitions are overloaded; the number of active class r jobs is equal to $n_r = \lfloor \gamma_r M / m_r \rfloor$ and each of them is allocated m_r pages ($r = 1, 2, \ldots, R$).

(iii) If there exists a subset of job classes S such that $N_r m_r < \gamma_r M$ for $r \in S$ and $N_r m_r \geq \gamma_r M$ for $r \in \{1, 2, \ldots, R\} - S$, then all jobs of classes in S are active and there is a pool of

$$\hat{M} = M - \sum_{r \in S} \lfloor \gamma_r M - N_r m_r \rfloor$$

pages available for allocation to the job classes in $\{1, 2, \ldots, R\} - S$. That pool is divided into fractions $\hat{\gamma}_r$ proportional to the weights α_r, for $r \in \{1, 2, \ldots, R\} - S$. The number of active class r jobs is then $n_r = \min\{N_r, \lfloor (\gamma_r M + \hat{\gamma}_r \hat{M})/m_r \rfloor\}$ and each of them is allocated m_r pages ($r \in \{1, 2, \ldots, R\} - S$). If, after that allocation, there are still pages left in the pool $\hat{M}$, these revert to their original partitions and are divided among the jobs there.

The above is called a "dynamic partitioning" strategy. In cases (i) and (ii) it acts exactly like a static partitioning one; in case (iii) it allows jobs from some classes to be admitted into partitions belonging to other classes but gives priority there to the "original owners".

One would expect that dynamic partitioning would lead to a more efficient utilisation of main memory and hence to better over-all system performance. This is true to a certain extent but the difference does not appear to be significant. This is illustrated in Fig. 9.8 for an example otherwise identical to that in Fig. 9.7 (two job classes, parameter γ_1 varying in range $0 \leq \gamma_1 \leq 1$, $m_1 = c_1$, $m_2 = c_2$). Part (a) shows the average response times W_1 and W_2 as functions of γ_1, while the set of achievable performance vectors $\mathbf{W} = (W_1, W_2)$ is shown in part (b).

If Figs. 9.7 and 9.8 are superimposed it can be seen that the performance of the dynamic partitioning strategies, over the whole range of γ_1, approximates very closely that of the static partitioning strategies for γ_1 in the neighbourhood of 0.5. What is happening here is that any unequal division of memory intended by the parameters α_1 and α_2 is counterbalanced by the dynamic memory allocation. The net effect is approximately the same as a static partitioning which divides the main memory equally among the classes. If the two families of scheduling strategies behave in general as in this example, we would be justified in claiming that there is not much point in dynamic partitioning. The same

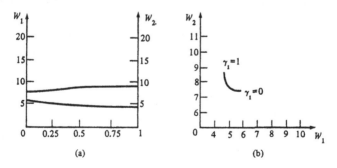

Fig. 9.8.

performance vectors can be achieved by static partitioning with a suitable choice of parameters while there are other, more extreme, performance vectors which are achievable by static but not by dynamic partitioning.

Another conclusion can be drawn from the strong non-linearity of the achievable performance curve in Fig. 9.7. Whereas in single-resource systems a decrease in one element of the performance vector is accompanied by a proportional increase in another, here a small improvement in the response time for one job class can lead to a disproportionate deterioration in the response time for the other.

In the next section we shall argue that such non-linear behaviour is likely to be observed in any multiclass terminal system, regardless of the scheduling strategy.

9.6. Towards a characterisation of achievable performance in terminal systems

In section 3.6 we derived a general relation (3.48) between node utilisations and response times in queueing networks. That relation can be used to shed some light on the nature of the set of performance vectors that is achievable in terminal-driven multiprogrammed systems (Hine [9]).

Consider a computer system where the input source (the outer system in Fig. 9.1) consists of R groups of terminals. There are N_1 terminals generating class 1 jobs, $\ldots, N_R$ terminals generating class R jobs. Class r terminals are characterised by their average think time τ_r $(r = 1, 2, \ldots, R)$. Denote by s_{ir} the total average service required by a class r job from node i in the inner system (e.g. $s_{0r} = 1/\mu_r$ is the total average CPU time required by a class r job). These are job characteristics which, with the exception of the paging drum's required service time s_{1r}, do not depend on the admission and scheduling policies. Denote, further, by U_{ir} the utilisation of node i in the inner system due to class r jobs $(i = 0, 1, \ldots, K; r = 1, 2, \ldots, R)$; that is, the proportion of time that node i spends serving class r jobs.

Equation (3.48) now expresses the average response time for class r jobs thus:

$$W_r = \frac{N_r s_{ir}}{U_{ir}} - \tau_r, \quad i = 0, 1, \ldots, K; \ r = 1, 2, \ldots, R. \tag{9.27}$$

Let us take a particular node in the inner system, for example the CPU $(i = 0)$, and solve (9.27) for the utilisation factor:

$$U_{0r} = \frac{N_r s_{0r}}{W_r + \tau_r}, \quad r = 1, 2, \ldots, R. \tag{9.28}$$

The total CPU utilisation U_0 is obtained by summing (9.28) over all job classes:

$$U_0 = \sum_{r=1}^{R} \frac{N_r s_{0r}}{W_r + \tau_r}. \tag{9.29}$$

This equation can be regarded as a conservation law conditioned upon the CPU utilisation: the performance vectors of all scheduling strategies which yield CPU utilisation U_0 must lie on the surface defined by (9.29). If one wishes to lower the average response time for a particular job class and keep the same CPU utilisation, then the response times of one or more other classes will increase in such a way that the vector $\mathbf{W}$ remains on that surface.

Consider the case of two-job classes ($R = 2$). Equation (9.29) now defines a hyperbola with asymptotes at

$$W_r = (N_r s_{0r}/U_0) - \tau_r, \quad r = 1, 2$$

and middle point of the convex region at

$$W_r = [(N_r s_{0r} + (N_1 N_2 s_{01} s_{02})^{\frac{1}{2}})/U_0] - \tau_r, \quad r = 1, 2.$$

When U_0 tends to zero, that curve moves away from the origin and "flattens out"; conversely, when U_0 increases the curve moves towards the origin and becomes more convex.

Thus, in a well-tuned system where the CPU utilisation is close to the maximum attainable, the performance vectors of all scheduling strategies which maintain that utilisation lie on a hyperbola. Of course, not all points on the hyperbola are achievable. As in the single-server case, the achievable performance vectors must satisfy inequalities of the type

$$W_r \geq W_r^{\min}, \quad r = 1, 2,$$

where $W_r^{\min}$ is the average response time for class r jobs in a system where the other job class does not exist and where the CPU utilisation is the maximum attainable. The set of achievable performance vectors is therefore contained in a region such as the shaded area in Fig. 9.9. The situation is similar when the number of job classes is $R > 2$.

We should point out that this characterisation of achievable performance has a limited, if any, practical value. The maximum attainable CPU utilisation is not usually known and the position of the bounding hyperbola (or R-dimensional surface) may be very sensitive to its estimate. Moreover, even if the constraints are calculated accurately there is no guarantee that

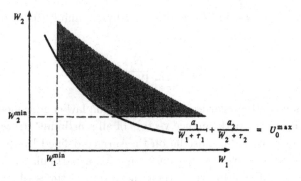

Fig. 9.9.

all points which satisfy them are, in fact, achievable. What we have obtained is an idea of the likely shape of the set of achievable performance vectors. That idea is consistent with the results of the last section (the curve in Fig. 9.7b closely resembles a hyperbola). It also confirms the observation made before, namely that the trade-offs between response times for different job classes are likely to be non-linear.

References

1. Adams, M. C. and Millard, G. E. (1975). "Performance Measurements on the Edinburgh Multi-Access System (EMAS)." Proc. ICS 75, Antibes.
2. Belady, L. A. and Kuehner, C. J. (1969). Dynamic space sharing in computer systems. *Comm. A.C.M.*, **12**, 282–288.
3. Buzen, J. P. (1976). Fundamental operational laws of computer system performance. *Acta Informatica*, **7**, 167–182.
4. Chamberlin, D. D., Fuller, S. H. and Lin, L. Y. (1973). "A Page Allocation Strategy for Multiprogramming Systems with Virtual Memory." Proc. 4th Symp. on Operations Systems Principles, pp. 66–72.
5. Denning, P. J. and Kahn, K. C. (1975). "A Study of Program Locality and Lifetime Functions." Proc. 5th Symp. on Operations Systems Principles, pp. 207–216.
6. Denning, P. J., Kahn, K. C., Leroudier, J., Potier, D. and Suri, R. (1976). Optimal multiprogramming. *Acta Informatica*, **7**, 197–216.
7. Gelenbe, E. and Kurinckx, A. (1978). Random injection control of multi-programming in virtual memory. *IEEE Trans. on Software Engng.*, **4**, 2–17.
8. Gelenbe, E., Kurinckx, A. and Mitrani, I. (1978). "The Rate Control Policy for Virtual Memory Management." Proc. 2nd Int. Symp. on Operations Systems, IRIA, Rocquencourt.
9. Hine, J. H. (1978). "Scheduling for Pre-specified Performance in Multiprogrammed Computer Systems." Research. Report., University of Wellington.

10. Hine, J. H., Mitrani, I. and Tsur, S. (1979). Control of response times in multi-class systems by memory allocation. *C.A.C.M.*, **22**(7), 415–423.

11. Leroudier, J. and Potier, D. (1976). "Principles of Optimality for Multiprogramming." Proc. Int. Symp. on Computer Performance Modelling, Measuring and Evaluation, pp. 211–218. Cambridge, Massachusetts.

12. Rodriguez-Rossel, J. and Dupuy, J. P. (1972). "The Evaluation of a Time Sharing Page Demand System." Proc. AFIPS, SJCC 40, pp. 759–765.

13. Sekino, A. (1972). "Performance Evaluation of a Multiprogrammed Time Shared Computer System." MIT Project MAC, Research Report MAC-TR-103.

Chapter 10

A Queue with Server of Walking Type

10.1. Introduction

Queues with autonomous service (QAS) represent service systems in which the server becomes unavailable for a random time after each service epoch. Such systems have been used to model secondary memory devices in computer systems (e.g. paging disks or drums) as was done in Chapter 2. The queue with "server of walking type" studied by Skinner [1] is a special instance of our model. This model has also been considered by Borovkov [4].

Assuming general independent interarrival times we obtain an operational formula relating the waiting time in stationary state of a QAS to the waiting time of the $GI/G/1$ queue. This result dispenses the need for analysis of the QAS in special cases and generalizes the result of Skinner [1], or that of Coffman [2] for a paging drum. Sufficient conditions for stability or instability of the system are also obtained.

10.1.1. *The mathematical model*

We examine a single server, first-come-first-served service center to which customers arrive according to a renewal process. Let $A_1, A_2, \ldots, A_n, \ldots$ denote the interarrival times, and denote by $s_1, s_2, \ldots, s_n, \ldots$ the service times of the successive customers. After serving the n-th customer the server becomes idle for a time $T_n \geq 0$. We write $S_n \equiv s_n + T_n, n \geq 1$, and assume that $S_1, S_2, \ldots, S_n, \ldots$ is a sequence of i.i.d. (independent and identically distributed) random variables, independent also of the interarrival times.

Suppose that the queue is empty at time $s_k + T_k$; the server becomes once again available for service at times

$$s_k + T_k + \bar{S}_1^k + \bar{S}_2^k, \ldots, s_k + T_k + \bar{S}_1^k + \bar{S}_2^k + \cdots + \bar{S}_n^k, \ldots$$

That is, service will resume for the $(k + 1)$-th customer which arrives at time $a_{k+1} \equiv \sum_1^{k+1} A_i$ at time $s_k + T_k + \sum_1^{l(a_{k+1})} \bar{S}_i^k$, where

$$l(a_{k+1}) = \inf \left\{ l : s_k + T_k + \sum_1^l \bar{S}_i^k \geq a_{k+1} \right\}.$$

We assume that the $\{\bar{S}_n^k\}_{n,k \geq 1}$ are i.i.d. and independent of the interarrival times and of the sequence $\{S_n\}_{n \geq 1}$. In the sequel, we shall drop the index k associated with $\bar{S}_n^k$ in order to simplify the notation, though it will be understood that the variables associated with the end of different busy periods are distinct.

The model we consider arises in many applications. In computer systems [2, 3, 5] it serves as a model of a paging drum (in this case S and $\bar{S}$ are constant and equal). In data communication systems it can serve to represent a data transmission facility where transmission begins at predetermined instants of time.

Using the terminology of Skinner [1] who analyzed the model assuming Poisson arrivals, we shall call it a queue with server of walking type: after each service the server "takes a walk". Borovkov [4] studies a related model which he calls a queue with "autonomous service".

The purpose of this paper is to obtain a general formula relating the waiting time W_n of the n-th customer in our model to the waiting time, of the n-th customer V_n in an equivalent GI/G/1 queue, $n \geq 1$. This equivalent GI/G/1 queue has the same arrival process, but the service times are $S_1, S_2, \ldots, S_n, \ldots$ and $V_{n+1} = [V_n + S_n - A_{n+1}]^+$. This result allows us to dispense with a special analysis of our queueing model in stationnary state since we can obtain the result directly from the known analysis of the corresponding GI/G/1 queue.

The formula (Theorem 4) is derived in section 2 together with sufficient conditions for ergodicity. Section 3 contains an application to the paging drum model.

10.1.2. *Relation to previous work*

Let us briefly review previous work on the subject. Borovkov ([4], Chapter 8) defines a system with arrivals according to a renewal process and in batches, and with service also in batches. According to the notations defined above, he assumes that the $T_n \equiv 0$ and that the $\bar{S}_n$ are distributed as the $S_n, n \geq 1$. Furthermore he considers various special cases for the distribution of the S_n and the A_n. His main result is that the queue length distribution (where the queue does not include the customers in service) of the above system is identical to the queue length distribution of a conventional queue (with batch arrivals and batch service) if the service times are exponentially distributed. The model considered by Skinner [1] is a special case of the one we study since he assumes that the arrival process is Poisson; otherwise it is identical to ours. He obtains the generating function for the queue length distribution in stationary state.

10.2. Properties of the waiting time process

Consider the sequence $W_1, W_2, \ldots, W_n, \ldots$ where W_n is the waiting time of the n-th customer arriving to the queue. We shall first prove that the $W_n, n \geq 1$, satisfy a simple recurrence relation. Let $\xi_n = S_n - A_{n+1}, n \geq 1$.

Lemma 1.

$$W_{n+1} = \eta(-W_n - \xi_n), \quad n \geq 1 \tag{10.1}$$

where $\eta(.)$ is defined by

$$\eta(x) = \begin{cases} -x & \text{if } x \leq 0 \\ \sum_1^{l(x)} \bar{S}_j - x, & \text{if } x > 0 \end{cases}$$

where we define for $x > 0$:

$$l(x) = \inf\left\{ l : \sum_1^l \bar{S}_i \geq x, l > 0 \right\} \tag{10.2}$$

Proof. The n-th customer arrives to the queue at time $\sum_1^n A_i$ and begins service at $\sum_1^n A_i + W_n$. The server will then be once again available (for the $(n+1)$-th customer) at time $\sum_1^n A_i + W_n + S_n$. Therefore

$$W_{n+1} = \begin{cases} \sum_1^n A_j + W_n + S_n - \sum_1^{n+1} A_j, & \text{if } W_n + S_n - A_{n+1} \geq 0 \\ \sum_1^{l(A_{n+1}-W_n-S_n)} \bar{S}_j - (A_{n+1} - W_n - S_n) & \text{if } W_n + S_n - A_{n+1} < 0 \end{cases} \tag{10.3}$$

where $l(x)$ is defined in (10.2).

This can be rewritten as

$$W_{n+1} = \begin{cases} W_n + \xi_n & \text{if } W_n + \xi_n \geq 0 \\ \sum_1^{l(-W_n-\xi_n)} \bar{S}_j - (-W_n - \xi_n) & \text{if } W_n + \xi_n < 0 \end{cases} \tag{10.4}$$

which is the formula (10.1) given in the lemma.

As a consequence of Lemma 1 we have the following result.   □

Lemma 2. *If* $E\xi_n > 0$ *for* $n \geq 1$ *then* $W_n \to \infty$ *with probability* 1 *as* $n \to \infty$.

Proof.   Notice from (10.1) that $\eta(x) \geq -x$ for all x with probability 1: if $x \leq 0$ the statement is obvious; since $\eta(x) \geq 0$ with probability 1 it follows that $\eta(x) \geq -x$ if $x > 0$. Therefore, by Lemma 1 we have

$$W_{n+1} \geq W_n + \xi_n, \quad n \geq 1$$

Therefore $W_{n+1} \geq \sum_1^n \xi_n$, $n \geq 1$. If $E\xi_n > 0$, then the sum on the RHS converges with probability 1 to $+\infty$ as $n \to \infty$.

Henceforth we shall assume that $E\xi_n < 0$ for all $n \geq 1$.   □

Remark 3. It is now clear that $W_1, W_2, \ldots, W_n, \ldots$ is a Markov chain since $\xi_1, \xi_2, \ldots, \xi_n, \ldots$ is a sequence of i.i.d. random variables and $\eta(.)$ is a random function which depends on $\bar{S}_1, \bar{S}_2, \ldots$, which are themselves independent of the $S_1, S_2, \ldots$, and of the $A_1, A_2, \ldots$.

We shall now study the characteristic function $Ee^{itW_{n+1}}$ for the waiting time process. Using (10.1) we have, for any real t

$$Ee^{itW_{n+1}} = Ee^{it(W_n+\xi_n)}I[W_n + \xi_n \geq 0] + \sum_{k=0}^{\infty} Ee^{it(W_n+\xi_n+\sum_1^{k+1}\bar{S}_i)}.I$$

$$\times \left[W_n + \xi_n + \sum_1^{k+1} \bar{S}_i \geq 0, \ 0 > W_n + \xi_n + \sum_1^k \bar{S}_i \right] \tag{10.5}$$

Let $f(t) = Ee^{it\bar{S}}$.

Then

$$Ee^{itW_{n+1}} = Ee^{it(W_n + \xi_n)} + [f(t) - 1] \sum_{k=0}^{\infty} Ee^{it(W_n + \xi_n + \sum_1^k \bar{S}_i)} . I$$

$$\times \left[W_n + \xi_n + \sum_1^k \bar{S}_i < 0 \right] \tag{10.6}$$

We are now ready to establish the main result of the paper.

Theorem 4. *Suppose that*

(a) *the random variable ξ is not arithmetic; that is $g(t) = Ee^{it\xi}$ has a single real value $t(t = 0)$ for which $g(t) = 1$,*

(b) *$E\xi < 0$, and $E\bar{S} < \infty$.*

Then:

(i) *$W \underset{p}{=} \lim_{n\to\infty} W_n$ exists and is a proper random variable ([1]),*

(ii) *$W \underset{p}{=} V + \gamma$, where $V \underset{p}{=} \lim_{n\to\infty} V_n$([1]),*

$$\gamma \underset{p}{=} \lim_{x\to\infty} \sum_1^{l(x)} \bar{S}_i - x,$$

and γ is independent of V.

That is, γ is the (limiting) forward recurrence time of the renewal process $\bar{S}_1, \bar{S}_1 + \bar{S}_2, \ldots, \bar{S}_1 + \cdots + \bar{S}_n, \ldots$ It is well known that

$$P[\gamma < x] = \int_0^x [1 - F_{\bar{S}}(y)]dy / E\bar{S}$$

Proof. Define

$$\phi_n(t) = \sum_{k=0}^{\infty} Ee^{it(W_n + \xi_n + \sum_1^k \bar{S}_i)} . I \left[W_n + \xi_n + \sum_1^k \bar{S}_i < 0 \right]$$

$$= \int_{-\infty}^{0-} e^{itx} d \left\{ \sum_{k=0}^{\infty} P \left[W_n + \xi_n + \sum_1^k \bar{S}_i < x \right] \right\} \tag{10.7}$$

---

[1] $\lim_{p} W \underset{p}{=}$ means limit in law.

Introduce the following notation:

$$\psi_n(t) = E e^{itW_n}$$

Then (10.9) becomes

$$\psi_{n+1}(t) = \psi_n(t)g(t) + (f(t) - 1)\phi_n(t) \qquad (10.8)$$

Our proof will be complete if we can prove the existence and uniqueness of the characteristic function $\psi(t) \equiv E e^{itW}$ of a positive random variable W, which is the solution of the stationary equation

$$\psi(t)(1 - g(t)) = (f(t) - 1)\phi(t) \qquad (10.9)$$

obtained from (10.8), such that (i) and (ii) are satisfied. $\square$

Uniqueness. We shall first show that if the solution $\psi(t)$ to (10.9) exists, then it is unique. If $\psi(t)$ exists, it must be continuous for real t and $\phi(t)$ must exist. Using (10.7):

$$\phi(t) = \int_{-\infty}^{0-} e^{ity} \, dG(y)$$

where

$$G(y) \equiv \sum_{k=0}^{\infty} P\left[W + \xi + \sum_{1}^{k} \bar{S}_i < y \right]$$

Let us first show that $\phi(t)$ is a continuous function of t.

Set $W = x$ in (10.6). Let us prove that the series on the right-hand-side of (10.7) is uniformly convergent on R^+ as function of x:

$$\left| \sum_{k=0}^{\infty} E e^{it(x+\xi+\sum_1^{k-1} \bar{S}_i)} I\left[x + \xi + \sum_{1}^{k} \bar{S}_i < 0 \right] \right|$$

$$\leq \sum_{k=0}^{\infty} P\left[x + \xi + \sum_{1}^{k} \bar{S}_i < 0 \right] < \sum_{k=0}^{\infty} P\left[\xi + \sum_{1}^{k} \bar{S}_i < 0 \right] = EH(-\xi)$$

where $H(.)$ is the renewal function for the renewal process $\bar{S}_1, \bar{S}_1 + \bar{S}_2, \bar{S}_1 + \bar{S}_2 + \bar{S}_3, \ldots$ and $EH(-\xi)$ is the expectation of $H(-\xi)$ with respect to the random variable ξ. But $H(y)$, which is the expected number of renewals in $[0, y]$ for $y > 0$ (and is zero for $y \leq 0$), is bounded by a function $\alpha + \beta y$ for $\alpha, \beta \geq 0$. This completes the proof since a similar argument can be applied to the second series.

Therefore $G(y)$ is a continuous function of y for almost all $y < 0$. It is obviously an increasing function of y and $G(-\infty) = 0$ and $G(0^-) < \infty$, since for $y < 0$

$$P\left[W + \xi + \sum_1^k \bar{S}_i < y\right] \le P\left[\xi + \sum_1^k \bar{S}_i < 0\right]$$

because $W \ge 0$. Also, $G(y)$ is bounded for $y < 0$. Thus we have established that $\phi(t)$ is a continuous function of t.

Rewrite (10.9) as

$$\phi(t) = (1 - g(t))\frac{\psi(t)}{f(t) - 1}$$

Since $\phi(t)$ is continuous and $g(t) \ne 1$ for $t \ne 0$ (by assumption (a)), it follows that every zero of $(f(t) - 1)$, if any, except $t = 1$, coincides with some zero of $\psi(t)$.

We now call upon a result of Borovkov [4]; if $E\xi < 0$ (Chapter 4, p. 103, equation (1)):

$$(1 - g(t)) = \frac{P(V = 0)}{Ee^{itV}}[1 - Ee^{itX}]$$

where X is a negative random variable. Therefore we may write,

$$\psi(t)\frac{P(V = 0)}{Ee^{itV}}[1 - e^{itX}] = (f(t) - 1)\phi(t)$$

or

$$\frac{\psi(t)P(V = 0)it}{(f(t) - 1)Ee^{itV}} = \frac{it\phi(t)}{1 - Ee^{itX}} \tag{10.10}$$

Consider the LHS of (10.10). $\psi(t)$, $f(t)$ and Ee^{itV} are characteristic functions of positive random variables; they are therefore analytic in the upper half-plane $(\mathrm{Im}(t) > 0)$ and continuous on the real line and bounded. Consider the RHS of (10.10). $\phi(t)$ is the characteristic function of a negative random variable and so is Ee^{itX}; therefore the RHS of (10.10) is analytic on the lower half-plane $(\mathrm{Im}(t) < 0)$ and continuous on the real line and bounded. Therefore by the Liouville's Theorem the expression (10.10) is a constant, call it C. Let us write:

$$\psi(t) = \frac{C(f(t) - 1)}{itP(V = 0)}Ee^{itV}$$

Taking

$$1 = \psi(0) = \frac{CE\bar{S}}{P(V = 0)}$$

we have $C = P(V = 0)/E\bar{S}$ and

$$\psi(t) = \frac{f(t) - 1}{itE\bar{S}} E e^{itV} \tag{10.11}$$

Therefore if $\psi(t)$ exists, then it is unique since it is given by (10.11). In fact, we have also shown that if it exists, it satisfies (ii) since (10.11) is simply the Fourier transform of the statement in (ii).

Existence. We must now prove the existence of the solution $\psi(t)$ given by (10.11), of the equation (10.9).

Using (10.7), we shall show that $\psi(t)$ of (10.11) is a solution to (10.9). We write, from (10.7):

$$\phi(t) = \int_{-\infty}^{0-} d\left[\sum_{k=0}^{\infty} P\left(W + \xi + \sum_{1}^{k} \bar{S}_n < x\right)\right] e^{itx} \tag{10.12}$$

It is the Fourier transform of the restriction to R^- of a mesure μ. μ is the convolution of two measures.

* μ_1, corresponding to the random variable ξ, on R
* μ_2, defined on R^+ with

$$\mu_2[0, x[= \sum_{k=0}^{\infty} P\left(W + \sum_{n=1}^{k} \bar{S}_n < x\right).$$

The Fourier transform of μ_2 is given by

$$\frac{\psi(t)}{1 - f(t)} (|f(t)| < 1 \quad \text{when } \mathrm{Im}(t) > 0)$$

But, from (10.11),

$$\frac{\psi(t)}{1 - f(t)} = \frac{-E e^{itV}}{itE(\bar{S})}$$

Using the fact that $-\frac{1}{itE(\bar{S})}$ is the Fourier transform of the Lebesgue measure on R^+, with density $\frac{1}{E(\bar{S})}$, μ_2 itself is obtained as the convolution of this Lebesgue measure and of the measure of V.

Hence, μ is σ-finite and its Fourier transform is

$$\int_R e^{itx}\mu(dx) = -g(t)\frac{Ee^{itV}}{itE\bar{S}} = [1 - g(t)]\frac{Ee^{itV}}{itE\bar{S}} + \left(-\frac{Ee^{itV}}{itE\bar{S}}\right)$$

$$= \frac{p(V=0).(1 - Ee^{itX})}{itE\bar{S}} + \int_{R^+} e^{itx}\mu_2(dx)$$

We deduce $\mu = \mu^* + \mu_2$, where

- μ_2 is μ restricted to R^+.
- μ^* is the restriction of μ to R^- and therefore has the Fourier transform $\phi(t)$ which is

$$\phi(t) = p(V=0)\frac{1 - E(e^{itX})}{itE\bar{S}}$$

Hence replacing $\phi(t)$ above and (10.11) in (10.9) we see that the equality (10.9) is satisfied completing the existence proof.

We have established the existence and uniqueness of the stationary solution $\psi(t)$ of equation (10.8). We now have to prove that

$$\lim_{n\to\infty} W_n \underset{p}{=} W$$

i.e. that this stationary solution is the limit in the above equation. For this we shall call upon general results on the ergodicity of Markov chains as presented by Revuz [6]. In particular:

① We first show that W_n is irreducible.

② We use the Theorem (Revuz [6], Theorem 2.7, Chapter 3) that states that if a chain is irreducible and if a finite invariant measure exists, then it is *recurrent in the sense of Harris* (i.e. a *Harris chain*). Thus we show that W_n is a Harris chain.

③ Finally we use Orey's theorem (Revuz [6], Theorem 2.8, Chapter 6) which states that if a finite invariant measure m exists for an aperiodic Harris chain W_n, then $W_n \underset{p}{\to} W$; if the measure m is a probability measure then it is the measure of W.

Let us proceed with this proof.

① To show irreducibility, consider the measure m whose Fourier transform is $\mu(t)$. By (10.11) we can write

$$m = v * s$$

where $*$ denotes the convolution, v is the measure whose transform is Ee^{itV} and s is the measure whose transform is $[f(t) - 1]/itE\bar{S}$. Clearly,

$$v_c(A) > 0 \Rightarrow m(A) > 0 \quad \text{where } v_c \text{ is the continuous component of } v$$

for a subset A of the non-negative real line. We shall show that, for each initial state $x \in [0, \infty[$, there exists a positive integer n such that

$$P(W_n \in A \,|\, W_0 = x) > 0.$$

For this, notice that V_n is ergodic (Borovkov [4], Theorem 7) if $a)$ and $b)$ are satisfied. Thus

$$v_c(A) > 0 \Leftrightarrow P(V \in A) > 0 \Rightarrow [\exists m \ni P(V_m \in A \,|\, V_0 = x) > 0]$$

But since $P(V_m = W_m \in A) > 0$ for each finite m (the case where the queue with automous server does not empty up to, and including, the m-th customer), then

$$v_c(A) > 0 \Rightarrow [\exists m \ni P(W_m \in A \,|\, W_0 = x) > 0]$$

Therefore (by Revuz [6], Definition 2.1 of Chapter 3) W_n is v_c-irreducible.

② Theorem 2.7, Chapter 3 of Revuz [6] states that W_n is a Harris chain if it is v-irreducible and if there exists finite invariant measure m such that $v(A) > 0 \Rightarrow m(A) > 0$ for all A ($m \gg v$, in Revuz's notation). This has already been proved. Therefore W_n is indeed recurrent in the sense of Harris.

③ We now have to show, in order to use Orey's theorem, that W_n is aperiodic. We call again upon the classical result that V_n is ergodic if $E\xi < 0$ and ξ is not arithmetic (both of which we have assumed). Therefore V_n is aperiodic, and so is W_n since for each finite m

$$P(V_m = W_m \in A) > 0$$

Thus, by Orey's theorem W_n is ergodic and

$$\lim_{n \to \infty} W_n \underset{p}{=} W$$

This complete the proof of Theorem 4.

10.3. Application to a paging drum model

In this section we shall apply the theoretical results obtained in the previous sections to the standard "paging disk" model arising in the analysis of computer system behaviour [2, 3, 5]. The customers are requests for the transfer of *pages* (blocks of information of fixed size) from a paging disk that in studied in section 2.2. For the purpose of efficiency, described in [2, 3, 5], page requests are addressed to one of N sector queues; each paging drum sector when traversed permits to deliver one page. Since the paging drum rotates at constant speed, if T is the time for one complete rotation then one page will be transfered in time T/N and service at this particular sector queue will not be available for a time $T(N-1)/N$ until the paging drum can be once again positioned at the beginning of the same sector.

Let W be the stationary waiting time at a sector queue with general independent interarrivals, and V be the stationary waiting time of the corresponding GI/D/1 queue with constant service time T. We then have:

Theorem 5. *If $EA < T$ and ξ is not arithmetic with $E\xi < 0$ then W and V are proper random variables related by the formula*

$$W \underset{p}{=} V + Y$$

where V and Y are independent and Y is uniformly distributed in $[0, T]$.

In particular we obtain the average waiting time for the case of Poisson arrivals studied in Chapter 2.

$$EW = \frac{T}{2} + \frac{\lambda T^2}{2(1 - \lambda T)}$$

where λ is the arrival rate of transfer requests.

Clearly, the response time R (waiting time plus service time) is simply

$$R = V + Y + \frac{T}{N}$$

References

1. Skinner, C. E. (1967). A priority queueing model with server walking type, *Operations Research*, **15**, 278–285.
2. Coffman, E. G. (1969). Analysis of a drum input-output queue under scheduled operation, *J.A.C.M.*, **16**(1), 73–90.
3. Gelenbe, E., Lenfant, J. and Potjer, D. (1975). Response time of a fixed-head disk to transfer of variable length, *S.I.A.M.J. on Computing*, **4**(4), 461–473.

4. Borokov, A. A. (1976). *Stochastic Processes in Queueing Theory*, Springer Verlag, New York.
5. Fuller, S. H. and Baskett, F. (1972). *An analysis of drum storage units*, Tech. Rep. 29, Digital Syst. Lab. Stanford University, Stanford, Cal.
6. Revuz, D. (1975). *Markov chains*, North Holland, Amsterdam.

Index

50% criterion, 279, 280

absorbing state, 186
achievable performance vector, *see* performance vector
active jobs, 269–271, 273–275, 277, 278, 281, 282, 286, 289
acyclic graph, 76
admission control policy, 270, 271
aggregate server, 282, 284, 285, 289
aggregate state, 104
aggregate/subsystem decomposition, *see* Decomposition
analytic, 303
arrival stream, 57, 63, 77–79, 237, 238

balance equations, 81, 83–85, 87, 91–93, 96, 97, 100–103, 284, 285, 289
BCMP theorem, 98, 101, 283, 289
boundary condition, 166–168, 175, 179, 257
bubble memory, 44, 58, 63, 64
buffer queue, 69–71, 197, 198
busy period, 166, 177, 235, 240, 241, 246, 247, 258

central limit theorem, 166, 167, 169, 170, 176
Chapman–Kolmogorov equations, 168
    differential, 215
    forward, 170
Characterisation theorems, 242, 248, 260, 287

characteristic function, 300, 302
charge-coupled device, 44, 64–67
circulating shift register, 44, 63, 64
coefficient of variation, 53, 62, 170, 186–188, 190, 199–201, 203, 204
communicating classes, 83, 87
communication channel, *see* Multiplexed communication channel
complete families of scheduling strategies, 249, 287
    $M/G/1$-complete, 249, 252, 253, 258, 259
    $M/M/1$-complete, 249, 250, 253–255, 258
computer system, 1, 43, 44, 58, 74, 93, 105, 112, 165, 201, 206, 207, 211, 231, 267, 269, 287, 292
conservation law, 233, 234, 236–238, 240–242, 250–252, 260, 263, 265, 267, 287, 293
    general, 234
    Kleinrock, 236, 237
    special, 236, 238, 241, 242
control of performance, 269, 287
    in multiple-resource systems, 269
    in single-resource systems, *see* Synthesis problems
Control of the degree of multiprogramming, *see* Degree of multiprogramming
convex hull, 245, 246
Coxian distributions, 95, 100, 106